STUDIES IN CHRISTIAN HISTORY AND THOUGHT

Pious Pastors

Calvin's Theology of Sanctification and the Genevan Academy

STUDIES IN CHRISTIAN HISTORY AND THOUGHT

Pious Pastors

Calvin's Theology of Sanctification and the Genevan Academy

Thomas Devonshire Hawkes

Copyright © Thomas Devonshire Hawkes 2016

First published 2016 by Paternoster

Paternoster is an imprint of Authentic Media Limited
PO Box 6326, Bletchley, Milton Keynes MK1 9GG

authenticmedia.co.uk

The right of Thomas Devonshire Hawkes to be identified as the Author of this Work has been asserted by him in accordance with the Copyright, Designs and Patents Act 1988.

All rights reserved. No part of this publication may be reproduced, stored in a retrieval system, or transmitted, in any form or by any means, electronic, mechanical, photocopying, recording or otherwise, without the prior permission of the publisher or a license permitting restricted copying. In the UK such licenses are issued by the Copyright Licensing Agency Ltd, Barnard's Inn, 86 Fetter Lane, London EC4A 1EN.

British Library Cataloguing in Publication Data
A catalogue record for this book is available from the British Library

ISBN 978-1-84227-984-7
978-1-78078-442-7 (e-book)

Printed and bound by Lightning Source

STUDIES IN CHRISTIAN HISTORY AND THOUGHT

Series Preface

This series complements the specialist series of Studies in Evangelical History and Thought and Studies in Baptist History and Thought for which Paternoster is becoming increasingly well known by offering works that cover the wider field of Christian history and thought. It encompasses accounts of Christian witness at various periods, studies of individual Christians and movements, and works which concern the relations of church and society through history, and the history of Christian thought.

The series includes monographs, revised dissertations and theses, and collections of papers by individuals and groups. As well as 'free standing' volumes, works on particular running themes are being commissioned; authors will be engaged for these from around the world and from a variety of Christian traditions.

A high academic standard combined with lively writing will commend the volumes in this series both to scholars and to a wider readership.

Series Editors

Alan P.F. Sell	Visiting Professor at Acadia University Divinity College, Nova Scotia
D.W. Bebbington	University of Stirling, Stirling, Scotland
Clyde Binfield	Professor Associate in History, University of Sheffield, UK
Gerald Bray	Anglican Professor of Divinity, Beeson Divinity School, Samford University, Birmingham, Alabama, USA
Grayson Carter	Associate Professor of Church History, Fuller Theological Seminary SW, Phoenix, Arizona, USA
Dennis Ngien	Professor of Theology, Tyndale University College and Seminary, Founder of the Centre for Mentorship and Theological Reflection, Toronto, Canada

Acknowledgments

John Donne famously said, "No man is an island." While researching and writing a book may at times be lonely work, when one pauses to consider those to whom thanks is due, even the writer is obliged to recognize that he stands on the shoulders of many others. First, there are the benefactors who kindly supply funding so that one may research and write at all. In that category I wish to thank the Elders of Uptown Church in Charlotte, N.C., who have graciously funded my studies with money and time. Then follows a host of individuals who have given generously: Mark and Tisha Bass, George and Elva Carpenter, Charlie and Lynne Hawkes, Rick and Sara Hawkes, Rob and Lisa Hawkes, Ed Reule, Ken and Ruth Samuelson, Stanton and Missy Vandenberg. Thanks to each of you.

Next I owe thanks to the various scholars who have helped me. First in that line is Dr. Tony Lane, who has guided and encouraged this work into being. Then I thank Dr. Douglas Kelly, who first put me in contact with Dr. Lane and encouraged me to press forward in this work. I would like to thank Drs. Wim Janse and Eddy Van der Borght of the Free University of Amsterdam for their encouragement in my early work on this subject and their excellent suggestion of adding a chapter on Calvin's view of the office of pastor. Drs. Michael Kruger and Richard Hawkes were very helpful in reading and critiquing the early chapters and encouraging me to keep at it. Thanks to each of you.

Writing of course comes down finally to words, which requires the assistance of proofreaders. Andy Pyrch helped with some early chapter editions, Jenni Pyrch, Aaron Gray, Andrew Shank and Angela Queen finished off the final edition. Thanks to you each.

Lastly, I would like to thank my family. I thank my sons: Collin, Taylor, Brandon and Preston, who never had a discouraging word but encouraged my research even when it cost them personally. Most of all I thank my dear wife Ann whose steady encouragement, sacrifice and more than occasional constructive comment made my work not only possible, but enjoyable.

Abbreviations

BLW	*The Bondage and Liberation of the Will.* Edited by A.N.S. Lane. Translated by G. I. Davies. Grand Rapids, Mich.: Baker, 2002.
CO	*Ioannis Calvini opera quae supersunt omnia.* Edited by G. Baum, E. Cunitz, E. Reuss. 59 vols. Brunswick: C.A. Schwetschke and Son, 1863-1900.
Commentary	*Calvin's Commentaries.* The Calvin Translation Society. 22 vols. Grand Rapids, Mich.: Baker, 2005.
CSW	*John Calvin, Tracts and Letters.* Edited by H. Beveridge and J. Bonnet. 7 vols. Edinburgh: Banner of Truth Trust, 2009.
Institutes	*Calvin: Institutes of the Christian Religion.* 2 vols. Edited by J.T. McNeill. Translated by F.L. Battles. Philadelphia, Pa.: Westminster, 1960.
OS	*Ioannis Calvini opera selecta.* Edited by P. Barth, W. Niesel, D. Scheuner. 5 vols. Munich: Christian Kaiser, 1926-52.
RCP	*The Register of the Company of Pastors of Geneva in the Time of Calvin.* Edited and translated by P.E. Hughes. Eugene, Oreg.: Wipf & Stock, 2004.

Table of Contents

Introduction 1

Section One

Chapter 1 -- The Divine Initiative in Sanctification 13

Chapter 2 -- Calvin's Anthropology and Its Implications for Sanctification ... 38

Chapter 3 -- Faith and Repentance 64

Chapter 4 -- The Life of the Christian Man within the Church 89

Section Two

Chapter 5 -- The Model of the Pious Pastor 114

Chapter 6 -- Calvin's Teaching to the Students of the Genevan Academy ... 141

Chapter 7 -- The Structures of the Genevan Academy which Enhanced Sanctification ... 167

Chapter 8 -- Comparing the Academies of Lausanne and Strasbourg with Geneva ... 197

Conclusions 227

Bibliography 237

Author Index 252

Introduction

"Donnez-moi du bois, et je vous envoie des flèches."[1]

From his refuge in Geneva, John Calvin lived with a burning passion—to reform his beloved French church. He had such a passion, in part, because he had been a true child of the church. He was reared in the shadows of the Cathedral Church of Noyon, whose steeples dominated the quiet village skyline as much as the church dominated its life and as much as the church would dominate Calvin's life. From her, Calvin's father earned his living as a kind of church accountant. Within her whitewashed walls, upon her stone floors, young Calvin studied and was nurtured, supported by her beneficence until he could no longer take her money in good conscience. He could easily write, with deep feeling for the church, "let us learn even from the simple title 'mother' how useful, indeed how necessary, it is that we should know her."[2] It was from this love for his Mother Church, who had given to him so much, that he desired to bring reform into her bosom.

To bring renewal Calvin not only strove to reform the theology of the church but desperately wanted to send to her pulpits a new kind of pastor, one marked by both a holy humility and a great boldness in preaching the Word. To accomplish this he would have to help produce such pastors. But where does one begin? Struck both by the lack of holiness in the Roman Catholic clergy, those "greedy priestlings" who are "prostituted to filthy gain,"[3] and by the lack of power in Roman practices of piety, Calvin charted a new course for sanctification among the clergy he would train, building on the lessons learned from earlier Reformers, the Church Fathers and Scripture itself. To assist this process, he utilized two tools. First, he developed in his writings a model of sanctification which fueled his teaching and educational practices. Second, he established the Genevan Academy in 1559 for the training of hundreds of Reformed pastors.

His approach to sanctification, which was outlined in the *Institutes*, exposited in sermons, and taught in lectures, was marked by two distinctives. First, under the influence of the *devotio moderna*,[4] he moved away from the emphasis on external disciplines and defined sanctification far more in terms of internal heart change, *pietas*.[5] "That reverence joined with love of God which the knowledge of his benefits induces."[6] Second, Calvin saw the general tendency behind Roman piety was toward exalting human ability, while simultaneously diminishing God's glory. Against this he rejected all efforts at flattering the

---

[1] Calvin to the churches of France, as cited by R.M. Kingdon, *Geneva and the Coming of the Wars of Religion in France, 1555-1563* (Geneva: Droz, 1956), Preface.
[2] *Institutes* 4.1.4.
[3] *Institutes* 4.10.15.
[4] A. Ganoczy, *The Young Calvin* (Philadelphia, Pa.: Westminster, 1987), 58.
[5] L.J. Richard, *The Spirituality of John Calvin* (Atlanta, Ga.: John Knox, 1974), 99.
[6] *Institutes* 1.2.1.

human condition and called for a radical humiliation of humanity with a simultaneous exaltation of God as the core condition for sanctification. This clear perspective, a two-fold knowledge of God and the self as they truly are, was not passive information. Rather, this knowledge should lead to a two-fold response: a movement of the human heart downward in humble prostration regarding oneself before God[7] and upward in reverence of God.[8] These two movements of the heart became the hallmark of his call to holiness.

By all accounts his efforts to train up godly pastors for France were met with great success. Students flocked to the Genevan Academy, for a year or perhaps even three, and then were sent out, mostly to France, where many were to face persecution and death.[9] But still they came to be trained and sent out. At its early height, some 200 were sent out in just a few years' time. They left Geneva with a boldness to preach the Word and with a holy humility regarding themselves. But how did this come to pass?

The rationale for this study

For 2000 years of church history, Christians have wondered how best to train and prepare Christian leaders. Within this development of the leader there has been a particularly pernicious issue: how to shape their character and heart, that is, how to enhance their holiness. From Origen's Alexandrian School, to Ignatius Loyola's Jesuits, to the founding of the Log College as precursor to Princeton, each generation has sought new answers to this age old question. With each new effort at perfecting our development of Christian leaders and their holiness something is gained and something is lost. Something is gained, for the Church tries new ways to train her leaders. Something is lost, for too often a new generation forgets what previous generations have understood. Often in the effort to try something new, something old, perhaps even more valuable, may well be lost. It is precisely toward this need, to understand what was known of old, that this book is written, in the hopes that something old might be understood about how John Calvin purposed to develop the holiness of pastoral candidates through the Genevan Academy, then, brought into the realm of modern scholarship, it may become useful again for our day. The insights that could be gained from a careful Historical/Theological analysis of Calvin's theology of sanctification, as expressed through the Genevan Academy, could potentially further a scholarly understanding of the theological inner workings of the Academy and might, as well, have implications for the theological underpinnings for modern Reformed educational institutions and may even illuminate how leaders are to be developed in the local church.

A word about definitions is in order. Calvin's distinguished between positional and progressive sanctification, but as we do today, often used the single term sanctification (*sanctificatio* in Latin, *sanctification* in French) to denote

---

[7] *Commentary*, Ps. 22:23; *CO* 31:232, "Iubet ab eo metuere, ut supplices coram eo se prosternant."
[8] "Sermon on Gen. 22:9-14," *CO* 23:775, "Au reste, l'amour de Dieu ne peut estre sans reverence."
[9] Kingdon, *Wars of Religion*, 144.

Introduction

either. Here he describes positional sanctification: "There is the word sanctify, which means that we should be separated from the world in order that we may be joined to the Son of God."[10] Calvin also recognized the progressive aspect of sanctification. "The meaning of the term sanctification we have already explained elsewhere in repeated instances—that renouncing the world, and clearing ourselves from the pollutions of the flesh, we offer ourselves to God as if in sacrifice, for nothing can with propriety be offered to Him, but what is pure and holy."[11] Further, while Calvin would clearly distinguish sanctification from justification,[12] he does not do so for regeneration and sanctification, tending to use several terms interchangeably, as Wallace points out. "Calvin, when he wishes to vary his language, can use many other terms such as repentance, mortification, new life, conversion, regeneration, to denote exactly the same as he means by the word sanctification."[13] For clarity in our writing, we will use Marcel's summary of Calvin's definition, referring in this work primarily to progressive and not positional sanctification. "Sanctification is that gratuitous and continuous operation of the Holy Spirit whereby He delivers the justified sinner from the defilement of sin, renews his whole nature after the image of God and enables him to perform good works."[14] Or as Calvin puts it: "Under the term *sanctification* is included the entire renovation of the man."[15] This is well justified by Calvin's frequent use of the term "sanctify" to denote the actual holiness of progressive sanctification. "We know that God is holy; thus we must be sanctified and holy too. For God cannot abide in the midst of our filth."[16]

Design of this book

We have taken as our overall task to answer the question: How did John Calvin encourage the sanctification of the candidates for pastoral office at the Genevan Academy? To explore this question we have divided our work into two sections. In the first we will explore the dynamics behind Calvin's theology of sanctification. In the second we will examine how his theology of sanctification shaped both the teaching and the educational methodologies which he used at the Academy in order to enhance his students' holiness. In addressing our central question we will attempt to advance the premise that Calvin's great concern for developing the holiness of the pastors at the Genevan Academy was shown

---

[10] J. Calvin, *Sermons on Ephesians* (tr. A. Golding; Edinburgh: Banner of Truth Trust, 1998), 577.
[11] *Commentary*, 1 Thess. 4:3.
[12] *Commentary*, 1 Cor. 6:11.
[13] R.S. Wallace, *Calvin's Doctrine of the Christian Life* (Edinburgh: Oliver and Boyd, 1959), 25.
[14] P. Marcel, "The Relation Between Justification and Sanctification in Calvin's Thought," *Evangelical Quarterly* 27 (1955), 133.
[15] *Commentary*, 1 Thess. 5:23.
[16] J. Calvin, *Sermons on the Book of Micah* (ed. and tr. B.W. Farley; Phillipsburg, N.J.: P&R, 2003), 134-35.

by the way his theology of sanctification was used to shape the teaching and educational structures of the Academy.

Section One: Defining principles from Calvin's theology of sanctification
In the first section, we attempt to answer the sub-question: What are the key principles of Calvin's theology of progressive sanctification which will shape his methods and teaching at the Genevan Academy? Since the first section is a broad survey of Calvin's mature theology of sanctification, we will draw primarily from his 1559 *Institutes*, his commentaries and his sermons. While much of Calvin research in our day is focused on the analysis of the various theological streams from which Calvin drank and the subsequent chronological development of his thought, necessary to understanding his life work, this project is less focused on the different phases of his development as it is on how his mature theology of sanctification came into play at the Academy during the final years of his life.

We will begin in Chapter 1 with Calvin's understanding of the divine role in sanctification, which shows our dependence on God. In Chapter 2 we will move to examine his view of humankind regarding our need for sanctification and so gain from that knowledge of self. Chapter 3 will describe his process of progressive sanctification. Chapter 4 will examine Calvin's disciplines of sanctification, both individual and corporate. In each of the chapters in Section One we will seek to define the key principles of Calvin's theology of sanctification in order to show in Section Two how his theology of sanctification informed his teaching and his methods of education at the Academy.

Section Two: Calvin's theology of sanctification as taught and practiced at the Genevan Academy
Having defined the principles of Calvin's theology of progressive sanctification in Section One, in Section Two we will use those principles to address the question: What were the specific teachings offered and the educational structures utilized by Calvin to enhance the *pietas* of the pastoral candidates he trained in the Genevan Academy? In addressing that question we must also ask: What is the model of the pious pastor toward which Calvin would train? The second section of this work will focus more narrowly on those sources which reveal both what Calvin taught and what educational methods were used at the Academy. To study his teaching, we will use as source material his lectures at the Academy, sermons given during this period and relevant correspondence. To understand the educational methods, we will examine the foundational documents of the Genevan Academy, as well as other historical documents, primarily correspondence to and from students, but also the *Registers of the Company of Pastors* and the *Registers of the Consistory of Geneva*.

In Chapter 5 we will outline the model of the pious pastor which formed the competency model toward which all of Calvin's training efforts were aimed. In Chapter 6 we will show how Calvin taught, with painstaking repetition, the theology around his view of sanctification. In Chapter 7 we will examine the educational structures designed to enhance the students' holiness, as illuminated by his theology of sanctification. In Chapter 8 we will compare the teaching and educational structures of the Genevan Academy with those of the Academies of Lausanne and Strasbourg, searching both for commonalities and any unique characteristics of the Academy in Geneva.

As we present the research on the educational methods and their influence on the students' holiness, particularly in Chapters 7 and 8, there are methodological limitations which must be acknowledged at the outset. While we may confidently discover the presence of any educational method—the use of pastoral mentors, for example—it is impossible to prove conclusively that any one method particularly contributed to the students' sanctification. To even attempt to assert proof of the effectiveness of these methods would require the ability to test each student before their attendance at the Academy in order to determine their level of holiness, could such a thing even be measured, and then to survey them again after their tenure at the Academy to ascertain what improvements had been made. Even then one could not scientifically assert that the change in their holiness was produced by the pastoral mentoring, rather than, for instance, the beauty of the sunsets in Geneva.

Given these limitations we expect our research to yield more suggestions rather than firm conclusions as to how useful any educational method or teaching was in enhancing holiness. This does not mean, however, that we will assert nothing regarding the educational structures and teaching. We will be able to show, for example, which educational structures were in place, the historical evidence supports this well. We will even be able to show, in most cases, that in line with Calvin's theology, he intended these structures to help in the students' sanctification. But then as to the effectiveness of these structures at actually producing sanctification, the historical data will suggest this rather than prove it.

Literature survey

As John Leith pointed out during the late 19th and early 20th centuries, the study of Calvin's theology revolved around the debate concerning Calvin's central organizing theological principle (*zentrale Dogma*).[17] Ferdinand Baur thought this central dogma was the absolute causality of God.[18] Karl Barth asserted that it was the Word of God.[19] Wilhelm Niesel said it was a Christo-centric focus.[20] Leith argued that it was "God's relationship to humankind and humankind's relationship to God" which served as Calvin's central focus.[21] Herman Bauke argued that Calvin lacked a central theme and instead had three forms that he

---

[17] J.H. Leith, *John Calvin's Doctrine of the Christian Life* (Louisville, Ky.: Westminster/John Knox, 1989), 28-35.
[18] F.C. Baur, "Über Princip und Charakter des Lehrbegriffs der reformirten Kirche in seinem Unterschied von dem der lutherischen, mit Rücksicht auf A. Schweizer's Darstellung der reformirten Glaubenslehre," *Theologische Jahrbücher* 6 (1847), 333.
[19] K. Barth, *The Word of God and the Word of Man* (tr. D. Horton; Grand Rapids, Mich.: Zondervan, 1935), 240.
[20] W. Niesel, *The Theology of Calvin* (tr. H. Knight; Philadelphia, Pa.: Westminster, 1956), 30.
[21] Leith, *Christian Life*, 16.

emphasized: the rational, the complex and the biblical.[22] Emile Doumergue goes further to say that Calvin's system is in fact only a collection of contrarieties defying systemization (*méthode des contrariétés*).[23]

In more recent years Calvin scholarship has turned away from the pursuit of a *zentrale Dogma* to focus on the developmental nature of Calvin's theology both by identifying the streams of thought which flowed into Calvin to shape his theology and by showing how his thinking progressed through the chronology of his writings. A.N.S. Lane, for example, intricately details Calvin's theological debt to the Church Fathers.[24] Irena Backus shows a similar dependence on the Fathers for Calvin's methodology.[25] Willem van 't Spijker has shown Calvin's dependence on contemporaries such as Luther and Bucer.[26] Wim Janse has shown the development of Calvin's thought on the Lord's Supper, including the somewhat surprising influence of Zwingli.[27]

Since our work is focused on Calvin's mature views and not his development, this review will primarily look at literature that touches upon Calvin's later views in three areas relevant to our goal: progressive sanctification, the pastoral office and the work of the Genevan Academy.

Calvin's theology of sanctification
Ronald Wallace's *Calvin's Doctrine of the Christian Life* is an admittedly uncritical and detailed rehearsal of every major feature in Calvin's theology of sanctification as seen through the lens of the *Institutes'* chapters on the *Life of the Christian Man*. Its chief value lies in its systematic presentation of Calvin's thought, drawing equally from the *Institutes*, commentaries and sermons. Wallace offers the "restoration of true order" as a possible central paradigm for Calvin's theology of sanctification.[28]

Leith's *John Calvin's Doctrine of the Christian Life*, by contrast with Wallace, takes a critical look at Calvin and finds six major inconsistencies in his doctrine of sanctification. For example, Leith says that Calvin will at one mo-

---

[22] H. Bauke, *Die Probleme der Theologie Calvins* (Leipzig: J.C. Hinrichs, 1922), 13-20.
[23] E. Doumergue, *Le caractère de Calvin* (Paris: Editions de Foi et Vie, 1921), 47.
[24] A.N.S. Lane, *John Calvin: Student of the Church Fathers* (Grand Rapids, Mich.: Baker, 1999).
[25] I. Backus, "Calvin's Patristic Models for Establishing the Company of Pastors," *Calvin and the Company of Pastors, Calvin Studies Society Papers 2003* (Grand Rapids, Mich.: CRC Product Services, 2004), 25-51.
[26] W. van 't Spijker, "Bucer's Influence on Calvin: Church and Community," *Martin Bucer Reforming Church and Community* (ed. D.F. Wright; Cambridge: Cambridge University Press, 1994), 32-44; "The Influence of Luther on Calvin According to the Institutes," *John Calvin's Institutes: His Opus Magnum* (ed. B.J. van der Walt; Potchefstroom, South Africa: Potchefstroom University for Christian Higher Education, 1986), 83-105.
[27] W. Janse, "Calvin's Eucharistic Theology: Three Dogma-Historical Observations," *Calvinus sacrarum literarum interpres, Papers of the International Congress on Calvin Research* (ed. H.J. Selderhuis; Göttingen: Vandenhoeck & Ruprecht, 2008), 37-69.
[28] Wallace, *Christian Life*, 101-22.

ment assert that the law is really the personal claim of God on humanity but then turn around and substitute the law for the relational aspect of God's claim, leading to a kind of legalism in practice.[29]

Paul Lobstein's *Die Ethik Calvins*[30] also uses the *Life of the Christian Man* as the lens through which to understand Calvin's theology of sanctification. Lobstein goes beyond Wallace and Leith by showing how vocation, church and state relate to the new life, offering a more complete understanding of Calvin's total theology of sanctification. Lobstein claims Calvin's theology contains a basic tension, teaching that sanctification is both God's work and something for which humanity must strive.[31] He asserts, as will we, that reverence becomes a key response of the Christian to God, and indeed to all authority. "This duty of reverence becomes for Calvin the general duty of obedience toward every authority."[32]

Roman Catholic scholar Lucien Richard[33] explains Calvin's theology of sanctification in light of major medieval spiritual sources such as the *devotio moderna*, the Brethren of the Common Life and Thomas à Kempis's *Imitatio Christi*. He asserts that Calvin, while deeply influenced by these movements, was an innovator who uniquely combined *sancta eruditio* and *pietas*, that is, a view of sanctification that called for progress in knowledge through the Word and also progress in holiness through the Spirit.

Edward Dowey's *The Knowledge of God in Calvin's Theology* focuses on the acquisition of the *duplex cognitio Domini*, that is, the knowledge of God as both Creator and Redeemer.[34] The *duplex cognitio*, though related to, is distinguished from the two-fold knowledge of God and self.[35] The growth in this knowledge leads to growth in worship and obedience, that is, in holiness.[36] Dowey makes important connections between the *duplex cognitio* and faith, as well as repentance and God's Word,[37] therefore his book is essential for understanding Calvin on sanctification.

T.F. Torrance's *Calvin's Doctrine of Man*[38] reveals the helplessness of humanity in its own sanctification, but always casts this helplessness on the background of God's hopeful grace.[39] He suggests a two-fold purpose to Calvin's anthropology: "by pointing the believer to his original creation in the image of

---

[29] Leith, *Christian Life*, 217-220.
[30] P. Lobstein, *Die Ethik Calvins in Ihren Grundzügen Entworfen* (Strasbourg: C.F. Schmidt's, 1877).
[31] Lobstein, *Die Ethik Calvins*, 72.
[32] Lobstein, *Die Ethik Calvins*, 49, "Diese Pflicht der Ehrfurcht wird von Calvin zur allgemeinen Pflicht des Gehorsams gegen jede Obrigkeit."
[33] Richard, *Spirituality of John Calvin*, 48-73.
[34] E.A. Dowey, Jr., *The Knowledge of God in Calvin's Theology* (New York, N.Y.: Columbia University Press, 1965).
[35] Dowey, *Knowledge of God*, 18-19.
[36] Dowey, *Knowledge of God*, 28, 50-52.
[37] Dowey, *Knowledge of God*, 172.
[38] T.F. Torrance, *Calvin's Doctrine of Man* (Westport, Conn.: Greenwood, 1997).
[39] Torrance, *Calvin's Doctrine of Man*, 20.

God to produce gratitude, and by pointing him to his present miserable condition to produce humility."[40] Calvin, it would appear, mirrors his two-fold knowledge of God and self with a two-fold response: gratitude and humility. Torrance casts these responses as movements, as will we. These are movements upward and downward, the appropriate "motions of grace,"[41] which lead humanity finally to the adoration of God's glory.[42]

Richard Muller's work in *Calvin and the Reformed Tradition* helps to bring clarity to the modern debate over the relationship between union with Christ and justification.[43] Carefully examining the Reformed scholars who followed Calvin, Muller is able to convincingly demonstrate that Calvin, in line with many of his successors, gave union with Christ great priority in the process of sanctification.

Dennis Tamburello thoroughly explores the *unio mystica* in *Union with Christ* demonstrating how Christ himself powers the transformation toward holiness, including the acquisition of the knowledge of God and the self.[44] He makes helpful observations on the relationship of God's love and progress in holiness,[45] though we will argue that even he understates the importance of love in Calvin's understanding of sanctification.[46]

Elsie McKee's work on pastoral piety does a marvelous job of bringing together the concept of piety and how Calvin hoped to encourage this in others through his specific teachings.[47] This is largely done through a collection of Calvin's works on the subject with some good commentary from her, which places his teachings in their historical settings.

Both Niesel and Barth offer important comments on Calvin's theology of sanctification. Barth, finding a tension between grace and legalism in Calvin's view of sanctification, asserts that Calvin seems to be at times a bitter moralist: "Calvin was a man over whose vitality a deep shadow lay."[48] This view, we will argue, is not well supported by the Calvin revealed in his pastoral correspondence and sermons. Niesel has a more positive evaluation of Calvin's theology of sanctification seeing in it the call to imitate Christ, not in slavish obedience, but as drawn by the power of Christ.[49]

In addition to these major works, many recent articles shed light on Calvin's understanding of sanctification, and among these, two stand out. First is Barba-

---

[40] Torrance, *Calvin's Doctrine of Man*, 13.
[41] Torrance, *Calvin's Doctrine of Man*, 115.
[42] Torrance, *Calvin's Doctrine of Man*, 17.
[43] R.A. Muller, *Calvin and the Reformed Tradition* (Grand Rapids, Mich.: Baker Academic, 2012).
[44] D.E. Tamburello, *Union with Christ: John Calvin and the Mysticism of St. Bernard* (Louisville, Ky.: Westminster/John Knox, 1994), 11.
[45] Tamburello, *Union with Christ*, 65, 105.
[46] Tamburello, *Union with Christ*, 105-07.
[47] E.A. McKee (ed.), *John Calvin: Writings on Pastoral Piety* (New York, N.Y.: Paulist, 2001).
[48] K. Barth, *The Theology of John Calvin* (Grand Rapids, Mich.: Eerdmans, 1995), 120.
[49] Niesel, *Theology of Calvin*, 127-29.

ra Pitkin's "Redefining Repentance" which demonstrates the centrality of repentance to Calvin.[50] Second, Herman Selderhuis's "Faith between God and the Devil" helpfully portrays sanctification as the struggle for faith against the demonic temptation to unbelief.[51]

These authors offer good agreement over Calvin's basic theology of sanctification. Wallace, Leith, Lobstein and Richard concur that Calvin calls for a dependence upon God while we are yet to actively mortify our flesh and quicken our spirit. This mortification, they agree, consists of the "denial of the self" and "bearing the cross;" while vivification consists of the "meditation on the future life."

There is, however, debate surrounding the question of Calvin's possible legalism. Barth, who will at points defend Calvin against the technical claim of legalism, says, "We cannot really learn to know the details of the Genevan system that is so much admired without words like, 'tyranny' and 'Pharisaism' coming almost naturally to our lips."[52] Leith, perhaps most clearly, charges Calvin with legalism: "Yet his writings and especially his practices reveal an unmistakable legalistic tendency."[53] Niesel defends Calvin saying that one who speaks so freely of the life of the Christian man should not be assumed to teach "a monastic outlook."[54] Torrance too defends Calvin asserting that the assumption behind all of Calvin's apparent moralism is "his great comprehensive inference from grace."[55]

Beyond the question of Calvin's possible legalism lies a more difficult one: What is the essence of Calvin's view of sanctification? Wallace offers the theme of the true order. Leith proposes the production of the person, both humble and confident, who emerges from the intense relationship with God.[56] Richard finds as key Calvin's equal emphasis on piety/Spirit and erudition/Word.[57] Niesel focuses on the imitation of Christ.[58] Ford Battles offers the theme of the double-knowledge of God's glory and of our sinfulness.[59] We will attempt to show, building upon both Battles and Leith, that the two-fold knowledge of God and self, leading to the two-fold movement of the human heart, downward

---

[50] B. Pitkin, "Redefining Repentance: Calvin and Melanchthon," *Calvinus Praeceptor Ecclesiae* (ed. H.J. Selderhuis; Geneva: Droz, 2004), 275-86.

[51] H.J. Selderhuis, "Faith Between God and the Devil: Calvin's Doctrine of Faith as Reflected in His Commentary on the Psalms," *Calvin, Beza and Later Calvinism, John Calvin and the Interpretation of Scripture, Calvin Studies Society Papers 2005, 2000, 2002* (Grand Rapids, Mich.: CRC Product Services, 2006), 188-205.

[52] Barth, *Theology of Calvin*, 122.

[53] Leith, *Christian Life*, 54.

[54] Niesel, *Theology of Calvin*, 141- 43.

[55] Torrance, *Calvin's Doctrine of Man*, 20.

[56] Leith, *Christian Life*, 107.

[57] Richard, *Spirituality of John Calvin*, 184-92.

[58] Niesel, *Theology of Calvin*, 143.

[59] F.L. Battles (tr.), *The Piety of John Calvin: An Anthology Illustrative of the Spirituality of the Reformer of Geneva* (Grand Rapids, Mich.: Baker, 1978), 14.

in prostration before God and upward in reverence, is the central pillar of Calvin's understanding of sanctification.

While these works offer insights in Calvin's view of sanctification, they offer neither an overarching taxonomy of his entire view of progressive sanctification nor do they show how his theology relates to his work at the Academy. Therefore our intended exploration could helpfully illuminate these two areas.

Calvin's view of the pastoral office
Calvin's view of the pastoral office has been studied with increasing popularity recently. Robert Kingdon's work serves as a foundation for studies on many aspects of church life in Geneva including the pastoral office and the work of the Consistory.[60] A thorough study of the Genevan pastorate is offered in the Calvin Studies Society's helpful collection.[61] There Darlene Flaming offers an in-depth understanding of the processes by which pastors were examined and approved for office.[62] R. Ward Holder presents a comprehensive framework of the pastor's call and work.[63] Erik de Boer shows how the *Congrégations* were used for the in-service training of pastors.[64] Beyond that collection, Andrew Pettegree has shown the transformation necessary to go from Roman priest to Reformed pastor.[65] McKee[66] and Holder[67] show the requirements for the pastoral office. Karin Maag has written extensively on the role and training of the

---

[60] R.M. Kingdon, "The Geneva Consistory in the Time of Calvin," *Calvinism in Europe, 1540-1620* (eds. A. Pettegree, A. Duke, G. Lewis; Cambridge: Cambridge University Press, 1996), 21-34.

[61] D. Foxgrover (ed.), *Calvin and the Company of Pastors, Calvin Studies Society Papers 2003* (Grand Rapids, Mich.: CRC Product Services, 2004).

[62] D.K. Flaming, "The Apostolic and Pastoral Office: Theory and Practice in Calvin's Geneva," *Calvin and the Company of Pastors, Calvin Studies Society Papers 2003* (Grand Rapids, Mich.: CRC Product Services, 2004), 149-72.

[63] R. W. Holder, "Calvin's Exegetical Understanding of the Office of Pastor," *Calvin and the Company of Pastors, Calvin Studies Society Papers 2003* (Grand Rapids, Mich.: CRC Product Services, 2004), 179-209.

[64] E.A. de Boer, "Calvin and Colleagues: Propositions and Disputations in the Context of the *Congrégations* in Geneva," *Calvinus Praeceptor Ecclesiae* (ed. H.J. Selderhuis; Geneva: Droz, 2004), 331-42; "The *Congrégation*: An In-service Theological Training Center for Preachers to the People of Geneva," *Calvin and the Company of Pastors, Calvin Studies Society Papers 2003* (Grand Rapids, Mich.: CRC Product Services, 2004), 57-87.

[65] A. Pettegree, "The Clergy and the Reformation: from 'Devilish Priesthood' to New Professional Elite," *The Reformation of the Parishes* (ed. A. Pettegree; Manchester: Manchester University Press, 1993), 1-21.

[66] E.A. McKee, "Calvin and His Colleagues as Pastors: Some New Insights into the Collegial Ministry of Word and Sacraments," *Calvinus Praeceptor Ecclesiae* (Geneva: Droz, 2004), 9-42; *Elders and the Plural Ministry* (Geneva: Droz, 1988).

[67] R.W. Holder, "Paul as Calvin's (Ambivalent) Pastoral Model," *Dutch Review of Church History/Nederlands Archief voor Kerkgeschiedenis* 84 (2004), 284-98.

Introduction

pastor.[68] Even more recently Scott Manetsch has rendered a careful examination of the life and work of the Company of Pastors.[69]

There is a clear consensus among these authors that Calvin meant to reform the pastoral office from what it had degenerated to under Rome into a new cadre of clergy who were both truly called and faithful to that call. These valuable resources, however, do little to address the question of how Calvin's view of sanctification was applied to the shaping of pastoral candidates at the Genevan Academy, hence the need for our study.

The work of the Genevan Academy
The work of the Genevan Academy is far less studied than either sanctification or the pastoral office. Though Charles Borgeaud[70] remains the standard in the field, thoroughly documenting the facts of the Academy, his account is at times clouded, if not by hagiography, then at least by reverent idealizing. "Les relations de disciple à maître sont infiniment plus faciles, plus intimes que de nos jours."[71] Maag's work offers the modern reader a rigorous understanding of the inner workings of the Academy through a thorough examination of primary source documents in Geneva.[72] She gives valuable insight into the intimate connection between the pastors of Geneva and the running of the Academy. Maag argues persuasively that the Academy was designed first to be a seminary,[73] an opinion held as well by Borgeaud,[74] and one which our research confirms.

There are, however, still unanswered questions: What were the students taught? What were the disciplines they kept? How did each of these contribute to the sanctification of these pastoral candidates? Though there is some good primary data with which to work, such as student letters and the lectures of Calvin at the Academy, it would appear that no one has yet attempted to piece together the available data in such a way as to reveal the correlation between Calvin's theology of sanctification and how the methods and teachings of the Academy were used to enhance the holiness of the students there.

---

[68] K. Maag, "Education and Training for the Calvinist Ministry: The Academy of Geneva, 1559-1620," *The Reformation of the Parishes* (ed. A. Pettegree; Manchester: Manchester University Press, 1993), 133-52; "Called to Be a Pastor: Issues of Vocation in the Early Modern Period," *Sixteenth Century Journal* 35 (2004), 65-78.
[69] S.M. Manetsch, *Calvin's Company of Pastors: Pastoral Care and the Emerging Reformed Church, 1536-1609* (New York, N.Y.: Oxford University Press, 2013).
[70] C. Borgeaud, *Histoire de l'Université de Genève. Tome 1: L'Académie de Calvin 1559-1798* (Geneva: Georg, 1900).
[71] Borgeaud, *Histoire de l'Université*, 138.
[72] K. Maag, *Seminary or University? The Genevan Academy and Reformed Higher Education, 1560-1620* (Aldershot, England: Scolar, 1995).
[73] Maag, *Genevan Academy*, 194.
[74] Borgeaud, *Histoire de l'Université*, 51.

Nexus of all three: Calvin's encouragement of the sanctification of pastoral candidates at the Genevan Academy

While there is little written directly on this topic, several articles explore Calvin's particular approach to education and at least touch upon his focus on holiness. T.M. Moore examines Calvin's work through an educational matrix rather than one of pastoral sanctification.[75] Frederick Eby helpfully places Calvin's educational philosophy among his contemporaries and rightly detects his unique success at "welding church, state and home into one combined institution for the purpose of instruction."[76] Stefan Ehrenpreis sheds light on the broad categories of content in Calvin's training.[77]

Although these sources offer pieces of the puzzle, no one has put them together in such a way as to answer our question: How did John Calvin encourage the sanctification of the candidates for pastoral office at the Genevan Academy? By correlating what Calvin taught about sanctification with what he taught at the Academy and the historical practices of the Academy, we will be able to gain a clearer understanding of exactly how Calvin intended to enhance the holiness of the pastors he hoped to unleash for the furtherance of the Reformation and the help of his beloved French church.

---

[75] T.M. Moore, "Some Observations Concerning the Educational Philosophy of John Calvin," *Westminster Theological Journal* 46 (1984), 140-55.
[76] F. Eby, *Early Protestant Educators* (New York, N.Y.: McGraw Hill, 1931), 235.
[77] S. Ehrenpreis, "Reformed Education in Early Modern Europe: A Survey," *Dutch Review of Church History/Nederlands Archief voor Kerkgeschiedenis* 85 (2005), 39-51.

Chapter 1 - The Divine Initiative in Sanctification

"Ero vobis in patrem."[1]

The Role of God the Father

The Father elects us to sanctification

Calvin wished to prove that God was the author of our sanctification, and that the methods of the Roman Church, the "satisfactions, superstitions and idolatry,"[2] were not only unhelpful, but hurtful to holiness, inasmuch as they gave humanity a false confidence in its own abilities. Calvin carefully builds his case by showing the role of the triune God in our sanctification: the Father decreeing our holiness, the Son achieving it and the Spirit applying it. In doing so Calvin will always aim to bring humankind to a true knowledge of self and God, the two-fold knowledge that will humble humanity and lead it to exalt God. As Wendel says, "Above all, God and man must again be seen in their rightful places."[3] Therefore, for Calvin, our holiness begins not with human effort but with Divine election.[4] "Our holiness flows from the fountain of divine election."[5] It is God's election that yields the fruit of holiness,[6] which even makes the Word of God bear fruit in our lives.[7] So great is Calvin's emphasis on election that some, such as Cottret, conclude that Calvin even went too far, terrifying believers for polemical purposes.[8] Niesel argues that in securing our holiness in the will of God, Calvin meant to counter the Roman idea that our holiness could be obtained by human effort,[9] for it is by mercy, not merit, that we progress.[10] "The doctrine of election…is an effectual antidote to every attempt on the part of man to elevate himself in terms of religious significance; it is the spearhead of the attack on the Romish doctrine of grace."[11] Calvin argued

---

[1] *Commentary*, 2 Cor. 6:18; *CO* 50:83.
[2] Ganoczy, *Young Calvin*, 195.
[3] F. Wendel, *Calvin: Origins and Development of His Religious Thought* (New York, N.Y.: Harper & Row, 1963), 151.
[4] So concludes Lobstein of Calvin: "We are chosen by God in order to live a holy and stainless life." Lobstein, *Die Ethik Calvins*, 23.
[5] *Commentary*, 1 Cor. 1:2. Cf. *Commentary*, 1 Pet. 1:3.
[6] *Commentary*, Eph. 1:4.
[7] *CO* 22:46, *French Catechism of 1537*, "La semence de la parolle de Dieu prent racine et fructifie en ceux la seulement lesquelz le Seigneur par son election eternelle a predestiné pour ses enfans et heretiers du royaulme celeste."
[8] B. Cottret, *Calvin: A Biography* (tr. M.W. McDonald; Grand Rapids, Mich.: Eerdmans, 2000), 322-23.
[9] H.J. Schroeder (tr.), *The Canons and Decrees of the Council of Trent* (Rockford, Ill.: Tan Books and Publishers, 1978), 46. "If anyone says that the good works of the one justified are in such manner the gifts of God that they are not also the good merits of him justified…let him be anathema."
[10] *Institutes* 3.22.1, 3.17.6.
[11] Niesel, *Theology of Calvin*, 168.

against the Catholic Schoolmen that it was God's will in election, not our good work, which makes us holy, and therefore, upon which we should lean.[12] This can be seen in his reply to Bishop Sadolet, "The end of gratuitous election…is, that we may lead pure and unpolluted lives before God."[13] Against those who cry "merit," Calvin would cry more loudly "mercy" (*misericordia*), for there is nothing but mercy on which we may stand.[14] First to last our holiness is the work of God, not our own, for "we are God's work, and … everything good in us is his creation."[15] So it is to God we must look for help in holiness.

The Father sanctifies us by his grace, not our works
Not only the beginning, but the progress of sanctification is dependent on God's grace rather than our good works.[16] For God, "whenever it pleases him, changes the worst men into the best."[17] Sanctification is a work wrought by God,[18] because he wants his children to be holy as he is holy.[19] Indeed, God freely justifies his own for this purpose, that he might "restore them to true righteousness by sanctification of his Spirit."[20] Since God is holy and abhors sin, yet desires to be joined to us as his people, he works to purify "by his Spirit those whom he has joined to himself."[21] The Christian must come to understand that God causes them to be holy so that they can "rest from all their affections and desires" and allow God to work in them.[22] For Calvin, justification and sanctification are both of grace.[23] Therefore Calvin fights just as doggedly to uphold sanctification by grace as he does to demonstrate justification by grace. This causes Marcel to observe that for Calvin, "In the justification of the righteous as in the sanctification of the righteous, all is grace."[24]

God begins sanctification in our lives by changing our wills
Calvin locates the beginning of God's gracious work of sanctification in the will, rather than the intellect,[25] agreeing with Paul's assertion in Phil. 1:6. "There is no doubt that through 'the beginning of a good work' he denotes the very origin of conversion itself, which is in the will."[26] God, in effect, gives us

---

[12] *Institutes* 3.17.15.
[13] *CSW*, Vol. 1, 44.
[14] *Commentary*, Rom. 9:11; *CO* 49:177.
[15] *Commentary*, Eph. 2:10.
[16] *Institutes* 3.3.1.
[17] *Institutes* 4.12.9.
[18] Wallace, *Christian Life*, 25.
[19] Battles, *The Piety of John Calvin*, 52.
[20] *Institutes* 3.3.19.
[21] *Institutes* 3.17.6.
[22] J. Calvin, *Sermons on the Ten Commandments* (ed. and tr. B.W. Farley; Grand Rapids, Mich.: Baker, 1980), 123.
[23] *Institutes* 2.1.7.
[24] Marcel, "Justification and Sanctification," 143.
[25] R.A. Muller, *The Unaccommodated Calvin* (New York, N.Y.: Oxford University Press, 2000), 171.
[26] *Institutes* 2.3.6.

a renewed will.²⁷ Calvin takes pains to explain that though we are given a new will, our will is not destroyed in the process, but rather a "new will" is a change of will, from an evil to a good will.²⁸

Yet God does change our will contrary to our own will, for we would have no inclination in us which would naturally submit to the change. Calvin wants to refute the Roman notion that we contribute something, even assent of our will, to our sanctification. He describes the conversion of Paul as the prototype for all repentance—unwilling. "Neither is our will one hair readier to obey than was Paul's, until such time as the pride of our heart be beaten down, and he has made us not only flexible but also willing to obey and follow."²⁹ It must be the case that God works above our will, for no good would come forth from us without God's intervention.³⁰

The Father produces good works in us

In his effort to leave nothing to the merit of good works, Calvin is concerned to relate evangelical obedience and good works back to God. Polemically it is important for Calvin to establish the connection between God and our good works for two reasons. First, as Niesel points out,³¹ Calvin has always to address those critics, such as Bishop Sadolet,³² who accused him of encouraging immorality by discouraging good works with his teaching on sanctification by grace. Second, while affirming the role of good works, he wanted to prove that they could never merit what Roman theology claimed. Calvin, himself careful of personal holiness, seemed deeply stung by criticism of licentiousness and was quick to affirm their importance. "If election has as its goal holiness of life, it ought rather to arouse and goad us eagerly to set our mind upon it than to serve as a pretext for doing nothing."³³

Calvin therefore calls the Christian to respond to God in faith-driven obedience. He will use a favorite term, "the obedience of faith" (*obsequium fidei*), to show that our obedience is only accomplished by God through faith. "When then the Lord goes before us with his instruction and shows the way," then we yield to him "the obedience of faith."³⁴ It is God's work that makes our new will turn in obedience toward him.³⁵ Yet even here Calvin attributes to humanity no ability apart from grace to obey. "The first part of a good work is will; the

---

[27] *Institutes* 2.3.10.
[28] *Institutes* 2.3.6.
[29] *Commentary*, Acts 9:5.
[30] *Institutes* 2.3.9.
[31] Niesel, *Theology of Calvin*, 130-31.
[32] Bishop Sadolet accused, "When I say by faith alone, I do not mean, as those inventors of novelties do, a mere credulity and confidence in God...it is not enough...Christ was sent that we, by well-doing, may, through him, be accepted of God. *CSW*, Vol. 1, 9, "Sadolet's letter to the Genevan Senate and People."
[33] *Institutes* 3.23.12.
[34] *Commentary*, Hos. 1:2.
[35] *CO* 1:30; 1536 *Institutes*.

other, a strong effort to accomplish it; the author of both is God."[36] Calvin is redundantly clear; God is the author of our good will and our good works, first to last. "If it is the part of God to renew the whole man, there is nothing left for free will. For if it had been our part to cooperate with God, Paul would have spoken thus—'May God aid or promote your sanctification.' But when he says, *sanctify you wholly*, he makes him the sole Author of the entire work."[37] Calvin asserts so completely that sanctification comes by God's grace and not our good works that he calls believers to actually rest in God. "If people were able on their own strength to fulfill the law, He would have said to them, 'Work!' But on the contrary He said: 'Rest in order that God might work.'"[38] This introduces a tension, perhaps even a paradox, in Calvin's thought, as Lobstein acknowledges.[39] For Calvin does not ultimately call for quietism but a very active pursuit of holiness. Calvin at least attempts to solve this conundrum by pointing out that our activity in sanctification (self-denial, cross-bearing, use of the sacraments, etc.) always relies on grace in such a way that it may be described as passive. "Believers act passively, so to speak, seeing that the capacity is supplied from heaven."[40]

Since even our obedience flows from God, it can bring no merit to the individual. Calvin will admit that in a state of grace believers have a new will which is "inclined to follow the action of grace." But even this inclination is from God, nourished by the Holy Spirit.[41] For even *in* the state of grace believers do not have within themselves the "power to work in partnership with God's grace."[42] We do not possess goodness as autonomous individuals, but rather our good works depend on a never-ending stream of grace to our will, such that "controlled by grace, it never will perish, but, if grace forsake it, it will straightway fall."[43] The one hoping to find some merit behind his good work is sternly quieted by Calvin, "When a person relying on his own strength wants to acquit himself before God, he cannot lift a finger or have one single good idea as to how it should be done."[44]

Regarding good works then, humanity is forced to look humbly to God for increase in holiness, and importantly for Calvin, left without any merit obtained from good works, thus rendering all satisfactions and penances moot. Sanctification is of God alone, from conception to completion. We are left in humility

---

[36] *Institutes* 2.3.9.
[37] *Commentary*, 1 Thess. 5:23.
[38] *Sermons on the Ten Commandments*, 118.
[39] Lobstein, *Die Ethik Calvins*, 72.
[40] *Institutes* 2.5.11. Cf. J. Boisset, "Justification et Sanctification chez Calvin," *Calvinus Theologus* (Neukirchen: Neukirchener Verlag, 1974), 18.
[41] *Institutes* 2.3.11.
[42] *Institutes* 2.3.11.
[43] *Institutes* 2.3.14.
[44] *Sermons on the Ten Commandments*, 118.

Chapter 1 - The Divine Initiative in Sanctification

to turn to God and ask for help to become holy.[45] "There is no other method of living piously and justly than that of depending upon God."[46]

We find here then our first principle from Calvin's theology of progressive sanctification, which however, we will assign the number 4, to build on other principles which may logically precede this one.

> **Principle 4: God Reliance. Because God is the one who sanctifies, therefore rely on God's powerful grace, and not yourself, to become holy.** God is the author of sanctification, working through the election of the Father, union with the Son and the indwelling of the Spirit to make the believer holy as he continuously relies on the grace of God and stops relying on his goodness or his own ability to improve himself.

The Father's love is key to our sanctification

Calvin will make clear that holiness–piety–begins with and grows to fruition only as we understand that God loves us, as a Father loves his children. "I call "piety" that reverence joined with love of God which the knowledge of his benefits induces. For until men recognize that they owe everything to God, that they are nourished by his fatherly care...they will never yield him willing service."[47] It is not until we know that we are "nourished by his fatherly care" that we truly know God as we ought, and then will look to him to further our holiness as our loving Father. "The first step toward godliness [is] to recognize that God is our Father to watch over us, govern and nourish us."[48] It is to this love that Calvin will point us again and again for furtherance in our sanctification.[49] Indeed, Calvin, who has been accused of possessing a certain emotional malaise,[50] could not sound healthier when it comes to reminding us of the Father's love for us, "We are indeed his children, whom he has received into his faithful protection to nourish and educate."[51]

Calvin, of course, did not invent the idea that God's love is a prime force behind our sanctification but, as Spijker observes, borrowed heavily from Luther. Calvin followed Luther's concept of God's fatherly goodness in the first edition of the *Institutes*, referring to God's *paterna benignitas ac clementia* (fatherly benevolence and mercy), as he explains the Apostles Creed.[52] Luther had made this emphasis clear, as well, in his landmark Galatians commentary. "The Father offers unto me, by His promise, His grace, and His fatherly favor. This remains then, that I should receive this grace. And this is done when I

---

[45] *Commentary*, 1 Thess. 3:12.
[46] *Commentary*, Gen. 17:1. Cf. *Commentary*, Jer. 17:6, 14; Eph. 2:10; 1 Cor. 1:2; 15:10; 2 Pet. 1:5.
[47] *Institutes* 1.2.1.
[48] *Institutes* 2.6.4.
[49] Leith, *Christian Life*, 21. Cf. *Commentary*, Jer. 16:10; Hos. 6:1; 14:4.
[50] "Calvin was a singularly anxious man and, as a reformer, fearful and troubled." W.J. Bouwsma, *John Calvin: A Sixteenth-Century Portrait* (New York, N.Y.: Oxford University Press, 1988), 32. Cf. Barth, *Theology of Calvin*, 120.
[51] *Institutes* 1.14.22.
[52] Spijker, "The Influence of Luther on Calvin," 89.

again with this groaning do cry, and with a childlike heart, do assent unto the name, Father."[53] Additionally, Ganoczy shows Calvin's close connection to this theme from the *devotio moderna*,[54] as represented by *The Imitation of Christ*.[55] "Ah, Lord God, my holy Lover, when You come into my heart, all that is within me will rejoice. You are my glory and the exultation of my heart."[56]

While following the lead of others in espousing God's love as central to our sanctification, it seems likely that Calvin was also reacting in part against the arid speculative theologies spun by the Sorbonne and other Catholic Scholastics, those "Questionarians," whom Calvin would note, had failed to produce vital religion.[57] Certainly, he meant as well to rebuff the Catholic dependence on making oneself holy by human effort, in order to better earn a place in the Father's heart, by countering that God's fatherly love has already been awarded to us.[58] Whatever the streams that fed into his thoughts, they flowed richly and deeply into this great theme of the Father's love as the ground of our sanctification. But how was the Father's love to be known?

God's love is seen most clearly in the Son
Calvin repeatedly asserts that the love of God for his children is primarily manifested in Christ. "Christ, then, is so illustrious and singular a proof of divine love towards us, that whenever we look upon him, he fully confirms to us the truth that God is love [*dilectio*]."[59] It is the sacrifice of Christ for us which proves God's fatherly love for us. "This distinction is inferred from very many passages of Scripture…'not that we first loved God, but that he first loved us,

---

[53] E. Middleton (tr.), *Martin Luther: Commentary on Galatians* (Grand Rapids, Mich.: Kregel, 1979), 251-52.

[54] The *devotio moderna*, flowing from the *Brethren of the Common Life*, founded by Geerte Groote (d. 1384), went beyond the more purely *external* forms of devotion, characteristic of the earlier medieval period, hence *moderna*, to emphasize a highly personal relationship with God through *inner-heart* devotion. Calvin came under the influence of the *devotio moderna* at the College of Montaigu in Paris, an influence which was later reinforced by Bucer's tutelage as well. (Ganoczy, *Young Calvin*, 58-59; R.C. Gleason, *John Calvin and John Owen on Mortification: A Comparative Study in Reformed Spirituality*, New York, N.Y.: Peter Lang, 1995, 47).

[55] Many have seen the influence of Thomas à Kempis's *Imitation of Christ* on the thoughts and spirituality of Calvin. (R.S. Wallace, *Calvin, Geneva and the Reformation*, Eugene, Oreg.: Wipf & Stock, 1998, 191) Required reading at Montaigu while Calvin was a student there, (Ganoczy, *Young Calvin*, 58) one can easily see Calvin's reliance on *Imitation* when we compare its description of self-examination with Calvin's. "Keep your eye upon yourself in the first place, and especially admonish yourself in preference to admonishing your friend." (Thomas à Kempis, *The Imitation of Christ*; trs. A. Croft, H.F. Bolton; Milwaukee, Wis.: Bruce, 1962, 1:21) Calvin writes: "For claiming as his own what pleases him, he censures the character and morals of others….Let us, then, unremittingly examining our faults, call ourselves back to humility." (*Institutes* 3.7.4).

[56] Thomas à Kempis, *The Imitation of Christ*, 3:5.

[57] *Commentary*, Tit. 3:9.

[58] *Commentary*, Col. 1:5.

[59] *Commentary*, 1 John 4:9; *CO* 55:353.

Chapter 1 - The Divine Initiative in Sanctification

and sent his Son to be the propitiation for our sins.'"[60] In this forgiveness of our sins God's love is seen, for he stands ready to pardon us.[61] Only as we fix our gaze on Jesus Christ can we be fully convinced of the Father's love,[62] for there the "paternal love of God is found."[63]

God's love is seen also in creation
To underscore God's love, Calvin points to it as well in creation and providence. "For if it be asked, why the world has been created, why we have been placed in it to possess the dominion of the earth...no other reason can be adduced, except the gratuitous love of God."[64] God's fatherly generosity, not just for the elect but toward all humanity, must be read clearly from the very fact that he has so amply furnished the world "with an immense profusion of wealth, before he formed man"[65] rather than bringing mankind into a barren place.[66] Were God's beneficence missed in the creation around us, then we need look no further than the creation of our own being to see God's fatherly love "which ought justly to strike us with amazement."[67] His children must recognize God's good purposes toward them by seeing what God has created for them,[68] and in seeing the "sweetness of his beneficence and goodness," they should respond to God's fatherly love with heartfelt thankfulness.[69]

God's love draws us toward him for sanctification
God's love acts as the motive force in our sanctification, exerting a kind of gravitational pull which sets the whole machine of sanctification into motion in our hearts. "That abundant sweetness which God has stored up for those who fear him cannot be known without at the same time powerfully moving us. And once anyone has been moved by it, it utterly ravishes him and draws him to itself."[70] This is not bare information but a deeply personal knowing, as we experience the favors of God, that cannot but "attract us toward him even more."[71] Even God's voice draws us, for perceiving the paternal affection in his voice, rather than running away, we are gently enticed toward him.[72] If we do not know this love, we will remain cold and unmoved toward God, but when we know his love toward us, "it is certain that this will draw us to him fully."[73]

---

[60] *Institutes* 2.17.2.
[61] *Commentary*, Hos. 6:1; cf. John 3:16.
[62] *Institutes* 2.16.3; *Commentary*, 1 John 4:10.
[63] *Commentary*, 1 John 4:16.
[64] *Commentary*, 1 John 4:9.
[65] *Commentary*, Gen. 1:26.
[66] *Institutes* 1.14.2.
[67] *Commentary*, Ps. 8:7.
[68] *Institutes* 1.14.21.
[69] *Institutes* 1.14.22.
[70] *Institutes* 3.2.41.
[71] *Sermons on the Ten Commandments*, 41.
[72] *Sermons on the Ten Commandments*, 258.
[73] "Sermon on Deut. 6:4-9," *CO* 26:439. Cf. *Commentary*, Mic. 7:19.

This wooing power of the love of God will become central to Calvin's schema of sanctification. While we must see our depravity to understand ourselves well, knowledge of depravity may only leave us in a morose heap. It has no power by itself to move us toward holiness, only God's love does. Therefore Calvin will repeatedly remind us that while God could be stern, he chooses rather to treat us graciously, so that "by doing so we see that he wanted to make them aware of his goodness in order to win them better."[74] So clearly does this theme occur throughout Calvin's writings, that Battles concludes that for Calvin, "God is first and foremost our father, our divine parent exceeding all human parents."[75]

Calvin returns to this theme, because he believes that it is love, not law, that will finally draw the individual to God and change them. "But because our sluggishness is not sufficiently aroused by precepts, promises are added in order, by a certain sweetness, to entice us to love the precepts."[76] Knowing that we are loved "because God's love is shedded into our hearts by the Holy Ghost,"[77] we cannot do anything other than be drawn to God for help in holiness.

Our obedience flows from God's fatherly love: "Ero vobis in patrem."
There can be no doubt that Calvin means for us to obey God, for we are meant to "serve him as a Father in holiness and righteousness."[78] But our obedience follows love *for* the Father, evoked by love *from* the Father. "When we are slow to obey God it is helpful to remember his gracious favors. For what could better stimulate our zeal for following what God commands?"[79] Our obedience follows our understanding of God's love for us as our Father, it does not precede it. "*I will be a Father unto you...* Paul has added it with this view, that a recognition of the great honor to which God has exalted us, might be a motive to stir us up to a more ardent desire for holiness."[80]

Indeed for Calvin, love must be the prime motive for obedience, since obedience is defined as our reciprocal love for God from the heart.[81] "He wants our hearts to be round and pure"[82] in our obedience toward him, that is, whole and having integrity of love through and through. Drawn to God by love, we are changed from the heart out, for it is the "inner disposition of the heart" that is

---

[74] *Sermons on the Ten Commandments*, 271.
[75] F.L. Battles, *Interpreting John Calvin* (ed. R. Benedetto; Grand Rapids, Mich.: Baker, 1996), 118.
[76] *Institutes* 2.5.10.
[77] J. Calvin, *Sermons on Galatians* (tr. A. Golding; Audubon, N.J.: Old Paths, 1995), 533.
[78] *Commentary*, Mark 1:14.
[79] *Sermons on the Ten Commandments*, 117.
[80] *Commentary*, 2 Cor. 6:18; *CO* 50:83.
[81] Wallace, *Christian Life*, 32.
[82] "Sermon on Deut. 26:16-19," *CO* 28:284, "Il veut le cœur soit rond et pur."

changed by God's love.[83] "True piety consists rather in a pure and true zeal which loves God altogether as Father."[84]

God's paternal love encourages our obedience in yet another way. For it is only out of his love that God accepts,[85] and rewards by grace,[86] our always imperfect obedience. As Barth points out, God's "fatherly leniency" toward our imperfect obedience motivates our further obedience such that "we may meet and obey the divine summons with great and joyous alacrity."[87] Confident because of our Father's love for us that our obedience is both graciously accepted and graciously rewarded, the Christian is spurred on to new heights of obedience.

God's love leads ultimately to the obedience of God's law. "We know that no one can with alacrity render service to God except he be allured by his paternal kindness."[88] When we find in our hearts any "idleness, any indifference" toward God's law, we must think of the many benefits which our loving Father has lavished on us, so that we are moved to be "that much more motivated to serve him."[89] God's love for us then leads finally to our loving obedience, the essence of sanctification. Leith explains this essential relationship in Calvin's thought: "The end of the law is that we should love God. True obedience arises when we hold God for our Father and live as his children. This indicates that the law expresses the content of the personal response of sonship to the fatherly love of God on the part of his children."[90]

God's love, not fear, is the primary motive for change
In Calvin, fear, the reverential awe and filial respect for God, plays a vital role in the life of the believer.[91] As a counter to disregard and disrespect for God, the believer must live with the constant awareness that he ought not to provoke discipline from his heavenly Father who stands ever-ready to bring needed correction. "When we see how David was dealt with, alas, what will it be like for us? Therefore, let us consider walking much more in the fear of God, in the future, not provoking him to anger...."[92] Yet the fear that the believer is to feel is directly related to a right apprehension of the love of God. Calvin continues in the above sentence with the lesson we are to draw from David, "... so that

---

[83] *Institutes* 3.3.17.
[84] P.T. Fuhrmann (tr.), *Instruction in Faith (1537)* (Louisville, Ky.: Westminster/John Knox, 1977), 22.
[85] *Institutes* 3.19.4-5.
[86] *Sermons on the Ten Commandments*, 284.
[87] Barth, *Theology of Calvin*, 196-97.
[88] *Commentary*, Jonah 4:2.
[89] *Sermons on the Ten Commandments*, 42.
[90] Leith, *Christian Life*, 47.
[91] Battles says that Calvin taught "the true nature of *pietas* is seen in the two marks of believers: (1) honor, the obedience rendered to Him as Father; (2) fear, the service done Him as Lord." Battles, *The Piety of John Calvin*, 14.
[92] J. Calvin, *Sermons on 2 Samuel Chapters 1-13* (tr. D. Kelly; Edinburgh: Banner of Truth Trust, 1992), 542.

after he has pardoned us, bestowed his fatherly goodness on us, he will not have to be so severe that there is nothing for us to do but gnash our teeth."[93] We fear God precisely because we know that it is in his love that God will bring discipline as often and as severely as it is needed to bring us back to him.

Further, the one who does not fear God rightly cannot know his love well. "Micah is able to show in general how estranged the people were from the fear of God. Therefore, it is no surprise that they were unable to taste God's goodness."[94] When we do not rightly fear God, we will find ourselves "frightened" by God as our enemy. For without the right fear of God, "We will always shun God; his majesty will frighten us, and when God addresses us, we will tremble."[95] Fear does have its proper place in the affective life of the believer alongside the right understanding of the paternal love of God. As Wallace observes, "Fear must always rest on a firm basis of confidence in God's mercy."[96]

As vital as fear is in the life of the believer, it is not the first mover in our sanctification but rather a response to God in the midst of sanctification. Calvin, against some popular notions in his day, taught that fear was not the primary motive behind any religion, much less Christianity. "False indeed is what is said, that fear is the cause of religion."[97] Calvin explains that love, rather than fear, serves to move us toward God. "When the love of God is by us seen and known by faith, peace is given to our consciences, so that they no longer tremble and fear."[98] God's love then is the firm basis for our sanctification.

God's love for us becomes a major theme in Calvin's preaching
This love of God for his people is among Calvin's most frequent themes in his sermons for good reason: "But first of all we see here which is the true manner of preaching the Gospel: namely to give knowledge of God's love towards us."[99] As he introduces the Ten Commandments, Calvin, at times accused of being a legalist,[100] strikes the theme of fatherly love at a point when a legalist might strike a very different chord. "God is revealed as liberal toward us, and ought that not attract us toward him even more?"[101] Expounding the law he decries our indifference to it and offers what he knows will warm the believer to obedience:

> Let us begin to enumerate the benefits which we have received from him: "Poor creature, how lax you are not to adhere to your God when he has revealed his will to you! Consider what you take from him. Consider the benefits which he has dis-

---

[93] *Sermons on 2 Samuel*, 542.
[94] *Sermons on Micah*, 111.
[95] *Sermons on Micah*, 112.
[96] Wallace, *Christian Life*, 223.
[97] *Commentary*, Jonah 1:5.
[98] *Commentary*, 1 John 4:18.
[99] *Sermons on Galatians*, 313.
[100] Barth, *Theology of Calvin*, 122; Leith, *Christian Life*, 152.
[101] *Sermons on the Ten Commandments*, 41.

tributed until now." There let each one of us examine how much we are indebted to him to the end that we might be that much more motivated to serve Him.[102]

Again and again in his preaching, Calvin will sound this same note: know that you are the beloved of God and let that knowledge move you to reciprocate this love in your obedience.[103]

Conclusions regarding the Father's role in sanctification

Calvin saw that from first to last our sanctification flows from the grace of God and is gained by faith and not works.[104] Given the picture he paints of human inability to obtain holiness, sanctification must lie in the hands of God. For the one who has elected us in love gracefully woos us with his love, by loving grace prompts our obedience, and by grace accepts our imperfect obedience with approval.

From this we will take another important principle forward in our search for the primary principles behind Calvin's paradigm for sanctification:

Principle 3: God's Love. Because God has elected us in love, therefore apprehend God's love to move us to love God in holiness. Knowledge of God's paternal love, most clearly seen in Christ and presented in covenant promises, serves as a primary motive force behind the believer's submission to God in sanctification.

For Calvin, if sluggishness is to be thrown aside, if apathy is to be overcome, if cold hearts are to be warmed then they must come to see the Father's role in our sanctification moved by his gracious love for us. As this doctrine was proclaimed clearly from the pulpits of Geneva, it is little wonder that Calvin found audiences eager to hear of the love of a God who destines them for holiness.

God's role in our sanctification does not stop with the Father, of course, for it is powerfully advanced by the Son as well.

The Role of God the Son

In Christ Calvin found not just another point of theology but the crown of his theology, as Niesel argues, "Jesus Christ…is the end of the law and the essence of the Gospel….Calvin in his theology is concerned fundamentally about this living Lord."[105] This Christ-centered focus of Calvin's is brought about by his view of the chasm that exists between God's holiness and our complete lack of holiness. Into this gulf, Battles asserts, Calvin could only conceive of placing Christ to bridge the gap. "These two movements of the human mind lead to the knowledge of God and the knowledge of ourselves, set in antithesis to one another: the gulf between the all-holy God and the fallen sinner which only the incarnate Son of God can bridge."[106]

---

[102] *Sermons on the Ten Commandments*, 42.
[103] See for example, *Sermons on Galatians*, 27, 533.
[104] *Institutes* 3.3.19.
[105] Niesel, *Theology of Calvin*, 27-28.
[106] Battles, *Interpreting Calvin*, 149.

Calvin would therefore insist on Christ's role in producing our holiness, in contrast to Rome which encouraged obtaining holiness through good works, satisfactions and observances of the mass.[107] "In the papacy...[t]hey must earn merits, so that they never find a true remedy to give them rest."[108] This Roman emphasis, Calvin believed, would keep people from ever properly obtaining the double-knowledge needed to proceed in holiness,[109] so he countered Rome with the work of the Son.[110]

The Son's goal in sanctification: restoring the imago Dei

Calvin recognized that Christ had one goal in our sanctification: "The end of regeneration is that Christ should reform us to God's image."[111] This restoration of the image of God means that we would return to the "true order"[112] (*verum ordinem*) and that Christ himself "restores us to true and complete integrity."[113] The perfect image of God to which we are restored is nothing other than the very image of Christ.[114] Christ's goal then is a natural one, to restore the order we once had, variously described in Calvin as the image of God, the true order, or even rightly understood, conformity to the law.[115] Christ then was to take the broken "children of hell" that the human race had become and turn them instead into children of God.[116] This Christ does by offering us full sanctification through a "double grace," his mystical union with us through his offices of prophet, king and priest.

The Son unites to us: mystica unio

Calvin, perhaps following the lead of Bucer,[117] attributed great importance to our mystical union with Christ for the advancement of our holiness. "Grafting designates not only a conformity of example but a secret union [*arcanam coniunctionem*], by which we are joined to him."[118] While Calvin acknowledges the mysterious nature of this union,[119] he does define it as union with the human nature of Christ, as Wallace concludes, "Our participation in the sanctification

---

[107] "If anyone says that the justice received is not preserved and also not increased before God through good works....let him be anathema." *Canons of Trent*, 45.
[108] *Sermons on 2 Samuel*, 569-70.
[109] *Institutes* 3.15.3.
[110] *Institutes* 3.11.1.
[111] *Institutes* 1.15.4.
[112] *Commentary*, Gen. 4:2.
[113] *Institutes* 1.15.4.
[114] *Institutes* 1.15.4.
[115] Wallace, *Christian Life*, 103-21.
[116] *Institutes* 2.12.2; *Commentary*, Eph. 1:19.
[117] M. Bucer, *Common Places of Martin Bucer* (ed. and tr. D.F. Wright; Appleford, England: Sutton Courtenay, 1972), 333-34.
[118] *Commentary*, Rom. 6:5; *CO* 49:106.
[119] "For we hold ourselves to be united with Christ by the secret (*arcana*) power of his Spirit." *Institutes* 3.11.5; "How this happens far exceeds the limits of my understanding." Letter to Peter Martyr, *CO* 15:723.

of Christ depends on our union with the human nature of Christ."[120] This union, though powerful, should not be mistaken for physical union,[121] for Christ is united with us spiritually.[122] We children of God "are not born of flesh and blood but of the Spirit through faith," for it is faith which engrafts us into Christ.[123] Indeed apart from union with Christ, all that he has done for us is "useless and of no value for us."[124]

Through this union, which Calvin typically calls "engrafting,"[125] the benefits of Christ's holiness become ours as his life continually flows into ours, transforming us into his image as the template of his life impresses its image onto our lives.[126] "Therefore, that joining together of Head and members, that indwelling of Christ in our hearts—in short, that mystical union [*mystica unio*]—are accorded by us the highest degree of importance, so that Christ, having been made ours, makes us sharers with him in the gifts with which he has been endowed."[127] Our union with Christ is so potent that we not only gain power and nourishment from him, "but we also pass from our own to his nature."[128] It is this union, not our good works, which effects the transformation of our character.[129] United with Christ we are transformed by our communion with him,[130] which he makes daily more complete, giving us confidence to hope for holiness.[131] We are so dependent on our union with Christ for our sanctification that Spijker declares that, for Calvin, sanctification of life *is* the result of communion with Christ.[132]

---

[120] Wallace, *Christian Life*, 17. "This life is placed in his flesh, that it may be drawn out of it." *Commentary*, John 6:51.

[121] Calvin's early usage of the term *substantia* led to some confusion, since this term could imply a fusing together of substances. After his debates with Osiander regarding the spiritual nature of our union with Christ (Wendel, *Origins*, 23) Calvin became more careful to show that the mystical union is spiritual. Writing in his 1553 commentary on John 17:21, Calvin clarifies by denying that Christ conveys his substance to us. "Hence, too, we infer that we are *one* with the Son of God; not because he conveys his substance to us, but because, by the power of his Spirit, he imparts to us his life and all the blessings which he has received from the Father." This important clarification makes a clear denial using the controversial term *substantia*: "non quia suam in nos substantiam transfundat" (*CO* 47:387).

[122] *Institutes* 4.17.33, 3.1.1; J. Calvin, *Sermons on Genesis Chapters 1-11* (tr. R.R. McGregor; Edinburgh: Banner of Truth Trust, 2009), 200-01.

[123] *Institutes* 2.13.2.

[124] *Institutes* 3.1.1.

[125] Tamburello, *Union with Christ*, 85. Cf. *Commentary*, Isa. 26:19; John 1:12; 1 Cor. 12:13; *Institutes* 3.2.25, 3.6.3, 3.15.6, 4.15.1, 4.16.12.

[126] *Commentary*, 1 John 2:6.

[127] *Institutes* 3.11.10.

[128] *Commentary*, Rom. 6:5.

[129] *Commentary*, John 17:19.

[130] *Institutes* 3.14.4.

[131] *Institutes* 3.2.24.

[132] Spijker, "Bucer's Influence on Calvin," 35.

The union with Christ serves to sanctify us by uniting us both to the death of Christ for our mortification and to the life of Christ for our vivification, apart from whom we can do nothing.[133] Christ's union with us allows his death to have the impact of crucifying our own flesh.[134] Not that our sin is killed all at once but that the "reign of sin and death ceases."[135] So too, by the power of union with the life of Christ, are we made more and more alive spiritually by him. "Transfusing us with his power, that he may quicken us to spiritual life, [and] sanctify us by his Spirit."[136]

The relationship between union with Christ and justification

There is a contemporary debate concerning the exact relationship between union with Christ and justification in Calvin's theology regarding the *ordo salutis*.[137] One side claims that in Calvin justification precedes union,[138] while the other asserts that union with Christ comes first.[139] We will examine five aspects of this argument, stating them first from the justification-prior viewpoint and then offering a union-prior response.

1) Calvin wrote more extensively on justification than union so justification appears to be primary.[140] However, since justification, not union, was the central debate with Rome, polemical success would dictate a focus on the former. Further, Calvin does regularly teach on union.[141]

2) Calvin presents justification as "the foundation for sanctification,"[142] and so it must precede union. The justification-prior advocates cite Calvin: "[Justification] is the main hinge on which religion turns."[143] Gaffin counters, that while justification may be the hinge, it is a hinge "anchored in union," and so

---

[133] *Institutes* 2.3.9, 2.16.19.
[134] *Institutes* 2.16.7.
[135] *Commentary*, Rom. 5:21.
[136] *Institutes* 2.16.16.
[137] Muller, *Reformed Tradition*; M. Horton, *Covenant and Salvation* (Louisville, Ky.: Westminster/John Knox, 2007); M. Horton, *The Christian Faith* (Grand Rapids, Mich.: Zondervan, 2011); C.R. Campbell, *Paul and Union with Christ* (Grand Rapids, Mich.: Zondervan, 2012); J.V. Fesko, "Sanctification and Union with Christ: A Reformed Perspective," *Evangelical Quarterly* 82 (2010), 197-214; R.B. Gaffin, Jr., "Calvin's Soteriology: The Structure of the Application of Redemption in Book Three of the *Institutes*," *Ordained Servant* 18 (2009), 68-77; M.A. Garcia, "Imputation and the Christology of Union with Christ: Calvin, Osiander, and the Contemporary Quest for a Reformed Model," *Westminster Theological Journal* 68 (2006), 219-51; T.L. Wenger, "The New Perspectives on Calvin: Responding to Recent Calvin Interpretations," *Journal of the Evangelical Theological Society* 50 (2007), 311-28.
[138] Horton, *Covenant and Salvation*, 139.
[139] Gaffin, "Calvin's Soteriology," 75.
[140] Wenger, "New Perspectives," 327.
[141] *Institutes* 3.1.1, 3.2.24, 3.11.10, 3.11.23, 3.17.8; *Commentary*, John 6:51; 15:1, 5; 17:26; Rom. 8:4, 28-30; Gal. 5:24; Eph. 5:32; 2 Peter 1:5.
[142] Fesko, "Sanctification and Union," 201.
[143] *Institutes* 3.11.1.

neither precedes union nor causes sanctification.[144] It is union which actually serves as the foundation for both sanctification and justification.[145] Calvin writes that to attain the righteousness of Christ one must "first possess Christ," for it is our "sharing in Christ, which justifies us," and which makes us partakers "in his sanctification."[146] Being "implanted in him" then, leads to our sanctification.[147] "There is no sanctification apart from communion with Christ."[148]

3) Calvin speaks of faith as prior to union so justification must be prior to union as well.[149] Calvin is cited, "The fellowship which we have with Christ is the consequence of faith."[150] Since faith precedes union, Horton avers, then "justification through faith alone is the fountain of union with Christ."[151] The union-prior advocates affirm that, in Calvin, faith precedes and achieves our union with Christ.[152] "All that he possesses is nothing to us until we grow into one body with him. It is true that we obtain this by faith."[153] However, they counter, faith and justification are not equivalent.[154] Rather, faith, grounding our union, leads to our justification. "You see that our righteousness is not in us but in Christ, that we possess it only because we are partakers in Christ."[155]

4) Calvin seems to assert the foundational priority of justification over the rest of the *ordo salutis*.[156] Horton writes that justification serves as the "basis for" our union with Christ.[157] Calvin, at first read, seems to concur: "It is necessary that the righteousness of faith alone so precede in order, and be so preeminent in degree, that nothing can go before it or obscure it."[158] The union-prior advocates counter that, on closer examination, union precedes justification in Calvin's thought.[159] It is our union with Christ, variously described as, "partaking of Christ,"[160] being "engrafted into his body,"[161] being "planted together"[162] with him and "become[ing] ours…to dwell with us,"[163] which allows us

---

[144] Gaffin, "Calvin's Soteriology," 74-75.
[145] Muller, *Reformed Tradition*, 211.
[146] *Institutes* 3.16.1.
[147] *Commentary*, John 15:1.
[148] *Institutes* 3.14.4; *CO* 2:566, "…sine Christi communicatione nulla est sanctificatio."
[149] Horton, *Covenant and Salvation*, 143.
[150] *Commentary*, Eph. 3:17.
[151] Horton, *Covenant and Salvation*, 143.
[152] Gaffin, "Calvin's Soteriology," 71.
[153] *Institutes* 3.1.1.
[154] Muller, *Reformed Tradition*, 209.
[155] *Institutes* 3.11.23.
[156] Fesko, "Sanctification and Union," 201.
[157] Horton, *Covenant and Salvation*, 143.
[158] *CSW*, Vol. 3, 128, "Acts of the Council of Trent with the Antidote;" cf. *Institutes* 3.17.9.
[159] Muller, *Reformed Tradition*, 209, note 27; Gaffin, "Calvin's Soteriology," 72.
[160] *Institutes* 3.11.1.
[161] *Institutes* 3.11.10.
[162] *Commentary*, Gal. 5:24.
[163] *Institutes* 3.1.1.

to "receive a double grace"[164] of justification and sanctification, so that his "righteousness overwhelms"[165] our sin and makes us holy.[166] Calvin teaches that justification is causally dependent upon our union with Christ. "I confess that we are deprived of this utterly incomparable good [justification] until [*donec*] Christ is made ours."[167] "He only begins to love us, when [*dum*] we are united to the body of his beloved Son."[168]

5) If union is prior to justification it poses a threat to imputed righteousness.[169] The union-prior advocates counter that union with Christ, rather than destroying, establishes our imputed righteousness,[170] which is "shared with believers through their spiritual union with him."[171] "Forensic justification is conceivable for Calvin only on grounds of communion with Christ by grace through faith."[172] Calvin seems clear, for it is only as we are joined in "mystical union" with Christ that "his righteousness may be imputed to us."[173]

Muller offers a helpful corrective for both parties regarding a proper understanding of Calvin and the *ordo salutis*. By framing the question carefully in the sixteenth-century context he demonstrates that while Calvin did have a concern to understand aspects of an *ordo salutis*, he was not concerned with establishing a rigid chronology, as are contemporary systematic theologians.[174] We concur with Muller who shows that Calvin had a loose, causal *ordo salutis*, which asserts union by faith as causally prior to, and the foundation of, justification and sanctification.[175] "We must be united to our Lord Jesus Christ, before [*devant*] we can be in God's favor."[176]

The Son works a "double grace"

Calvin taught that we are both justified *and* sanctified by grace as a kind of "double grace."[177] "By partaking of him, we principally receive a double grace: namely, that being reconciled to God through Christ's blamelessness, we may have in heaven instead of a Judge a gracious Father; and secondly, that sanctified by Christ's spirit we may cultivate blamelessness and purity of life."[178] This double grace, coming through the work of Christ, means that we can only

---

[164] *Institutes* 3.11.1.
[165] *Institutes* 3.2.24.
[166] *Commentary*, Gal. 5:24.
[167] *Institutes* 3.11.10; *CO* 2:540.
[168] *Commentary*, John 17:26; *CO* 47:391.
[169] Wenger, "New Perspectives," 325; Horton, *The Christian Faith*, 708.
[170] Garcia, "Imputation and the Christology of Union," 249.
[171] Campbell, *Paul and Union with Christ*, 404.
[172] Muller, *Reformed Tradition*, 209, note 27.
[173] *Institutes* 3.11.10.
[174] *Commentary*, Rom. 8:28-30; Muller, *Reformed Tradition*, 165-66, 240, 281.
[175] Muller, *Reformed Tradition*, 240.
[176] *Sermons on Galatians*, 488-89; *CO* 50:563.
[177] J.H. Rainbow, "Double Grace: John Calvin's View of the Relationship of Justification and Sanctification," *Ex Auditu* 5 (1989), 104. Cf. Niesel, *Theology of Calvin*, 137; Gleason, *Reformed Spirituality*, 57.
[178] *Institutes* 3.11.1. Cf. 3.11.6.

look to Christ for our continued progress in holiness. "Let then the faithful learn to embrace him, not only for justification, but also for sanctification."[179] Calvin could not imagine Christ beginning a work in our justification then not completing it in our sanctification.[180]

Justification, through both the forgiveness of sin and the imputation of righteousness[181] only from Christ,[182] grants us the position of being righteous in the presence of God. Justified before the presence of God, we are able to enter into relationship with him, rather than flee from him, for we now stand before him by grace alone in the work of Christ. Thus in relationship with God through justification, God continues the work he has begun, through Christ, by applying the sanctifying work of Christ to our lives that we might grow in piety.[183] It is both improper and impossible to tear asunder the two concepts as though having been justified by faith we now progress in sanctification by our good works. "We cannot be justified freely through faith alone without at the same time living holily. For these fruits of grace are connected together, as it were, by an indissoluble tie."[184] Calvin has in mind defending the reality that good works flow from, rather than are hindered by, free justification when he explains the necessity of co-joining, while yet distinguishing, justification and sanctification.

> Why, then, are we justified by faith? Because by faith we grasp Christ's righteousness, by which alone we are reconciled to God. Yet you could not grasp this without at the same time grasping sanctification also. For he "is given unto us for righteousness, wisdom, sanctification, and redemption" [1 Cor. 1:30]. Therefore Christ justifies no one whom he does not at the same time sanctify. These benefits are joined together by an everlasting and indissoluble bond.[185]

Calvin, ever-warring against the notion of sanctification by human effort through the idolatrous triumvirate of "satisfactions, superstitions and idolatry," opposed to them this "double grace" which includes our entire sanctification by grace. This doctrine of sanctification by grace left the believer doubly thankful, doubly humble and in a position then to receive from Christ even more grace to draw them along in sanctification.

The Son works continually in our sanctification as Prophet, King and Priest
Christ advances his people's holiness in his offices of Prophet, King and Priest.[186] This threefold office, unmentioned in the 1536 *Institutes*, appeared in the 1539 edition and then was fully developed in the 1559 version, perhaps

---

[179] *Commentary*, Rom. 8:13.
[180] Gleason, *Reformed Spirituality*, 57.
[181] *Institutes* 3.11.2.
[182] *Institutes* 2.16.3.
[183] *Institutes* 3.11.1.
[184] *Commentary*, 1 Cor. 1:30. Cf. *Commentary*, John 13:8; 17:19.
[185] *Institutes* 3.16.1.
[186] *Institutes* 2.15.1.

under the influence of Martin Bucer's *Commentary on the Gospels*.[187] In these offices Christ continually works to purify his people who are, without doubt, still deeply in need of daily purification and just as certainly assured that Christ will finish their holiness.[188]

As our Prophet, Christ continually teaches us everything "worth knowing" through his Spirit.[189] We come by no helpful truth of salvation by our own effort, but all is revealed by Christ as our teacher who "impresses his word on our hearts by his Spirit."[190] The truth taught to us by our Prophet is not bare information but has real power to transform us by freeing us from the slavery to sin, including sinful thought patterns, "so that, loosed from the snares of Satan, we willingly obey righteousness."[191]

As our King, Christ rules over us, subduing all his enemies including the world, the devil and our own flesh, and equipping us for battle, that his kingdom might advance both within us and outside of us. "Now he arms and equips us with his power, adorns us with his beauty and magnificence, enriches us with his wealth."[192] It is as our King that Christ constantly "enriches his people with all things necessary for the eternal salvation of souls and fortifies them with courage to stand unconquerable against all the assaults of spiritual enemies."[193]

As our High Priest, Christ has interceded for us, through the consecration of offering himself, so we are made partakers of his High-Priestly holiness.[194] As our Priest only Christ can purify us, for "having washed away our sins"[195] he furthers our sanctification, which the saints could never do alone.[196] Christ then is completely active, not only in the establishing, but in completing the sanctification of his people.

Conclusions regarding the Son's role in sanctification

Calvin puts forth the efficacy of Christ's sanctification of his people both to defend the glory of Christ and to steer believers away from attempts to obtain holiness through the use of the false Roman methodology, which produced not holiness but hypocrites.[197] Defending the glory of Christ, Calvin would write with fury against all efforts to diminish His role as sole savior. "Let Papists

---

[187] Wendel, *Origins*, 225. Bucer's *Enarrationes in Evangelia*, 1536, 606, says: "Rex regum Christus est, summus sacerdos, et prophetarum caput."
[188] *Institutes* 4.8.12.
[189] *Institutes* 2.15.2.
[190] *Commentary*, John 8:32.
[191] *Commentary*, John 8:32.
[192] *Institutes* 2.15.4.
[193] *Institutes* 2.15.4.
[194] *Institutes* 2.15.6.
[195] *Institutes* 2.15.6.
[196] *Institutes* 3.20.21.
[197] *Institutes* 4.10.12, 4.13.7.

now go and proudly vaunt of their free-will, but let us, who are conscious of our own slavery, glory in none but Christ our Deliverer."[198]

Calvin hated Roman devices not only for the harm done to the glory of Christ but the harm done to believers, who were led astray in the quest for holiness when only the cross of Christ could help.[199] While the Roman church offered satisfactions and indulgences, Calvin fought back, showing that holiness could be found nowhere but in the blood of Christ. "Indulgences proclaim: Sanctification, otherwise insufficient, is perfected by the martyrs. John says that 'all the saints have washed their robes...in the blood of the Lamb.'"[200]

Calvin wanted to steer his readers away from any idea that they can sanctify themselves by mere human effort but pointed them rather to Christ.[201] We can add nothing to the glorious work of Christ to sanctify ourselves.[202] True, the sinner may repent of sin, but he may not offer any work as a "satisfaction" for that sin. Calvin assures his readers that when Daniel (Dan. 4:27) seems to indicate that Nebuchadnezzar might, by his own effort of showing mercy to the poor, make satisfaction for his sin, this could not be the case: "Banish the thought that there should be any other ransom than the blood of Christ!"[203] "Banish the thought," cries Calvin, for anything that would subtract from the glory of Christ in either justification or sanctification must not even be considered as a possible solution.

Because Calvin wants believers to see that Christ is, as it were, the only grounds for our sanctification, apart from human effort, he will focus our attention on Christ's supremacy more and more clearly in his teaching and preaching.

> For this is eternal life: to know the one true God, and him whom he has sent, Jesus Christ, in whom he has formed the beginning, the middle and the end of our salvation. It is he who is Isaac, the beloved Son of the Father, who was offered in sacrifice....He is the vigilant shepherd Jacob, taking such great care of the sheep that are in his care....He is the faithful captain and guide Joshua, to lead us into the promised land. He is the noble and victorious King David subjecting with his hand all rebellious power.[204]

In Christ we gain the knowledge of the glorious mercy and love of the Father, along with his justice, all played out in the cross. In Christ we also gain a

---

[198] *Commentary*, John 8:32.
[199] *Institutes* 4.18.3.
[200] *Institutes* 3.5.2.
[201] Commenting on 2 Cor. 7:11, Calvin will pause to take Erasmus to task for translating ἀπολογίαν as "satisfaction" because, "ignorant persons, misled by the ambiguity of the term, have applied it to popish satisfactions." Calvin could not tolerate a translation of the biblical text that might support a Roman approach to sanctification. He takes the trouble to correct this single word, preferring Jerome's *defensionem*, explaining that Paul actually means here, "a kind of *defense* that consists rather in supplication for pardon, than in extenuation of sin."
[202] *Institutes* 3.15.3.
[203] *Institutes* 3.4.36.
[204] Calvin's Preface to Olivetan's New Testament, *CO* 9:813.

knowledge of ourselves. As we gaze upon his perfect obedience, we see what we are designed to be, the true order for humanity. In the cross we see the agony of how far we have fallen short of the mark. We see, as well, our helplessness at self-improvement, our total inability to sanctify ourselves. We are reduced to humble dependence on the glorious Christ for our sanctification.

The Role of God the Holy Spirit

The Holy Spirit gives us a new will

For Calvin it is the Holy Spirit who brings the electing love of the Father and the gracious work of the Son to bear in our lives.[205] It is the Holy Spirit who actually effects the change in the human will, converting it from a bad to a good will. "Hence it appears that God's grace...is the rule of the Spirit to direct and regulate man's will. The Spirit cannot regulate without correcting, without reforming, without renewing....At the same time a new will is said to be created in man."[206] Our sanctification is dependent, foundationally, on this work of God through his Spirit which allows us to respond to him with repentance.[207] It is the Spirit who not only restrains our will from evil but also regenerates us to walk in righteous obedience.[208] The Spirit, having begun the good work of regeneration by the shaping of a new will in the individual, presses on in this work by producing faith.

The Holy Spirit produces faith

The Holy Spirit is the one who brings about the inception and growth of faith as his "principal work."[209] "For the Spirit is not only the initiator of faith, but increases it by degrees, until by it he leads us to the Kingdom of Heaven."[210] Human effort can never produce faith, no matter how often we are commanded to believe.[211] It is the Holy Spirit who, giving us eyes to see and ears to hear, works in our hearts "to conceive, sustain, nourish, and establish faith."[212] Barth rightly concludes that, for Calvin, faith comes as God's imposition upon us. "It is the nature of faith to pierce the ears, close the eyes, wait upon the promise, and turn aside from all thoughts of human worth or merit."[213]

It is then through the work of the Holy Spirit that all the benefits of Christ are attained by us through faith,[214] including assurance of our adoption as God's children.[215] As Muller says, "Faith is a gift that awakens all the powers

---

[205] *Institutes* 3.1.1.
[206] *Institutes* 2.5.15.
[207] J.K.S. Reid (ed.), *Calvin: Theological Treatises* (Louisville, Ky.: Westminster/John Knox, 2006), 197, "Articles Concerning Predestination."
[208] *Institutes* 2.5.14.
[209] *Institutes* 3.1.4.
[210] *Institutes* 3.2.33.
[211] *Institutes* 3.2.35.
[212] *Institutes* 4.14.9.
[213] Barth, *Theology of Calvin*, 168.
[214] *Institutes* 3.3.1.
[215] *Commentary*, Rom. 8:16.

of the soul, intellect and will, so that both are enlightened and moved, each in its own way, to grasp the gift of God in Christ."[216] Since faith is "a firm and certain knowledge of divine benevolence toward us...sealed upon our hearts through the Holy Spirit,"[217] this increase in faith is both the measure of and the result of sanctification.[218]

The Holy Spirit unites us to Christ

Calvin sees the Holy Spirit as the one through whom the believer is given real spiritual unity with Christ.[219] "To sum up, the Holy Spirit is the bond by which Christ effectually unites us to himself."[220] This union is effected through faith, as Tamburello asserts, "The Holy Spirit brings the elect, through the hearing of the Gospel, to faith; in so doing, the Spirit engrafts them into Christ."[221] It is the Holy Spirit who, by making us "true members of Christ,"[222] then unites us to his life which sanctifies us, "that as he has sanctified himself on our account, we may also through his Spirit be made partakers of the same sanctification."[223]

The Holy Spirit directly mortifies and vivifies

Calvin will argue that the very work of sanctification—mortification and vivification—are carried on for us by the Holy Spirit. Against all the Roman inventions, useless to fight our concupiscence, Calvin offers the work of the Spirit, who is not only "opposed to the old man and to the flesh" but works in us for the "reformation of all the parts."[224] Indeed it is the "Spirit of sanctification through whom we are consecrated as temples to God,"[225] so that we will no longer be "dragged to and fro by wandering lusts."[226] As Niesel summarized, "The death of the old man and the resurrection of the new...happens through the Spirit of Christ who binds us to Him and evokes in us faith and obedience."[227]

While putting to death concupiscence in us, the Spirit works at the same time to vivify a new principle of life within us, such that "we are no longer actuated by ourselves, but are ruled by his action and prompting."[228] It is the Spirit who washes us with clean water to make us clean and to make us "fruitful to bring forth the buds of righteousness."[229] It is the Spirit who kindles a holy fire within us so that "he enflames our hearts with the love of God and with zealous devo-

---

[216] Muller, *Unaccommodated*, 172.
[217] *Institutes* 3.2.7.
[218] Wallace, *Christian Life*, 327.
[219] *Institutes* 1.15.5.
[220] *Institutes* 3.1.1.
[221] Tamburello, *Union with Christ*, 86.
[222] *Institutes* 4.1.7.
[223] *Commentary*, Jer. 11:17; *Institutes* 3.1.3, 3.1.1.
[224] *Institutes* 2.1.9.
[225] *Institutes* 2.2.16.
[226] *Institutes* 2.5.14.
[227] Niesel, *Theology of Calvin*, 128.
[228] *Institutes* 3.1.3.
[229] *Institutes* 3.1.3.

tion."[230] It is the Spirit of sanctification who not only "quickens and nourishes us" but sows the heavenly seed in us.[231] It is the Holy Spirit who brings to bear the very holiness of Jesus Christ which has a powerful cleansing and purifying effect.[232] From the Spirit flows our regeneration, justification and sanctification.[233] Indeed we are so dependent upon the Holy Spirit to transform us that we must ask God to "help us through his Holy Spirit, and not simply for him to make up for our frailty, but for him to begin and perfect everything in us."[234]

While it is the Spirit who does the work of sanctification, Calvin is clear that we are to play a role inasmuch as we are to submit to the Spirit's work.[235] Thus when Scripture warns us to "grieve not the Holy Spirit of God" (Eph. 4:30), Calvin will agree that we are commanded to submit to the Spirit's direction. "As God has sealed us by his Spirit, we grieve him when we do not follow his guidance, but pollute ourselves by wicked passions."[236] However, even this submission by faith[237] is part of the Spirit's work, so that "the Spirit claims for himself alone the office of sanctifying."[238] Calvin, always cautious of appearing to attribute sanctification to any work in human nature, drives home the point that our submission is drawn from us by God's Spirit. Commenting on 1 Thess. 5:19, "quench not the Spirit," a text which clearly lends itself to emphasizing human responsibility in sanctification, Calvin goes to great lengths to show that we cannot even truly quench the Spirit when he is at work.

> Those, however, who infer from this that it is in man's option either to *quench* or to *cherish* the light that is presented to him, so that they detract from the efficacy of grace, and extol the powers of free will, reason on false grounds. For...God works efficaciously in his elect...and...causes them to see, opens the eyes of their heart, and keeps them open....What God commands by Paul's mouth, He himself accomplishes inwardly.[239]

What then is left for us to do in submission? It is our part to ask help from the Lord. Yet even when Calvin examines our call to repentance, he finds here again not human effort at improving ourselves but the Holy Spirit at work. "For although we are urged to come to him, we would remain obstinate, and never take the right steps unless we are touched by his Holy Spirit. Therefore, repentance is already a gift of God."[240] Calvin even hesitates to call our role cooperation, which seems to imply more innate ability than we possess.[241] All our good

---

[230] *Institutes* 3.1.3.
[231] *Institutes* 3.2.2.
[232] *Commentary*, John 12:19.
[233] *Institutes* 1.13.14.
[234] *Sermons on the Ten Commandments*, 274.
[235] Gleason, *Reformed Spirituality*, 61.
[236] *Commentary*, Eph. 4:30.
[237] Marcel, "Justification and Sanctification," 139.
[238] *Institutes* 2.5.11.
[239] *Commentary*, 1 Thess. 5:19.
[240] *Sermons on 2 Samuel*, 567.
[241] *BLW*, 195.

works then, including repentance, come from the Spirit who "forms us anew unto good works,"[242] leaving finally no grounds for claiming merit.

The Holy Spirit renews our mind

The Spirit also powerfully brings about our vivification by renewing our very minds that we might come to a true two-fold knowledge of God and self. It is impossible, apart from the Spirit, to ever come to the truth of God and self, for these truths are not accessible to the natural mind, which is blind to the light of the Gospel,[243] until they are "enlightened by the Spirit of God."[244] The Spirit allows us to see ourselves as we are. As Wendel points out, "Sanctification consists partly then, in recognizing how far we still are in fact from true righteousness."[245] The Spirit, in renewing our minds, allows us to comprehend and apply the Word of God to our lives, "sealing our minds with that very doctrine which is commended by the gospel."[246] Indeed, "unless animated by the power of the Spirit," the Word would be of no profit.[247] Apart from the Spirit we could never derive right doctrine from Scripture, for unless "the Spirit of wisdom be present, to have God's word in our hands will avail little or nothing."[248] With Holy Spirit illumination, the minds of the elect may also resist the temptation of Satan since they are able "readily to distinguish between light and darkness, because they had the Spirit as their guide."[249] And what is it from the Scriptures that we learn of God by the Spirit? "This knowledge of divine love towards us is instilled into our hearts by the Spirit of God."[250] The Holy Spirit does not just communicate bare information to us about God's love but moves us to respond to that knowledge of God's love with a reciprocal love toward him.[251]

Conclusions regarding the Holy Spirit's role in sanctification

The Spirit becomes Calvin's refutation of the Roman technologies of sanctification.[252] It is not human assent to the teachings of the Church that produces faith ("implicit" faith), but the Spirit. It is not the human effort of meditating upon Christ that unites us to him, but the Spirit. It is not attempts at fasting that mortify our flesh, but the Spirit. It is not our effort at good deeds that make us better people, but the Spirit. It is not our power to understand God in nature, nor even our ability to see our own frailty that brings us to the true knowledge of God and self, but the Spirit. Hence we must "lay aside all confidence in our own abilities, and seek light from heaven," allowing ourselves to be governed

---

[242] *Commentary*, Rom. 6:14.
[243] D. Steinmetz, *Calvin in Context* (New York, N.Y.: Oxford University Press, 1995), 29.
[244] *Commentary*, 1 Cor. 2:14; 1 John 2:20.
[245] Wendel, *Origins*, 243.
[246] *Institutes* 1.9.1.
[247] *Commentary*, Ezek. 2:2.
[248] *Commentary*, 1 John 4:1.
[249] *Commentary*, 1 John 2:21.
[250] *Commentary*, Rom. 5:5.
[251] *Commentary*, 1 John 2.3.
[252] Wendel, *Origins*, 248.

and directed by the Spirit of God.[253] We are entirely dependent on God, not human effort, to make us holy. "Indeed, instead of being able to perfect to the end what we have been commanded, we don't even know where to begin. We can't even conceive of one single good idea until God has reformed us, until he has drawn us to himself and given us the heart to do it; and then at the same time he must add the ability to put into practice what we will."[254]

Conclusion

From this study of God's role in the sanctification of his people, we have seen that God is the author of our sanctification. In describing God's role in our sanctification, Calvin means to help lay the groundwork for our understanding of the first half of the two-fold knowledge, knowledge of God. As Jones has argued persuasively, Calvin meant for knowledge of God to precede knowledge of self logically, if not rhetorically, in the *Institutes*.[255] We must see God rightly in his glory before we can see ourselves accurately in our need.[256] "It is certain that man never achieves a clear knowledge of himself unless he has first looked upon God's face, and then descends from contemplating him to scrutinize himself [*se ipsum inspiciendum descendat*]."[257] As Torrance comments on this passage, he concludes that, according to Calvin, one cannot see oneself rightly until he has first seen the grace of God in sanctification. "A true knowledge of man is not only reflexive of the divine self-revelation but also of the divine action in grace. There is no true knowledge of man, therefore, unless it is conceived as grounded upon the downward motion of grace."[258] It is only in knowing God that we truly know ourselves, as Calvin concludes in his 1560 French *Institutes*: "C'est qu'en cognoissant Dieu, chacun de nous aussi se cognoisse."[259]

We are not brought to this God-given two-fold knowledge for knowledge's sake. Rather, this true knowledge of God above ourselves brings us, as Richard says, to "the humble dependence upon God."[260] That is, we are forced by God in this knowledge to acknowledge him as Savior and turn to him, away from human effort and Rome, for help in holiness.[261] For in describing human sanctification first in terms of God's role, as Father, Son and Spirit, Calvin very much

---

[253] *Commentary*, Luke 24:45.

[254] *Sermons on the Ten Commandments*, 274.

[255] Jones solves this puzzle by demonstrating that Calvin begins his discussion of the two-fold knowledge of God and self in 1.1.1, focusing on knowledge of self as a rhetorical device, designed both to engage fellow French humanists and to avoid estranging those who might have favored Zwingli's openness to an initial inward look. S. Jones, *Calvin and the Rhetoric of Piety* (Louisville, Ky.: Westminster/John Knox, 1995), 90-93.

[256] Dowey, *Knowledge of God*, 18-19.

[257] *Institutes* 1.1.2. Cf. *Commentary*, 1 Cor. 8:2.

[258] Torrance, *Calvin's Doctrine of Man*, 14.

[259] *CO* 3:37.

[260] Richard, *Spirituality of John Calvin*, 99.

[261] *Commentary*, Mic. 7:9.

Chapter 1 - The Divine Initiative in Sanctification

means to force humankind away from its natural, but erroneously exalted, view of its own role and to see, rather, that God is the one who plays the exalted role in human sanctification.[262] As Battles concludes, "The lesson of this knowledge is that we learn to humble ourselves, cast ourselves before God, seek His mercy."[263] Turning to God for help in sanctification, we are transformed by the mercy of God as we see him and ourselves rightly, our hearts are round and pure, the image of Christ is established in us and from whole hearts we love the God who has loved us so well.[264]

The implications of the two principles we have discovered in this chapter for Calvin's teaching and training for the men of the Genevan Academy are profound and sweeping when contrasted to the sixteenth-century Roman understanding of sanctification. To believe Calvin one must simply discard all Roman methods of advancing in holiness. Gone are satisfactions and indulgences. Gone are good works for merit. Gone are prayers to Mary and the saints. None but God can help. If the pastors of the Academy are to become holy men, they will need to look to God, Father, Son and Spirit, in deep and more dependent ways than they had been previously taught. Calvin will not, however, dismiss all external means as aids to sanctification; rather he will replace Roman methods with biblical methods. For Calvin will only offer approaches to sanctification which are God's own, that is, which are taught or derived directly from Scripture, such as prayer, the Word, church discipline and sacraments to replace the human inventions of Rome.

In understanding Calvin's view of God's role in our sanctification, one is forced to a clear conclusion: people are helpless to sanctify themselves apart from the work of God. This knowledge, of human inability and God's ability, is a two-fold knowledge that is driven home even further by Calvin's view of anthropology in sanctification.

---

[262] Torrance, *Calvin's Doctrine of Man*, 56.
[263] Battles, *The Piety of John Calvin*, 16.
[264] Wallace, *Christian Life*, 322.

Chapter 2 - Calvin's Anthropology and Its Implications for Sanctification

"Stare tantum Dei misericordia, quum a nobis ipsis non nisi mali simus."[1]

Introduction

In order to understand Calvin's view of sanctification, one must understand his anthropology, for therein we discover the ideal state of human holiness, the current condition of sinfulness and the inability of humankind to help itself toward holiness. Calvin will paint a picture of humanity in four states: creation, sin, grace and glory, all in order to help us gain a true understanding of God and ourselves. This double-knowledge allows us to understand both, "in this sad ruin what our nature in its corruption and deformity is like"[2] and also what God can do to change us "that we may be made like God."[3] This understanding, which comes by grace alone, leads one to an inescapable conclusion: we must stop trusting in our own goodness, or our own ability to make ourselves good, and instead continually turn to God's grace for help in holiness. "Man, rendered utterly destitute in his own right, should learn to depend wholly upon God."[4]

Calvin would war against all the more flattering views of humanity not only among the Scholastics[5] but even with the humanists, such as Erasmus.[6] Calvin leaned heavily on Augustine for his anthropology,[7] who himself fought with Pelagius to establish the depth of the fallen nature. Calvin went to great lengths to prove the absoluteness of the fallen nature, a logical necessity if he is to refute Catholic approaches to sanctification, which depended on some human ability to perform rites such as satisfaction and penance. The absoluteness of the fall also established the necessity of his alternate approach to sanctification by grace.[8]

In all his anthropology, Calvin will repeat two themes, as Torrance rightly observes, "The purpose of a Christian anthropology is twofold: by pointing the believer to his original creation in the image of God to produce gratitude, and

---

[1] *Institutes* 2.2.11, "By God's mercy alone we stand, since by ourselves we are nothing but evil."
[2] *Institutes* 1.15.1.
[3] *Commentary*, Col. 3:10.
[4] *Institutes* 2.2.9.
[5] *Institutes* 2.3.5.
[6] It was in order to refute an argument in Erasmus's *De libero arbitrio* that Calvin wrote: "Our adversaries usually say that after we have accepted the first grace, then our own efforts co-operate with subsequent grace." *Institutes* 2.3.11.
[7] *Institutes* 2.3.5, 2.3.14.
[8] This polemical necessity explains the length of this argument in the *Institutes* (eight chapters with 159 sections) and his frequent use of the Church Fathers (with over 75 mentions of Augustine on this topic, alongside of Jerome, Chrysostom, Bernard and others) and Scripture (5 verses cited in just one of the typical 159 sections, 2.1.9), all used to build an unassailable case for his view of humanity.

by pointing him to his present miserable condition to produce humility."[9] It is precisely these two movements, prostrated before God in humility and exalting God in thankfulness, that we argue are the keys to Calvin's entire scheme of sanctification. Humbled, we no longer rely on our own righteousness; exalting in God, we turn to him for help.

In each of the four states Calvin drives home the necessity of this double-knowledge. In presenting humanity in its original creation, he shows both how good God is to create us with such majesty and from what a lofty height humanity has fallen, so that we might humbly seek help from God to return to holiness. Humanity's fallen state, when viewed next to its created glory, proves that no human effort could ever repair the damage done in the fall, thus requiring us to turn to God for sanctification. The state of grace reveals a transformation so profound, in contrast to the state of sin, that clearly no human effort could produce it or sustain it, leading us to a constant reliance on grace to conquer sin. The state of glory shows that humanity's current state is so far from perfection that, again, we must rely on God to bring us to holiness.

To help us toward holiness, Calvin will try to lead us to an accurate two-fold knowledge of God and ourselves. Humankind, who consists of both body and soul,[10] suffers the effects of the fall in both. But it is the soul, comprised of reason and will,[11] with will subordinate to reason,[12] that most needs reformation from its corruption. Both our reason and will are affected by our rejection of the truth, so that we no longer see ourselves, or God, rightly. "Having forsaken the truth of God, they turned to the vanity of their own reason...[and were carried away] into errors and delusions."[13] Central to Calvin's understanding of sanctification then is the necessity of reversing this delusion, to restore humankind to a true double-knowledge which leads to both humility regarding our own virtue and gratitude as we turn to the grace of God for holiness. "By God's mercy alone we stand, since by ourselves we are nothing but evil."[14]

Calvin's understanding of the double-knowledge
The precise etymology of Calvin's understanding of the double-knowledge is uncertain. If Battles is correct, it may be that Calvin's view of the double-knowledge was shaped in part by his own personal encounter with the text of Rom. 1:18-25.[15] Yet, as Serene Jones makes clear, the same idea was used by many before Calvin, from whom he may have borrowed the concept.[16] We read, for example, in Clement of Alexandria, "If one knows oneself, one will

---

[9] Torrance, *Calvin's Doctrine of Man*, 13.
[10] *Institutes* 1.15.2.
[11] Niesel, *Theology of Calvin*, 65. Cf. *Institutes* 1.15.7.
[12] A.N.S. Lane, "Calvin's Doctrine of Assurance," *Vox Evangelica* 11 (1979), 42.
[13] *Commentary*, Rom. 1:21.
[14] *Institutes* 2.2.11.
[15] Battles, *Interpreting Calvin*, 142.
[16] Jones, *Rhetoric*, 92.

know God."[17] Augustine writes, "I desire to know God and the soul."[18] Bucer, as well, sees a two-fold knowledge, "If we know God and ourselves we will ascribe to God glory in all things, but to ourselves confusion."[19] We also find similar thoughts in Basil of Caesarea. "If we are penetrated by these truths, we shall know ourselves, we shall know God, we shall adore our Creator."[20] We may cautiously conjecture, warned by Lane,[21] that here, as was often the case, Calvin built his ideas on others. As Muller notes, Calvin became increasingly attuned to the "insights both of the patristic and of the medieval periods."[22]

While it has been debated which precedes the other for Calvin, knowledge of God or knowledge of self,[23] Calvin finally explains himself. For a proper double-knowledge, knowledge of God must precede knowledge of self, for "the beginning of religion is the knowledge of God."[24] "Yet, however the knowledge of God and of ourselves may be mutually connected, the order of right teaching requires that we discuss the former first, then proceed afterward to treat the latter."[25] This is the correct way, Spijker argues, in which to understand Calvin's *ordo docendi*.[26]

Understanding that the core of humanity's fall was found in the rejection of the true knowledge of God and self, Calvin saw that being brought back to this right knowledge was the way back to holiness, to restoring the image of God. "Newness of life consists in *knowledge*...transforming the whole man...that we are *renewed after the image of God*."[27] It is God, of course, who must restore our reason, bringing us from the lie that we are great and he is small to the truth: God is great and we are small before him. "We cannot attain to the full knowledge of God's works...until we be transformed into His image."[28]

The true double-knowledge aids our sanctification first by showing us our need.[29] "This knowledge of ourselves...shows us our nothingness."[30] Seeing

---

[17] Clement, "Instructor" 3.1, *The Ante-Nicene Fathers* (eds. A. Roberts, J. Donaldson; Peabody, Mass.: Hendrickson, 1994), 2:271.
[18] Augustine, "Soliloquies" 1.2.7, *The Nicene and Post-Nicene Fathers* (ed. P. Schaff; Peabody, Mass.: Hendrickson, 1994), Series1:7:539.
[19] M. Bucer, *Enarrationes perpetuae in sacra quatuor Evangelia, recognitae nuper et locis compluribus auctae* (Strasbourg: Georg Ulricher,1530), fol. 66v, 25-28.
[20] Basil of Caesarea, Hexaemeron, "The Creation of Luminous Bodies," *NPNF2*, 8:309.
[21] These assumptions must be balanced with Lane's important Thesis VIII: "A critical approach is necessary to determine which authors influenced Calvin, even where Calvin cites them extensively." Lane, *Student of the Church Fathers*, 8.
[22] Muller, *Unaccommodated*, 57.
[23] Jones, *Rhetoric*, 87-88.
[24] *Commentary*, Jer. 10:25.
[25] *Institutes* 1.1.3.
[26] Spijker, "The Influence of Luther on Calvin," 97. Muller concurs, see *Unaccommodated*, 95.
[27] *Commentary*, Col. 3:10.
[28] J. Calvin, *Sermons on Job* (tr. A. Golding; Edinburgh: Banner of Truth Trust, 1993), 384.
[29] *Commentary*, Jer. 14:21.
[30] Fuhrmann, *Instruction*, 27.

our inability to meet God's righteous demands in the law, we are forced to recognize that we are sinners in need of help. "In considering our powers, we learn that they are not only too weak to fulfill the law, but utterly nonexistent."[31] Showing us our helplessness before God, a right double-knowledge also brings us to understand that we have no hope but to turn to God's grace for help. "Yet, O Lord, thou art our Father, and we are but earth and mire."[32] It is there in the tension within "the gulf between the all-holy God and the fallen sinner"[33] that we are forced to reach out to Christ, who alone can bridge the gulf and make us holy.

The double-knowledge is not bare information but a relational understanding that leads us to a proper relational response to God.[34] This relational response is the two-fold movement of the human heart, which we have asserted is essential to Calvin's theology of sanctification: a downward movement, prostrating ourselves before God, accompanied by a simultaneous movement of the heart upward to exalt God in thankful reverence.[35] "These two things then ought not to be separated, and cannot be—the acknowledgment of our sins, which will humble us before God—and the knowledge of his goodness, and a firm assurance as to our salvation."[36]

To be sanctified, to be as we were in creation, as we shall be in glory, is to see God and ourselves rightly and to respond rightly to that knowledge of God and self. The double-knowledge then is both the medicine that cures us and the health we have once cured, which both flow from God. "The true knowledge of God is that which regenerates and renews us, so that we become new creatures; and that hence it cannot be but that it must conform us to the image of God."[37] To aid the cure, Calvin would convey the desperate nature of the human condition so we can, with proper humility, seek the right help.[38]

The Created State

Knowledge of God's goodness in creating us so well leads us to piety
Calvin pointedly describes the glory of humankind's creation. He wishes to show not only God's goodness but, by contrast to our created state, the depth of our eventual fall. "We shall see how far away men are from the purity that was bestowed upon Adam."[39] We were made in the very image of God,[40] such that "the likeness of God extends to the whole excellence" of humankind.[41] Our

---

[31] *Institutes* 2.8.3.
[32] "La Forme des Prieres et Chantz Ecclesiastiques," 1543, *OS* 2:28.
[33] Battles, *Interpreting Calvin*, 149.
[34] Battles, *Interpreting Calvin*, 173. Cf. Dowey, *Knowledge of God*, 20.
[35] *Commentary*, 1 Pet. 5:5. Cf. Lobstein, *Die Ethik Calvins*, 49.
[36] *Commentary*, Mic. 7:9.
[37] *Commentary*, 1 John 4:7.
[38] Torrance, *Calvin's Doctrine of Man*, 13.
[39] *Institutes* 1.15.1.
[40] Wallace, *Christian Life*, 105.
[41] *Institutes* 1.15.3.

soul was upright, our mind sound and our will "free to choose the good."[42] Our essential integrity included "right understanding," "reasonable affections" and a basic orientation of thankfulness toward God for all his good gifts.[43] Humanity was a glorious "world in miniature."[44]

Humanity's "right understanding" was comprised of a right knowledge of God and of the self, the original double-knowledge, revealing that humanity is fearfully and wonderfully made in order to serve and worship God.[45] Reflecting Anselm, who taught that man "was made holy for this end, that he might be happy in enjoying God,"[46] Calvin asserts that we originally knew to "reverence his Deity."[47] This double-knowledge led humanity not to pride but humility, for while humanity is created in God's image, it was, after all, "formed of clay" that man should not "exult beyond measure in his flesh."[48]

This original double-knowledge drew forth relational responses from humankind such as humility, thankfulness, dependence and obedience, those "reasonable affections." Humility came as humanity saw itself in comparison to its creator.[49] A heart of thankfulness was produced as humanity rightly beheld "the wonderful works of God."[50] Dependence came in knowing that all good originated from God, seeking it there and "having received it, to credit it to his account."[51] In that God had ordained the use of all creation for us, man felt the desire to "devote and dedicate himself entirely to obedience towards God."[52]

This response of reverence and love toward God—piety—is the description of our original rightness. Piety at its simplest is "that reverence we owe God."[53] More elaborately Calvin writes, "I call 'piety' that reverence joined with love of God which the knowledge of his benefits induces."[54] Piety then is the heart orientation toward God that looks to him in reverent faith, or reverential fear,[55] to provide, and returns to him love born of gratitude.[56] Piety is affective, "a pure and true zeal which loves God altogether as Father, and reveres him truly as Lord."[57] Piety, *pietas*, will serve for Calvin as theological shorthand to describe the state of the human in created perfection and the state toward which we press in sanctification.

---

[42] *Institutes* 1.15.8.
[43] *Institutes* 1.15.3.
[44] *Commentary*, Gen. 1:26.
[45] *Institutes* 1.15.3.
[46] Anselm, *Cur Deus Homo* (tr. S.N. Deane; Fort Worth, Tex.: RDMc, 2005), 82.
[47] *Commentary*, Gen. 2:16.
[48] *Commentary*, Gen. 2:7.
[49] *Institutes* 2.1.3.
[50] *Commentary*, Calvin's introductory argument to Genesis.
[51] *Institutes* 1.2.2.
[52] *Commentary*, Calvin's introductory argument to Genesis.
[53] *Sermons on the Ten Commandments*, 138.
[54] *Institutes* 1.2.1.
[55] Fuhrmann, *Instruction*, 23.
[56] *Commentary*, 1 Thess. 3:6.
[57] Fuhrmann, *Instruction*, 22.

Note in his definition, however, from whence *pietas* emerges: "which the knowledge of his benefits induces." The true knowledge of God, and ourselves in sight of God, is meant to bring forth not just correct understanding but piety. Reverence (*reverentiam*) and love (*amore*) are responses to God from the affective domain. Each glance up at God and down at ourselves drives us to these responses. The double-knowledge we possessed at creation was not just information but a deep understanding that produced a heart response from us, those "reasonable affections," from which we "bestir ourselves to trust, invoke, praise, and love him."[58]

Conclusion: Knowledge of our creation leads to humble exalting in God
Knowledge of the glory of our created state is useful to our sanctification, first, because it produces thankfulness toward God for having created us so wonderfully.[59] Second, knowledge of our created state humbles us as we see how far we have fallen and thus how unable we are to restore ourselves apart from God's help.[60] This logically discourages humanity from seeking human solutions but rather encourages them to turn to God for holiness "that they should seek nothing beyond him."[61] Knowledge of our fall from such a lofty height, while it strips us of our pride, does not leave us hopeless but will rather, as Torrance says, "lead men to the acknowledgment of the pure grace of God, and the adoration of His glory."[62] Third, seeing in the original blueprint of piety how we are called to reverence God, having been created in his very image, we should "be all the more moved to love him."[63] This true knowledge of our created state then brings us to a proper double-knowledge which brings forth the right response for relationship with God, *pietas*. We are humble, prostrating ourselves before God as we recognize that we cannot restore ourselves to such perfection, and at the same time exalting in God such that we in reverence and love turn to him for our sanctification.[64] "He admonishes us from what excellence we have fallen, that he may excite in us the desire of its recovery."[65]

The Fallen State

The nature of our condition: Misery and helplessness

Humankind is so thoroughly corrupt that it possesses no absolute good
Calvin believed that after the fall humankind was so utterly sinful that, apart from the intervention of grace, there was nothing that humanity could do to help itself. "Nothing has remained in the heart of man but corruption, since the

---

[58] *Institutes* 1.14.22.
[59] Torrance, *Calvin's Doctrine of Man*, 18.
[60] *Institutes* 2.1.1.
[61] *Institutes* 1.2.1.
[62] Torrance, *Calvin's Doctrine of Man*, 17.
[63] "Sermon on Deut. 6:4-9," CO 26:439.
[64] *Institutes* 2.1.3.
[65] *Commentary*, Gen. 1:27.

time in which Adam lost the image of God."[66] Calvin drove this point home in order that humanity would give up all hope of self-improvement and turn to God for help. Torrance writes, "Calvin insists again and again that man must be reduced to nothing in his own estimation."[67] To reduce humankind to nothing Calvin would describe humanity's sin, often and in great depth.

Humankind is corrupted entirely, heart, mind and soul by original sin.[68] "Unspeakable impiety occupied the very citadel of his mind, and pride penetrated to the depths of his heart."[69] Stemming from a heart of unbelief,[70] with our initial act of prideful "unfaithfulness" in disobeying God,[71] human nature was corrupted by "concupiscence" (*concupiscentia*).[72] This term describes not so much the actions of sin but the ever-present tendency to gratify the flesh, "fertile and fruitful of every evil,"[73] against the will and glory of God.[74] This cupidity restlessly lusts for more and more (*cupidité de gagner*) that the self might be built up in the pride of life.[75] In sin we "feel nothing but the flesh" and naturally hate the goodness of God and move "furiously towards iniquity."[76] This sin nature continually generates new sins "just as a glowing furnace continually emits flame and sparks."[77] Humankind is so sinful "they cannot help but tumble from one sin into another, until they have exhausted them all."[78] Indeed for Calvin, as for Augustine, humanity is *una massa peccati* and therefore *una massa damnati*.[79] To understand Calvin's program for sanctification, one must first see that "in us there is nothing but sin,"[80] so that humanity will be entirely disinclined to look inward for help.

Yet God's image is not totally removed, so that humankind might hope for restoration
Calvin shows that while the *imago Dei* is broken in humankind,[81] yet some hints of it still linger.[82] "Should any one object, that this divine image has been obliterated [*deletam*], the solution is easy; first, there yet exists some remnant

---

[66] *Commentary*, Rom. 7:15.
[67] Torrance, *Calvin's Doctrine of Man*, 94.
[68] *Institutes* 2.1.5. Cf. *Commentary*, Gen. 8:21; Jer. 17:9; John 3:6.
[69] *Institutes* 2.1.9.
[70] *Commentary*, Gen. 3:6. Cf. Niesel, *Theology of Calvin*, 81; *Commentary*, Eph. 2:2.
[71] *Institutes* 2.1.4.
[72] *CO* 2:183, "Qui dixerunt esse concupiscentiam, non nimis alieno verbo usi sunt."
[73] *Institutes* 2.1.8.
[74] Fuhrmann, *Instruction*, 26.
[75] *Sermons on the Ten Commandments*, 192.
[76] Fuhrmann, *Instruction*, 25.
[77] *Institutes* 4.15.11.
[78] *Sermons on Micah*, 68.
[79] D.N. Bell, *Many Mansions, An Introduction to the Development and Diversity of Medieval Theology West and East* (Kalamazoo, Mich.: Cistercian, 1996), 324.
[80] *Commentary*, 1 Cor. 1:30.
[81] *Commentary*, Gen. 3:1.
[82] *Commentary*, Jas. 3:9; Gal. 5:14.

of it."[83] The remnants of that image were to be found both in humanity's ability to reason, for it still "sees and understands"[84] and in its ability to conduct itself in "earthly things" toward some common social goods.[85] Neither could Calvin, trained as a humanist, deny the relative splendor of human achievement, for "we cannot read the writings of the ancients on these subjects without great admiration."[86] Hence Calvin will conclude that "he, then, who truly worships and honors God, will be afraid to speak slanderously of man."[87]

This respectful view of fallen humanity, along with his obvious cultural appreciations,[88] has caused some to conclude that Calvin might rightly be called a humanist. Hence Wendel[89] points to Calvin's philological methods and Ganoczy[90] to Calvin's theological influences. Muller is more circumspect placing Calvin "at the center of a significant confluence of nominally humanistic...patterns of discourse."[91] Cottret, while acknowledging humanism's deep influences, correctly nuances the label in Calvin's case. "If by humanist one means a concern for fine literature and the restoration of texts, Calvin was unquestionably a Renaissance humanist....If, on the other hand, one means by humanism faith in man...Calvin was the absolute opposite of a humanist."[92]

This opposition to humanism is clear in Calvin's handling of the *imago Dei*, first in his downgrading of the natural gifts in contrasts to the spiritual. As Torrance writes, "Any remnant of the image must refer to man's natural gifts, which...are not in any sense the spiritual image or part of it."[93] Second, Calvin is clear that pointing to the *imago Dei* is not for man to take pride in himself but rather that he may hope toward the restoration of that image, "the end of his original creation," by the grace of God.[94]

Our will is in bondage to sin, such that we cannot will well apart from grace
Calvin steers between two extremes in describing the fallen will, maintaining that the will still functions as a will, yet it is so corrupt that it never cooperates with God. Against critics, such as Pighius, who charged Calvin with destroying human will by making us into "stones,"[95] Calvin maintained that the will still functioned even in depravity.[96] Neither the fall, nor the grace of God, can efface

---

[83] *Commentary*, Gen. 9:6.
[84] *Commentary*, John 1:5.
[85] *Institutes* 2.2.13.
[86] *Institutes* 2.2.15.
[87] *Commentary*, Jas. 3:9.
[88] See, for example, Calvin's lengthy defense of knowledge and learning where he says, "Knowledge is good in itself," *Commentary*, 1 Cor. 8:1.
[89] Wendel, *Origins*, 31.
[90] Ganoczy, *Young Calvin*, 180-81.
[91] Muller, *Unaccommodated*, 157.
[92] Cottret, *Calvin*, 331.
[93] Torrance, *Calvin's Doctrine of Man*, 83.
[94] *Commentary*, Gen. 9:6.
[95] *BLW*, 200.
[96] *BLW*, 231.

our will.[97] While detesting the confusion of the term "free will," lest man thinks he can "turn himself toward either good or evil,"[98] Calvin concurs with Augustine[99] that the will has a certain freedom: either free from righteousness, or by grace, free from sin.[100]

Precisely because we still possess a working will, we are rightly held responsible for our willful sin.[101] "No one can claim that anything else is responsible for his sinning except an evil will."[102] While the will sins of necessity, the necessity is found in our own evil nature, not in some outside coercion,[103] so that we are responsible for our willful sin.[104] We are no more excused by necessity than is the devil.[105] Calvin, who takes Anselm to task at other points, agrees here: the necessity of our sin derives from our own sinfulness and so rightly condemns us, not God.[106] Therefore the root of blame remains firmly with us, for we will with "deliberate evil intent"[107] and thus sin voluntarily.[108]

Calvin fought the Roman concept that the will possessed enough goodness to cooperate with grace, and thus warrant merit from God, because he did not want humanity claiming credit for good works or relying on its own power to do good.[109] He would argue against Pighius, "The human will should not even be considered a follower of grace's leadership, as though it cooperated by itself."[110] Since the fallen human will always sins[111] and wills only evil,[112] rather than cooperating with God, it always defies him in every way.[113] Humans are, in Niesel's words, "cramped within themselves instead of being expanded outwards to God in the desire to do His will."[114]

Since we are not capable of cooperating with God, then any move toward holiness must flow from the power of God whose Spirit directs our will to any good.[115] It is God who makes us will to obey him,[116] who "arouses then guides

---

[97] *BLW*, 123.
[98] *Institutes* 2.2.7.
[99] *Institutes* 2.2.8.
[100] *BLW*, 130.
[101] *Commentary*, John 8:34.
[102] *BLW*, 169.
[103] *Institutes* 2.3.5.
[104] *BLW*, 68-69.
[105] *BLW*, 147.
[106] *BLW*, 169; Anselm, *Cur Deus Homo*, 76, "So inexcusable is man, who has voluntarily brought upon himself a debt which he cannot pay, and by his own fault disabled himself, so that he can neither escape his previous obligation not to sin, nor pay the debt which he has incurred by sin."
[107] *BLW*, 37.
[108] *Commentary*, Rom. 1:28.
[109] Tamburello, *Union with Christ*, 31.
[110] *BLW*, 225.
[111] *BLW*, 183.
[112] *BLW*, 115.
[113] *BLW*, 213.
[114] Niesel, *Theology of Calvin*, 89.
[115] *BLW*, 231.

Chapter 2 - Calvin's Anthropology and Its Implications for Sanctification

man's will to do good."[117] We must look to God to sanctify us,[118] relying moment by moment on his grace to produce a good will.[119] Calvin quotes Bernard with favor: "Therefore simply to will is of man; to will ill, of a corrupt nature; to will well, of grace."[120] It is only as we rely on grace, not on our ability to will well, Calvin agrees with Augustine, that our will itself is liberated "from the bondage that made it the slave of sin."[121]

Our reason is corrupted, such that only God can heal our thinking
The "whole of their mental system"[122] was corrupted by sin, for "sin properly belongs to the mind."[123] As a result our minds cannot, apart from grace, understand the things of God well enough for salvation. "Their foolish mind, being involved in darkness, could understand nothing aright."[124] Ironically, our reason was destroyed by our original sinful desire "to know more than was lawful, in order that they might become equal with God."[125]

Human reason, while fallen, still functions in part.[126] Humankind "still sees and understands"[127] well enough that it can reasonably conduct itself in the daily world. Also, human conscience, the seed of religion (*semen religionis*) and the sense of the divine (*sensus divinitatis*) still operate.[128] The conscience is the moral part of human reasoning, telling us that God's law should be obeyed,[129] while the *sensus divinitatis* pertains to our intellectual understanding of God,[130] informing us that God should be worshipped.[131] "The impious themselves therefore exemplify the fact that some conception of God is ever alive in all men's minds,"[132] for they cannot open their eyes "without being compelled to see him."[133]

It is, however, debated just how much efficacy Calvin attributed to either conscience or the *sensus divinitatis* to help humanity understand God apart from grace. While Brunner found much in Calvin to suggest that natural humanity may understand God and Barth found little,[134] Bouwsma concludes that

---

[116] *BLW*, 211.
[117] *BLW*, 177.
[118] *BLW*, 174.
[119] *BLW*, 114.
[120] *Institutes* 2.3.5.
[121] *BLW*, 92.
[122] *Commentary*, Col. 1:21.
[123] *Commentary*, Rom. 2:1.
[124] *Commentary*, Rom. 1:21.
[125] *Commentary*, Gen. 3:6.
[126] *Commentary*, John 1:4.
[127] *Commentary*, John 1:5.
[128] *Commentary*, John 1:5; Jonah 1:5. Cf. Dowey, *Knowledge of God*, 51-52.
[129] *Commentary*, Gen. 4:9; *Institutes* 1.3.2.
[130] Tamburello, *Union with Christ*, 38.
[131] Dowey, *Knowledge of God*, 71-72.
[132] *Institutes* 1.3.2.
[133] *Institutes* 1.5.1; *Commentary*, John 3:16; Rom.1:19.
[134] Steinmetz, *Context*, 24.

the debate is futile because Calvin "can be cited on both sides of the issue."[135] We would concur with Steinmetz, however, that Calvin distinguishes between what is offered to natural reason and what is received—too little to help—due to "culpable human blindness."[136] Fallen humanity has some capacity to understand about God, who is clearly manifested, yet humanity willfully refuses to accept true knowledge of God "since their mind is corrupted with contempt of God."[137] Human conscience and *sensus divinitatis* lead finally to a dead end, bearing no fruit, for "conscience perverts every decision" and "natural reason never will direct men to Christ."[138] Since impiety, rather than *pietas*, holds sway over the human mind,[139] we are willfully blind to the light of God[140] and persist in our blindness until grace frees us.[141]

Humankind does perceive just enough of the knowledge of God that "the ignorance of the ungodly is without excuse."[142] Niesel concurs that "in face of God we cannot shelter behind the excuse that we have no knowledge of Him."[143] Humanity's natural knowledge of God serves not to save them, but so they "cannot allege anything before God's tribunal for the purpose of showing that they are not justly condemned."[144]

Fallen human reason "enveloped in hypocrisy and deceitful craft"[145] offers us no hope for attaining true knowledge of God or self but, as with the fallen will, only shows how dependent we must be on the grace of God for both salvation and sanctification. The human mind, unable to find a saving knowledge of God on its own, must be entirely transformed, renewed by grace through faith so that we can come to a true knowledge of God and ourselves.[146] It is faith then which overcomes our blindness and becomes "the light by which man can gain real knowledge from the work of creation."[147] Faith, a kind of knowledge itself, is not gained by our fallen reason but is a gift "acquired by the teaching of the Holy Spirit."[148] Faith, aided by the Holy-Spirit-illuminated-Scriptures, serves as a kind of "spectacle" which allows humanity to see and finally under-

---

[135] Bouwsma, *Sixteenth-Century Portrait*, 262, note 51.
[136] Steinmetz, *Context*, 29. Cf. Niesel, *Theology of Calvin*, 46.
[137] *Commentary*, Gen. 8:21.
[138] *Commentary*, John 1:5. Cf. *Commentary*, John 11:25; Acts 14:17; 17:27; 1 Cor. 1:21; *Institutes* 1.5.11.
[139] *Institutes* 2.1.9.
[140] Battles, *Interpreting Calvin*, 269.
[141] *BLW*, 77.
[142] *Commentary*, Heb. 11:3. Cf. Tamburello, *Union with Christ*, 37.
[143] Niesel, *Theology of Calvin*, 49.
[144] *Commentary*, Rom. 1: 20. Cf. *Commentary*, Jonah 1:5; Rom. 1:21; 2:15; *Institutes* 1.5.15.
[145] *Institutes* 2.5.19.
[146] *Commentary*, Rom. 12:2.
[147] *Commentary*, Rom. 1:20.
[148] *Commentary*, Eph. 3:19.

stand God.[149] Humanity, once it is rightly humbled about its own reason,[150] may finally find the needed help in the grace of God to think aright.

The results of the fallen state: Enmity toward God and self-reliance

Regarding God: Hating God we create idols, cannot please God, suffer his wrath

Our rejection of God leads us to hate God as our enemy with "every affection of our heart."[151] We reject the authority of God's Word which might require us to reform or submit.[152] Determined to live in unbelief, humankind wants freedom to give full reign to the flesh.[153] We are hateful to God as well, who only loves purity.[154] "Abhorrent to God"[155] we are subject to his wrath. Counting God our mortal enemy, we flee his presence.[156]

Having rejected the truth of God's Word, humanity scrambles to create order out of its own chaos by devising its own idolatrous religions. "All who forsake the word fall into idolatry."[157] This basic human tendency, to fashion and worship idols, is "the root of all evil" which must inevitably occur once we have turned "aside from knowledge of God."[158] It takes no prompting for us to "contaminate ourselves with idolatry,"[159] such that we are "a perpetual factory of idols."[160]

Rather than turn to God for help, motivated by the "irreligious affectation of religion," humanity will only turn to its own idols in order to acquire "righteousness apart from God's Word."[161] We learn to turn to idols for righteousness naturally "without ever having to go to school."[162] Because Calvin identified the Catholic practices of penance and indulgences as the very heart of idolatry, that is, superstitious human efforts to secure righteousness apart from Christ through reliance on human ability and goodness,[163] he would consider them lethal to sanctification.

Idolatry creates a kind of addiction that keeps us bound to it. "All are nevertheless addicted to idolatry."[164] Idolatrous to the core, man continuously robs

---

[149] *Institutes* 1.6.1.
[150] *Institutes* 2.2.1.
[151] *Commentary*, John 5:25.
[152] *Institutes* 2.1.4.
[153] Niesel, *Theology of Calvin*, 81.
[154] *Institutes* 4.15.10.
[155] *Institutes* 2.1.8.
[156] *Sermons on the Ten Commandments*, 257.
[157] *Commentary*, John 4:22.
[158] *Sermons on Micah*, 30.
[159] *Sermons on Micah*, 57.
[160] *Institutes* 1.11.8.
[161] *Institutes* 2.8.5.
[162] *Sermons on Micah*, 37-38.
[163] *Institutes* 3.5.2.
[164] *Commentary*, 1 Thess. 1:9.

God of his glory, "transferring to himself what belongs to God."[165] In the end we are "brute beasts" who cannot help but flee the presence of God.[166] Humankind's idolatry renders it doubly helpless. Refusing to turn to God for help, we turn to idols which are powerless to help and only drag us deeper into the rebellion of self-reliance.

In our state of rebellion there is nothing we can do which could ever merit "the favor of God by works."[167] Even our best works "are without exception sinful,"[168] so that they "derive no praise at all."[169] Yet while humanity has no ability to merit God's favor, it is rightly held responsible for its willful rebellion.[170] Nor can we object that God is unreasonable to command us to do what we cannot do in our own strength, since the very purpose of the command is "that we should know what we ought to seek from [God]."[171] Humanity is left a helpless, but culpable, sinner. An enemy of God, who can do nothing to please God, humanity flees his presence and creates idols which bind us to their worthless rituals, leaving us even more helpless and guiltier before God.

Regarding one's self: Humanity blindly imagines itself good, and God evil, so it futilely turns to itself for help in holiness
Calvin finds a bitter irony in fallen human nature: it includes a deep blindness, such that it cannot perceive its own sin but rather dupes itself into believing well of itself.[172] As Battles summarizes, "We suffer from *lippitudo*, blearedness."[173] We have such a wrongly inflated opinion of ourselves that we seek nothing "more eagerly than to be flattered."[174] We are so blinded that, "there is not a single person who does not deceive himself or become a deceiver."[175]

Since we perceive ourselves as being good, and we perceive God, opposed to us in our sin, as being evil, we turn "upside down all the heavenly wisdom,"[176] which leads us to a kind of insane hatred of his glory.[177] Unable to see our sin or God's goodness, we are rendered incurable on two counts. Thinking we are healthy, we will not seek a cure. "Through this subtlety Satan attempted to cover up the disease and thus to render it incurable."[178] Thinking God evil,

---

[165] *Commentary*, Rom. 1:18.
[166] *Sermons on Job*, 605.
[167] Reid, *Treatises*, 199, "Necessity of Reforming the Church," 1543.
[168] *BLW*, 28.
[169] *Institutes* 2.2.16. Cf. *Commentary*, Rom. 7:19; Jonah 1:15.
[170] *Institutes* 1.5.1.
[171] *BLW*, 141-42.
[172] *Institutes* 3.2.10.
[173] Battles, *Interpreting Calvin*, 130.
[174] *Institutes* 2.1.2.
[175] *Sermons on Micah*, 59.
[176] Fuhrmann, *Instruction*, 24.
[177] *Commentary*, Rom. 11:36.
[178] *Institutes* 2.1.5.

Chapter 2 - Calvin's Anthropology and Its Implications for Sanctification

we will avoid the only one who can cure us, "for when our minds are inflated with foolish self-confidence, we neglect God."[179]

The corruption in human nature leaves us in an unnatural state regarding our self-understanding. At one moment humanity will strive to achieve honor,[180] fill its every desire[181] and boast[182] of its own vain power,[183] being filled with "irrational self-confidence."[184] At the next moment, humanity finds itself cast down in despair, for while we boast vainly, we live in the real world where the law of God, written on all hearts, convicts our imperfect conscience of our own miserable failure. This awareness is made more acute by the fact that even fallen humanity will "naturally long for the undamaged condition."[185] Unable to rid our conscience of this sense of failure, we vacillate[186] between two equally unhelpful positions: overly-confident boasting and hopeless despair.[187]

This internal warfare also drives people into conflict with others, to gain self-esteem at others' expense. "Such arrogance indwells us, that we each want to be elevated over our neighbors."[188] Their slightest failing becomes an opportunity to exalt ourselves over them,[189] for we are "inclined to speak indiscreetly and heap blame and scandal"[190] on others. Rather than actually improving us, these conflicts, as with all our efforts at self-improvement, only make us guiltier.

Feeling his internal conflict and wanting to improve his righteousness, humanity turns to self-help which is finally futile because original sin has rendered humans unable to help themselves. "When we are taught to wage our own war, we are but borne aloft on a reed stick, only to fall as soon as it breaks!"[191] Blinded to its true condition, humanity cannot see that it is beyond its own ability to cure itself, but rather in its self-dependency, makes matters worse. "Born we have been with no power to do what is acceptable or pleasing to our God, yet the very thing we cannot supply we do not cease to owe."[192] We are unable to take what good God has graciously allowed to remain in us and stir it up to piety,[193] for we are "so far from making progress in piety, that [we]

---

[179] *Commentary*, Mic. 5:11.
[180] *Sermons on 2 Samuel*, 13.
[181] *Commentary*, 1 Thess. 4:3.
[182] *Sermons on 2 Samuel*, 13.
[183] *Commentary*, Ps. 94:4.
[184] *Commentary*, Hos. 13:6.
[185] *Institutes* 3.25.2.
[186] *Institutes* 3.3.12.
[187] *Sermons on 2 Samuel*, 24.
[188] *Sermons on the Ten Commandments*, 125.
[189] *Sermons on 2 Samuel*, 26.
[190] *Sermons on the Ten Commandments*, 217.
[191] *Institutes* 2.2.1.
[192] Battles, *The Piety of John Calvin*, 45.
[193] *Institutes* 1.4.1.

fall into what is worse."[194] There is nothing that humankind can do to sanctify itself apart from God granting regeneration.[195]

Nowhere did Calvin fight the notions of self-help more powerfully than against the Roman "satisfactions, superstitions and idolatries,"[196] which had reduced holiness to the point that it could rightly be said that there were "none with disciplined character, none knowledgeable in sacred literature, none reverent in divine things."[197] Theologically, these Roman practices were sympathetic toward the semi-Pelagian notion that humanity could perform works which merited God's favor,[198] rendering humanity capable of self-improvement. This idea Calvin endlessly opposed as a kind of dark cancer that ate away souls.[199] Against all notions of self-sanctification, he declared that the Lord "both begins and completes the good work in us."[200] Methodologically, Rome relied too heavily on the external disciplines of penance, allowing sinners to progress in their holiness through contrition, confession and satisfaction. Calvin understood these disciplines as failing to touch the heart of humankind and therefore the heart of the issue, the need for God to grant true repentance.[201] Contrition could never be full and true,[202] confession never complete enough[203] and satisfactions an affront to the free grace of Christ.[204] The most extreme example of satisfactions, the practice of purchasing indulgences, he would denounce as a "profanation of the blood of Christ" which only serves to turn people "aside from the true way of salvation."[205] Seeing the lost sheep of the church being led away from true holiness toward futile human efforts, Calvin would call them to see their own inability so as to drive them to seek the help of grace.[206]

Conclusion: Seeing our misery turns us toward God for help
This proper double-knowledge of our fallen nature makes us "doubly ashamed."[207] We must admit that any good in us is from God, not ourselves.[208] We must also admit that we are helpless and have to rely on God's grace[209] to

---

[194] *Commentary*, 1 Thess. 1:9.
[195] *Institutes* 2.2.12.
[196] Ganoczy, *Young Calvin*, 195.
[197] C. Bellarmine, *Opera* (Cologne: 1617), Vol. VI., Col. 296, as cited by Fuhrmann, *Instruction*, 78, note 2.
[198] *Sermons on the Ten Commandments*, 285.
[199] *Institutes* 3.17.15.
[200] *Institutes* 2.3.9.
[201] *Institutes* 3.4.1.
[202] *Institutes* 3.4.3.
[203] *Institutes* 3.4.16.
[204] *Institutes* 3.4.29.
[205] *Institutes* 3.5.2.
[206] *Commentary*, Rom. 4:14.
[207] "Sermon on Job 33:1-7," CO 35:47; cf. *Sermons on Job*, 576.
[208] *BLW*, 162.
[209] *BLW*, 114.

"recover us from that bottomless pit."[210] As Niesel summarizes, "The independence of man is crushed into dust in the presence of the majesty of God."[211] Calvin does not intend to leave humanity crushed but, properly humbled, he aims to show us that our only source of hope is "not partially but wholly from God."[212] People are brought finally to a contrite submission before the hand of God,[213] wherein they "stake their entire refuge on God's loving-kindness."[214] We must always understand Calvin's doctrine of the fall in light of God's grace, both in creating us in his image and redeeming us through his Son,[215] rather than, as some have thought, as something morosely negative.[216] Calvin painted such a bleak picture of human nature precisely so we might turn from human efforts and turn to grace for help in holiness. "Goodness results from the grace of the Holy Spirit and so is his own work."[217]

The State of Grace

Only God's grace can transform the mind and will to a true double-knowledge
Humanity, in a state of grace, is so altered by the work of God's redemption that will and mind are transformed "from their innate wickedness to obedience of his law."[218] We who were hateful as God's enemies "now begin to bear the image of Christ,"[219] so that seeing the "features of his own countenance"[220] we are lovely to God.

The will, regenerated through the Holy Spirit,[221] is set free from sin "that man reflects, like a mirror, the wisdom, righteousness, and goodness of God."[222] Our mind is also freed, so we can think "free from guile and feigning" and seek from God "the cultivation of holiness and righteousness."[223] The end result of the renewed will and mind is the "transforming [of] the whole man"[224] from a state of rebellion against God to a state of humility before him. It is only by the work of God that we come to a real double-knowledge, which is not a

---

[210] J. Calvin, *Sermons on Election and Reprobation* (tr. J. Fielde; Willowstreet, Pa.: Old Paths, 1996), 42.
[211] Niesel, *Theology of Calvin*, 167.
[212] Reid, *Treatises*, 198, "Necessity of Reforming the Church," 1543.
[213] *Institutes* 2.1.2.
[214] *Sermons on the Ten Commandments*, 299.
[215] Torrance, *Calvin's Doctrine of Man*, 20.
[216] Barth, *Theology of Calvin*, 120.
[217] *BLW*, 115.
[218] *BLW*, 124.
[219] *Commentary*, 1 Cor. 15:49.
[220] *Institutes* 3.17.5.
[221] *Institutes* 2.2.12; *BLW*, 226.
[222] *Commentary*, Col. 3:10.
[223] *Institutes* 3.6.5.
[224] *Commentary*, Col. 3:10.

"simple and bare knowledge,"[225] but leads us to respond to God as we rightly prostrate ourselves before God and adore his glory.[226]

Only the grace of God can transform humankind into the image of God

Grace transforms us into the image of God and conformity to the law
In this state of grace, God begins to restore us to what we were in the Garden,[227] to the "true order"[228] (*verum ordinem*) wherein we bear with increasing clarity the image of God, or the image of Christ,[229] which is "stamped anew upon us."[230] This restoration of the true order is "the idea that dominates the whole of Calvin's theological exposition,"[231] as Wendel suggests. Within the true order, God and humanity move toward their proper relationship. Humanity, with "eyes prepared to see God,"[232] is humble, thankful and dependent on God; God is glorified and exalted by humanity.

The restoration to the image of God, or to the true order, is the same as being restored to the pattern of the law.[233] "The law of God contains in itself that newness by which his image can be restored in us."[234] The law, which is the "perfection of wisdom,"[235] was always the pattern to which the people of God were to conform, so "there was good reason why all the precepts of the law should be observed."[236] The law, never intended to be set aside, remains inviolable as the plan for our lives,[237] any deviation from which is certain to lead us to "nothing but ruin."[238]

Our conformity to the law is not merely external but a change in our very "affections and cupidity,"[239] such that the law finds "a seat and resting place in the inmost affection of the heart."[240] External conformity, "false appearances in order to be approved,"[241] could never be enough, for without the right motive, external obedience becomes disobedience.[242] We are transformed internally, into those who love and long to obey the law,[243] for it arouses us "to a zeal for

---

[225] *Commentary*, Col. 3:10.
[226] *Institutes* 2.2.10; Torrance, *Calvin's Doctrine of Man*, 17.
[227] *Commentary*, Eph. 4:24.
[228] Wallace, *Christian Life*, 107.
[229] *Institutes* 3.6.3.
[230] *Commentary*, 2 Cor. 3:18.
[231] Wendel, *Origins*, 151.
[232] *Commentary*, 1 John 3:2.
[233] *Institutes* 4.13.13.
[234] *Institutes* 3.6.1.
[235] *Sermons on the Ten Commandments*, 291.
[236] *Commentary*, Deut. 6:20-25. Cf. Lobstein, *Die Ethik Calvins*, 46.
[237] *Institutes* 2.7.14.
[238] *Sermons on the Ten Commandments*, 244.
[239] *Sermons on the Ten Commandments*, 219.
[240] *Institutes* 3.6.4. Cf. *Commentary*, Rom. 6:15; 7:3-4.
[241] *Sermons on 2 Samuel*, 111.
[242] *Sermons on 2 Samuel*, 109-11.
[243] *Institutes* 2.7.12, 3.14.9.

holiness and innocence."[244] Since we love the law we hate any transgression of it but desire purity,[245] holiness and to avoid all corruptions.[246] Calvin follows the sentiment of Bernard regarding loving the law: "It is given them as to willing subjects, with a freedom equal to the sweetness with which it is breathed into them."[247]

Through grace, our growing obedience to the law is rewarded by God who gives us "the blessings which under the covenant were owed to the observance of his law."[248] Our imperfect obedience is really blessed, but not for its own merit.[249] Rather our obedience of faith is kindly rewarded by our Father because of Christ[250] "to make us aware of the fruits of his grace."[251] While the reward is far beyond what the good works actually merit, the reward will not come without the good works produced by Christ, through the obedience of faith, so that it is rightly said that people are "crowned according to their own works."[252] God intends for his blessing also to stir us to greater obedience.[253] "When he bestows his favor on us in this way it serves to move us more effectively and results in our serving him with far more ardent heart."[254]

In grace, while we are conforming more to the law, we have the blessing of freedom of conscience before the law, two aspects of which are relevant here.[255] First, the conscience is free from the law's power to condemn, finding its justification in faith alone.[256] Second, the conscience is free to obey from a willing heart and not under the constraint of perfect obedience.[257] As Leith explains, "They do not have to earn salvation by obeying every jot and tittle of the law."[258]

Freedom of conscience before the law of God also renders us free from manmade laws, such as "abominable" monastic regulations,[259] that would restrict us beyond the law of God.[260] While we rightly observe local statutes, they have no power over our consciences.[261] This freedom of conscience before the

---

[244] *Institutes* 3.19.2. Cf. Lobstein, *Die Ethik Calvins*, 52.
[245] *Commentary*, 1 John 3:1.
[246] McKee, *Pastoral Piety*, 257, 264.
[247] Bernard of Clairvaux, *On the Love of God* (tr. T.L. Connolly; New York, N.Y.: Spiritual Books Assoc., 1937), 59-60.
[248] *Institutes* 3.17.3.
[249] *Institutes* 3.18.3; *Commentary*, 1 John 2:17.
[250] *Institutes* 3.17.8, 3.17.3, 3.17.5.
[251] *Sermons on the Ten Commandments*, 284. Cf. Barth, *Theology of Calvin*, 170.
[252] *Institutes* 3.18.1.
[253] *Institutes* 3.19.5.
[254] *Sermons on the Ten Commandments*, 296.
[255] Calvin speaks of three Christian freedoms, but the third, freedom in things indifferent, does not pertain to our discussion here. Cf. *Institutes* 3.19.7.
[256] *Institutes* 3.19.2.
[257] *Institutes* 3.19.4, 3.19.5.
[258] Leith, *Christian Life*, 49.
[259] *Institutes* 4.13.12.
[260] *Institutes* 4.10.8.
[261] *Institutes* 3.19.14.

law of God and humankind ultimately leads to a good conscience, which is "nothing but inward integrity of heart."[262] Our good conscience does not encourage laxity towards either God's law or human law, but rather, knowing we are graciously forgiven "renders us far more prompt to obey."[263] Thus, as people are transformed into the image of God, or the law, they receives a double blessing: from outside, God pours blessing upon their obedience, and internally, they are given an untroubled conscience, both results that could come to sinful humanity only by reliance on God's grace.

We become lovers of God
Finally recognizing that "he will provide all that we need,"[264] we respond to God with a sincere love.[265] No longer passing over "in ungrateful thoughtlessness"[266] his many kindnesses, but seeing that "God has destined all things for our good,"[267] we are prodded on to love him even more. Loving him, we trust him as the sole source of every good in our lives.[268] Love for God grows, forcing out anything in us that may "conflict with this love for him."[269] Neither is our love a repayment for the gifts rendered by God, a spiritual *quid pro quo*. Rather, we delight in him as our Father, beyond his bounty to us, and grow in heartfelt love for him.[270] It is from this new heart, "aflame with a love and desire to walk in all holiness,"[271] that we grow in loving obedience.

Love for our Father runs so deep that we have a "zeal to illustrate the glory of God"[272] above all other good in our lives,[273] gladly ascribing to him any glory we might have claimed.[274] Thus we fulfill our created purpose, the true order, that God "might be glorified in us."[275] Seeking God's glory leads us to a grateful worship of God[276] which flows naturally from the regenerate soul,[277] such that we "gather every day to call upon the name of God."[278] Worship from the whole person, "prompt and active in rendering thanks,"[279] becomes the only

---

[262] *Institutes* 3.19.16.
[263] *Commentary*, 1 John 5:3; *Institutes* 3.19.8.
[264] *Sermons on the Ten Commandments*, 196.
[265] *Institutes* 3.6.5.
[266] *Institutes* 1.14.21.
[267] *Institutes* 1.14.22.
[268] Niesel, *Theology of Calvin*, 27.
[269] Reid, *Treatises*, 117, "Catechism of the Church of Geneva," 1545.
[270] *Commentary*, 1 John 2:5.
[271] *Sermons on the Ten Commandments*, 221.
[272] *CSW*, Vol. 1, 33, "Reply to Sadolet."
[273] McKee, *Pastoral Piety*, 169.
[274] McKee, *Pastoral Piety*, 163.
[275] Reid, *Treatises*, 91, "Catechism of the Church of Geneva," 1545.
[276] *Sermons on the Ten Commandments*, 228.
[277] Fuhrmann, *Instruction*, 29.
[278] *Sermons on the Ten Commandments*, 118.
[279] *Commentary*, 2 Cor. 4:15.

Chapter 2 - Calvin's Anthropology and Its Implications for Sanctification

rational response for anyone who realizes the goodness of God as Father. "Then knowing that we owe our life to Him, we ought to do homage to Him."[280]

We become lovers of others
Love for our neighbor springs from the reality that "we have been loved freely"[281] and therefore comes from the pure motive of Christ's love for us "as an instance of perfect love."[282] In the state of grace, we are freed from self-love, such that love of neighbor will be "the principle of all our purposes and all our actions."[283] Loving our neighbor also ensures we will not sin against them in violation of any of the other commandments.[284]

This love can only be lived out in the context of the church and society and not in monastic isolation,[285] for true Christianity "is lively and full of vigor, so that it spares no labor, when assistance is to be given to one's neighbors."[286] This is easily seen as we are moved to supply their material needs,[287] particularly by giving to the poor among us, which "the Lord reckons as given to himself."[288]

We become moderate in all of life
The "true order" brings us to moderation in emotions, desires and conduct as an expression of our newfound humility.[289] Emotionally, while we are not "stones," neither are we to be carried away by extreme emotions, even grief, for God "requires moderation in our mourning."[290] Calvin rebukes King David for the depth of his lament over the deaths of Jonathan and Saul, for he showed "excessive grief, with complete lack of self-control."[291] But Calvin applauds Christ whose "feelings were adjusted and regulated in obedience to God" as he mourned Lazarus.[292] Not only grief, but our joy must not depart from an even keel lest we display an "unseemly levity."[293]

Along with moderate emotions, our very desires proceed from a well-regulated heart that has no "uncontrolled desire" or "immoderate prodigality."[294] Christ models for us the moderation of desire, for when he was "dis-

---

[280] *Sermons on the Ten Commandments*, 122.
[281] *Commentary*, 1 John 4:11; Acts 2:46.
[282] *Commentary*, 1 John 3:16.
[283] Reid, *Treatises*, 117, "Catechism of the Church of Geneva," 1545.
[284] *Sermons on the Ten Commandments*, 191.
[285] *Institutes* 4.13.10.
[286] *Commentary*, 1 Thess. 1:3. Cf. Wallace, *Christian Life*, 157; *Sermons on Micah*, 120.
[287] *Commentary*, 1 John 3:17.
[288] *Institutes* 3.18.6. Cf. *Sermons on Micah*, 114-16.
[289] *Commentary*, Rom. 12:16.
[290] *Commentary*, 1 Thess. 4:13.
[291] *Sermons on 2 Samuel*, 23.
[292] *Commentary*, John 11:33.
[293] *Institutes* 3.19.11.
[294] *Institutes* 3.19.9.

tressed by grief and fear, he did not rise against God, but continued to be regulated by the true rule of moderation."[295]

This inner temperance is accompanied by moderation of conduct, particularly public conduct, touching on clothing, food, drink, parties, ambition and even war.[296] We will be moderate with our wealth, not increasing it too much, but will be "tighter" with ourselves,[297] excluding "luxuries and overflowing abundance."[298] Calvin holds up Jethro's preservation of the true order in discreetly advising Moses and not upsetting "the due order [*verum ordinem*] of things."[299]

We follow God's calling in life
Each Christian, created for the "purpose of laboring, and of being vigorously employed, in his work,"[300] is called by God to contribute to the good of society. Hence it is true that "no sacrifice is more pleasing to God, than when every man applies diligently to his own calling."[301] This calling is into the world, not the monastery, which, as Torrance observed, "...cast a slur on the ordinary life and work of men."[302] Women, too, should be in the world, not induced to take on the "cursed halter"[303] of a nunnery. The most humble calling in society far outstrips the monastery in holiness.[304]

Our vocation marks out the particular path of obedience that each is to walk, unique in many respects to the one called.[305] "The Lord bids each one of us in all life's actions to look to his calling."[306] To deviate outside our particular calling would be sinful,[307] "let no man go beyond his own bounds."[308] The "true order" finds us pursuing our calling as a good citizens, generally enjoying a good reputation,[309] as we attend to all the duties of our vocation.[310]

This restoration to the image of God is pietas
As we have said, Calvin often uses one single concept to summarize the life of humanity in a state of grace: piety. The pious will look for all good from God, "confide in his power, trust in his goodness, depend on his truth, and turn to

---

[295] *Commentary*, Matt. 26:37.
[296] Wallace, *Christian Life*, 170-80. See this for one of the best presentations of moderation in Calvin.
[297] *Sermons on the Ten Commandments*, 195.
[298] *Commentary*, 1 Tim. 6:8.
[299] *Commentary*, Ex. 18:17.
[300] *Commentary*, Luke 17:7.
[301] *Commentary*, Luke 10:38.
[302] Torrance, *Calvin's Doctrine of Man*, 64.
[303] *Institutes* 4.13.19.
[304] *Institutes* 4.13.16.
[305] Lobstein, *Die Ethik Calvins*, 140-45.
[306] *Institutes* 3.10.6.
[307] *Institutes* 4.13.3.
[308] *Commentary*, John 7:30.
[309] *Commentary*, 2 Cor. 8:21.
[310] Ganoczy, *Young Calvin*, 73-74.

him with the whole heart."[311] Because piety is primarily a heart condition, it grows as we obtain a true knowledge of God as our loving Father, who wants "to watch over us, govern and nourish us"[312] and a true knowledge of ourselves as his dependent children. Loving God means the pious will "make true holiness their concern,"[313] for it is God's intention in calling us to make us holy.[314]

In a state of continuous dependence on God, we render the obedience of faith
Even renewed in a state of grace, Calvin is clear; humanity is still entirely a dependent creature who must, in order to think clearly and will well, rely on God's grace "without interruption."[315] The renewed will relies on grace,[316] as God "both prepares a good will in man, so that it may be helped, and helps it when it has been prepared."[317] Calvin, who parts with some Church Fathers over Romans 7, interprets it as a description of the Christian struggle to constantly depend on grace to defeat sin.[318] Torrance argues that this state of constant dependence is, in fact, the natural order to which grace restores us from the disorder of rebellious independence.[319] We are forced to humbly recognize our complete dependence on God's grace for all good in us. "If God has implanted in us anything that is good, we are so much the more debtors to his grace."[320] We can never wean ourselves from grace, for our fruitfulness depends on the "continuous supply of his aid"[321] and his "constant activity."[322] We have nothing good but what God's grace has given us, and "we do nothing good but what he *worketh in us.*"[323]

Having reduced our role in sanctification to one of utter dependence upon God, Calvin is left with a conundrum: What role is left to humankind in sanctification? Although he wanted to dispel sluggishness,[324] Calvin could not bear to dispel it by insisting that God needed our "cooperation" or that our will is even "attendant" to grace.[325] Rather he will present a more dependent posture, as Tamburello states, "Calvin...wants nothing to do with any notion of 'cooperative' grace."[326] Rejecting cooperation Calvin still maintains our wills are active in sanctification. "Having now been reformed, the will presents itself as ready

---

[311] Reid, *Treatises*, 187-88, "Necessity of Reforming the Church," 1543.
[312] *Institutes* 2.6.4.
[313] *Institutes* 3.14.1.
[314] *Commentary*, 1 Thess. 4:3. Cf. *Institutes* 3.6.2.
[315] *BLW*, 114.
[316] *BLW*, 68-69.
[317] *BLW*, 162.
[318] Steinmetz, *Context*, 111.
[319] Torrance, *Calvin's Doctrine of Man*, 47.
[320] *Commentary*, 1 Cor. 4:7.
[321] *BLW*, 123.
[322] *BLW*, 230.
[323] *Commentary*, 1 Cor. 15:10.
[324] *Institutes* 2.5.14.
[325] *Institutes* 2.3.7.
[326] Tamburello, *Union with Christ*, 39.

and compliant to the Spirit."[327] But Calvin will not allow this to be called cooperation, because it concedes too much to humanity, which would then share credit with God for its good works and would therefore have a basis for merit, unthinkable for Calvin.[328]

Rather than cooperation Calvin will prefer terms such as service, submission and obedience to describe our role in sanctification.[329] Most often he will resort to the concept of obedience, itself a gift of God.[330] "Through the Spirit of sanctification, [God] guides the faithful to obedience."[331] Calvin will further qualify obedience, modifying it as the "obedience of faith" (*obedientiam fidei* or *obsequium fidei*).[332] The "obedience of faith" is the term that suits our humble role and denotes that everything we do in sanctification comes only in response to the initiation of God in our salvation.

Conclusion: Humankind must constantly depend on God
With a growing and proper double-knowledge, humankind can come to God, not in cooperation, but depending on God for the continual grace to render the obedience of faith. Human will, freed from rebellion against God, can finally desire and follow the truth. The human mind, freed from vain pride, can rightly see its poverty and God's great goodness. Being restored to the image of God, humanity loves God and neighbor freely, no longer constrained by a slavish obedience to the law or futile Roman ritual. Each person humbly lives out their own calling from their Father among their neighbors, not driven by passions but moderate in all things, returning thanks to God from a heart of piety. The totality of these transformations, from the impiety of the fall to the growing *pietas* of grace, argues against the possibility of external human means ever effecting such a change. We are forced to look to God's grace alone to make us not just children of Adam but "brothers of angels."

> We have said that regeneration is like another creation; and if we compare it with the first creation, it far surpasses it. For it is much better for us to be made children of God, and reformed after his image within us, than to be created mortal: for we are born children of wrath, corrupt and degenerate; since all integrity was lost when God's image was removed. We see, then, the nature of our first creation; but when God re-fashions us, we are not only born sons of Adam, but we are the brothers of angels, and members of Christ; and this our second life consists in rectitude, justice, and the light of true intelligence.[333]

Here with a true double-knowledge, humankind lives in response to God's grace with the two-fold movement of *pietas*: downward, prostrating itself as helpless before God, and upward, exalting in God's transforming grace.

---

[327] *BLW*, 225.
[328] *Institutes* 2.3.11.
[329] *Institutes* 3.7.1.
[330] *Institutes* 3.8.4.
[331] *BLW*, 231.
[332] *Institutes* 3.2.8.
[333] *Commentary*, Ezek. 18:32.

Chapter 2 - Calvin's Anthropology and Its Implications for Sanctification

The State of Glory

Glory is so beyond us, we see our need for God's grace

Calvin held a real hope for the complete sanctification of humanity in the state of glory. "Let us imagine...enjoyment, clear and pure from every vice."[334] His occasional mentions of glory served both to show us the lofty goal of sanctification and to demonstrate the inadequacy of human-centered approaches to sanctification. To achieve both ends, Calvin will contrast the "holiness" in the Roman Church with true glory, where humanity is restored to God's image, perfectly fulfilling the law to love God and neighbor.

The definition of glory, complete sanctification, is to be restored to the image of God as we were originally made.[335] In this Calvin follows such Church Fathers as Anselm of Canterbury: "For if man is to be perfectly restored, the restoration should make him such as he would have been had he never sinned."[336] Our nature must be changed into sinless perfection in order to be "admissible into the kingdom of God."[337] We will only know the joys of sinless holiness as we emerge renewed from the grave,[338] a reality adumbrated by the immortality of our souls.[339] Then we will be in the most beautiful place, free from immoderate want, with every true desire met perfectly by our Father.[340]

Calvin was no Platonic dualist; the glory of heaven will not find us disembodied souls but reunited with our bodies.[341] For it could not be that our flesh, in which we bear the "death of Christ," should fail to experience his same resurrection[342] but must, like his, be made incorruptible.[343] In glory the saints will finally know the joy of experiencing all the excellences of God as he "will somehow make them to become one with himself."[344]

To be restored into the image of God is to look like Christ.[345] Not that we will be equal to Christ but rather, holy as he is holy,[346] putting off all sin[347] and taking on all righteousness so we might resemble him entirely.[348] We must also look to Christ in order to gain the assurance that we will be like him, for he is the "pledge of our coming resurrection."[349] For Calvin there is a neat symmetry.

---

[334] *Institutes* 3.25.11.
[335] Marcel, "Justification and Sanctification," 133; *Commentary*, Gen. 1:26.
[336] Anselm, *Cur Deus Homo*, 84.
[337] *Commentary*, 1 Cor. 15:53.
[338] *Commentary*, 1 Cor. 15:54; *Institutes* 3.25.5.
[339] *Institutes* 3.25.6.
[340] *Institutes* 3.25.11.
[341] *Institutes* 3.25.7; Tamburello, *Union with Christ*, 15.
[342] *Institutes* 3.25.7.
[343] *Institutes* 3.25.8.
[344] *Institutes* 3.25.10.
[345] *Institutes* 1.15.4, 3.25.5.
[346] *Commentary*, 1 John 3:2.
[347] *Sermons on the Ten Commandments*, 98-99.
[348] *Commentary*, 1 John 3:2.
[349] *Institutes* 3.25.3.

Christ, who restores us to the "proper order"[350] (*verum ordinem*), is at last the true order to which we are restored.

We finally become true lovers of God and neighbor

Restoration of the true order brings humanity back to its original creation design where people love "God in sincerity of heart"[351] and acquiesce "to his good will"[352] with thankfulness for all of God's blessings.[353] Then God gives us the greatest reward of all: himself.[354] United to God we cannot but love others, for "brotherly love flows immediately from the love of God."[355] In glory the law of God is completed, for love of God and neighbor "is right fulfillment of the law."[356]

Conclusion: Knowledge of glory leads us to depend on grace

Calvin's portrait of glory aids the proper double-knowledge and our response to it. God is exalted in his goodness as he recreates heavenly perfection out of fallen humanity. Humankind is humbled as it sees both the contrast of its present and future states and its inability to reform itself. From this double-knowledge, humankind has a two-fold response: a movement of the heart upward in exaltation and a downward movement in humble prostration. The move upward has us longing for heaven, such that we "always have in mind the eternal happiness,"[357] a necessity in order to advance in holiness.[358] The promise of heaven draws us upward toward life with God and away from sin in the world,[359] while also giving us courage here that we "may not fail in this race."[360] The downward movement forces us to "groan and travail" over our current miserable state of sin which appears in sharp contrast.[361] This negative comparison forces us to repent in humility, for we are "ashamed to languish in our corruption."[362] Forced to recognize our inability to close the gap between what we are and what we are to be, we must turn to God, who alone "accomplishes the salvation of his people,"[363] a salvation that only grace, never human good works or Roman methods, could ever procure.

---

[350] *Commentary*, Isa. 35:1.
[351] *Commentary*, 1 John 2:5.
[352] *Sermons on 2 Samuel*, 119-20.
[353] *Institutes* 1.14.22.
[354] *Institutes* 3.25.10.
[355] *Commentary*, 1 John 2:5.
[356] *Commentary*, 1 John 3:10.
[357] *Institutes* 3.25.10.
[358] *Institutes* 3.25.1.
[359] *Institutes* 3.25.2, 3.25.10.
[360] *Institutes* 3.25.2.
[361] *Institutes* 3.25.11.
[362] *Institutes* 3.25.2.
[363] *Commentary*, 1 Cor. 15:54.

Implications for Sanctification from Calvin's Anthropology

We have seen in Chapter 1 the work of God in sanctification; to this we must add the insights of Calvin's anthropology. In his anthropology Calvin patiently builds a case for the absolute necessity for divine help toward holiness. This help comes here in the form of God's regenerating grace which allows the renewed mind and heart to gain a true two-fold knowledge of God and self. Humanity, in a state of creation, shows us both God's greatness in creating us so well and our own present littleness by contrast. The state of sin shows us how incapable we are of curing our sinfulness. The state of grace shows how continually dependent we are upon grace for our ongoing transformation into the image of God. The state of glory forces us to realize we cannot obtain the perfection we long for apart from depending on God. The new heart, mind and will, illuminated with the two-fold knowledge of God and self, is moved by grace to return to the true order, rendering God glory through the obedient movements of faith: downward in humble prostration before him and upward in thankful exaltation.

From these observations and from those in Chapter 1, we deduce a new principle from Calvin's theology of progressive sanctification which is so foundational we number it as Principle 1:

> **Principle 1: Two-fold Knowledge. Because God created us to lovingly revere him, therefore gain knowledge of God and self thus to offer God prostration and reverence.** The two-fold knowledge, of God's greatness and of human depravity and inability to improve itself, leads the believer to respond to God with the two-fold motion of faith: downward in humble prostration before God and upward in thankful and loving reverence to God.

As Calvin turned his hand to enhance the sanctification of the pastors he prepared for the ministry, he knew too well what he was up against. Sitting before him in his lectures and sermons were men filled with concupiscence,[364] who cast down the name of God in order to lift up their own, who outstripped one another in pride and arrogance. His understanding of human nature in its four states applied directly to the sanctification of the students he would train in the Genevan Academy. He knew that he must convince them of their need to turn to Christ for holiness. "Therefore, if he seeks resources to succor him in his need, he must go outside himself and get them elsewhere."[365] These were the men he was soon to release on his beloved France, his beloved church. However, before he would they would require a cure, and the only cure that Calvin knew was the holiness that came from God, sought through faith and repentance.

---

[364] *Institutes* 3.2.18.
[365] *Institutes* 3.20.1.

Chapter 3 - Faith and Repentance

"Or nous-nous prosternerons devant la Maiesté de nostre bon Dieu."[1]

While we have seen both the divine role in making humanity holy and the human need for holiness, it is as Calvin looks at faith and repentance that we see more precisely how the work of God comes to fruition in the souls of humankind to make them holy. Faith and repentance become the essential gifts from God through which the benefits of Christ are applied to the lives of believers. Here we see the two-fold knowledge of God and self, leading one to the proper two-fold response before God. With faith people are made to stop trusting in either their own goodness or ability to improve themselves and trust rather in the mercy of God in Christ for help. With repentance people are made to humble themselves before God and to turn to God for help.

Faith

Faith is knowledge of God's goodness that bids us look to Christ
Calvin will define faith as knowledge. It is a "firm and certain knowledge of God's benevolence toward us, founded upon the truth of the freely given promise in Christ, both revealed to our minds and sealed upon our hearts through the Holy Spirit."[2] This is not just any knowledge, such as assenting to the historical facts about Christ, but a certainty that God will be benevolent towards us because of Christ.[3] Faith entails a two-fold movement: downward, we cease to trust in our ability to improve ourselves; upward, we look to Christ to transform us.[4] As Dowey explains, "This knowledge involves a conscious turning away from false gods and an awareness of the promise of mercy of the true God as revealed in Christ."[5] Here we will explore the relationship of faith to sanctification by looking at the nature of faith by itself and the impact of faith on sanctification.

In the logic of Calvin, faith precedes repentance,[6] for no sinner would be willing to turn from their self-trust to trust in God until they first believed that God would receive and pardon sinners because of Christ.[7] "Repentance not

---

[1] "Sermon on Gen. 25:21-22," *CO* 58:44, "Now let us prostrate ourselves before the majesty of our good God."
[2] *Institutes* 3.2.7.
[3] *Commentary*, Rom. 4:14. Cf. W.R. Godfrey, "Faith Formed by Love or Faith Alone? The Instrument of Justification," *Covenant, Justification, and Pastoral Ministry: Essays by the Faculty of Westminster Seminary California* (Phillipsburg, N.J.: Presbyterian & Reformed, 2007), 271.
[4] *Institutes* 3.2.8.
[5] Dowey, *Knowledge of God*, 172.
[6] Lobstein, *Die Ethik Calvins*, 64.
[7] *Commentary*, Jer. 26:3.

only constantly follows faith, but is also born of faith."[8] Repentance must also always be accompanied by faith for it to be true repentance and not a work of the flesh which can bear no fruit.[9] It is the promise of faith that allows us to face our sin honestly and, seeing it as it is, to turn from our sinful self-confidence to rely wholly on the promises of God in Christ.[10]

The nature of faith

Faith, a gift of God, is knowledge, certainty and trust
While we must have faith for sanctification to move forward in our lives, we cannot create faith by ourselves—faith is the gift of God.[11] Neither is faith synergistic, partly God's contribution and partly ours, but it is all of God.[12] "Faith is a work of God."[13]

The Holy Spirit is the author of faith in the life of God's elect, since our minds are "too rude to be able to grasp the spiritual wisdom of God which is revealed to us through faith."[14] Faith is knowledge, but a higher knowledge.[15] While reasonable, it is beyond the confines of human reason,[16] for no one "can arrive at faith by his own sagacity."[17] This knowledge is assurance more than simply comprehension,[18] persuasion more than just cognition,[19] involving the will and reason.[20]

True faith must consist of certainty—assurance.[21] "For Calvin it was not possible to partake of salvation without being sure of it."[22] Thus he argued with Rome, which saw the Reformer's certainty as a "vain and ungodly confidence,"[23] since Rome maintained only pure holiness could ever make one certain of salvation.[24] Calvin's certainty, however, was founded upon election,[25]

---

[8] *Institutes* 3.3.1.
[9] *Commentary*, Jer. 23:22.
[10] *Institutes* 3.2.8.
[11] *Commentary*, Rom. 1:8.
[12] *Commentary*, John 6:29; 2 Pet. 1:3; Niesel, *Theology of Calvin*, 123.
[13] *Commentary*, John 6:38.
[14] Reid, *Treatises*, 105, "Catechism of the Church of Geneva," 1545.
[15] *Institutes* 3.2.3.
[16] *Institutes* 3.2.14.
[17] *Commentary*, John 6:65.
[18] *Institutes* 3.2.14.
[19] Richard, *Spirituality of John Calvin*, 152; Dowey, *Knowledge of God*, 184.
[20] Muller, *Unaccommodated*, 170-72.
[21] *Institutes* 3.2.15; *Commentary*, John 6:40; Rom. 10:10.
[22] Lane, "Assurance," 32.
[23] *Canons of Trent*, 35.
[24] S. Schreiner, "Calvin's Concern with Certainty in the Context of the Sixteenth Century," *Calvin, Beza and Later Calvinism, John Calvin and the Interpretation of Scripture, Calvin Studies Society Papers 2005, 2000, 2002* (Grand Rapids, Mich.: CRC Product Services, 2006), 118.
[25] D.B. McWilliams, "Calvin's Theology of Certainty," *Resurrection and Eschatology: Theology in Service of the Church, Essays in Honor of Richard B. Gaffin, Jr.* (Phil-

based upon Christ,[26] given by the "inward and secret testimony of the Spirit"[27] and arising from the doctrines of Scripture as applied to the individual believer.[28] "It is the knowledge of my salvation...of God as my Father."[29] As Beeke writes, faith "contains personal, *subjective* assurance," so that the believer may know that God is gracious toward him.[30] While assurance is not grounded upon either an internal self-examination or a survey of one's good works,[31] either may serve to confirm assurance.[32] Such an examination may lead us to a right faith which will "repose in [the] safety and favor of God...with a firm and steadfast assurance."[33] This is not to say that an imperfect faith is not real faith, for Calvin was careful to distinguish between our always imperfect faith and counterfeit faith.[34]

Faith is not only a higher knowledge than reason alone can comprehend, but faith also includes a "devout disposition"[35] of the mind and heart toward God—trust.[36] Faith in its essence contains not only assent (*assensus*) to objective knowledge (*cognitio*)[37] but also subjective trust (*fiducia*).[38] "Faith is trust. It is a trusting and confident knowledge."[39] This trust cannot be trust in the abstract; one must personally trust in Christ for mercy.[40] This trust requires the heart to turn from all other trusts to trust in God alone,[41] and therefore faith must reside "not in the ears, but in the heart."[42]

Faith leads to more faith, which is more knowledge and more trust, "a lively and real sense of his power, which produces confidence."[43] This trust of God spills over into love for him as well. "To believe is to love God on account of his goodness toward us."[44]

---

lipsburg, N.J.: Presbyterian & Reformed, 2008), 521; Lane, "Assurance," 36; *Sermons on Ephesians*, 25.

[26] *Commentary*, Rom. 4:21; 1 John 2:3.
[27] *Commentary*, John 15:26. Cf. Schreiner, "Certainty," 117.
[28] *Institutes* 3.2.6.
[29] Lane, "Assurance," 43.
[30] J.R. Beeke, "Does Assurance Belong to the Essence of Faith? Calvin and the Calvinists," *The Master's Seminary Journal* 5 (1994), 50.
[31] Lane, "Assurance," 35.
[32] McWilliams, "Certainty," 525-26; Beeke, "Assurance," 58.
[33] *Commentary*, 2 Cor. 13:5.
[34] *Commentary*, John 2:23-24. Cf. Beeke, "Assurance," 68.
[35] *Institutes* 3.2.8.
[36] *Institutes* 3.3.2.
[37] Beeke, "Assurance," 49.
[38] Lane, "Assurance," 43.
[39] Godfrey, "Faith Alone," 272.
[40] Dowey, *Knowledge of God*, 182; *Commentary*, John 6:69; 14:21; 16:33.
[41] Dowey, *Knowledge of God*, 172.
[42] *Commentary*, John 5:24; Fuhrmann, *Instruction*, 38.
[43] *Commentary*, 1 John 2:28.
[44] Selderhuis, "Faith Between God and the Devil," 192. Calvin appears to concur with Aquinas on this, insisting, however, that love only follows faith. Cf. Godfrey, "Faith Alone," 270; *Institutes* 3.2.41.

Faith rests on the Word of God which promises us mercy in Christ
Faith always arises from the Word of God and depends upon it for its continued existence.[45] "The same Word is the basis whereby faith is supported and sustained."[46] As sun rays are dependent on the sun, as the fruit depends on the fruit tree, so is faith dependent on the Word.[47] Faith, however, does not arise from the Word impersonally but as God's Word is personally apprehended and applied.[48]

While faith is wholly dependent on Scripture, it is not faith in the Bible, *per se*, but faith in Christ as presented in Scripture to which one must look as the final object of faith.[49] "It is Christ alone on whom, strictly speaking, faith ought to look."[50] More than that, it is Christ who creates the "experiential certitude of faith in the heart."[51] Mere belief in the facts of Scripture could never be enough.[52] Faith must look through Scripture to see Christ.[53]

It is Christ to whom faith must look, yet not all of Scripture holds forth, with equal clarity, the truth of the mercy of God in Christ. While faith accepts all of God's Word, it does not spring from commandments and threats, true as they may be, but from the freely given promise of Christ.[54] Even in the Old Testament era, faith was only truly faith as it looked to Christ, though he was seen less clearly.[55] We may rightly teach all the Word of God with its call to good works, but it is ultimately to have our hearers "contemplate the grace of Christ" that we teach.[56] To grow in faith we must be fed on a constant diet of Christ.[57]

Faith and prayer
For Calvin faith and prayer are tied together. "But after we have been instructed by faith to recognize that whatever we need…is in God…it remains for us…in prayers to ask of him."[58] Prayer relies on faith since prayer is not the "idle lifting up of the voice, but the presentation of our petitions from an inward principle of faith."[59] While prayer, as "the expression of a living faith,"[60] should be

---

[45] *Commentary*, John 5:39; 6:27; 15:27; Rom. 10:17. Cf. W. Kolfhaus, *Christusgemeinschaft bei Johannes Calvin*, Beiträge zur Geschichte und Lehre der Reformierten Kirche, Vol. 3 (Neukirchen: Buchhandlung des Erziehungsvereins, 1938), 43.

[46] *Institutes* 3.2.6. Cf. Selderhuis, "Faith Between God and the Devil," 194.
[47] *Institutes* 3.2.31.
[48] Wallace, *Christian Life*, 213.
[49] According to Dowey, *Knowledge of God*, 159 and contra Gerrish, cf. B.A. Gerrish, "The Gift of Saving Faith," *Christian Century* 116 (1999), 968.
[50] *Commentary*, John 3:16; cf. Jonah 3:5; Gen. 12:2.
[51] Schreiner, "Certainty," 117.
[52] *Institutes* 3.2.30.
[53] *Institutes* 3.2.31; Niesel, *Theology of Calvin*, 124.
[54] *Institutes* 3.2.29.
[55] Dowey, *Knowledge of God*, 164-65.
[56] *Commentary*, 1 John 2:12.
[57] *Institutes* 3.2.7.
[58] *Institutes* 3.20.1. Cf. Lobstein, *Die Ethik Calvins*, 94.
[59] *Commentary*, Ps. 140:6. Cf. Wallace, *Christian Life*, 272.

constant, it is wise to have times during the day when one especially focuses on prayer: in the morning, before starting work, at meals and bedtime.[61] Prayer, while in essence humble, should be at the same time bold, based on God's promises in Scripture.[62] "A dauntless spirit of praying rightly accords with fear, reverence, and solicitude."[63] In a way prayer, being connected to faith, was the "vital heart of piety for Calvin"[64] and underscored all the virtues of the Christian life.[65] Self-denial, cross-bearing, meditation on the future life, repentance—all of the Christian life involves this essential dialogue with God in prayer. "The primary exercise which the children of God have is to pray; because here indeed is the true proof of our faith."[66]

The result of faith

Through faith we are sanctified by Christ

As Calvin considers the role of faith in sanctification, he has a simple conclusion: sanctification is growth in faith, growth in faith is sanctification.[67] It is as the Lord "breathes faith into us" that we have "newness of life."[68] Godfrey correctly concludes, "True faith is also the fountain of sanctification, love, and repentance."[69] Every aspect of our new life, regeneration, forgiveness, repentance, is all "attained by us through faith."[70] All our progress in holiness is linked directly to our growth in faith,[71] which is sanctification's "subjective" cause.[72]

It is not that faith possesses some magical power to improve us, but rather that faith is the conduit through which Christ flows to us,[73] and he does have the power to make us holy.[74] "For since faith...receives Christ, it puts us in possession...of all his blessings."[75] The more faith we have, the more we are

---

[60] Wallace, *Christian Life*, 271.
[61] *Institutes* 3.20.50; cf. E.A. McKee, "Spirituality," *The Calvin Handbook* (ed. H.J. Selderhuis; Grand Rapids, Mich.: Eerdmans, 2009), 467.
[62] Wallace, *Christian Life*, 279.
[63] *Institutes* 3.20.14.
[64] McKee, "Spirituality," 466.
[65] Lobstein, *Die Ethik Calvins*, 94.
[66] "Sermon on 1 Tim. 2:1-2," *CO* 53:125.
[67] *Institutes* 3.2.17.
[68] *Commentary*, John 1:13.
[69] Godfrey, "Faith Alone," 274.
[70] *Institutes* 3.3.1.
[71] Selderhuis, "Faith Between God and the Devil," 197; Marcel, "Justification and Sanctification," 134.
[72] Lobstein, *Die Ethik Calvins*, 28.
[73] Kolfhaus, *Christusgemeinschaft*, 40. Cf. Wendel, *Origins*, 262.
[74] Marcel, "Justification and Sanctification," 139.
[75] *Commentary*, John 1:13.

Chapter 3 - Faith and Repentance

united to Christ,[76] who transforms us and advances us in holiness.[77] "We conquer by faith, because we derive strength from Christ."[78]

We must never think or act as though we could become holy by the effort of flesh and blood.[79] While conformity to the law from the heart outward is God's plan for us, he accomplishes this not by human power but through faith in Christ. "Faith achieves what the law commands."[80] Nor should we expect, as did Rome, that we must add to faith our love, rather it is faith which produces love.[81] As we are justified by faith, so too are we sanctified by faith, the double grace given to us by Christ.[82] Faith mortifies the old man and quickens the new,[83] it leads us to humility,[84] it obtains what we ask in prayer,[85] and it quiets our mind with a "firm and steady conviction"[86] so that we may boldly face any foe.[87]

Sanctification is a struggle for growth in faith against unbelief
Faith does not exist in a placid pool in the heart of the believer. Rather faith is constantly engaged in a battle, a struggle in the human heart, always fighting against doubt and unbelief. Indeed, *the* Christian struggle is not primarily for outward morality but "the struggle between faith and doubt, certainty and fear, belief and unbelief."[88] We rightly aim for an increase in faith, but the increase itself is a struggle.[89] "Our faith cannot and should not exist without battle."[90] This is not a struggle that we enter into episodically but a battle that must be fought each hour of each day.[91]

There is an apparent contradiction in Calvin,[92] who asserts that faith is assurance yet acknowledges that all believers have a "perpetual conflict with their own unbelief"[93] as they struggle for a "fuller confirmation."[94] "While we teach that faith ought to be certain and assured, we cannot imagine any certainty that is not tinged with doubt, or any assurance that is not assailed by some anxie-

---

[76] Kolfhaus, *Christusgemeinschaft*, 35-36.
[77] *Institutes* 3.2.19.
[78] *Commentary*, 1 John 5:5.
[79] *Institutes* 3.1.4. Cf. Kolfhaus, *Christusgemeinschaft*, 52.
[80] *Institutes* 2.5.7.
[81] Godfrey, "Faith Alone," 274.
[82] *Institutes* 3.11.1.
[83] *Institutes* 3.3.3.
[84] *Commentary*, Ps. 37:7.
[85] *Institutes* 3.20.11.
[86] *Commentary*, Eph. 1:13.
[87] *Institutes* 3.2.15.
[88] Schreiner, "Certainty," 119.
[89] *Commentary*, John 2:11.
[90] "Sermon on 1 Tim. 1:5," *CO* 53:29.
[91] *Institutes* 4.17.40.
[92] Lane, "Assurance," 33.
[93] *Institutes* 3.2.17.
[94] *Commentary*, 1 John 5:13.

ty."[95] The contradiction is, however, only apparent. Calvin carefully defines faith as being comprised of certainty in its essence,[96] yet he recognizes that the whole of the human soul is not possessed by faith, because unbelief, doubt, dwells right beside it.[97] While faith possesses assurance by nature, humanity possesses doubt by its fallen nature. It is the presence of unbelief in the fleshly heart of humanity, not any defect in faith proper, that causes the struggle within us.[98]

This struggle between faith and doubt is a struggle between two worldviews,[99] one which doubts God's goodness and one which believes in it.[100] "In the struggle of faith there are internal conflicts."[101] Our flesh, the world and, in particular the devil, want to draw our attention to the hardships and disappointments of life to convince us that God cannot be trusted.[102] "Satan hunts for nothing more than to involve us in various and intricate disputes, and he is an acute disputant, yea, and a sophist."[103] Selderhuis explains this "theology from below." "Satan takes advantage of such a theology and the feelings generated by it. We do not feel anything of God's benefits, and so, we think, he has probably forgotten us."[104] Exacerbating this state, those who prosper are tempted to think it is by their own hand alone, and therefore discount God's role.[105] The Lord, however, wants to draw our attention to the promise of His Word, to assure us that he can be trusted despite any circumstance.[106]

We must struggle all our lives with doubt as part of the normal Christian life,[107] yet unbelief "does not hold sway within believers' hearts" but assails us, as it were, from outside.[108] The simple struggle for faith is itself the victory, for when we strive for faith we are "already in large part victorious."[109] The struggle for faith against unbelief is necessary for faith to grow, just as exercise is necessary for an athlete, it is the very struggle for faith that changes us.[110] Without the struggle faith would not only fail to advance but atrophy.[111] While we always struggle for faith, we always triumph by faith in Christ.[112]

---

[95] *Institutes* 3.2.17.
[96] *Institutes* 3.2.15.
[97] *Institutes* 3.2.4.
[98] Lane, "Assurance," 33; Beeke, "Assurance," 54.
[99] Steinmetz, *Context*, 117.
[100] Beeke, "Assurance," 53-54.
[101] *Commentary*, Jonah 2:4.
[102] *Commentary*, Dan. 11:32; Rom. 1:21. Cf. Wallace, *Christian Life*, 256.
[103] *Commentary*, Jer. 16:19.
[104] Selderhuis, "Faith Between God and the Devil," 200.
[105] Selderhuis, "Faith Between God and the Devil," 204-05.
[106] *Institutes* 3.2.6.
[107] *Institutes* 3.2.17.
[108] *Institutes* 3.2.21.
[109] *Institutes* 3.2.17.
[110] *Institutes* 3.2.19.
[111] Wallace, *Christian Life*, 252.
[112] *Institutes* 3.2.18.

Growth in faith means an increase in two aspects of faith: we move from ignorance of God to knowledge of him and we move from uncertainty to certainty in that same knowledge.[113] As we fight for more certainty, we fight for more of what is known by faith: that God will keep all of his promises to us.[114] Even while in the struggle, the promises of God give us the repose of certainty. "As soon as the promises have been embraced, souls that were restless and uneasy are made calm."[115]

It is precisely at this point that Calvin faults the Roman doctrine of *fides implicita*, even while acknowledging that faith is always imperfect and in some way "implicit."[116] Whereas *fides implicita* calls for faith in the Church and leaves faith stagnated in uncertainty, true faith, as distinguished from false,[117] must be both placed in the right object—Christ—and growing in certainty[118] that his promise applies to us.[119] From this we derive our next principle concerning the struggle for faith.

> **Principle 6: Faith. Because God sanctifies by giving more faith, therefore struggle daily for more faith to become more holy.** Holiness grows with faith, and faith, as a gift of God, arises from hearing the Word of God while also ignoring the world, the flesh and the devil, which all bid us to doubt God by focusing on negative circumstances.

The godly teacher will teach of Christ to increase faith

Since we must have more faith for growth in holiness, and since we cannot create faith ourselves, we must seek faith from God[120] by hearing the "preaching of the Gospel" which grows faith,[121] "that our faith may increase through the whole course of our life."[122] Because of this dynamic, Calvin was certain that the Roman Catholic approaches to sanctification, which failed to rightly grasp the role of preaching Christ, could not possibly increase faith, the essential goal *and* means of sanctification, and were therefore contrary to holiness.[123]

Because faith only rightly takes Christ as its object, then the faithful pastor only rightly has one subject which to emphasize: "God's benevolence toward us, founded upon the truth of the freely given promise in Christ."[124] It is only as we are taught of the "office and power of Christ" that faith grows, and therefore sanctification presses forward in our lives.[125] The godly teacher must therefore

---

[113] *Commentary*, Eph. 1:13. Cf. Wallace, *Christian Life*, 328.
[114] *Commentary*, 1 John 5:13.
[115] *Commentary*, Isa. 30:15.
[116] Dowey, *Knowledge of God*, 171.
[117] Beeke, "Assurance," 56.
[118] *Institutes* 3.2.19.
[119] *Institutes* 3.2.16; Selderhuis, "Faith Between God and the Devil," 195.
[120] *Commentary*, Mark 9:24.
[121] *Commentary*, Heb. 3:15. Cf. *Institutes* 3.2.21.
[122] *Commentary*, 1 John 5:13.
[123] *Commentary*, 1 John 5:13.
[124] *Institutes* 3.2.7.
[125] *Commentary*, 1 John 5:13; John 6:29.

return constantly to this one theme: "It is therefore the duty of a godly teacher, in order to confirm disciples in the faith, to extol as much as possible the grace of Christ, so that being satisfied with that, we may seek nothing else."[126]

Repentance

Gospel repentance was Calvin's answer to Roman penance
As with the other reformers who preceded him, Calvin would emphasize the vital role of repentance for progress in sanctification.[127] "For Calvin, the Christian life is simply the constant practice of repentance."[128] While modern Reformed theologians define repentance as a narrow subset of sanctification,[129] Calvin, while sometimes using the term that way, often uses it to represent sanctification in its entirety. Similarly, Calvin will at times use the terms repentance and regeneration synonymously.[130] However, in general, regeneration is used to refer to God's work in making us holy, and repentance is used to describe the human response to God's work.[131] Calvin does offer a succinct working definition of repentance, which mirrors the modern emphasis on turning: "It is the true turning of our life to God, a turning that arises from a pure and earnest fear of him; and it consists in the mortification of our flesh and of the old man, and in the vivification of the Spirit."[132] Repentance then contains a twofold movement, a sorrowful turning from sin and a hopeful turning to God, both of which have a view to the mercy of God in Christ.[133] Calvin will often use repentance in two distinct senses: he refers to the "first repentance" of conversion[134] and then to the daily repentance needed throughout the Christian life.[135] It is this later use which we explore.

---

[126] *Commentary*, 1 John 5:13.
[127] Consider Martin Luther's first of his Ninety-Five Theses, "When our Lord and Master Jesus Christ said, 'Repent,' he willed the entire life of believers to be one of repentance." M. Luther, "Disputation on the power and efficacy of indulgences," *Luther's Works, American Edition*, 55 vols. (eds. J. Pelikan, H.T. Lehmann; Philadelphia, Pa.: Muehlenberg and Fortress, and St. Louis, Mo.: Concordia, 1955-86), 31:25.
[128] Wallace, *Christian Life*, 99.
[129] As does the Westminster Shorter Catechism Question 87: "Repentance unto life is a saving grace, whereby a sinner, out of a true sense of his sin, and apprehension of the mercy of God in Christ, doth, with grief and hatred of his sin, turn from it unto God, with full purpose of, and endeavor after, new obedience." P. Schaff (ed.), *The Creeds of Christendom*, 3 vols. (Grand Rapids, Mich.: Baker, 1977), 3:695.
[130] Such as *Institutes* 3.3.9, "Therefore, in a word, I interpret repentance as regeneration, whose sole end is to restore in us the image of God."
[131] C.P. Venema, *Accepted and Renewed in Christ: The "Twofold Grace of God" and the Interpretation of Calvin's Theology* (Göttingen: Vandenhoeck & Ruprecht, 2007), 111-12.
[132] *Institutes* 3.3.5.
[133] *Institutes* 3.3.3.
[134] *Commentary*, Heb. 6:1.
[135] *Commentary*, Luke 5:7.

Repentance relates to faith as a stream does to a spring, for repentance flows from faith.[136] While repentance and faith "are so linked together that they cannot be separate,"[137] they must be distinguished. They are distinguished by their nature: repentance is a turning to God, faith a receiving of grace "offered us in Christ."[138] They are distinguished as well by their order: repentance both follows faith and is "born of faith."[139] Repentance cannot precede faith, for we must first understand God's gracious mercy before we can avail ourselves of it in repentance.[140]

Repentance occurs primarily in the grieving heart rather than externally
Calvin differed sharply with Rome over the nature of repentance, as did the other Reformers.[141] The Roman notion of penance emphasized external contrition manifested by "many tears and labors"[142] and the "outward fruits of penitence,"[143] often to the exclusion of "the inward renewal of the mind, which bears with it true correction of life."[144] Calvin, following in line with the *devotio moderna*, emphasized the internal life of the heart in relationship with God.[145] "In order to serve God properly our hearts must be surrendered to him...affection must precede [everything else]."[146] True repentance is the "rending not of garments but of the heart,"[147] for repentance occurs "in the soul itself,"[148] so that a person is "renewed in the spirit of his mind."[149]

True repentance must include grief, for "repentance takes its rise in grief,"[150] along with a "dissatisfaction and hatred of sin,"[151] such that we are "made sore by the sting of sin,"[152] and angry with our sin,[153] we turn to the Lord for relief.[154] When we do experience the sorrow of repentance it both flows from a heart changed by God and changes our heart for God.[155]

Calvin draws several careful distinctions between a heart that rightly hates sin in Gospel repentance and the Roman Catholic desire to self-flagellate in

---

[136] *Institutes* 3.3.1.
[137] *Commentary*, Acts 20:21.
[138] *Commentary*, Acts 20:21.
[139] *Institutes* 3.3.1.
[140] *Institutes* 3.3.2. Cf. *Commentary*, Hos. 6:1.
[141] D.C. Steinmetz, "Reformation and Conversion," *Theology Today* 35 (1978-79), 25.
[142] *Canons of Trent*, 90.
[143] *Commentary*, Ezek. 18:30.
[144] *Institutes* 3.4.1.
[145] *Sermons on 2 Samuel*, 109.
[146] *Sermons on the Ten Commandments*, 293.
[147] *Institutes* 3.3.17.
[148] *Institutes* 3.3.6.
[149] *Commentary*, Acts 2:38.
[150] *Commentary*, 2 Cor. 7:10.
[151] Reid, *Treatises*, 107, "Catechism of the Church of Geneva," 1545.
[152] *Institutes* 3.3.4.
[153] *Commentary*, 2 Cor. 7:11.
[154] *Commentary*, 2 Cor. 7:10; Jer. 14:20.
[155] *Commentary*, 2 Cor. 7:10.

order to atone for sins with contrition. First, while Trent proclaimed that one must, "with a hatred of sin and a sincere sorrow of heart, detest so great an offence against God,"[156] Calvin asserted that this was for Rome generally only a superficial exercise.[157] Second, our hatred of our sin cannot be considered in any way to "compensate to God for the punishment due to him."[158] Third, contrition, "repentance of the law," would always leave the Christian unsure if his grief had been deep enough, producing "truly miserable consciences,"[159] "stricken by dread of God's wrath."[160] By contrast, Gospel repentance makes the conscience quiet with assurance before God.[161]

Repentance produces deep changes in behavior and is life long
While Calvin will insist that true repentance occurs first in the heart,[162] he will equally insist that repentance must then demonstrate itself outwardly, as the "fruits and proofs of repentance"[163] which are "proved by the conduct"[164] that is, a life conformed more and more toward obedience.[165] The fruit of repentance can never be merely some "frivolous works" of satisfactions, assigned by a confessor; rather it must be a real turning away from the sins which had been committed toward "innocence and holiness."[166]

Though Roman penance was practiced over the entire lifetime, it was often relegated to an annual observance during Lent, rather than a daily, even hourly, struggle.[167] Calvin recognized that since we will never be sinless in this world,[168] expecting Christ to perfect us in heaven,[169] we must continually,[170] daily,[171] even "every moment,"[172] practice repentance to make progress in holiness.[173]

---

[156] *Canons of Trent*, 89.
[157] *Institutes* 3.4.1.
[158] *Commentary*, 2 Cor. 7:11.
[159] *Institutes* 3.4.2.
[160] *Institutes* 3.3.4.
[161] *Institutes* 3.4.3.
[162] *Institutes* 3.3.6.
[163] *Commentary*, Ezek. 18:30.
[164] *Commentary*, Matt. 3:8.
[165] Reid, *Treatises*, 107, "Catechism of the Church of Geneva," 1545; cf. *Commentary*, Acts 5:31.
[166] *Commentary*, Acts 2:38.
[167] *Institutes* 3.3.2; *Canons of Trent*, 94.
[168] *Institutes* 3.17.15.
[169] *Institutes* 3.25.10.
[170] *Commentary*, Heb. 6:1.
[171] *Institutes* 4.1.23.
[172] *Commentary*, Jer. 14:20.
[173] *Commentary*, 1 Cor. 1:8.

Chapter 3 - Faith and Repentance

Repentance is a work of God yet requires human effort

Repentance is gift of God, by grace, given through the Holy Spirit
Although we are active in repentance, it is not a work accomplished by our power but rather "a singular gift of God,"[174] "attained by us through faith,"[175] such that "it cannot be ascribed to human powers."[176] Even the command to repent does not prove our ability to repent by human effort.[177] Rather, the command is meant to underscore our inability to *even* repent on our own, so that we must seek God's help more fully[178] and appreciate his help more deeply.[179]

If repentance "is given by God,"[180] then what does God give us in repentance? God confronts our sin, externally through his Word and internally through his Spirit.[181] He grants us the conviction that we have sinned against him, so we no longer blame others for our sin.[182] Having been confronted by God, he holds out "the hope of pardon" to us, turning us toward him[183] to "implore God's forgiveness."[184] God softens our heart[185] toward him, so we are not only able to turn to him in repentance[186] but will actually do so.[187]

Repentance calls for the individual to participate in response to God's work
As clearly as Calvin will assert that repentance is a work of grace, he will argue that humanity has a role.[188] He says, "We must strive toward repentance itself."[189] We are to humble ourselves before God asking him to make us feel our sins all the more.[190] We must always "shake off sloth and carelessness," standing guard against sin[191] and praying that God will turn us from sin.[192] We must heed God's condemnation of our sin, confessing them rather than clinging to them,[193] lest God proves himself "far more obdurate than we"[194] in forcing us to

---

[174] *Institutes* 3.3.21. Cf. *Commentary*, Matt. 3:2; Rom. 6:21.
[175] *Institutes* 3.3.1.
[176] *Commentary*, Jer. 31:19.
[177] *Commentary*, Jer. 31:19.
[178] Calvin, *BLW*, 141-42.
[179] *Institutes* 3.2.23.
[180] *Commentary*, Heb. 6:6.
[181] Calvin, *BLW*, 163-64.
[182] *Commentary*, Ezek. 18:32.
[183] *Commentary*, Jer. 8:4-5.
[184] *Sermons on Micah*, 11.
[185] *Commentary*, Acts 5:31.
[186] *Sermons on Micah*, 7; *Commentary*, Jer. 31:19.
[187] Calvin, *BLW*, 211.
[188] *Institutes* 2.16.13.
[189] *Institutes* 3.3.20.
[190] McKee, *Pastoral Piety*, 265.
[191] *Institutes* 3.3.14.
[192] *Commentary*, Ps. 19:13.
[193] *Sermons on Micah*, 133, 152; *Commentary*, 1 John 1:9.
[194] *Sermons on Micah*, 11.

repent. We are to "struggle manfully"[195] for holiness, actively resisting sin,[196] all the while trusting that God will complete his good work in us.[197]

We must not make the mistake of Rome,[198] however, thinking that our repentance purchases for us the grace of God by merit,[199] for it is God's grace, in both faith[200] and forgiveness,[201] which leads us to repentance.[202] Our repentance, always imperfect,[203] could not merit grace[204] but flows from the grace we have already received,[205] inviting yet more unmerited grace.[206]

Repentance flows from fear of God's judgment, with an eye to mercy
Repentance emerges from the belief that God will punish the unrepentant sinner. "Repentance proceeds from an earnest fear of God."[207] We must believe we are sinners, for the man who judges himself righteous will detect no cause to repent.[208] We must believe that God's word of judgment threatens us, a regular theme in Calvin's sermons.[209] We only truly learn to hate our sin and turn from it when we see how it invites God's judgment.[210]

Not all fear of God leads to godly repentance, however. There is a fear which does not view God's mercy but rather leaves the sinner "tormented by a sense of their own punishment."[211] This fear, a repentance of the law, may lead the sinner to temporarily flee the sin but always leads to fleeing God's presence,[212] trapping the sinner "in that disturbed state."[213]

Therefore, we must not think of repentance as being exclusively attached to judgment and faith to mercy, for repentance, too, has its origin in grace.[214] Un-

---

[195] *Institutes* 4.15.11.
[196] *Commentary*, Rom. 6:11.
[197] *Institutes* 3.6.5.
[198] *Institutes* 3.3.1.
[199] *Institutes* 3.4.27.
[200] *Commentary*, Matt. 4:17.
[201] *Commentary*, 2 Cor. 7:10.
[202] *Commentary*, Matt. 3:2.
[203] *Institutes* 3.4.27.
[204] Calvin, *BLW*, 152.
[205] V.A. Shepherd, *The Nature and Function of Faith in the Theology of John Calvin* (Macon, Ga.: Mercer University Press, 1983), 35.
[206] Calvin, *BLW*, 175.
[207] *Institutes* 3.3.7.
[208] *Commentary*, Acts 20:21.
[209] *Sermons on Micah*, 51.
[210] *Commentary*, Jer. 31:19.
[211] *Commentary*, Heb. 12:17.
[212] *Commentary*, Heb. 12:17.
[213] *Institutes* 3.3.4.
[214] Wallace, *Christian Life*, 97. We would contend that Leithart overstates, or at least over simplifies, the role of fear when he states, "Calvin claimed that the Christian life of repentance is motivated by fear." Certainly fear is an element but so is mercy, and perhaps an even greater one. P.J. Leithart, "Stoic Elements in Calvin's Doctrine of the Christian Life, Part 2: Mortification," *Westminster Theological Journal* 55 (1993), 195.

less we first believe that God will be gracious to us, we will not repent.[215] Even God's wrath and our subsequent fear are meant to lead us to mercy.[216] Repentance only comes as faith in God's judgment on our sin intersects with faith in God's mercy to us.[217] There is an "inseparable link"[218] between God's love and our repentance: "The foundation of repentance is the mercy of God."[219]

Repentance entails two motions: downward in prostration and upward in reverence

The downward movement: prostration
Calvin called for the downward movement before God in his earliest version of the *Institutes*. "From this knowledge of our poverty and calamity we learn to humble ourselves and to cast ourselves before God to seek his mercy."[220] He will use one term in particular to describe this downward movement of the human soul: prostration (La.: *prosterno*, Fr.: *prosterner*). As they come to a true knowledge of God and self, people are "to prostrate themselves before God."[221]

Everyone must prostrate themselves before God.[222] "He exhorts them to stand in awe of him, and to prostrate themselves [*se prosternant*] humbly before him."[223] Calvin would typically close each sermon with a call to prostration. "But now let us fall down [*nous-nous prosternerons*] before the majesty of our good God, in acknowledging our faults."[224]

The call to prostration before God is no accident; it is a return to the natural order which was supplanted in the fall by the unnatural act of humankind standing in arrogance before God. Humanity must be humbled before God, as reflected in the requirement for humility before a parent,[225] in order that the kingdom of Christ may be established. Indeed, Christ came to restore humankind to its rightful place—kneeling before God.[226]

The upward movement: reverence
Several terms compete, in Calvin's usage, to describe the upward turn to God: fear, love, trust, thankfulness, reverence and piety.[227] While Gerrish has made an argument for describing this upward movement with the term thankful-

---

[215] *Institutes* 3.3.2; *Commentary*, Jer. 18:11; 26:3; Mark 1:14; Lobstein, *Die Ethik Calvins*, 66.
[216] *Commentary*, Ezek. 14:6.
[217] *Commentary*, Acts 8:22; Venema, *Accepted and Renewed*, 118.
[218] *Sermons on 2 Samuel*, 569.
[219] *Commentary*, Matt. 3:2.
[220] 1536 *Institutes, CO* 1:31.
[221] *Commentary*, Ps. 22:27.
[222] *Commentary*, Ps. 72:11.
[223] *Commentary*, Ps. 22:23; *CO* 31:232.
[224] "Sermon on Gen. 25:20-22," *CO* 58:44.
[225] *Institutes* 2.8.35.
[226] *Commentary*, 1 Cor. 10:4.
[227] *Institutes* 1.2.2, 2.8.16, 1.2.1.

ness,[228] we find another term more dominant in Calvin: reverence (La.: *reverentia*, Fr.: *révérence*).[229] Selderhuis concurs, "The attitude we must assume toward God is best expressed in the word 'reverence.'"[230] Reverence more easily encompasses love, fear, trust and thankfulness.[231] It captures more neatly the relationship that we are to have with God in sanctification: "to reverence him as our Father."[232]

Reverence, born of God's benevolence[233] yet with an appreciation of his wrath,[234] leads us to glorify God and worship him for his mercy rather than to glory in any work of our own.[235] Reverence calls us to obey and serve our God,[236] in order to bring him honor,[237] as we did at creation.[238] This reverence, though similar to the filial love for a parent, must exceed all earthly loves[239] and thus fulfill the whole duty of the first table of the law "by showing him reverence."[240]

The two-fold movement is simultaneous
These two movements of the heart—prostration and reverence—are to occur simultaneously and constantly in repentance.[241] "Now let us fall down before the majesty of our good God...and give ourselves wholly to our Lord Jesus Christ."[242] Knowledge of ourselves before God will lead us simultaneously to "arouse" ourselves to divine worship (reverence) and to prostrate ourselves in "extreme confusion."[243] These right motions of repentance stand in contrast to the wrong motion of sin, as Torrance points out. "That is the essential motion of sin, unthankful arrogance and self-glorification, which runs directly contrary to the very motion of the grace of God."[244] Torrance describes another motion, the motion of grace, which initiates the two-fold motion of repentance.[245] We

---

[228] B.A. Gerrish, *Grace and Gratitude, the Eucharistic Theology of John Calvin* (Eugene, Oreg.: Wipf & Stock, 2002), 41.
[229] *Sermons on the Ten Commandments*, 293, "Accordingly, if we want to keep the law correctly and want our life acceptable to God, then we must begin in this way: by showing him reverence." Cf. *Commentary*, Luke 1:46-50; Rom. 4:23-25; 1 Cor. 3:16-23; Eph. 3:1-6.
[230] Selderhuis, "Faith Between God and the Devil," 192.
[231] *Institutes* 2.8.1.
[232] *Institutes* 3.17.6.
[233] *Commentary*, Gen. 4:2.
[234] *Commentary*, Jonah 1:16.
[235] *Sermons on the Ten Commandments*, 298.
[236] *Sermons on Micah*, 55.
[237] *Institutes* 3.20.41.
[238] *Commentary*, Gen. 2:16.
[239] *Commentary*, Matt. 10:37.
[240] *Sermons on the Ten Commandments*, 293.
[241] *Institutes* 3.20.42.
[242] *Sermons on Galatians*, 498; cf. *Sermons on Election and Reprobation*, 47.
[243] *Institutes* 2.1.3.
[244] Torrance, *Calvin's Doctrine of Man*, 115.
[245] Torrance, *Calvin's Doctrine of Man*, 115.

will find these two motions connected repeatedly in Calvin's thought and exhortations. "To despair in ourselves so that we may be comforted in him; to abase ourselves so that we may be lifted up by him; to accuse ourselves so that we may be justified by him."[246]

Prostration is necessary because humankind is naturally proud
The original order of humanity was one of humility before God, an order which was entirely reversed by the fall such that humanity lives in a state of arrogant pride and self-exaltation, denying God his rightful place.[247] Because "humanity craves to be flattered,"[248] man must be "brought to nothing in his own estimation."[249] Humans must be stripped entirely of any thought of their own glory, for any good in them comes from God[250] and only makes them "debtors to his grace,"[251] that they might live sanely in the real universe with a God who alone is all glorious. Humanity's pride in trusting its own reason must be humbled too,[252] in order that it may meekly receive the Word of God.[253] Since humility is contrary to fallen human nature, God must work to humble humanity, by opposing its "in-turned understanding and self-grounded reason" in order to reduce humanity to dependence on the Word and Spirit[254] that it might be filled with truth.[255] We must come to an accurate self-assessment, wherein we see ourselves in our lowly estate[256] in order to make "any approach to the doctrine of Christ."[257] This humility must never be merely a lowly appearance but a true lowness of spirit,[258] an "unfeigned submission of our heart," arising from true knowledge of our "own misery and want."[259]

Humility is given to us as we gain a true knowledge of ourselves before God as totally dependent creatures.[260] We are dependent moment by moment on the sustaining hand of God just to exist.[261] Even the immortality of our souls is borrowed from the continued power of God who maintains them.[262] We are dependent on God's providence who orders our lives as he wills, so we must "render subjection to him in all humility and obedience."[263] We are dependent

---

[246] *Institutes* 4.17.42.
[247] *Institutes* 2.1.2.
[248] *Sermons on Micah*, 9.
[249] *Commentary*, 1 Cor. 1:31.
[250] *Commentary*, Isa. 2:22.
[251] *Commentary*, 1 Cor. 4:7.
[252] Calvin, *BLW*, 25.
[253] *Sermons on Micah*, 50.
[254] "Sermon on Deut. 4:19-24," *CO* 26:160.
[255] *Commentary*, 2 Cor. 10:5.
[256] *Commentary*, 2 Cor. 10:4.
[257] *Commentary*, 2 Cor. 10:5.
[258] *Sermons on Micah*, 23.
[259] *Institutes* 3.12.6.
[260] Selderhuis, "Faith Between God and the Devil," 190.
[261] *Commentary*, Ps. 103:15.
[262] "Sermon on 1 Tim. 1:17-19," *CO* 53:89-100.
[263] "Sermon on Job 1:1," *CO* 33:21.

upon God for all our good and success in this world,[264] for "just one little breath of God can remove our glory for eternity."[265]

Scripture, too, humbles us by comparing us to God, rather than to other sinful people whom we may outshine.[266] Compared to the spotless purity of God, we are dark blotches on his universe, even our best deeds pale next to his holiness.[267] Scripture humbles us by appraising us of our current "miserable ruin,"[268] comparing it to our created state, so that we have nothing left in which to take pride[269] and must "humble ourselves…before God."[270] "Its whole end is to restrain our pride, to humble us, cast us down, and utterly crush us."[271] Scripture convinces us of sin and reduces us to humility before God that we might "flee to grace,"[272] through repentance.[273]

People, however, will not yield themselves easily to this understanding of sin and will at times need the church to confront their sinfulness when they obstinately refuse to yield to God's Word on its own merit. Steinmetz suggests, "Repentance is, if you will not misunderstand me, a churchly function."[274] The church is given clear instructions as to how to confront one caught in sin[275] so as to lead them to repentance.[276] Aware of this need, it was arranged that both the members of the Company of Pastors[277] and the students of the Academy would have ample opportunity for their sins to be personally confronted by others.[278]

Humility comes from self-examination and confession
Because humility is given to us as we are convicted by the Word, we must be willing to examine ourselves for the least sin.[279] Self-examination, supplemental for assurance of faith,[280] is essential to the humility of repentance. "If they descended within themselves, and sincerely examined their whole life, they would be instantly humbled before God; hence that thought should stimulate them to repentance."[281] This descent into the self, or *descensus in se*, is part of the downward motion where the person, after looking at God, must descend

---

[264] *Institutes* 3.20.27.
[265] *Sermons on Micah*, 60.
[266] *Institutes* 3.12.2.
[267] *Institutes* 3.12.4.
[268] *Institutes* 1.1.1.
[269] *Institutes* 2.1.3.
[270] 1536 *Institutes*, *CO* 1:31.
[271] *Institutes* 3.18.4.
[272] *Institutes* 2.7.9.
[273] *Commentary*, Jer. 15:10; 26:3.
[274] Steinmetz, "Reformation and Conversion," 29.
[275] *Commentary*, Matt. 18:15-20.
[276] *Commentary*, Ezek. 14:6.
[277] Reid, *Treatises*, 61, "Ecclesiastical Ordinances," 1541.
[278] Maag, *Genevan Academy*, 122.
[279] *Institutes* 2.1.2.
[280] Beeke, "Assurance," 56; cf. Lane, "Assurance," 46-47.
[281] *Commentary*, Ezek. 18:30.

"from contemplating him to scrutinize himself."[282] Battles describes this in saying, "Two movements, as we have seen, mark for John Calvin the initial steps of the soul's return to God: our upward vision of God as he accommodates himself to our feeble capacity, and our downward contemplation of ourselves within...the...*descensus in se*."[283]

While some self-examination may take place in a corporate confession of sin,[284] each one must examine "his own case" to be brought to genuine repentance.[285] Our standard for judging ourselves can be none other than the objective Word of God, a light to expose sin accurately in the dark recess of our soul.[286] This soul-searching cannot be superficial but must be done seriously[287] and regularly, each morning and evening,[288] so that our consciences may "straightway smite" us,[289] that displeased with ourselves[290] we are forced to seek God's mercy.[291] When we are reproved by God,[292] or discover a sin, we must be "doubly critical"[293] to search for other hidden sins so we might "prostrate ourselves before God."[294]

In order for self-examination to have its fully-humbling impact, and thus lead us to grace, we must confess the sins we discover.[295] Evangelical confession, unlike the Catholic practice, was no effort to merit grace but rather to seek it.[296] Confession must be made primarily to God, not a priest, since God is the most aggrieved party and the one who can grant forgiveness.[297] After we have confessed to God we may confess to a fellow believer[298] and to our pastor, if the sin is grievous or our conscience is still burdened.[299]

While man will confidently endeavor to rid himself of vices and by his own power "to exert himself with all his ardor" toward the good, self-examination brings him to the end of such self-confidence and self-help.[300] "Convinced that they cannot deliver themselves,"[301] believers turn to God from sin,[302] crying out

---

[282] *Institutes* 1.1.2.
[283] Battles, *Interpreting Calvin*, 237.
[284] *Institutes* 3.4.11.
[285] *Commentary*, Jer. 26:3.
[286] Wallace, *Christian Life*, 227. Cf. *Sermons on the Ten Commandments*, 269.
[287] *Commentary*, John 9:2.
[288] "Sermon on Deut. 9:6-7," *CO* 26:657.
[289] *Commentary*, Lev. 4:13.
[290] *Commentary*, Gen. 3:22.
[291] Reid, *Treatises*, 234, "Reply to Sadolet."
[292] *Commentary*, Jonah 1:7.
[293] *Sermons on the Ten Commandments*, 231.
[294] *Commentary*, Ps. 51:6.
[295] *Institutes* 4.15.12. Cf. *Commentary*, Ps. 51:3.
[296] *Institutes* 3.4.27.
[297] *Institutes* 3.4.9.
[298] *Institutes* 3.4.10.
[299] *Institutes* 3.4.12.
[300] *Institutes* 2.1.3.
[301] Selderhuis, "Faith Between God and the Devil," 189.
[302] *Commentary*, Ezek. 18:30.

from the depth of their heart.[303] As they cry out to God in faith and repentance, God extends grace to help make them holy.[304] Though pride will try to convince us to find life by deflecting all accusations of sin, since grace only comes to the humble, we must seek life through self-examination which leads to repentance and therefore healing.[305]

Reverence is necessary because humankind naturally despises God
Sanctification not only calls us to humbly prostrate ourselves before God but bids us as well to move up toward God in newness of life, "to live to God"[306] in reverence. This upward movement toward God is only possible for believers[307] as a thankful sacrifice of the heart to God by faith in Christ.[308] Reverence, which must arise from a sincere heart,[309] is the very goal of sanctification, reversing humanity's natural belittling of God.[310] As such reverence includes worship of God, obedience to him,[311] trust and hope in him and thanksgiving for all his grace to us,[312] so that all the rest of our lives "become sacred offerings"[313] for his glory.[314] Repentance leads to a reverence which thanks God for all the good we receive from him,[315] our very lives, even down to the details of food and shelter which he provides.[316] In yielding our lives to God in gratitude, our lives are to "express Christ," to show forth the same attitude of love and gratefulness that the life of Christ evidenced,[317] that we might come to know and be more like Christ.[318]

How Repentance Aids in Sanctification: Grace Flows Down to the Lowly

Repentance puts us in the low place so God can lift us up
As we consider how repentance aids in our sanctification, Calvin offers a very simple insight, critical to his understanding: God humbles the proud but lifts up the humble, offering them his grace.[319] Hence Calvin cites Augustine with glowing approbation, "If you ask me concerning the precepts of the Christian

---

[303] Battles, *Interpreting Calvin*, 239.
[304] Reid, *Treatises*, 234, "Reply to Sadolet."
[305] *Commentary*, Jer. 8:4-5.
[306] *Institutes* 3.3.3.
[307] *Institutes* 3.3.2; *Sermons on Micah*, 98-99.
[308] Wallace, *Christian Life*, 28.
[309] *Sermons on the Ten Commandments*, 292.
[310] *Commentary*, 1 Thess. 4:3; 1 John 2:5. Cf. *Sermons on Micah*, 107.
[311] *Institutes* 3.3.14, 3.14.9.
[312] Fuhrmann, *Instruction*, 29. Cf. Wallace, *Christian Life*, 34.
[313] Wallace, *Christian Life*, 33.
[314] *Institutes* 3.20.43.
[315] *Sermons on Micah*, 55.
[316] *Sermons on Micah*, 51.
[317] *Institutes* 3.6.3.
[318] Niesel, *Theology of Calvin*, 27.
[319] *Institutes* 3.12.5-6.

Chapter 3 - Faith and Repentance

religion, first, second, third, and always I would answer, 'Humility.'"[320] Calvin's very first thoughts in the 1536 *Institutes* show this pattern. "After we descend in this humility and submission, then our Lord smiles on us, he shows himself lenient, merciful, gentle."[321] God has two hands with which he deals with humanity, one hand with a hammer to beat down the proud and "the other, which raises up the humble."[322]

God actively opposes and abases all those who do not fear him but wish to exalt themselves.[323] He "uncovers their crime by force. When they wish to advance themselves, he throws them back."[324] The proud heart, full of itself, has no room for the grace of God.[325] God will gravely wound all those who are proud in order that they may be "completely humbled."[326] Since the proud will be brought down by God, we must "walk in such humility" so as to remove God's need to humble us.[327]

Just as certainly as God will abase the proud, he will lift up the humble.[328] It is only the heart that is "utterly empty of all opinion of its own worth" that is opened to receive God's mercy and grace.[329] God will "raise us up when he sees that our proud spirits are laid aside."[330] Grace is not, as had taught Gabriel Biel (d. 1495), the reward for those strong in their own virtues,[331] rather it is offered to those who are "overwhelmed with shame, and flee to the undeserved mercy of God."[332]

Here we find the beating heart of Calvin's sanctification—humility. The two-fold knowledge of God and self destroys our self-assurance and humbles us.[333] In the humble, the *verum ordinem* is restored: humankind humbled, God glorified. Humility is the essential ingredient in piety as we correctly see ourselves before God,[334] looking up into his face with full reverence, knowing that God is "glorified in our littleness."[335] These two are ever-linked in our sanctification: our humility before God which leads to God's grace for us.[336] "No one

---

[320] *Institutes* 2.2.11. Calvin's citation of Augustine can be found in: Augustine, *Epistolae*, 118.3.22.
[321] *CO* 1:30, 1536 *Institutes*.
[322] *Commentary*, 1 Pet. 5:5.
[323] *Institutes* 3.12.8.
[324] *Sermons on 2 Samuel*, 128.
[325] "Sermon on Gen. 25:24-28," *CO* 58:62.
[326] *Sermons on 2 Samuel*, 567-68.
[327] *Sermons on Micah*, 23.
[328] *Institutes* 3.12.6. Cf. Selderhuis, "Faith Between God and the Devil," 189.
[329] *Institutes* 3.12.7.
[330] *Commentary*, Jas. 4:10.
[331] Steinmetz, "Reformation and Conversion," 27.
[332] *Commentary*, John 5:44.
[333] Fuhrmann, *Instruction*, 27.
[334] *Institutes* 1.2.1.
[335] "Sermon on Gen. 25:24-28," *CO* 58:62.
[336] *Commentary*, Hos. 14:3.

is permitted to receive God's blessings unless he is consumed with the awareness of his own poverty."[337]

The help God gives the humble: sanctification
God does not humble men to leave them in disgrace "but that they may seek a better glory, for God delights not in the degradation of men."[338] God wants people humble in order that "humbled by a true knowledge of themselves, they flee to the grace of Christ."[339] God then "cares for all who humble themselves before his majesty,"[340] offering them grace.[341] Because the rain flows to the valleys more than the mountain tops, we must, therefore, "become a *valley*...to receive the heavenly rain of God's spiritual grace."[342]

As God's grace is poured out upon us, the work of sanctification is accomplished. He gives the humble more faith to know his mercy. "Humility is the best preparation for faith."[343] Through increased faith we receive the blessings of union life with Christ, such as an increase in holiness[344] and a soft heart which buds with the fruit of repentance.[345] Attracted by his "gentle kindness," we are eager to serve him in the obedience of faith,[346] which God then lavishly rewards with a rounder heart from which flows yet more obedience.[347]

Since humility comes by grace, always seek the grace of humility
We do not gain even humility by our own power; it is the work of God, who grants this through his Holy Spirit,[348] to bring us low enough to receive grace.[349] It is God's Spirit who humbles us internally, taming us[350] as God's providential hand, through trials, forces us externally to our knees before him.[351] God grants humility in response to dependent prayer,[352] as we ask God for the very grace of humility,[353] "that we may be humbled so much that we experience his salvation."[354]

---

[337] *Institutes* 2.2.10.
[338] *Commentary*, Jer. 9:24.
[339] *Commentary*, Heb. 4:12.
[340] *Sermons on Micah*, 20.
[341] *Sermons on 2 Samuel*, 569. For Calvin's personal application of this see: *CSW*, Vol. 4, 75, Letter from Calvin to Farel, Aug. 4, 1538.
[342] *Commentary*, 2 Cor. 12:9.
[343] *Commentary*, Jer. 16:21.
[344] Wallace, *Christian Life*, 78.
[345] *Institutes* 3.3.16.
[346] *Sermons on the Ten Commandments*, 298; *Commentary*, Rom. 1:5.
[347] *Sermons on the Ten Commandments*, 284.
[348] *Commentary*, Acts 5:31.
[349] *Commentary*, Isa. 40:7; Luke 5:32. Cf. Niesel, *Theology of Calvin*, 129.
[350] Calvin, *BLW*, 193.
[351] "Sermon on Gen. 25:24-28," CO 58:63-64.
[352] *Institutes* 3.20.9.
[353] *Institutes* 3.20.8.
[354] *Sermons on 2 Samuel*, 564.

Humility must be the aim of the Christian life, for it both leads to, and follows from, true knowledge of God and self and is thus the restoration of the true order.[355] We must seek humility because "salvation has been prepared for the humble people"[356] who recognize how far they are from true righteousness.[357] We can never seek any other worthiness before God than to offer him our weak selves in full humility.[358] We should aim for humility whether God is blessing or disciplining us. Blessings, even receiving mercy,[359] may lead us to pride, unless we hold ourselves in check by humbly recognizing that all blessings come from God.[360] When we are under discipline, we may want to rise up against God but again must check our pride and humble ourselves in true repentance.[361]

Because of our need for humility and our natural disinclination towards it, Calvin will persistently call us away from the insanity of pride to the sanity of humility,[362] for "there is no other means of serving God except in humility."[363] Calvin will pray ceaselessly for humility: "But now let us fall down before the high majesty of our good God, with acknowledging of our faults."[364]

Repentance as a Vital Christian Response to God

Repentance a vital key to the whole Christian life

Because repentance leads us to experience more and more grace from God, it holds a prominent place in Calvin's theology of sanctification.[365] Through repentance we "are being purged from…sins" and made more holy.[366] Repentance is central to virtually all Christian counsel, teaching and worship. Although Calvin did not think all suffering was caused by some immediate sin, yet, as a matter of spiritual discipline, he encouraged anyone undergoing suffering to examine their life to see if there were some sin God wished to chastise, and then repent.[367] For the Christian to make progress there is a daily and lifelong necessity of self-examination and repentance.[368]

Since God's Word brings about "our humiliation and sighing and true repentance,"[369] we must hear the Word preached to grow in holiness. The sermon should not only show us our sin, and the hope of mercy, but call to repentance.

---

[355] *Commentary*, Ps. 22:27.
[356] *Institutes* 3.12.6; cf. *Commentary*, Jas. 4:10.
[357] Wendel, *Origins*, 243.
[358] *Institutes* 4.17.42.
[359] *Institutes* 3.23.12; cf. 3.21.1.
[360] *Sermons on Micah*, 55.
[361] Wallace, *Christian Life*, 258.
[362] *Commentary*, Ps. 22:23.
[363] "Sermon on Deut. 5:13-15," *CO* 26:304.
[364] *Sermons on Election and Reprobation*, 234.
[365] Niesel, *Theology of Calvin*, 128-29.
[366] *Commentary*, 1 Cor. 1:8.
[367] *Commentary*, John 5:14; *Sermons on Micah*, 99-100.
[368] *Institutes* 3.3.9, 3.3.10.
[369] *Sermons on the Ten Commandments*, 107.

"This sermon must continually sound in the Church, repent."[370] So sermon after sermon in Geneva called the people to repentance. "Every time he gives us the opportunity to repent, let us learn that he wants us to think of our sins, and…to bow our head in utter humility."[371]

Calvin's Bible lectures also called the hearers not just to understand the passage but to practice repentance. Consider these teachings from his 1563 lectures on Jeremiah, "Let us then know that this is necessary in repentance—that he who has offended God should present himself willingly."[372] Calvin explains that God invites us to repentance,[373] brings us suffering to produce repentance,[374] stimulates us to repentance[375] and judges our sin to lead us to repentance.[376]

Worship, both public and private, should be marked with repentance in the form of a confession of sin, a distinctive trait in Calvin's form of worship.[377] Sermon, commentary, worship and even prayer will drip with a call to repentance, "praying him that…we may more and more be brought both to repentance and to humility."[378] Calvin would echo with Luther that the whole of the Christian life must be one of repentance.

We derive from the necessity of having the Word instruct us in humility for repentance, as seen here, and from its role in giving faith, as seen earlier, a new principle from Calvin's theology of progressive sanctification:

Principle 2: Bible Preaching. Because God has given his Word to lead us to life, therefore submit to the preaching of the Word of Christ. Bible preaching proclaims both God's judgment on sin, and an offer of God's grace in Christ, calling the believer to turn in faith and repentance to the grace of God, who makes them holy for the obedience of faith.

Repentance leads to humble boldness

One feature peculiar to Calvin's call to humble ourselves before God is that in doing so the humble are made confident, even bold.[379] The humility and confidence, however, have essentially different orientations. We are humble regarding ourselves—our sins, our words—but we are confident in God—his salvation and his Word. Humbled by our sin, we lose confidence in our goodness[380] and no longer lean on it,[381] but we gain confidence in God's grace, upon which

---

[370] *Commentary*, Acts 2:38.
[371] *Sermons on 2 Samuel*, 573.
[372] *Commentary*, Jer. 10:24.
[373] *Commentary*, Jer. 1:10; 3:4.
[374] *Commentary*, Jer. 3:3.
[375] *Commentary*, Jer. 3:22.
[376] *Commentary*, Jer. 24:7.
[377] *Institutes* 3.4.11, 3.4.14.
[378] *Sermons on Election and Reprobation*, 142.
[379] Leith, *Christian Life*, 107.
[380] *Institutes* 3.12.8.
[381] *Institutes* 3.12.4.

we do firmly lean.[382] With consciences quieted by grace,[383] we have full confidence to approach the throne of grace[384] and thus to boldly face any future circumstance.[385] The result of the certainty that accompanies faith was, according to McWilliams, "incredible boldness in Christian living."[386] Those who were humbled in Geneva would go forth to exhibit an unusual boldness in the world. "It followed naturally for the Calvinist to exhibit an unusual aggressiveness in history."[387]

All the disciplines of the Christian life are part of repentance
The disciplines of the Christian life—self-denial, cross-bearing and even meditation on the future life—can all be seen as applications of repentance.[388] We find repentance at the very heart of self-denial.[389] To deny one's self is to repent,[390] turning from the self-centeredness of our sin.[391] Similarly, cross-bearing is both an act of, and an aid to, repentance, wherein God allows the elect to endure their sufferings as his discipline.[392] "Thus repentance does ever of itself lead to the bearing of the cross."[393] God uses cross-bearing to wake us from our slumber in sin,[394] forcing us to examine ourselves and discover that our cross is "an invitation to repentance."[395] Repenting of our sins allows us to submit to the cross; the cross trains us to be conscious of our sins, from which we must repent. Meditation on the future life requires us to turn from our hope in this world and look to the hand of God for our blessing in the next.[396] It is this repenting of our hope in the present life which allows us to "exercise ourselves on earth in meditating on the heavenly life."[397] The disciplines of the Christian life then are all simply applications of repentance.

From repentance we derive this new principle:

Principle 7: Repentance. Because God gives grace to the lowly, therefore repent humbly to find more grace. The grace of God for sanctification only flows to the humble penitent who, through self-examination, based on the Word preached, read and held forth by others in the church, seeks out all sin in his life so that in seeing his sin, he will ask God for the humility to turn from sin to Christ and there receive forgiveness and grace to make him holy.

---

[382] *Institutes* 1.2.2.
[383] *Institutes* 3.2.15.
[384] *Institutes* 3.20.11.
[385] *Institutes* 1.17.7.
[386] McWilliams, "Certainty," 530-31.
[387] Leith, *Christian Life*, 82.
[388] *Commentary*, Acts 20:21.
[389] Wallace, *Christian Life*, 99.
[390] *Commentary*, Acts 5:31.
[391] Wallace, *Christian Life*, 60-61.
[392] *Commentary*, Jer. 31:19.
[393] *Commentary*, Mic. 7:9.
[394] *Commentary*, Jer. 31:19.
[395] *Commentary*, Luke 13:2; Jer. 15:7.
[396] *Institutes* 3.20.42.
[397] *Commentary*, Matt. 3:2.

Having seen how faith and repentance work together to produce holiness, it remains next to see how they are lived out daily in the life of the Christian within society and the church, which we now explore in Chapter 4.

Chapter 4 - The Life of the Christian Man within the Church

"Summa vitae christianae: ubi de abnegatione nostri."[1]

Introduction

In this chapter we move from the theology of sanctification to the practice of sanctification in the daily life of the Christian. Here we will see the essential paradigm of Calvin's sanctification lived out: growth in the two-fold knowledge of God and self, leading to the two-fold movement of the heart toward piety, downward in prostration and upward in reverence. "The reaction is twofold: man stands awestricken in fear, and yet is drawn in love. These two responses are not antithetical, but belong side by side in the pious heart."[2] We will do this by exploring two topics: first, Calvin's chapters on the Life of the Christian Man and second, how the church was to contribute to that life. The few short chapters on the Christian Life, which first appeared in the 1539 *Institutes*, perhaps influenced by reading Bucer,[3] were only ever slightly revised[4] and reveal "a pattern for the conduct of life."[5] His four practices, drawn from Matthew 16:24,[6] self-denial, cross-bearing, meditation on the future life and proper use of this life, hold together as a unified approach to yielding oneself to the work of God. Each leads to a humble prostration before God and reverent turning upward toward him for help, thus restoring us our "rightful places"[7] in the true order (*verum ordinem*),[8] the natural way of being.[9] For Calvin the experience of sanctification was far from individualistic but could only take place in the church, as Luke indicated in Acts 2:47. "He teaches that this is the means to attain salvation, if we be incorporated into the Church."[10] It is within the church that Christ engenders growth in faith through her Word,[11] shepherds us with her pastors[12] and strengthens his union with us through her sacraments.[13] But before we begin these topics we must understand the role of human effort in sanctification.

---

[1] *CO* 2:505, "The sum of the Christian life: whereof we deny ourselves." *Institutes* 3.7.1.
[2] Dowey, *Knowledge of God*, 30.
[3] Wendel, *Origins*, 142.
[4] Wendel, *Origins*, 246.
[5] *Institutes* 3.6.1.
[6] *Commentary*, Matt. 16:24.
[7] Wendel, *Origins*, 151.
[8] Wallace, *Christian Life*, 107.
[9] Wallace, *Christian Life*, 53-60.
[10] *Commentary*, Acts 2:47.
[11] Wallace, *Christian Life*, 207.
[12] T.H.L. Parker, *Calvin, An Introduction To His Thought* (Louisville, Ky.: Westminster/John Knox, 1995), 144.
[13] Niesel, *Theology of Calvin*, 221.

Christian life requires desire and effort, but these depend upon grace
Calvin definitely calls the believer to be active in the pursuit of holiness, "that ye may *sanctify* yourselves to *God*"[14] and thus "make some unceasing progress in the way of the Lord."[15] Our effort must start with the God-given desire to actually become more holy so that we will turn to God to make us holy. "The highest perfection of the godly in this life is an earnest desire to make progress."[16] Seeing from Scripture that God is holy and desires his people to become holy, human effort is birthed in a desire to be like the Father.[17] Because this desire is such an essential part of Calvin's understanding of the right pursuit of the Christian life, we derive from this another principle from his theology of progressive sanctification.

> **Principle 5: Desiring Holiness. Because God is holy and loves holiness, therefore desire deeply to become holy.** The believer must see God's intention to conform his people to the Scriptural standard of holiness and thus desire to become more holy, rendering the obedience of faith from a heart of integrity.

Though we must desire holiness and make an effort to grow in holiness, since conformity to the law/the pattern of Christ is still required,[18] we should not confuse our role as "cooperation" with God.[19] While we do make "a deliberate and continuous conscious effort,"[20] our effort only proceeds by continually relying on the grace of God.[21] We should not think, even as Christians, that we have the inherent ability to obey God, for we are still totally dependent upon God, "drawing all our help from him."[22] The new life in us is precisely this: a true knowledge of our inability to obey and Christ's ability, which leads us to turn to Christ for help to "conquer the will of the flesh."[23] We work, but our work is turning to Christ and resting in his power that he may work in us through his Spirit.[24] "We must rest entirely, in order that God may work in us; we must resign our own will, yield up our heart, and abandon all the lusts of the flesh. In short, we must desist from all the acts of our own mind, that God working in us, we may rest in him."[25] Our effort is entirely based upon God's prior efforts in

---

[14] *Commentary*, 1 Thess. 4:3.
[15] *Institutes* 3.6.5.
[16] *Commentary*, Eph. 3:16.
[17] *Commentary*, Rom. 12:1.
[18] Lobstein, *Die Ethik Calvins*, 148. Cf. R.C. Zachman, "'Deny Yourself and Take up Your Cross': John Calvin on the Christian Life," *International Journal of Systematic Theology* 11 (2009), 469-70.
[19] This has not prevented others from using the term in reference to Calvin: "Sanctification becomes a work in which the believer cooperates by faith." Marcel, "Justification and Sanctification," 139.
[20] Wallace, *Christian Life*, 59.
[21] *Institutes* 3.6.3.
[22] *Sermons on Micah*, 183.
[23] Wallace, *Christian Life*, 66.
[24] *Commentary*, 1 John 3:9.
[25] *Institutes* 2.8.29.

Christ and comes in response to his effort.[26] As Lane has written, "We act only to the extent that we are acted upon."[27]

We are active, but Calvin directs our activity toward faith, faith that looks to God's grace to make us holy. "The denial of ourselves...is impossible except by faith in Christ."[28] Sanctification only proceeds from faith which looks to Christ to work,[29] vivifying our spirit[30] and mortifying our flesh.[31] Our activity in sanctification is to make way for God to transform us. Niesel notes this dynamic: "The substance of Christian ethics is in no sense the positive shaping of life by the initiative of the pious man. The essential action which we are called upon to perform is rather the renunciation of all that is our own, that we may give scope to the action of God."[32]

The origins of Calvin's thoughts on self-denial, cross-bearing, etc.
Calvin's thoughts on the Christian life were not new, but rather drew upon a long Christian tradition highlighted with Augustine[33] and culminating with medieval monasticism, as Lucien Richard has shown.[34] Regarding self-denial, we find that Benedict of Nursia (480-543) taught of this in "the twelve steps of humility."[35] Similarly, the *Imitation of Christ* bid one to find grace by shrinking "from all self-esteem and account myself as the dust which I am."[36] Bernard called for self-denial by losing "yourself as though you were not."[37] When we consider cross-bearing, we find that Gregory the Great had written, "The sick are to be admonished to realize that they are sons of God by the very fact that the scourge of discipline chastises them."[38] As well we read in à Kempis, "In the cross is salvation, in the cross is life...in the cross is perfect holiness."[39] The concept of meditating upon the heavenly life was found in Bernard as in others: "The remembrance of eternity should prove a source of delight."[40]

While Calvin did not invent any new Christian disciplines, he did take them in new directions relevant to the general concerns of his fellow reformers. Cal-

---

[26] Leithart, "Stoic Elements," 194.
[27] A.N.S. Lane, "Anthropology," *The Calvin Handbook* (ed. H.J. Selderhuis; Grand Rapids, Mich.: Eerdmans, 2009), 286.
[28] Wendel, *Origins*, 248.
[29] *Commentary*, Rom. 6:7.
[30] *Sermons on the Ten Commandments*, 42.
[31] *Commentary*, 1 Pet. 4:1.
[32] Niesel, *Theology of Calvin*, 144.
[33] *Institutes* 2.2.11.
[34] Richard, *Spirituality of John Calvin*, 50-51.
[35] T. Fry (ed.), *The Rule of St. Benedict* (New York, N.Y.: Random House, 1998), 16-20.
[36] *Imitation of Christ*, 3.8.
[37] Bernard, *Love of God*, 44-45.
[38] Gregory the Great, *Pastoral Care* (ed. and tr. H. Davis; New York, N.Y.: Newman, 1950), 122-23.
[39] *Imitation of Christ*, 2.12.
[40] Bernard, *Love of God*, 17.

vin would argue that self-denial best occurs in community,[41] not the monk's cell.[42] He transformed what had been in the fourteenth century an absolute *contemptus mundi* into a comparative one, hating this world only relative to the glory of the world to come.[43] He broke with the medieval ascetic view[44] that the holy life was primarily to focus on the future, and he taught that the right use of this present life was a holy calling.[45]

Self-Denial

Understanding self-denial

Self-denial contains both a negation and an affirmation; we must first deny our own wills so that we may take up in its place the will of God. "We are not our own: in so far as we can, let us therefore forget ourselves and all that is ours. Conversely, we are God's: let us therefore live for him and die for him."[46] Since we are a "perpetual factory of idols,"[47] who live in defiance of God's will, the first step to return to the obedience of faith is to renounce our own will and reason, submitting rather to God in his Word,[48] offering ourselves as living sacrifices to God.[49] Self-denial, then, is a first Christian discipline for sanctification,[50] the principle move away from self and toward the grace of God. "Self-denial may be said to be the commencement of piety."[51]

How we should practice self-denial

Self-denial begins with a heart-felt desire to deny our own will, even our own good,[52] which may be thought of as self-hatred. "We must transfer the hatred that we naturally feel for God and our fellow man back on ourselves."[53] This even entails denying what the world suggests ought to be ours,[54] so that we never seek any blessings apart from God's Word[55] but take from the world only what is delivered by God's hand.[56] Self-denial requires us to understand what Scripture[57] and a careful *descensus in se*[58] reveal as evil in our own will. Dis-

---

[41] *Institutes* 3.7.7.
[42] *Imitation of Christ*, 1.20.
[43] Richard, *Spirituality of John Calvin*, 104.
[44] Wendel, *Origins*, 247.
[45] *Institutes* 4.5.8.
[46] *Institutes* 3.7.1.
[47] *Institutes* 1.11.8.
[48] Zachman, "Deny Yourself," 471.
[49] *Commentary*, Rom. 12:1.
[50] Lobstein, *Die Ethik Calvins*, 149. Cf. *Commentary*, 1 Cor., "Introduction."
[51] *Commentary*, John 3:12.
[52] *Institutes* 3.7.1.
[53] Wallace, *Christian Life*, 61.
[54] *Institutes* 2.15.5.
[55] *Institutes* 3.7.9.
[56] *Institutes* 3.7.8.
[57] *Institutes* 3.7.2, 3.7.8.
[58] *Commentary*, 1 John 3:21.

covering this evil we are to confess and deny it, turning from it to seek God's revealed will for his glory.[59]

Self-denial demands that we submit to God's will by recognizing that all life circumstances are really God's providence,[60] to which one must submit,[61] since "it is with God he has to deal."[62] This favorite concept of Calvin's is witnessed in his own readiness to return to Geneva, against his own will but in subjection to God's. "I am well aware, however, that it is God with whom I have to do."[63] As we seek God's will, we offer ourselves to his service,[64] as in our Sabbath observance,[65] and thus experience what Wallace describes as self-immolation, being consumed into the will of God.[66] It was on this concept that Calvin founded his personal motto and the signet for his ring, "cor meum velut mactatum Domino in sacrificium offero."[67]

Self-denial also requires that we yield to the will of our neighbor[68] for the "dethroning of self in face of the claims of our fellow man,"[69] which fulfills the second great commandment.[70] We must do anything we can to help our brothers no matter how great an inconvenience to ourselves.[71] Indeed, the more inconvenient, the deeper the self-denial. "Whatever man you meet who needs your aid, you have no reason to refuse to help him."[72]

How self-denial works in the process of sanctification

Self-denial is faith and repentance at work
Self-denial is both the fruit and the practice of faith, for without faith in Christ, no one would imagine denying them self.[73] We must first believe that we are not our own but the Lord's,[74] and that his will for us is better than our own, before we will deny ourselves and trust him to prosper us.[75] Faith is required to believe that in all circumstances we are dealing with God,[76] who will reward[77]

---

[59] *Institutes* 3.7.2. Cf. Barth, *Theology of Calvin*, 171.
[60] *Institutes* 2.15.5.
[61] Wendel, *Origins*, 249.
[62] *Institutes* 3.7.2.
[63] *CSW*, Vol. 4, 281.
[64] Lobstein, *Die Ethik Calvins*, 69.
[65] *Commentary*, Jer. 17:24-25.
[66] Wallace, *Christian Life*, 29-30.
[67] Barth, *Theology of Calvin*, 117, "My heart I offer as though slain in sacrifice to God." *CO* 11:100, Letter to Farel, Oct. 24, 1540.
[68] Parker, *Calvin's Thought*, 89; *Institutes* 3.7.5.
[69] Wallace, *Christian Life*, 62.
[70] Lobstein, *Die Ethik Calvins*, 81.
[71] *Institutes* 3.7.5. Cf. Zachman, "Deny Yourself," 472-73.
[72] *Institutes* 3.7.6.
[73] Wendel, *Origins*, 248.
[74] *Institutes* 3.7.1.
[75] *Institutes* 3.7.8.
[76] *Institutes* 3.7.2.
[77] *Institutes* 3.7.9.

those who, "with Christ, voluntarily abase themselves."[78] We must believe that the "hope of blessed immortality"[79] awaits before we will see the benefit in denying ourselves temporally. Human reason must give way to faith and "submit and subject itself to the Holy Spirit."[80] Self-denial is faith, which, looking to Christ to bring life, allows the Christian to abandon all other self-oriented schemes of grasping for life.

In calling us to self-denial, the practice of repentance becomes a real and daily affair as we "unremittingly examining our faults call ourselves back to humility."[81] Self-denial is repentance in that we turn from our sinful "ambition and all craving for human glory"[82] to Christ, in order to find life.[83] As repentance, self-denial turns us toward God to serve him and his desires. "We are God's: let us therefore live for him and die for him."[84] The effort required for self-denial, always reliant on Christ,[85] is primarily of a negative nature: we yield our sinful passions to God in order that he might subdue them.[86]

Self-denial humbles us before God who makes us into happy people
Self-denial, as the daily practice of humbling ourselves before God,[87] empties oneself of "all opinion of its own worth," and opens up the heart to receive God's mercy.[88] In this humble posture God can and will work to transform us into holy creatures[89] as he pours out his grace.[90] "Having prostrated ourselves in the dust before him, he may raise us up."[91]

God's grace to the humble restores them to happiness before God, who leads them in the good way (*qu'il nous ait ramenez au bon chemin*).[92] "Man becomes happy by self-denial."[93] This is entirely contrary to the world's way, which tells us we find happiness in self-indulgence and self-absolution, covering our sins. Calvin will suggest that peace is found in accusing oneself through self-denial and allowing Christ to absolve us.[94] As we cease managing our lives by enforcing our wills and yield to God's will,[95] he gives us a "peaceful and grateful

---

[78] *Commentary*, Phil. 2:9.
[79] *Institutes* 3.7.3.
[80] *Institutes* 3.7.1.
[81] *Institutes* 3.7.4.
[82] *Institutes* 3.7.2.
[83] Wallace, *Christian Life*, 59.
[84] *Institutes* 3.7.1.
[85] D.K. Winecoff, "Calvin's Doctrine of Mortification," *Presbyterion* 13 (1987), 98.
[86] Wallace, *Christian Life*, 60-61.
[87] *Institutes* 3.7.2.
[88] *Institutes* 3.12.7.
[89] Wallace, *Christian Life*, 65.
[90] Battles, *The Piety of John Calvin*, 4.
[91] *Commentary*, Ps. 34:18.
[92] "Sermon on Gen. 26:6-10," *CO* 58:116.
[93] *Commentary*, Heb. 4:10.
[94] *Commentary*, 1 John 3:21.
[95] *Institutes* 3.7.10.

mind," no matter what the circumstances.[96] Though there are superficial similarities here to the Stoic ideal of tranquility, the joys of self-denial are so God-oriented that it is clearly distinct from Stoicism, despite Leithart's claims.[97] Made free of the "deadly pestilence of love of strife and love of self," we become those who love their neighbors, having "a heart imbued with lowliness and with reverence for others."[98]

Implications for Calvin's model of sanctification

Self-denial becomes the active obedience of faith that the Christian renders to the Lord, so Calvin will call for it often in his writings and sermons. The true order is restored through self-denial: humanity moves downward in prostration before God, denying its own will, while God is rightly lifted up in reverence before humanity, as it submits to God's will. Here we derive another principle:

> **Principle 8: Self-denial. Because God gives life to those who lose it, therefore deny yourself as a practice of faith and repentance.** To progress in holiness the believer must practice faith and repentance by constantly considering the interests of God and others before his own and yielding to God's will, as it is revealed in Scripture, through his neighbor's needs and to his conscience.

Cross-bearing

Understanding cross-bearing

While self-denial has to do with the internal voluntary struggle to submit to the rule of God, cross-bearing pertains to the external trials—crosses—that God in his providence sends our way, in order to tame us to his will.[99] Thus mortification always proceeds on two fronts: internally and externally.[100] Cross-bearing is the willing submission to the external trials as we come to understand they are all actually from God's loving hand.[101] Cross-bearing must involve real suffering, whether physical, spiritual, social or economic,[102] accompanied by emotional pain,[103] which must be endured.[104]

Since cross-bearing requires faith that God is behind and working through suffering,[105] only believers can rightly be said to bear the cross,[106] for while God burdens all people with suffering, "unless they willingly bend their shoulders to it, they are not said to *bear the cross*."[107] In the unbeliever suffering will

---

[96] *Institutes* 3.7.10.
[97] Leithart, "Stoic Elements," 200.
[98] *Institutes* 3.7.4.
[99] Wallace, *Christian Life*, 68.
[100] Winecoff, "Mortification," 92.
[101] *Sermons on Micah*, 101. Cf. *Commentary*, Hos. 9:7.
[102] *Institutes* 3.8.10.
[103] Wallace, *Christian Life*, 183.
[104] *Commentary*, Rom. 8:24.
[105] *Institutes* 3.8.10.
[106] Lobstein, *Die Ethik Calvins*, 85.
[107] *Commentary*, Matt. 16:24.

have a deleterious effect, hardening them toward God,[108] "like an anvil under the blows of a hammer."[109] It is not the suffering *per se* that produces holiness but rather the work of the Holy Spirit[110] who bears us up under the load.[111]

Every Christian *must* bear the cross as a normal, although not constant, part of life,[112] in order to put to death the old nature.[113] "Christ calls his disciples: that each must bear his own cross."[114] Cross-bearing is so important to growth in holiness that it may appear that God "treats his children more harshly than he does strangers," but we must always understand that God uses our crosses for our good.[115] We are to bear the cross even to death,[116] because Jesus went this way before us.[117]

Three types of cross-bearing
Calvin outlines three types of cross-bearing: 1) suffering to cure us from the disease of sin, 2) suffering as direct chastisement for sin and 3) suffering for righteousness.[118] In the medicinal use of the cross, since we all have different sin patterns in our lives,[119] God individualizes each person's "remedy of the cross" according to their type of sin, treating "this one with greater harshness, that one with more kindly indulgence."[120] God will use for one poverty, for another shame, or disease, or family suffering, or hard labor, but in each instance God will apply precisely the "appropriate remedy,"[121] which is "healthful for each man,"[122] to best foster holiness.

When we bear the cross as chastisement for sin,[123] it would be "utterly foolish to think"[124] that chastisement is a judicial penalty for sin, because Christ has already born the penalty due our sin. Here Calvin draws a fine distinction, which at first may seem as though he were quibbling over words, but in the end the distinction is central to his understanding of cross-bearing. Calvin will assert that fatherly chastisements (*paternis castigationibus*[125]) are different from

---

[108] *Commentary*, Jas. 1:3.
[109] Wallace, *Christian Life*, 71.
[110] Wallace, *Christian Life*, 72.
[111] *Commentary*, Rom. 8:26.
[112] *Commentary*, 1 Cor. 16:24.
[113] *Institutes* 3.8.1. Cf. Wallace, *Christian Life*, 44-45.
[114] *Institutes* 3.8.1.
[115] *Sermons on Micah*, 61.
[116] *Commentary*, John 12:26.
[117] *Institutes* 3.8.1. Cf. Wallace, *Christian Life*, 44-45.
[118] Wallace, *Christian Life*, 69.
[119] Wallace, *Christian Life*, 254-55.
[120] *Institutes* 3.4.35.
[121] *Commentary*, Ps. 119:67.
[122] *Institutes* 3.8.5.
[123] David is a favorite example; see *Institutes* 3.4.35 and *Sermons on 2 Samuel*, 579: "When David's child died, the result was that David felt how much God detested the sin that he had committed."
[124] *Institutes* 3.4.35.
[125] *CO* 2:486; *Institutes* 3.4.35.

the punishments of iniquity (*supplicia iniquitatis*[126]). Judicial punishment (*poena*[127]) is vengeance taken on God's enemies and accompanied with his wrath. Fatherly chastisement (*castigatio*[128]) is correction offered to God's children from a heart of love,[129] to train them for the future.[130] While both may rightly be called punishment, it is God's intention that distinguishes a "judgment in vengeance" from a "judgment in chastisement."[131] "The one is the act of a judge; the other, of a father."[132] The distinction is critical for the believer to comprehend, for it is only as we see the cross as loving correction and not penalty that we can come to trust God during suffering.[133]

Believers will be called to suffer for righteousness' sake, as was Christ, and this should both comfort us and cause us to rejoice.[134] We should always anticipate that the world may rise up against us,[135] ready to "vomit out their venom" in slander, attacks, or opposition.[136] Yet, we may find real "spiritual joy"[137] in bearing this cross, even as it holds "bitterness and pain,"[138] for we are united with Christ who, sanctifying us like Job,[139] will one day "turn reproaches, slanders, and mocks of the world, into great honor."[140]

How we should practice cross-bearing

We can only bear the cross by faith in the good providence of God
Cross-bearing is supremely an act of faith.[141] We must believe that God is both sovereignly in control[142] and working for our good,[143] such that any trial in our life is finally seen as a providential good from his hand.[144] As we believe in God's providence,[145] his absolute control over every aspect of life,[146] we can

---

[126] *CO* 2:485; *Institutes* 3.4.33.
[127] *CO* 2:483; *Institutes* 3.4.32.
[128] *CO* 2:483; *Institutes* 3.4.32.
[129] *Institutes* 3.4.31.
[130] Parker, *Calvin's Thought*, 91.
[131] *Institutes* 3.4.32.
[132] *Institutes* 3.4.31.
[133] *Institutes* 3.4.34.
[134] *Institutes* 3.8.7.
[135] *Commentary*, Matt. 5:10.
[136] *Commentary*, 2 Tim. 3:12.
[137] *Commentary*, Acts 5:41.
[138] *Institutes* 3.8.8.
[139] *Commentary*, John 9:2.
[140] *Commentary*, Acts 5:41.
[141] Wallace, *Christian Life*, 73.
[142] *Commentary*, Lam. 3:37-38.
[143] *Institutes* 1.17.8.
[144] *Institutes* 3.8.11.
[145] *Institutes* 1.16.2.
[146] *Commentary*, Gen. 2:2. Cf. Torrance, *Calvin's Doctrine of Man*, 61. This concept of *creatio continua* is important for Calvin who writes, "We and all the creatures do not, strictly speaking, live, but only borrow life from Him." *Commentary*, 1 Tim. 6:16.

submit to any difficulty, whether arising from enemies or inanimate objects,[147] knowing they occur not by blind fortune,[148] or even by God's mere permission, but by his decree.[149]

God providentially manages all the activities in the world in such a way as to benefit the church.[150] "The church is indeed the real object of divine providence."[151] While God governs all his creatures through his providence he shows special "vigilance in ruling the church, which he deigns to watch more closely."[152] God is a Father who, while being fair to all people, is careful to preserve his best inheritance for his own children.[153] However, since God is more concerned for the church's holiness than her ease, his providence for the church, rather than simply pleasant, is often brutal in appearance.[154]

We must learn to submit to God in difficult providences
There is one single overarching response necessary for the Christian in cross-bearing: we must submit to God under his difficult providences.[155] God has designed the cross that his people "might resignedly and humbly submit to the condition allotted to them"[156] with trust, patience and joy. The essence of submission is an attitude of trust.[157] Our heart must not be allowed to complain bitterly toward God, seeking escape from our circumstances, as is our natural tendency.[158] "If God singles us out first for chastisement and in the meantime we observe that others are enjoying their ease we murmur: 'Whoa! What is this? What's going on here?'"[159] We are called "with becoming humility"[160] to submit to the level of health, wealth, popularity and success God grants us.[161] This trust is faith lived out, believing God's Word[162] rather than "believing" negative circumstances or our own limited understanding,[163] from which the devil would encourage our doubt.[164]

We must be patient[165] because the cross always has a temporal aspect. Our crosses will both arrive at inopportune moments and remain for inordinate

---

[147] *Institutes* 1.16.8.
[148] *Commentary*, John 5:14.
[149] Wallace, *Christian Life*, 260. Cf. *Institutes* 1.17.8.
[150] Wendel, *Origins*, 179.
[151] Niesel, *Theology of Calvin*, 74.
[152] *Institutes* 1.17.1.
[153] *Commentary*, Ps. 31:19.
[154] Niesel, *Theology of Calvin*, 75.
[155] *Commentary*, Gen. 3:19; 8:1; Hos. 7:12.
[156] *Commentary*, Rom. 8:30.
[157] Wallace, *Christian Life*, 182.
[158] Lobstein, *Die Ethik Calvins*, 88.
[159] *Sermons on Micah*, 53.
[160] *Institutes* 1.17.2.
[161] *Sermons on Micah*, 43.
[162] *Institutes* 3.8.11.
[163] *Institutes* 1.16.9.
[164] Selderhuis, "Faith Between God and the Devil," 201.
[165] Lobstein, *Die Ethik Calvins*, 84.

lengths of time, such that we must "languish long under them,"[166] until they become effective.[167] We must learn to "bear with patience whatever it pleases God to send us,"[168] for however long he pleases.[169] This endurance is not, however, an emotionless,[170] stoical self-reliance, but rather a "humility that prostrates itself in the dust before God."[171]

We are to welcome the cross, which "renders tribulations to be loved by us,"[172] so we may persevere in hope,[173] gratitude[174] and even joy.[175] Since the cross conforms us to the image of Christ, we "should lovingly kiss the cross rather than dread it."[176] Kissing the cross we reject impatience and insolence, and instead, consoled that God is at work for our salvation,[177] "undergo them with a thankful and quiet mind."[178] Each cross can be honestly welcomed as an opportunity to find and mortify sin in our lives.[179] Even while welcoming the cross, we may still ask God to deliver us from it, moved by the cross to pray,[180] as long as our prayers are humble and submissive, readily accepting "no" for the answer.[181]

This submission to God in difficult providences will form the cornerstone of Calvin's understanding of the role of suffering in our sanctification, and therefore is the bedrock of his pastoral counsel.[182] It is this lesson Calvin taught all those around him, perhaps one of his most profound. As he dealt with his own grief over the death of Calvin, Beza wrote, "I would also have profited very little from his teaching…if I had not learnt through all these means to submit to God's providence and be completely satisfied and content."[183]

How cross-bearing works in the process of sanctification

We are mortified, brought to the end of ourselves and prostrated before God
Cross-bearing, a kind of enforced repentance from pride[184] and encouragement to turn to God in faith,[185] is used by God to return humanity to a properly pros-

---

[166] *Commentary*, John 11:15.
[167] *Commentary*, John 12:25.
[168] *Sermons on Micah*, 54.
[169] *Commentary*, Rom. 14:8.
[170] Zachman, "Deny Yourself," 476.
[171] Wallace, *Christian Life*, 191.
[172] *Commentary*, Rom. 5:5.
[173] *Sermons on Election and Reprobation*, 127.
[174] *Institutes* 3.7.10.
[175] *Institutes* 1.17.7. Cf. Lobstein, *Die Ethik Calvins*, 86.
[176] *Commentary*, Heb. 2:10.
[177] *Institutes* 3.8.8.
[178] *Institutes* 3.8.11.
[179] *Institutes* 3.8.6.
[180] Wendel, *Origins*, 253.
[181] *Commentary*, John 5:11.
[182] Wendel, *Origins*, 178. For an example see *CSW*, Vol. 7, 70-71, Letter of Calvin to Madame Grammont, Oct. 28, 1559.
[183] T. Beza, *The Life of John Calvin* (Durham, England: Evangelical, 1997), 12.
[184] *Institutes* 3.4.33; *Commentary*, Hos. 2:7.

trated place before him.[186] When life is easy, humanity may remain in its proud self-confidence, but God brings the cross to humble the proud.[187] "He can best restrain this arrogance when he proves to us by experience not only the great incapacity but also the frailty under which we labor."[188] To end our self-confidence, the cross threatens us with death, for our flesh will only finally yield under such duress.[189] It is the threat of death which forces people to see their own weakness,[190] and "falling into utter despair,"[191] they no longer consider their power up to the task and will turn to God.[192] Thus the cross mortifies our old nature. "The resultant humiliation [from suffering] forces us not to trust ourselves for the needs of this life, but rather transfer our trust to His love and grace."[193]

We are vivified, brought to reverence God and seek him for help
Broken down by the cross, we turn toward God in reverence,[194] seeking from him deliverance from the cross.[195] "Our experience of affliction reveals to us our own weakness and nothingness, so that we abandon all trust in ourselves, and are more deeply humbled by the true knowledge of ourselves."[196] This enforced prostration is critical to turn us toward God and away from our self-confidence.

> And it is of no slight importance for you to be cleansed of your blind love of self that you may be made more nearly aware of your incapacity; to feel your own incapacity that you may learn to distrust yourself; to distrust yourself that you may transfer your trust to God; to rest with a trustful heart in God that, relying upon his help, you may persevere unconquered to the end.[197]

In looking to God, we see not only his ability to deliver us but always "the fatherly love of God,"[198] who in using the cross "is actually encouraging them by these things to return to himself."[199] Seeing God's loving hand behind each blow of the cross, all history teaches us to trust God,[200] and so come to transfer our confidence from ourselves to him, as the one who can deliver us from suf-

---

[185] *Commentary*, Ps. 119:67.
[186] *Commentary*, Jonah 1:5.
[187] *Institutes* 3.8.2, 1.17.1; *Sermons on 2 Samuel*, 576.
[188] *Institutes* 3.8.2.
[189] *Commentary*, 2 Cor. 1:9; *Institutes* 3.8.3.
[190] *Commentary*, 2 Cor. 1:8.
[191] *Commentary*, 2 Cor. 1:9.
[192] *Institutes* 3.8.2. Cf. Wallace, *Christian Life*, 258-59.
[193] Winecoff, "Mortification," 101.
[194] *Institutes* 3.8.2.
[195] Wallace, *Christian Life*, 258.
[196] Zachman, "Deny Yourself," 475.
[197] *Institutes* 3.8.3.
[198] Wallace, *Christian Life*, 263.
[199] *Sermons on 2 Samuel*, 577. Cf. *Sermons on Micah*, 83.
[200] *Institutes* 1.17.6.

fering by his grace.[201] Indeed, we come to see that it has been our lack of submission which has often invited the cross from God,[202] who uses it to lead us back to him,[203] even as a donkey must be lead with blows.[204]

God extends his grace and remolds us in the image of Christ
As we humbly and reverentially turn to God for help, our Lord is kindly to extend his grace to us and change us more and more into his own image.[205] He works to produce in us more faith in Christ[206] by continually bringing us to circumstances where we can only live by faith.[207] Through faith we are made holy, conformed more to the image of God.[208] We are transformed bit by bit into those who obey God, having been "instructed by the cross to obey."[209] We are brought to a place of peaceful rest,[210] knowing that no matter what tempests rage around us, "a constant quiet and serenity ever remain in heaven."[211] We rest knowing that God is at work, making us holy by his cross,[212] giving us a future and a hope.[213]

Implications for Calvin's model of sanctification
There is no way to be made holy other than by cross-bearing, which yields a faith-filled submission to God who mortifies and vivifies us by the cross.[214] Hence Calvin will consistently call his hearers to submit to God in the difficult providence of cross-bearing.[215] From this we derive another principle:

Principle 9: Cross-bearing. Because God mortifies through suffering, therefore bear the cross to mortify our flesh. God sanctifies the believer by providentially bringing him the sufferings of the cross, which he should bear with joy and patience, as he submits to God in difficult providences.

Meditation on the Future Life

Understanding meditation on the future life
Meditation on the future life involves the two-fold movement: first downward, away from a love for this life,[216] as we consider its miseries, and then upward

---

[201] Wallace, *Christian Life*, 76.
[202] *Institutes* 3.4.35; *Commentary*, Hos. 5:13.
[203] *Institutes* 3.8.6.
[204] *Sermons on 2 Samuel*, 580-81.
[205] *Institutes* 3.8.2.
[206] *Institutes* 3.8.11.
[207] Wallace, *Christian Life*, 252-53.
[208] *Commentary*, Rom. 8:29. Cf. Winecoff, "Mortification," 98.
[209] *Institutes* 3.8.4. Cf. *Commentary*, Heb. 2:10; *Sermons on Micah*, 124.
[210] *Commentary*, Matt. 5:3; 10:29.
[211] *Institutes* 1.17.1.
[212] *Institutes* 3.2.28; *Commentary*, John 12:24.
[213] *Commentary*, Rom. 5:4.
[214] *Commentary*, Ps. 119:166.
[215] *CSW*, Vol. 5, 407.
[216] *Institutes* 3.9.4.

as we contemplate the glorious life to come.[217] This two-fold movement begins with our thought patterns but must include a two-fold affective response: a repentant groaning over our love for this world and a faith-filled longing for the next.[218] Meditation on the future, or heavenly life,[219] requires us to "strive with all our heart"[220] to consistently contemplate the reality and glory of the life to come, in order to overcome the natural domination by thoughts of this present life.[221] Looking ahead we long to dwell with Christ in his glory,[222] with "the unspeakable sweetness of his delights"[223] and all the blessings of God.[224]

How we should practice meditation on the future life

Beginning from youth[225] the believer is to think of the glories of the world to come in real and concrete terms, which can draw their hearts heavenward.[226] We are to meditate constantly on the promise of heaven,[227] not only when we are tempted with this world, or forced by death, to think of the next.[228] When the "many allurements"[229] of this world do capture us, we should recognize that temporary bliss is nothing without eternity,[230] and so lay up our treasure in heaven.[231] When trials assail us, we use them to launch us into thoughts of heaven.[232] When blessings please us, we use them to "whet our hope and desire" for the even greater blessings to come.[233] Any bodily infirmity is reason enough to think upon the glorified state of our body.[234] Even the Lord's Supper is to become a "serious exercise of meditation on the heavenly life."[235] We can materially focus our attention on heaven by sending "our possessions thither"[236] as we provide for the poor.

Meditation on the future life requires a consistent *contemptus mundi* in which we despise the present world due to our own sin[237] and trials, such as

---

[217] Wallace, *Christian Life*, 91.
[218] *Commentary*, Rom. 8:23.
[219] Wallace, *Christian Life*, 88.
[220] *Institutes* 3.9.2.
[221] Wallace, *Christian Life*, 90.
[222] *Commentary*, 1 Thess. 1:9.
[223] *Institutes* 3.9.6.
[224] *Commentary*, 1 Thess. 1:9.
[225] Reid, *Treatises*, 104, "Catechism of the Church of Geneva," 1545.
[226] *Commentary*, Rom. 8:17.
[227] *Commentary*, Rom. 8:17.
[228] Reid, *Treatises*, 228, "Reply to Sadolet."
[229] *Institutes* 3.9.2.
[230] *Sermons on Micah*, 79-80.
[231] *Commentary*, Matt. 6:20.
[232] *Institutes* 3.9.2.
[233] *Institutes* 3.9.3; *Sermons on the Ten Commandments*, 286.
[234] Zachman, "Deny Yourself," 477.
[235] Reid, *Treatises*, 266, "Partaking of the Flesh and Blood."
[236] *Institutes* 3.18.6.
[237] *Commentary*, John 12:25.

disease, want and the vicissitudes of this world.[238] However, contempt for this life is not absolute but only relative to the glory of the future life,[239] since even this life is to be received as God's good gift.[240] Hence meditation on the future life actually enables one to live righteously in this life,[241] by allowing the focus on the ultimate to add perspective for existence in the penultimate.[242]

How meditation on the future life works in the process of sanctification
Meditation on the future life becomes another way to apply faith and repentance. In faith we "turn our eyes to the glory of the life that is to come," and God replaces our hopes and fears in this world with hope in the world to come.[243] As we look forward to Christ's final triumph over our flesh,[244] we behold him more clearly[245] and are united to him more completely,[246] thus he transforms us into his likeness.[247]

As repentance, meditation on the future life leads us away from self-confidence to look to Christ. We naturally love this world, confident that we can achieve "immortality for ourselves on earth."[248] This confidence must be pried out of our hearts[249] by coming to a true knowledge, both of our despised condition here, relative to heaven,[250] and of our inability to manufacture heaven on earth.[251] Meditation on the future life leads us to this knowledge and to humbly repent of our worldly affections.[252] Humbled before God in acknowledging our inability to derive full pleasure from this world, we turn to him, trusting him to create a perfect life for us in the next.

Implications for Calvin's model of sanctification
Calvin will constantly call his hearers to contemplate the reality of their future life with God, in order to draw them away from the world and toward heaven thus leading them toward holiness.[253] From this we derive another principle:

Principle 10: Future Life. Because God grants us an eternal inheritance, therefore meditate on the future life with Christ. The believer progresses in holiness as he is constantly drawn through public preaching and private meditation

---

[238] Fuhrmann, *Instruction*, 27.
[239] *Commentary*, John 12:25. Cf. *Institutes* 3.9.4.
[240] *Institutes* 3.9.3.
[241] Venema, *Accepted and Renewed*, 126, note 68.
[242] K.Y. Shin, "Calvin's Theology of Holiness," PhD. thesis (University of Aberdeen, 2002), 86.
[243] Wallace, *Christian Life*, 267.
[244] *Institutes* 3.9.6.
[245] *Commentary*, Col. 3:1.
[246] Wallace, *Christian Life*, 87.
[247] *Institutes* 3.9.5.
[248] *Institutes* 3.9.2.
[249] *Institutes* 3.9.1.
[250] *Institutes* 2.1.3.
[251] Wallace, *Christian Life*, 268.
[252] *Commentary*, Acts 20:21.
[253] *Commentary*, Gen. 5:22; John 20:17.

Use of this Present Life

Understanding the proper use of this life

Calvin's paradigm for sanctification included careful instruction in the right use of the present life as a good gift from God,[254] since Christ and his people are supposed to possess and enjoy the earth.[255] In sharp distinction from the monkish ideal[256] and Platonic dualism,[257] Calvin called his hearers to walk a tightrope, a *via media*,[258] of thankfully enjoying the pleasures of this world, such as the arts,[259] fine food and beauty,[260] as blessings to God's children,[261] while always avoiding hedonism.[262] "To love this life is not in itself wrong, provided that we only pass through it as pilgrims."[263] God filled the earth with beautiful and delightful things for our benefit, exceeding bare necessity, that we might enjoy them thankfully.[264]

How we should properly use this present life

Calvin lays down several rules to guide our proper use of this life. First, we must hold this life loosely.[265] As pilgrims we "should not be too much at home upon this earth,"[266] remembering that God may always take it away.[267] Second, we are to use things in this life according to our vocation,[268] which requires using them moderately for their intended design.[269] "The Lord bids each one of us in all life's actions to look to his calling."[270] What is moderate for a prince would be indulgence for a pauper.[271] As we look to our calling we may enjoy good food and drink, moderately,[272] for our body's health and our soul's delight.[273] Third, we are to use this world as accountable stewards in order to meet

---

[254] *Institutes* 3.10.2.
[255] Wallace, *Christian Life*, 131.
[256] Lobstein, *Die Ethik Calvins*, 139.
[257] Tamburello, *Union with Christ*, 15.
[258] Battles, *Interpreting Calvin*, 152-54.
[259] *Commentary*, Gen. 4:20.
[260] Lobstein, *Die Ethik Calvins*, 109.
[261] *Commentary*, Ps. 25:13.
[262] Wallace, *Christian Life*, 138.
[263] *Commentary*, John 12:25. This is contra Shin, who claimed that Calvin relatively neglected the present life, Shin, "Calvin's Theology of Holiness," 75.
[264] *Institutes* 3.10.2. Cf. Wallace, *Christian Life*, 137-38.
[265] *Institutes* 3.10.4. Cf. *Commentary*, John 12:25.
[266] Wallace, *Christian Life*, 134.
[267] Wallace, *Christian Life*, 126-27.
[268] *Institutes* 3.10.1; *Commentary*, Gen. 2:15; Jonah 3:1, 4:2.
[269] Zachman, "Deny Yourself," 480.
[270] *Institutes* 3.10.6.
[271] *Institutes* 3.10.4, 3.10.6.
[272] *Institutes* 3.10.3.
[273] *Commentary*, John 4:32.

the needs of others.[274] "Let him have pity and compassion on those in need, in order to help them."[275] This charity includes the sharing of one's material[276] and spiritual[277] resources to help others, for true holiness is lived out in family and community.[278]

How use of this present life works in the process of sanctification
A cursory reading of Calvin's call to moderation produces the sense of a man fearful of excess. A more careful understanding finds in Calvin's call to moderation his essential paradigm for living by faith and repentance. "The chief virtue of the faithful is moderation."[279] The right use of this present life becomes the training ground in which God teaches us, and we practice, a humble, prostrating moderation within our calling.[280] God helps us by bringing periods of material dryness—an enforced moderation[281]—to bring us low before him in repentance.[282] As we are humbled in our moderation,[283] God meets us and helps us let go of the world even more.[284]

The right use of this present life is an exercise in faith, only possible for the faithful.[285] They reverently look to God for, and serve him with, all the blessings in this life.[286] The ungodly may glut themselves like pigs, but they are never satisfied in their souls, for they do not know God's fatherly love.[287] It is only faith that allows us to submit to our vocation and puts an end to craving for the world's goods,[288] knowing that we may rest in God's providence.[289] "If a man knows to make use of present abundance in a sober and temperate manner, with thanksgiving, prepared to part with everything whenever it may be the good pleasure of the Lord, giving also a share to his brother, according to the measure of his ability, and is also not puffed up, that man has learned to *excel*, and to *abound*."[290]

---

[274] *Institutes* 3.10.5.
[275] *Sermons on Micah*, 146.
[276] *Commentary*, Ps. 23:5.
[277] *Commentary*, Rom. 12:4.
[278] Lobstein, *Die Ethik Calvins*, 104-05. Cf. Shin, "Calvin's Theology of Holiness," 40.
[279] *Commentary*, Rom. 12:16.
[280] *Sermons on Micah*, 71.
[281] Wallace, *Christian Life*, 132, note 4.
[282] *Commentary*, Ps. 25:13.
[283] *Commentary*, Ps. 25:13.
[284] *Commentary*, Ps. 128:3.
[285] *Commentary*, Ps. 36:8.
[286] Wallace, *Christian Life*, 126.
[287] *Commentary*, Ps. 36:8.
[288] *Commentary*, John 3:27.
[289] *Sermons on Micah*, 71.
[290] *Commentary*, Phil. 4:12.

Implications for Calvin's model of sanctification

In the right use of this present life, God transforms his children into the true order for humanity: those who use this life moderately, thankfully and for others.[291] Here we discover another principle:

Principle 11: Present Life. Because God providentially guides all of life, therefore rightly use this present life to love others. God produces holiness as the believer practices the obedience of faith in the schoolroom of this daily life: enjoying life without lusting, being moderate within his vocation and benefiting others as a steward of his resources.

How the Life of the Christian Man Works Together

All four aspects of the life of the Christian work together as exercises in faith[292] and repentance,[293] contributing to growth in holiness.[294] "The doctrine of repentance containeth a rule of good life; it requireth the denial of ourselves, the mortifying of our flesh, and meditating upon the heavenly life."[295] Cross-bearing aids self-denial by forcing us beyond what we would voluntarily demand of our selves.[296] As we meditate on our "future blessedness," our hearts are given faith to endure even greater crosses here,[297] for crosses here "stir us up to meditation on the future life."[298] Both self-denial and meditation on the future life increase our satisfaction with, and thus moderate use of, this present life.[299] Calvin will freely associate these four aspects of the Christian life. "No man will indeed calmly and quietly submit to bear the cross, but he who has learnt to seek his happiness beyond this world."[300]

The Church

The church and sanctification

Calvin's view of sanctification, while intensely personal, was never individualistic but always looked to the "community of faith."[301] The church, the primary institution created by God to sanctify,[302] aids our sanctification as she provides the authoritative teaching of the Word, the sacraments[303] and discipline, by which Christ transforms us into his holy people. While each church has free-

---

[291] *Commentary*, Rom. 13:14.
[292] Leith, *Christian Life*, 76; Wallace, *Christian Life*, 92.
[293] *Institutes* 3.8.2, 3.9.4.
[294] Niesel, *Theology of Calvin*, 149; Lobstein, *Die Ethik Calvins*, 14.
[295] *Commentary*, Acts 20:21.
[296] Wallace, *Christian Life*, 74-75.
[297] Wendel, *Origins*, 252; *Commentary*, Rom. 8:25; 2 Cor. 4:17.
[298] Wallace, *Christian Life*, 89; *Institutes* 3.9.1.
[299] *Institutes* 3.10.4.
[300] *Commentary*, Rom.12:12.
[301] McKee, *Pastoral Piety*, 4.
[302] Niesel, *Theology of Calvin*, 185. Cf. Wendel, *Origins*, 292.
[303] *Institutes* 4.1.1.

Chapter 4 - The Life of the Christian Man within the Church

dom to establish its particular organization,[304] Christ's presence is especially realized within the church through the Gospel and sacraments,[305] the two marks whose presence shows that "a church of God exists."[306] However, the right use of the Word is the primary mark, without which there can be no church.[307] "We may discern which is the true Church of God, namely one that follows the pure truth."[308] Discipline, while not listed formally as a mark of the church, was, however, critical to Calvin's understanding of the work of the church. "There are three things on which the safety of the Church is founded and supported: doctrine, discipline, and the sacraments."[309]

God sanctifies his people within the church.[310] God first sanctifies his people by setting them apart[311] from the "degrading pollutions of the world" that they may then be joined to his church, the "holy and peculiar people of God."[312] The very gathering of a people for God as his holy people is the fulfillment of the plan of redemption which culminates finally in the heavenly church.[313] God continues to sanctify his people only as they are part of the church,[314] where he uniquely produces holiness among his elect.[315] The church, as our mother, is absolutely necessary for our growth in holiness, thus she must "keep us under her care and guidance" until death and glory.[316] As God gathers his people for biblical corporate worship,[317] which humbles them even as it exalts God,[318] God is present to transform them in holiness.[319] However, for participation in the church's life to be beneficial,[320] one must truly love the church[321] and should love her more than life,[322] submitting to her as unto the Lord, since he reigns as her head.[323]

Because the Christian cannot hope to grow in holiness outside the church, "it becomes his duty to adhere loyally to the visible Church."[324] Calvin did not

---

[304] *Commentary*, Acts 8:38; 1 Cor. 11:12.
[305] Parker, *Calvin's Thought*, 131.
[306] *Institutes* 4.1.9.
[307] *Institutes* 4.2.1.
[308] "Sermon on Dan. 8:1-7," *CO*, 41:482.
[309] Reid, *Treatises*, "Reply to Sadolet," 232.
[310] *Commentary*, 1 Cor. 11:17.
[311] Wallace, *Christian Life*, 203-205.
[312] *Commentary*, Ps. 16:3.
[313] *Commentary*, John 11:51.
[314] Wallace, *Christian Life*, 198.
[315] *Institutes* 4.1.20; Wallace, *Christian Life*, 197.
[316] *Institutes* 4.1.4.
[317] *Sermons on Micah*, 36.
[318] *Sermons on Micah*, 37-38.
[319] McKee, *Pastoral Piety*, 4.
[320] Wallace, *Christian Life*, 243.
[321] *Commentary*, Ps. 102:3.
[322] Wallace, *Christian Life*, 248.
[323] Wallace, *Christian Life*, 195; *Sermons on Micah*, 207.
[324] Wallace, *Christian Life*, 232.

take schism lightly, warning against it by the monk's bad example[325] and maintaining that one should only depart from the church when she was, in effect, no longer the church, having abandoned God's Word.[326] Calvin therefore felt it necessary to defend his break from Rome, making himself the faithful soldier who, seeing the troops scattered, raises "the leader's standard, and recalls them to their posts."[327] He encouraged his fellow pastors to remain in the Genevan Church after he was cast out, so as not to harm the unity of the church.[328] For her health and witness, and for ours, we must not abandon the church.[329] Hence we find another principle:

> **Principle 12: Church. Because God sanctifies his church, therefore engage fully in the life of church.** The believer is sanctified by Christ only as he fully participates in the life of the church, in its preaching of the Word, its right administration of the sacraments and its shepherding through discipline.

The church provides feeding on God's Word

The church will nurture us by feeding us on the Word, "a live and efficacious force,"[330] which she has uniquely been given in order to teach her children[331] as they are gathered corporately.[332] The authoritative ministers of the church preach the Word,[333] with the power of the Holy Spirit,[334] such that her members advance in faith, "solely by outward preaching."[335]

Because the preaching of the Word is so vital for the Christian life, Calvin has clear duties for both hearer and preacher. The hearer, understanding that his private reading by itself is inadequate for holiness[336] and may lead to error, must attend public preaching to be conformed to God's truth.[337] He must receive the sermon as the Word of God,[338] even from flawed pastors,[339] and must apply it to himself deeply to change mind and heart.[340] Pastors must constantly provide preaching to give the flock "their proper food."[341] They must preach

---

[325] Steinmetz, *Context*, 194. In *Institutes* 4.13.14, Calvin calls monks a "conventicle of schismatics."
[326] *CO* 10:310, Letter of Calvin to Antonio Pignaeo, Jan. 1539.
[327] *CSW*, Vol. 1, 58-59, "Reply to Sadolet."
[328] Niesel, *Theology of Calvin*, 196.
[329] Wallace, *Christian Life*, 237-38.
[330] Niesel, *Theology of Calvin*, 183.
[331] *Institutes* 4.1.1.
[332] *Sermons on the Ten Commandments*, 268-69.
[333] Barth, *Theology of Calvin*, 198.
[334] Calvin, *BLW*, 33.
[335] *Institutes* 4.1.5.
[336] Wallace, *Christian Life*, 244.
[337] *Institutes* 4.1.5.
[338] Ganoczy, *Young Calvin*, 193; *Institutes* 4.3.3.
[339] *Sermons on 2 Samuel*, 122.
[340] Wallace, *Christian Life*, 219.
[341] *CO* 9:819, "Preface to New Testament."

Chapter 4 - The Life of the Christian Man within the Church

only from the Word and focus on the love of God in Christ[342] to be "faithful stewards of God's Word."[343]

The Word, preached faithfully and received humbly, is quickened by the Holy Spirit to transform believers by giving them more faith by which they embrace Christ[344] and his kingship,[345] and thus they are conformed more to his image.[346] "It is [Christ] who must rule over us and in us, in order that by his teaching our lives might conform to his Father's will for us."[347] Since we must receive the preached Word to grow holy, "everyone is to be present at the Sermon when the prayer is begun…everyone is to pay attention during Sermon."[348] We see here clearly reinforced our aforementioned Principle 2 on the necessity of submitting to Bible preaching.

The church provides the sacraments

The Sacraments as a means of grace are "instruments of the Spirit whereby God sanctifies us."[349] Sacraments, the visible Word,[350] united with the spoken Word[351] and faith in the believer,[352] set Christ before us such that we receive his power[353] for sanctification.[354] By increasing our faith in Christ,[355] the sacraments unite us more fully with Christ,[356] who transforms us by union with him through the Holy Spirit.[357]

The sacraments wrongly used, rather than helping us in holiness, are defiled by our pollution.[358] Calvin, therefore, set out to correct Rome's *ex opere operato* view.[359] Denying that the Lord's Supper was a literal sacrifice which contained inherent power,[360] he argued it was effective only by God's appointment[361] and only for those who had faith to feed upon Christ.[362] He said to re-

---

[342] *Sermons on Galatians*, 313.
[343] *Sermons on the Ten Commandments*, 269.
[344] *Commentary*, 1 John 3:23.
[345] Ganoczy, *Young Calvin*, 192.
[346] *Commentary*, John 13:10.
[347] *Sermons on Micah*, 136.
[348] Reid, *Treatises*, 77, "Ordinances for the Supervision of Churches in the Country," 1547.
[349] *Commentary*, Lev. 16:16.
[350] Gerrish, *Eucharistic Theology*, 108; *Institutes* 4.17.3.
[351] Niesel, *Theology of Calvin*, 213.
[352] Wallace, *Christian Life*, 208.
[353] Niesel, *Theology of Calvin*, 221.
[354] Parker, *Calvin's Thought*, 157.
[355] *Institutes* 3.1.3, 4.14.9.
[356] Gerrish, *Eucharistic Theology*, 73; *Institutes* 4.14.16; Niesel, *Theology of Calvin*, 219.
[357] *Institutes* 4.14.7; Niesel, *Theology of Calvin*, 217.
[358] *Commentary*, Lev. 16:16.
[359] Steinmetz, *Context*, 72; Reid, *Treatises*, 205, "Necessity of Reforming the Church," 1543; Reid, *Treatises*, 282-85, "Partaking of the Flesh and Blood."
[360] Reid, *Treatises*, 203-04, "Necessity of Reforming the Church," 1543.
[361] Niesel, *Theology of Calvin*, 194.

ceive the sacrament worthily, one is required only to come aware of their unworthiness,[363] rather than attempting to make the full penance of Rome.[364]

Baptism unites us to the death and resurrection of Christ by faith, such that our sins are mortified and our spirit is given life as our faith is increased, "just as the twig draws substance and nourishment from the root to which it is grafted."[365] This union with Christ increases our faith by confirming our place in Christ[366] and by assuring us our sin no longer dominates us. It is vanquished by Christ and not sacramental water,[367] awaiting the day of its complete destruction.[368]

Through the Lord's Supper, we partake of the real body and blood of Christ, spiritually.[369] The Holy Spirit, through faith, unites us spiritually to Christ's humanity, his flesh,[370] but not such that our flesh is commingled with his.[371] It is as we are united to Christ's human nature that we benefit from him.[372] Therefore, as we are united to Christ's humanity more fully through the Lord's Supper,[373] Christ increasingly communicates his vivifying life to us.[374] "While [Christ] alone has life in himself, he shows how we may enjoy it, that is, by *eating his flesh.*"[375]

How the sacraments work in the process of sanctification
The sacraments, rightly offered by the church for those within the church, are effective for our sanctification[376] by bringing Christ[377] to us through the work of the Holy Spirit[378] and the Word.[379] United to Christ by faith, his life is powerful to transform us, giving us more faith and holiness.[380] The sacraments also serve as an exhortation,[381] which excites an internal desire for more holiness as

---

[362] *Institutes* 4.14.7.
[363] *Institutes* 4.17.42.
[364] Reid, *Treatises*, 152, "Treatise on the Lord's Supper," 1541.
[365] *Institutes* 4.15.5.
[366] *Institutes* 4.15.6.
[367] *Commentary*, 1 John 5:16.
[368] *Institutes* 4.15.11.
[369] Gerrish, *Eucharistic Theology*, 126-27; *Commentary*, 1 Cor. 11:24.
[370] *Commentary*, Matt. 26:26; John 6:56.
[371] *Commentary*, 1 Cor. 11:24.
[372] Winecoff, "Mortification," 86; *Commentary*, John 6:51.
[373] Gerrish, *Eucharistic Theology*, 134.
[374] Parker, *Calvin's Thought*, 156
[375] *Commentary*, John 6:56.
[376] *Commentary*, Rom. 2:25.
[377] Wendel, *Origins*, 342.
[378] Niesel, *Theology of Calvin*, 223.
[379] *Commentary*, John 20:22.
[380] *Commentary*, Gen. 17:9; Reid, *Treatises*, 141, 152-53, "Treatise on the Lord's Supper," 1541; Reid, *Treatises*, 267, "Partaking of the Flesh and Blood."
[381] *Institutes* 4.17.38.

the life of Christ is given to us in new portions.[382] Here we find another principle from Calvin's theology of progressive sanctification:

Principle 13: Sacraments. Because God offers grace sacramentally, therefore commune regularly with Christ through the sacraments. The sacraments, properly administered and worthily received, communicate the grace of Christ, which actually puts to death sin and engenders faith, by which Christ is received more and more.

The church provides discipline and pastoral care

Calvin's movement was a reformation of pastoral care

The church helps our holiness through her pastoral care and discipline.[383] "Discipline is like…a spur to arouse those of little inclination; and also sometimes like a father's rod to chastise mildly…those who have more seriously lapsed.[384] Calvin advocated a reformation of pastoral care,[385] not for the sake of strictness but in the pursuit of holiness.[386] Since sin blinds us first to our own sin, we need the church community,[387] under holy leaders,[388] to show us our failings,[389] and pointing us to Christ, help us to grow in holiness.[390]

The idea of close pastoral care had been suggested to Calvin by predecessors such as Seneca,[391] Gregory the Great, who called it the "art of arts,"[392] and by John Oecolampadius,[393] whom Calvin had watched mobilize elders as shepherds in Basel. Likely it was in Strasbourg, where Bucer put into practice his *Concerning the True Care of Souls*, that Calvin found his pattern for Geneva,[394] including the distinct roles of church and state for moral oversight.[395]

The church has been given a unique judicial authority[396] to discipline the life and doctrine of her members[397] as a kind of spiritual police,[398] much as the police and courts govern the world.[399] The power to purify her people, ulti-

---

[382] Reid, *Treatises*, 149, "Treatise on the Lord's Supper," 1541.
[383] Wendel, *Origins*, 298.
[384] *Institutes* 4.12.1.
[385] Wallace, *Calvin and Geneva*, 169.
[386] Niesel, *Theology of Calvin*, 73.
[387] Wallace, *Christian Life*, 233-36.
[388] Ganoczy, *Young Calvin*, 228.
[389] Wallace, *Christian Life*, 196-97; *Commentary*, 1 Cor. 12:12.
[390] *Commentary*, 1 Cor. 12:11.
[391] "It is therefore indispensable that we be admonished." L.A. Seneca, *Moral Epistles* (tr. R.M. Gummere; Cambridge, Mass.: Harvard University Press, 1917-25), 3:48-49; Epistle 94, 59.
[392] Gregory the Great, *Pastoral Care*, 21.
[393] Ganoczy, *Young Calvin*, 91-92.
[394] H.J. Selderhuis, *John Calvin, A Pilgrim's Life* (Downers Grove, Ill.: InterVarsity, 2009), 89.
[395] Wendel, *Origins*, 65.
[396] Lobstein, *Die Ethik Calvins*, 123.
[397] Parker, *Calvin's Thought*, 140-41.
[398] *Institutes* 4.11.1.
[399] Wendel, *Origins*, 308.

mately expressed in excommunication,[400] is a responsibility that the church must fulfill or face correction herself.[401] The church's standard of discipline is the Word of God, such that she may discipline no further, nor less than, it directs.[402] The purpose of church discipline was threefold: upholding the glory of God, maintaining the peace and purity of the church and wherever possible, to call the wayward back to repentance and holiness.[403]

How pastoral care and discipline were exercised
Calvin's program of pastoral care began with the Word preached, continued with the use of elders to check on conformity to the Word in life and doctrine and culminated with the Consistory, which enforced the Word in the life of those who refused the milder warnings.[404] The teaching of the Word, in church and from house to house,[405] was the foundation of pastoral care, laying out the demands of the law, explaining how the congregation had failed to meet those demands and pointing them to Christ for help toward new obedience.[406]

Within Geneva 12 men, by 1541 called "elders,"[407] chosen from the various councils, were assigned to watch over their flocks in each quarter[408] and to "admonish amicably those whom they see to be erring."[409] They checked on the people regularly, particularly in preparation for the quarterly Lord's Supper,[410] gently recalling the sinner to Christ with "no rigor by which anyone may be injured."[411] It was as the elders sat together with the pastors of the city, each Thursday morning in the *Consistoire*, that they served as the collective moral governors of the city, in subordination to the city councils.[412] Exercising the authority of the keys of the kingdom,[413] they pronounced God's judgment on sin within the church to purify her.[414] Serious about discipline the Consistory was busy, for example, handling 556 cases in 1557,[415] or nearly four percent of the entire population of Geneva.[416]

---

[400] Barth, *Theology of Calvin*, 185; Reid, *Treatises*, 51, "Articles Concerning the Organization of the Church," 1537.
[401] *Commentary*, 1 Cor. 5:2.
[402] Parker, *Calvin's Thought*, 141; *Institutes* 4.12.9.
[403] *Institutes* 4.12.5.
[404] *Institutes* 4.1.22.
[405] Lobstein, *Die Ethik Calvins*, 126.
[406] *Institutes* 4.1.5; Niesel, *Theology of Calvin*, 197.
[407] Battles, *Interpreting Calvin*, 323.
[408] Reid, *Treatises*, 52, "Articles Concerning the Organization of the Church," 1537.
[409] Reid, *Treatises*, 63, "Ecclesiastical Ordinances," 1541.
[410] Reid, *Treatises*, 66, "Ecclesiastical Ordinances," 1541.
[411] Reid, *Treatises*, 71, "Ecclesiastical Ordinances," 1541. Cf. Wendel, *Origins*, 78.
[412] Reid, *Treatises*, 70, "Ecclesiastical Ordinances," 1541.
[413] *Institutes* 4.11.1.
[414] Wallace, *Christian Life*, 198.
[415] J. Witte, Jr. and R.M. Kingdon, *Sex, Marriage, and Family in John Calvin's Geneva: Courtship, Engagement, and Marriage* (Grand Rapids, Mich.: Eerdmans, 2005), 75-76.
[416] Assuming roughly 15,000 residents, Selderhuis, *Pilgrim Life*, 58.

The pastors were subject to discipline as well. Four times per year the Company of Pastors used their meeting to examine their own lives and doctrine.[417] Held to a higher standard than the laity, the pastors would admonish one another to repentance.[418] Failing repentance they would suspend the recalcitrant from the Lord's Supper and report him to the magistrate.[419]

Individual Christians, in many ways true ministers,[420] were expected to provide pastoral care as well, first by their example[421] and then by watching for sin or bad doctrine in one another's lives.[422] Finding failure they were to offer corrections in accord with Matthew 18.[423] This correction was to be offered humbly, having first removed the log from one's eye, and gently, so as to not discourage the offender but "retrieve them from the road of perdition."[424] Only if gentle rebuke failed should one attempt to wake the sinner from their slumber with "great hammer blows."[425]

How pastoral care and discipline work in the process of sanctification
Pastoral care is yet another call to faith and repentance. The discipline of the church, which we all need,[426] forces us to turn from our sins,[427] which we see only with help,[428] to Christ, believing he alone can sanctify.[429] Brought to repentance in the midst of the church, we turn to Christ, who in grace[430] forgives and builds up the penitent,[431] leading to new obedience.[432] Another principle emerges from these observations:

Principle 14: Church Discipline. Because God shepherds us through his leaders, therefore seek pastoral care and church discipline. Church discipline and pastoral care, when received in submission, confront the believer with particular sins to which he is blind and leads him toward the cure of Christ.

Here we have seen that for Calvin one cannot hope to grow in holiness apart from full participation in the life of the church. For churches to be effective, however, they must have good pastors. In Chapter 5 we will see Calvin's understanding of the true pastor.

---

[417] T.H.L. Parker, *John Calvin, a Biography* (Philadelphia, Pa.: Westminster, 1975), 89; Reid, *Treatises*, 61, "Ecclesiastical Ordinances," 1541.
[418] Reid, *Treatises*, 61, "Ecclesiastical Ordinances," 1541.
[419] Reid, *Treatises*, 70, "Ecclesiastical Ordinances," 1541.
[420] Ganoczy, *Young Calvin*, 218-19.
[421] *Sermons on Micah*, 12.
[422] *Commentary*, 1 John 4:1.
[423] *Institutes* 4.12.1.
[424] *Sermons on the Ten Commandments*, 208.
[425] *Sermons on the Ten Commandments*, 213.
[426] Wallace, *Christian Life*, 246-47.
[427] *Institutes* 4.12.1.
[428] *Institutes* 4.12.5.
[429] Wallace, *Christian Life*, 243.
[430] *Institutes* 3.3.20.
[431] *Sermons on 2 Samuel*, 562; *Institutes* 4.12.1.
[432] Lobstein, *Die Ethik Calvins*, 129.

Chapter 5 - The Model of the Pious Pastor

"Donnez-moi du bois, et je vous envoie des flèches."[1]

Introduction

While more attention has been given through the years to Calvin's effort to reform medieval Roman Catholic theology, increasingly Calvin's passion to reform the Roman priesthood by institutionalizing the development of Reformed pastors in the Genevan Academy has gained study. Ganoczy understood Calvin's passion: "It seems that Calvin is thinking more or less explicitly of a solution through new leadership."[2] As Calvin gazed upon the landscape of sixteenth-century Europe, he saw the crying need for pastors, pious and well-trained. "You can hardly be persuaded how great is the scarcity of ministers, considering the multitude of churches who need pastors."[3] From nearly his first to his last editions of the *Institutes*, Calvin named as his chief goal the instruction of future pastors.[4] "It has been my purpose in this labor to prepare and instruct candidates in sacred theology for the reading of the divine Word."[5]

Yet as Calvin surveyed the scene, he realized that the great Roman training centers, with their deeply flawed theology,[6] such as the Sorbonne, would never produce the kind of pastors which he saw described in Scripture and embodied by many of the Church Fathers.[7] Calvin had the vision of reforming pastoral training with the creation of an academy at least from 1541, when he returned to Geneva, fresh from teaching at the Academy of Strasbourg.[8] It would not be until 1559, however, that his vision came into being with the establishment of the Genevan Academy. At the Academy Calvin hoped to raise up a new breed of pastors, who, unlike their Roman counterparts, were marked with *pietas*. Calvin would regularly pray as he began his lectures to the students of the Academy, "May the Lord give us so to wrestle with the secrets of his heavenly wisdom that our piety truly progresses to his glory and our edification."[9] His prayers, as we shall see, were largely answered.

To understand what Calvin was trying to accomplish at the Academy, we must understand the kind of pastor he meant to produce. For Calvin the Reformed pastorate did not simply spring from the pages of the Bible but rather

---

[1] Kingdon, *Wars of Religion*, Preface, "Calvin to the churches of France."
[2] Ganoczy, *Young Calvin*, 228.
[3] *CO* 10b:64, Calvin to François Daniel, Oct. 13, 1536.
[4] *CO* 1:256, Introduction to 1539 *Institutes*, where Calvin calls the students the "sacrae theologiae candidatos." Cf. Muller, *Unaccommodated*, 141.
[5] Preface to the 1559 *Institutes*, 4.
[6] Muller, *Unaccommodated*, 50-52.
[7] *Institutes* 2.3.13.
[8] Reid, *Treatises*, 63, "Ecclesiastical Ordinances," 1541.
[9] *CO* 37:463.

formed in his mind over against the failings of the Roman clergy[10] and was informed by the Church Fathers as well.[11] Calvin's standard was as clear as it was simple: a real pastor, a pious one, must have a true call from God and faithfully follow that call. "There are two things necessary to prove a person to be [a true minister]—a divine call, and faithfulness."[12]

We will show in this entire second section of the book that Calvin's theology of sanctification, highlighted in the fourteen principles from Section One, was not checked at the door of the Academy but rather was built into its warp and woof, in its teaching and structures.[13]

In this chapter we will argue that Calvin's very model of a pious pastor, understood in the context of his theology of sanctification, served both to call and to lead the students to higher levels of holiness as pastors. The basic dynamics of Calvin's understanding of sanctification are necessarily magnified in the life of pastors, who were compelled to a clearer double-knowledge of their own sin and God's greatness. They were compelled to see their own sin, for they were held to a higher standard of holiness, had their motives dissected more regularly, were supervised more closely and disciplined more severely. They were compelled to see God's greatness as they relied on him to achieve any effectiveness in preaching, shepherding and administering the sacraments. Calvin's model of a pious pastor ultimately produced a pastor that was both bolder and more humble than his Roman counterpart. He was more humble regarding himself, because he would see the incredibly high standard for a Reformed pastor. He was bolder regarding God's Word, for he would see God's wisdom in preaching. This ideal was seen in Calvin himself. "The apprehensive Calvin, who still regarded himself as a shy schoolboy, was the fearless preacher of grace at the same time!"[14]

The High Standard of a True Call Led Pastors to Holiness

The high view of the role of pastor enhanced holiness
Setting aside the extraordinary offices of apostle, evangelist and prophet,[15] Calvin taught that there were four offices in the church: pastor, teacher, elder and

---

[10] Reid, *Treatises*, 240, "Reply to Sadolet."
[11] Reid, *Treatises*, 206, "Necessity of Reforming the Church."
[12] *Commentary*, Jer. 23:21. Cf. *Commentary*, Jer. 18:18; John 5:43; 1 Cor. 1:1; *Institutes* 4.3.10; *Sermons on Micah*, 157.
[13] Sources for Calvin's instruction to the students of the Academy include his lectures on Daniel, Jeremiah, Lamentations and Ezekiel, as well as sermons (regularly attended by students) delivered on the Gospels, Genesis, 1 and 2 Samuel, and 1 and 2 Kings. T.H.L. Parker, *The Oracles of God* (Cambridge: James Clarke, 2002), 162; T.H.L. Parker, *Calvin's Old Testament Commentaries* (Louisville, Ky.: Westminster/John Knox, 1986), 29.
[14] W. van 't Spijker, "Calvin's Friendship with Martin Bucer: Did it Make Calvin a Calvinist?" *Calvin and Spirituality, Calvin and His Contemporaries, Calvin Studies Society Papers, 1995, 1997* (Grand Rapids, Mich.: CRC Product Services, 1998), 183.
[15] *Institutes* 4.2.4.

deacon,[16] or three if one conflates pastor and teacher as two types of presbyter, as Calvin sometimes did.[17] Calvin will focus his efforts primarily on the office of the pastor[18] because of its central role in building the church from the Word of God.[19] The pastor represents God on earth by speaking God's Word authoritatively to his people,[20] something personal Bible reading cannot do.[21] The pulpit is therefore "the seat of God from which he wants to govern our souls."[22] Hence, the church must meekly receive the Word preached by pastors,[23] for to reject it is to reject God.[24] Because the pastor speaks *for* the Father, we are to regard him *as* a father to be respected in and outside of the pulpit.[25] God chooses to speak to us through other humans, not because he is incapable of speaking directly to us, but because we would be annihilated by the majesty of God.[26] "God accommodates himself to our lowliness and weakness."[27] The pastoral ministry itself is the end of a lengthy process of God's accommodation, which moves from creation, to Scripture, to Christ, to pastor and culminates in the sermon and sacrament, which finally we may receive.[28]

The pastor's role was more than preaching, however. While Calvin will maintain two marks of the church, Word and sacrament, when it comes to defining the duties of a pastors, Calvin, following Bucer, would add to the duties of preaching and administering the sacraments a third duty: discipline.[29] Calvin defines discipline as one duty which separates "teachers" from "pastors."[30] The true pastor is "to instruct the people to true godliness, to administer the sacred mysteries and to keep and exercise upright discipline."[31] Though Calvin may at

---

[16] *Institutes* 4.3.4.
[17] *Institutes* 4.4.1; Reid, *Treatises*, 58, "Ecclesiastical Ordinances," 1541; cf. Niesel, *Theology of Calvin*, 202; Parker, *Calvin's Thought*, 136.
[18] I. Backus, "Calvin's Patristic Models," 28-31; cf. *Institutes* 4.3.8, Calvin will call pastors interchangeably bishops, presbyters or ministers.
[19] Parker, *Calvin's Thought*, 136.
[20] *Institutes* 4.1.5; *Commentary*, Jer. 43:10; 50:2. Cf. Selderhuis, *Pilgrim Life*, 110.
[21] *Sermons on the Ten Commandments*, 252.
[22] "Sermon on 1 Tim. 5:17-20," *CO* 53:520.
[23] *Sermons on Micah*, 158.
[24] *Sermons on the Ten Commandments*, 261-62.
[25] *CSW*, Vol. 4, 144, Calvin to the Church of Geneva, June 25, 1539, *CO* 10b:352; cf. *Commentary*, 1 Thess. 5:12.
[26] *Sermons on the Ten Commandments*, 259.
[27] *Sermons on the Ten Commandments*, 257; cf. *Institutes* 4.1.1.
[28] L. Carrington, "Calvin and Erasmus on Pastoral Formation," *Calvin and the Company of Pastors, Calvin Studies Society Papers 2003* (Grand Rapids, Mich.: CRC Product Services, 2004), 142-43.
[29] M. Bucer, *Praelectiones doctiis, in epistolam D. P. ad Ephesios* (Basel: Peter Perna, 1562), 107: "Truly there are three kinds of ministries: of teaching, of sacraments, and of discipline." Cf. Holder, "Exegetical Understanding," 181; McKee, *Elders and the Plural Ministry*, 25.
[30] *Institutes* 4.3.4.
[31] *Institutes* 4.3.6.

times have subsumed discipline under the role of teaching to individuals,[32] as in the annual pastoral home visit,[33] pastors were required to "enjoin brotherly corrections,"[34] to know their flock[35] and grieve over the sins of individuals,[36] all functions of pastoral care and discipline.

All three duties of the pastor had one core purpose: to build up the church. Preaching "is the edification of the Church."[37] The right administration of the sacraments was to nourish and protect the church, lest the Supper be "profaned by being administered indiscriminately."[38] Disciplining the morals of the church was necessary in order to build up the church as the holy bride of Christ.[39] The pastor was therefore central to the life and health of the church. "Thus the renewal of the saints is accomplished; thus the body of Christ is built up."[40]

This lofty understanding of the role of pastor as mouthpiece of God and builder of the Church of God would have a sanctifying effect. Men, realizing they were unworthy, would be humbled by a true call to such a lofty role (Principle 1, Two-fold Knowledge and Response). "We know that the whole authority belongs entirely to God, with regard to the doctrine of religion, and that it is not in the power of men to blend this or that, and to make the faithful subject to themselves. As God, then, is the only true teacher of the Church, whosoever demands to be heard, must prove that he is God's minister."[41] At the same time, pastors must look upward to God for the ability to fulfill such a high calling (Principle 4, Rely on God). "There are peculiar endowments required for the prophetic, the apostolic, and the pastoral office, which are not in the power or at the will of men. We hence see that the hidden call of God is ever necessary, in order that any one may become a prophet, or an apostle, or a pastor."[42]

The true call from God enhanced holiness

Calvin requires that a man be truly called by God[43] for one simple reason: no man is qualified by any human ability to serve as a pastor, a spokesman for God.[44] He must be called of God and come not only by his own choosing,[45] as do the Roman priests, who "boast themselves to be the successors of the Apos-

---

[32] *Institutes* 4.3.6.
[33] *CO* 18:236, Calvin's letter to Olevianus, Nov. 1560; cf. Selderhuis, *Pilgrim Life*, 249.
[34] Reid, *Treatises*, 58, "Ecclesiastical Ordinances," 1541.
[35] *Sermons on 2 Samuel*, 177.
[36] *Commentary*, 2 Cor. 12:21.
[37] *Commentary*, 1 Thess. 5:12.
[38] *Institutes* 4.12.5.
[39] Reid, *Treatises*, 58, "Ecclesiastical Ordinances," 1541.
[40] *Institutes* 4.3.2.
[41] *Commentary*, Jer. 1:2.
[42] *Commentary*, Jer. 23:21.
[43] *Commentary*, Jer. 26:2.
[44] *Commentary*, Jer. 25:4; John 20:22.
[45] *Commentary*, Ezek. 2:3.

tles."[46] Self-appointed leaders are unworthy. "We ought boldly to reject all who exalt themselves."[47]

A true call has two aspects, external and internal.[48] Externally the church must recognize God's calling and gifting of the minister. This external calling produces holy pastors by screening out those sinfully pursuing the office (Principle 14, Church Discipline). However, a true call usually starts internally, in the heart of the one called, and is testified to by a clear conscience, which knows itself moved not by "ambition and avarice" but by God.[49] The discernment of this internal call was an important aid to pastoral holiness, requiring the *descensus in se* to discern one's motives, which naturally led to repentance and holiness (Principle 7, Repentance).

The true call from the church enhanced holiness

The true call of God, while it originates with God and not humankind, must be confirmed externally by the church, both in the "approval of the people"[50] and in the approval of the other pastors in cooperation.[51] Usually the Company of Pastors had the principal role in calling,[52] nominating a candidate who would be approved by the Council and finally gain congregational assent.[53] If the Company did not concur with the Council, the question of call remained open, and in one notable case, that of François Bourgoin in 1552, went in favor of the Company.[54] It is necessary to have the church legitimize the call so that "noisy and troublesome men" do not grab for office.[55] For the church to discern if a man is truly called requires that the man must be examined by proper biblical criteria,[56] sound doctrine and a holy life,[57] to see if God has supplied the necessary gifts for the office of pastor.[58] Since God will always supply pastoral gifts to those whom he calls,[59] the presence of those gifts serves as an indication of a possible call; while if a man lacks those gifts, he cannot be called.[60]

---

[46] *Commentary*, Rom. 1:1.
[47] *Commentary*, John 5:43.
[48] *Commentary*, Jer. 14:14.
[49] Parker, *Calvin's Thought*, 138; *Commentary*, Jer. 43:3.
[50] *Institutes* 4.3.15.
[51] Niesel, *Theology of Calvin*, 204; *Commentary*, Jer. 29:31.
[52] Flaming, "The Apostolic and Pastoral Office," 167.
[53] Reid, *Treatises*, 59, "Ecclesiastical Ordinances," 1541; cf. Bouwsma, *Sixteenth-Century Portrait*, 226.
[54] Carrington, "Calvin and Erasmus," 159-60; cf. *RCP*, 189: "Bourgoin now informed the brethren that, as he had no testimony to this call other than the wish of the Messieurs, he could not vacate his present post to go to the country."
[55] *Institutes* 4.3.10.
[56] Reid, *Treatises*, 59, "Ecclesiastical Ordinances," 1541.
[57] *Institutes* 4.3.12; cf. Maag, "Education and Training," 135.
[58] Reid, *Treatises*, 207, "Necessity of Reforming the Church." Cf. *Commentary*, Jer. 28:15.
[59] *Commentary*, Ezek. 3:19; *Institutes* 4.3.11; Niesel, *Theology of Calvin*, 204.
[60] *Commentary*, John 20:22; Eph. 4:11.

Chapter 5 - The Model of the Pious Pastor

Woven into a true call was proper preparation, again under the direction of the Company of Pastors.[61] Calvin believed that a good pastor required thorough training, both to shape his character and to instruct his mind, in order to teach the Bible well.[62] "Learning joined with piety and the other gifts of the good pastor are a sort of preparation for it."[63] The training was intensive, requiring the mastery not only of biblical content, theology and languages, but erudition in reading, writing and speaking classical Latin as well.[64] Since this training was to be thorough it would take some time. Ideally young men were apprenticed by godly, well-trained pastors,[65] who were in good supply in Geneva[66] and who gave "sacred instruction and strict training."[67] Properly examined and trained, the truly called pastor was to be duly ordained by the other pastors,[68] as Calvin had learned from the Council of Nicea and Cyprian.[69]

The external call, with its examination, training and ordination, is an implementation of Calvin's understanding of communal sanctification (Principle 10). The close examination of a candidate's life and doctrine, with the inevitable exposure of some areas of weakness, led a candidate to new areas of humility, repentance and turning to Christ (Principle 7). The careful training in life and doctrine would be a fleshing out of Principle 2 (Bible Preaching). The true calling served as a form of the double-knowledge of God and self, bringing forth the two-fold response of prostration and reverence (Principle 1). It helped to humble a man to know that he was called, not based on any great quality in himself but by God's mercy.[70] At the same time, the true call rendered a man bold, not in himself, but in God's call[71] and God's Word.[72] "Strength shall never be wanting to God's servants, while they derive courage from the conviction that God himself is the author of their calling and become thus magnanimous;

---

[61] J.D. Small, "A Company of Pastors," *Calvin and the Company of Pastors, Calvin Studies Society Papers 2003* (Grand Rapids, Mich.: CRC Product Services, 2004), 11.
[62] Flaming, "The Apostolic and Pastoral Office," 163.
[63] *Institutes* 4.3.11.
[64] Kingdon, *Wars of Religion*, 14; cf. *Institutes* 4.3.12.
[65] K. Maag, "Preaching Practice: Reformed Students' Sermons," *The Formation of Clerical and Confessional Identities in Early Modern Europe* (eds. W. Janse, B. Pitkin; Leiden: Brill, 2005), 134-35.
[66] A.N. Burnett, "A Tale of Three Churches," *Calvin and the Company of Pastors, Calvin Studies Society Papers 2003* (Grand Rapids, Mich.: CRC Product Services, 2004), 118. Fully half of the Genevan pastors from 1536-1566 were educated beyond the norm.
[67] *Institutes* 4.4.9.
[68] Reid, *Treatises*, 58, "Ecclesiastical Ordinances," 1541; *Institutes* 4.19.28; *Commentary*, Acts 13:3.
[69] Backus, "Calvin's Patristic Models," 42-43.
[70] *Sermons on Micah*, 165.
[71] *Commentary*, Jonah 1:2.
[72] Wallace, *Christian Life*, 303.

for God will then supply them with strength and courage invincible, so as to render them formidable to the whole world."[73]

The High Standard of Pastoral Faithfulness Led to Holiness

The high standard of faithfulness

In addition to being truly called, Calvin believed that a pastor must also live out that call in faithfulness. To be faithful a pastor must be prompt in teaching the Word, careful in administering the sacrament, loving in shepherding the flock and personally holy. We may observe this emphasis on faithfulness by studying Calvin's direct practical applications to pastors as he lectured at the Academy. In one lecture series, the series on Jeremiah delivered between April 1560 and September 1562,[74] out of 84 specific applications to pastoral ministry we found 29 related to the personal holiness and faithfulness of the pastor.[75] Another 29 addressed the issue of preaching the Word faithfully.[76] This means that nearly 70 percent of his practical applications to his pastoral students in this two-year period had to do with faithfulness, demonstrating Calvin's concern for the development of faithful pastors.

Calvin set before his pastoral candidates an incredibly high standard of pastoral faithfulness as seen in the pastoral ordination vow:

> I promise and swear that in the Ministry to which I am called I will serve faithfully before God, setting forth purely his Word for the edification of this church to which he has bound me; that I will in no way abuse his doctrine to serve my carnal affections or to please any living man; but that I will employ it with pure conscience in the service of his glory and for the profit of his people to which I am a debtor.[77]

The pastor must give himself wholeheartedly to the ministry no matter his level of success,[78] not for personal gain but for God's glory, undistracted by other interests,[79] while leading a life of exemplary personal holiness.[80] Should he fail on any point, the pastor is held to a higher standard, accountable for the souls that perish due to his neglect,[81] for an unfaithful pastor destroys the church.[82] What person would ever think they could meet such an absurdly high standard

---

[73] *Commentary*, Jer. 1:17.
[74] Parker, *Old Testament Commentaries*, 29.
[75] *Commentary*, Jer. 1:2, 6, 7, 8, 10, 18; 3:15; 9:17; 11:19; 13:18; 15:10, 19, 21; 16:10; 17:16; 18:18; 23:1, 4, 11, 21; 25:9; 26:17; 34:9; 36:23; 37:14; 38:6; 42:5; 43:2-3.
[76] *Commentary*, Jer. 1:2, 9, 11, 17; 5:14, 31; 7:27; 9:6; 11:20; 14:14; 15:16, 19; 17:16-17; 19:2; 20:7; 23:10, 16; 26:2, 6, 7, 17, 19; 28:11; 29:10, 31; 32:3; 36:29; 43:10.
[77] Reid, *Treatises*, 72, "Ecclesiastical Ordinances," 1541.
[78] *Commentary*, Ezek. 2:3.
[79] *CSW*, Vol. 7, 270, Calvin to the Church of Lyons, May 13, 1562. Calvin castigates a pastor who has taken up arms.
[80] *Commentary*, 1 Cor. 4:2.
[81] *Institutes* 4.3.6.
[82] *Commentary*, Lam. 4:13.

Chapter 5 - The Model of the Pious Pastor

by human effort? Like the law of God,[83] the high standard for the pastor was never to be accommodated downward so they could fulfill its demands on their own power, rather the high pastoral standard was meant to drive them to seek God's grace. Calvin taught the students at the Academy that the work of the pastor was beyond human ability *precisely* so they would turn to Christ, depending on him for the power and authority to pastor aright.[84] "Scripture joins the power of Christ with the ministry of man; as, indeed, man is nothing else than the hand of Christ. Such modes of expression show, not what man can of himself accomplish, but what Christ performs by man, and by the sign, as his instruments."[85] Presented with such a high calling to faithfulness, Calvin's students would be encouraged to turn to God's grace (Principle 4). It is only inasmuch as the pastor in humility turns to and relies upon God's grace to make him able that he is faithful.[86] "By these words God exhorts his Prophet to prayer; for we know how dangerous is self-security to all the children of God, and especially to teachers."[87]

The high standard of faithful preaching enhanced holiness

The high standard of faithful preaching would create dependence on God
Calvin called pastors to such a high standard of preaching that it would have had the effect of sending them humbly to God for help. Pastors must be very knowledgeable of God's Word,[88] and they must also faithfully teach that Word to the church or risk being useless.[89] Calvin would often hold up the Roman clergy as failed preachers to warn his students. The priests, concerned about their benefices[90] and tied up in "the administration of cities," neglected the essential work of preaching.[91] When they did preach, they often preached wrongly, as false teachers.[92] Calvin's practice of using the Roman clergy as negative examples for his students would have had a sanctifying impact. Fearing such failure themselves, they would be driven to God for help to become faithful preachers.

There was only one proper source for faithful preaching—the Bible. "No one then ought to be deemed a sound teacher, but he who speaks from God's mouth."[93] The pastor must not share from his wisdom but only from God's Word.[94] Neither should the pastor substitute emotionalism for biblical content

---

[83] Battles, *Interpreting Calvin*, 134.
[84] *Commentary*, Jer. 17:16.
[85] *Commentary*, John 1:26; cf. *Commentary*, Jer. 2:33.
[86] *Commentary*, Jer. 3:15.
[87] *Commentary*, Jer. 15:20.
[88] *Commentary*, Jer. 26:16; 27:26.
[89] *Commentary*, 1 Thess. 5:12.
[90] *Institutes* 4.5.13.
[91] *Institutes* 4.11.9.
[92] *Commentary*, Jer. 5:31.
[93] *Commentary*, Jer. 23:16.
[94] *Sermons on the Ten Commandments*, 268-69; *Commentary*, Jer. 1:2.

in the vain effort to produce emotional responses in the hearers.[95] Any addition to the Word[96] or subtraction from it[97] would dilute or destroy its pure doctrine. The Word must be delivered whole and unpolluted, for amendment or abridgement places the pastor over it as judge.[98] "Those who are charged with proclaiming the Word of God should offer nothing except what they have received from God."[99]

Old or New Testament,[100] Calvin was clear as to the central biblical theme which must be preached: "To extol as much as possible the grace of Christ."[101] Calvin will so frequently repeat to his students the instruction to preach only from the Word of God that it could not have failed to find the mark.[102] "Ministers are to bring forward nothing but what they have learnt from God himself."[103]

Given such severe warnings and frequent exhortations to faithful preaching, pastors under Calvin's tutelage would have been humbled and led to Christ for help (Principle 4). They would not dare to speak relying on wit and wisdom, but with proper reverence, they would have trembled to do other than hold forth the pure Word of God,[104] which would also directly benefit them (Principle 2).

The goal of faithful preaching, making people holy, humbles pastors
The very goal of preaching, in Calvin's schema, was never just to impart information[105] but rather to increase the holiness of an individual.[106] Calvin was "convinced that the way to build up piety and restore the church was to open access to the fountains of pious doctrine."[107] Preaching is designed to mature the church, as the people partake of the heavenly doctrine,[108] sermon by sermon.[109] The sermon would impart "wisdom tempered with sobriety and discretion," which will "fortify us against all the snares of the devil."[110]

To aim at the holiness of the hearers, the pastor must understand sin in his congregation, not just superficially, for "the innermost recesses of the heart

---

[95] *Commentary*, Jer. 9:17.
[96] *Commentary*, Jer. 1:9; 1 Thess. 2:13; *Sermons on Micah*, 161.
[97] *Sermons on the Ten Commandments*, 267-68.
[98] *Sermons on the Ten Commandments*, 279.
[99] *Sermons on Micah*, 15.
[100] *Commentary*, Rom. 10:5.
[101] *Commentary*, 1 John 5:13; cf. Holder, "Exegetical Understanding," 195.
[102] *Commentary*, Jer. 1:9; 14:14; 15:17; 17:16; 26:2, 16, 19.
[103] *Commentary*, Jer. 19:2.
[104] *Sermons on Micah*, 165.
[105] *Commentary*, Ezek. 1:26.
[106] *Institutes* 1.14.4; *Commentary*, Jer. 51:56; Ezek. 3:20.
[107] R.C. Zachman, "Restoring Access to the Fountain: Melanchthon and Calvin on the Task of Evangelical Theology," *Calvin and Spirituality, Calvin and His Contemporaries, Calvin Studies Society Papers 1995, 1997* (Grand Rapids, Mich.: CRC Product Services, 1998), 205.
[108] *Institutes* 4.1.5.
[109] *Commentary*, 1 Thess. 3:9.
[110] *Commentary*, Ezek.1:26.

must be probed and searched."[111] The pastor must not only know sin but must zealously oppose it in the life of his congregation,[112] connecting with his hearers in such a way that they are brought to see the sin they do not want to see.[113] "For until a sinner knows his sinfulness, he will never really and from the heart return to God."[114] Made aware of their sin, the people were then to be urged toward repentance, however distasteful that might be to the human heart.[115] The call to repentance was never a mild one but must be "urgent on every occasion."[116] It was to be intense. "It is necessary to prick them sharply and even deeply to wound them,"[117] since "excitements are daily necessary to rouse us up."[118] Ultimately, the sermon is to lead the believer to Christ who sanctifies.[119]

Since the preacher's goal was to serve as an instrument of God to bring about holiness in his hearers, it would quickly be made apparent that the preacher must always rely on God,[120] not his ability, to achieve such an end.[121] "Those are *ministers* whose services God makes use of, not as though they could do anything by their own efforts, but in so far as they are guided by his hand, as instruments."[122] The pastor's preaching depends on God, for "he will have its success depend exclusively upon his blessing, that he may have the entire praise."[123] This dependence on God is not merely external, that is an additive to the words that come from the mouth of the pastor, but must come from within, as God feeds the heart of the pastor on His Word first. "God's servants ought to speak from the inmost affection of their heart."[124] Without this feeding from God, the preacher is useless; with it the preacher may perform "in real earnest the office committed to him…as a faithful and true minister of God."[125] Finally, the pastor must acknowledge his dependency on God formally, by requesting God's help in prayer after each sermon.[126] This dependence on God to make the preacher effective places the pastor in the proper relationship to God, one of dependent humility which recognizes one's inability (Principle 1).[127] The pastor must repose entirely and humbly in the hands of God so their confi-

---

[111] *Commentary*, Jer. 9:6.
[112] *Commentary*, Jer. 23.10; 1 Thess. 2:12.
[113] Holder, "Pastoral Model," 287.
[114] *Commentary*, Jer. 3:13.
[115] *Commentary*, Jer. 3:13.
[116] *Commentary*, Ezek. 3:18.
[117] *Commentary*, Jer. 3:13.
[118] *Commentary*, Ezek.13:9.
[119] D. DeVries, *Jesus Christ in the Preaching of Calvin and Schleiermacher* (Louisville, Ky.: Westminster/John Knox, 1996), 95.
[120] *Commentary*, Ezek. 11:5.
[121] *Commentary*, 1 Cor. 1:17.
[122] *Commentary*, 1 Cor. 3:5.
[123] *Commentary*, 1 Cor. 3:7.
[124] *Commentary*, Ezek. 3:3.
[125] *Commentary*, Jer. 15:16.
[126] *Commentary*, Acts 20:36.
[127] *Commentary*, 1 Cor. 9:1.

dence is not in "their own industry or virtue, but on the assistance of God."[128] Such repose places a pastor squarely into the hands of the only one who may transform him, bit by bit, into a truly faithful and holy pastor (Principle 4).

The weighty responsibility of faithful preaching would humble pastors
Faithful preaching was so powerful in Calvin's view that it carried with it an inhuman weight of responsibility. Preaching was seen to be the very word of life and death, by which individuals were either saved or condemned.[129] "The minister of the word is said in some way to save those whom he leads to the obedience of faith."[130] Since God uses faithful preaching to lead people to salvation,[131] faithful preaching is essential to the health of the church, the individual and the entire world.[132]

If the majesty of the preaching challenge did not humble a pastor then the penalty for failing to preach faithfully certainly must have. Calvin would repeatedly warn that pastors who fail to preach faithfully will be held accountable for the blood of their hearers[133] and serve as examples of God's harshness toward faithless shepherds.[134] With so much on the line, the salvation of souls, the health of the church, the Kingdom of God, with blood guilt in the balance, the pastor would likely be humbled, falling prostrate before God, even to consider mounting the steps into the pulpit (Principles 4 and 1).

The fact that people should listen to imperfect pastors humbles pastors
Calvin would emphasize the duty of parishioners to attend to the preaching of a pastor even though he might have visible flaws. "Those who think the authority of the Word is dragged down by the baseness of the men called to teach it disclose their own ungratefulness."[135] People must listen to the faithful pastor preach, despite a list of flaws that a pastor may have, such as imperfections in speaking,[136] some persistent ignorance[137] or even character flaws.[138]

However, while there is no perfect pastor, God's people must distinguish between the pastors who are "altogether blind" and those who are only "blind in part." The former are hirelings "and know nothing," while the "good and faithful Ministers," aware of their partial blindness, are yet useful to God.[139] The method of discernment is simple: the faithful pastor is the one who teaches only the Word of God.[140] Once a sound, though imperfect, preacher is found, we

---

[128] *Commentary*, 1 Tim. 3:1.
[129] *Commentary*, Jer. 5:14.
[130] *Commentary*, Rom. 11:14; cf. *Commentary*, Jas. 5:20; Jude 1:22.
[131] *Commentary*, Jer. 3:15; Rom. 10:17.
[132] *Commentary*, 1 Thess. 5:12.
[133] *Commentary*, Jer. 1:17; Ezek. 3:21.
[134] *Sermons on Micah*, 156-57.
[135] *Institutes* 4.1.5; *Commentary*, Ezek. 3:20.
[136] *Commentary*, Jer. 20:7.
[137] *Sermons on Election and Reprobation*, 252-53.
[138] *Sermons on 2 Samuel*, 122.
[139] *Sermons on Election and Reprobation*, 271.
[140] *Commentary*, Ezek. 2:8; Jer. 23:21.

Chapter 5 - The Model of the Pious Pastor

must submit to their teaching,[141] for rejecting it is tantamount to rejecting God himself,[142] a danger to our souls.[143]

Being required to listen to imperfect preachers is humbling, and therefore sanctifying, to both the hearer and the preacher. For the hearer it is humbling to sit under the teaching of men "like us and sometimes even by those of lower worth than we,"[144] and yet we find that God blesses through them.[145] For the preacher this doctrine is humbling, first, in the very fact that Calvin is careful to repeatedly point out the universality of pastoral failings. Calvin will describe his fellow pastors as "'vessels of clay' indeed, fragile and of nothing,"[146] "a contradiction between their life and their doctrine,"[147] "examples unto us, of the fragility and weakness of men,"[148] "altogether mean and despicable to instruct us"[149] and "the greatest dangers to the church."[150] This message would be difficult for any pastoral candidate to miss: there is no cause for you to think highly of yourself. Second, the pastor is led toward humility in the very fact that his congregation must humble themselves in order to listen to him, "a puny man risen from the dust!"[151] Where one might consider followers a cause for boasting, the pastor, reminded that his parishioners must stoop low in order to receive his teaching, must himself be humbled. Third, Calvin will proclaim that God's ability to use such broken people as his servants is a testimony to God's power, not theirs.[152] "As the voice of man is in itself inefficacious and lifeless, the work of cleansing really and properly belongs to the Spirit."[153] This teaching leaves no room for inflated egos but deflates and humbles the pastor. Fourth, the pastor is humbled as he realizes that he is used by God, only inasmuch as he is faithful to preaching the Word of God "rightly and sincerely."[154] The power of his ministry is totally dependent on the Word of God, before which the pastor himself must sit and submit or be found useless.[155] Calvin's teaching here leaves no room for the pastor to develop pride but rather gives him every reason to enter the pulpit with genuine humility, prostrated before God, even as he stands before God's people (Principle 1).

---

[141] *Commentary*, Jer. 11:20.
[142] *Commentary*, Jer. 5:13; 29:19.
[143] *Commentary*, Ezek. 2:5.
[144] *Institutes* 4.3.1.
[145] *Sermons on 2 Samuel*, 302-03.
[146] *Sermons on 2 Samuel*, 302-03.
[147] *Sermons on 2 Samuel*, 122.
[148] *Sermons on Election and Reprobation*, 252.
[149] *Commentary*, John 9:34.
[150] *Institutes* 4.9.4.
[151] *Institutes* 4.3.1.
[152] *Sermons on 2 Samuel*, 302-03.
[153] *Commentary*, Rom. 15:16.
[154] *Commentary*, Jer. 11:20.
[155] *Sermons on 2 Samuel*, 299.

The requirement to preach boldly in the face of opposition sanctified pastors
Calvin required, as one of the highest standards for preaching, that the faithful preacher must boldly preach the Bible no matter what opposition he might face.[156] Preaching boldly in the face of opposition is a logical imperative for one simple reason, God's Word will always meet some level of opposition, since both believers[157] and non-believers chafe at hearing God's requirements of them.[158] God's Word preached in the face of opposition serves both to redeem the elect and to condemn the obstinate who will not repent.[159] Were the pastor silent in the face of opposition, he would work against God's intention of proclaiming to the resistant, from whom God would remove all excuses for sinning[160] and so "doubly prove them to be unhealable."[161] Preaching the Word to opposition serves to crush the lies and objections of God's enemies,[162] while it pleases God who finds it "a sweet and good savor."[163]

While it might appear at first that a call to boldness in preaching would produce pride, as understood by Calvin, it would actually produce humility. First, the pastor must humbly accept that bold preaching is dependent on the inerrant and powerful Word, while he is prone to error and weakness (Principle 1).[164] Second, the pastor could only preach with true boldness, while humbly relying on the strength of the Lord (Principle 4).[165] Third, the pastor is humbled by the opposition, which inevitably includes personal attacks and slanders (Principle 9, Cross-bearing).[166] Finally, the preacher is humbled to realize that the results of his work may not be apparent in this world but only the next, so he must find his satisfaction not in the applause of humanity, but of God (Principle 10, Meditate on Future Life).[167]

In the end the requirement to preach boldly in the face of opposition would produce a pastor who was humble as regards himself and bold as regards the power of the Word of God. He would be humble as he is forced to rely on God, "convinced that they are supported by the hand of God."[168] Yet he would be bold, inasmuch as relying on God, he believes that God's mighty Word will prevail.[169] This boldness was bolstered by two key assurances: God would care for and protect the faithful preacher against all foes,[170] and the Word preached

---

[156] *Commentary*, Jer. 1:17; 17:16; 28:11; 29:8-10; 32:3; 36:29.
[157] *Sermons on Micah*, 122.
[158] *Commentary*, Jer. 15:19.
[159] *Commentary*, Ezek. 13:19.
[160] *Commentary*, Ezek. 2:5.
[161] *Commentary*, Jer. 7:27.
[162] *Commentary*, Jer. 1:11; Rom. 3:8.
[163] *Commentary*, Jer. 7:27.
[164] *Commentary*, Jer. 1:9; 20:7.
[165] *Commentary*, Ezek. 3:9.
[166] *Commentary*, Ezek. 2:6.
[167] *Commentary*, Jer. 11:20; 15:19; 20:9; 27:15.
[168] *Commentary*, John 8:29.
[169] *Commentary*, John 8:29.
[170] *Commentary*, Jer. 1:8,18-19.

boldly would be effective either "to slay all the ungodly"[171] or for salvation.[172] This bold preaching in the face of opposition required more than human courage to steady the knees of a pastor facing harsh opposition from Rome; it required deep faith in God,[173] a faith that would itself produce holiness in the humbly bold pastor (Principle 6, Struggle for Faith).

The high standard of faithful shepherding enhanced holiness

The requirement to pastor one church was sanctifying
Calvin would call his pastors to a high standard of faithfulness as shepherds, which would enhance their holiness. Calvin's understanding of the pastor as a shepherd, who diligently and humbly cared for his own flock, led him to despise the Roman system, which found priests serving several parishes, absent from parishes or moving freely and often between parishes in an effort to climb up the ecclesiastical ladder and reap financial reward.[174] These were "monstrous abuses, which are utterly contrary to God, nature, and church government."[175] The absentee pastorates were abominable because they encouraged an independent and arrogant spirit, while a settled pastor, "content with his limits," would be led to humility.[176]

The pastor is a shepherd bound to lengthy service for one flock, which he may leave only when duly dismissed by the Lord (Principle 12, Church). "When our Lord appoints a man as pastor in a church...he may not lightly withdraw."[177] A pastor was to have a settled ministry since the days of the itinerant apostles, whose authority extended over many churches, had long since passed.[178] The pastors were to conceive of themselves as humbly obliged to one congregation[179] and not as "drifters," who might fancy themselves superstars as they pass from church to church.[180] Calvin demonstrated such humility, even while exiled from Geneva, he felt bound to the Genevan Church, "for God, when he charged me with it, bound me to be faithful to it forever."[181]

While Calvin wanted each pastor to be bound to his own church, he recognized that this did not preclude the pastor's obligation to be concerned for the church at large.[182] Calvin would also grant that a call to one church was not

---

[171] *Commentary*, Jer. 5:14.
[172] *Commentary*, John 8:29.
[173] *Commentary*, Jer. 16:10; Ezek. 2:6.
[174] P. Schaff, *History of the Christian Church*, Vol. 7 (Peabody, Mass.: Hendrickson, 2002), 9.
[175] *Institutes* 4.5.7.
[176] *Institutes* 4.3.7.
[177] *CSW*, Vol. 4, 209, Calvin to the Senate of Geneva, Oct. 13, 1540, *CO* 11:96.
[178] *Commentary*, 1 Cor. 12:28; T.J. Davis, "A Response to the Apostolic and Pastoral Office," *Calvin and the Company of Pastors, Calvin Studies Society Papers 2003* (Grand Rapids, Mich.: CRC Product Services, 2004), 173.
[179] *Institutes* 4.5.4; *Commentary*, 1 Cor. 9:16.
[180] Holder, "Exegetical Understanding," 192-93.
[181] Reid, *Treatises*, 222, "Reply to Sadolet."
[182] *Institutes* 4.3.7; McKee, "Calvin and His Colleagues," 40.

necessarily for a lifetime, for a pastor is not "an ecclesiastical serf"[183] but may take a new call when he is rightly released by the former.[184] Neither did Calvin insist that a pastor must stay at a church when his life was in danger, provided *the church* thought it best that he leave to preserve his life.[185] Caveats included, this call to pastor one church for a long period was a call to humble self-denial peculiar to pastors, who must turn aside ambition for the sake of being faithful (Principle 8, Self-denial). Yet this teaching would also produce boldness, for seeing that it is God himself who assigned him his charge, the pastor could boldly execute that charge in Christ's name.

The requirement to work hard was sanctifying
The pastor must work hard and persevere long,[186] giving himself fully,[187] because he is a servant to Christ, who is worthy of diligence.[188] The pastor will face endless troubles *within* the life of the church, which require "fidelity, diligence, watchfulness, prudence, and unwearied constancy."[189] Similarly, the forces which attack the church from *without* will require that "all who undertake the office of feeding must be prepared for death."[190] Calvin would remind his students at the Genevan Academy to persevere in the office no matter what hardships arose.[191] So he prayed, "May we learn so entirely to devote ourselves to thy service, and each of us be so attentive to the work of his calling, that we may strive with united hearts to promote the honor of thy name."[192]

By word and by example Calvin set the tone for hard pastoral labors, rising at four in the morning and working hard until late in the evening.[193] His schedule often required five or more sermons per week, many weddings (24 during 1553[194]), baptisms, letter writings, lectures to students, weekly *Compagnie* and *Consistoire* meetings and visitation of the sick.[195] This model of hard work was lived out by the other pastors of Geneva. In one case a pastor baptized four babies at three different services of two churches and preached a sermon, all before 8:00 AM on a weekday.[196]

The requirements of perseverance in this hard labor would have had distinctly sanctifying movements in the pastors' lives. Here we see pastoral work as a

---

[183] Parker, *Calvin's Thought*, 137.
[184] Carrington, "Calvin and Erasmus," 159; *Commentary*, Acts 13:1; *CSW*, Vol.7, 97, Calvin to the Montelimart Church, Apr. 1560.
[185] *Commentary*, Acts 1:8.
[186] *Commentary*, 1 Tim. 4:15.
[187] *Commentary*, 2 Tim. 4:2.
[188] *Commentary*, 1 Thess. 5:12; 1 Tim. 3:1.
[189] *Commentary*, 2 Tim. 3:1.
[190] *Commentary*, John 21:18; Jer. 26:14.
[191] *Commentary*, Jer. 11:20.
[192] *Commentary*, Jer. 1:7.
[193] Selderhuis, *Pilgrim Life*, 220.
[194] McKee, "Calvin and His Colleagues," 29, note 62.
[195] *CSW*, Vol. 4, 132, Calvin to Farel, Apr. 20, 1539.
[196] McKee, "Calvin and His Colleagues," 37, Pastor Macur, the morning of Wed., May 17, 1557.

kind of cross-bearing (Principle 9) to which the pastor must submit and therein find grace. We see as well the two-fold knowledge of God and self (Principle 1) offered to the pastor who daily realizes he is the servant while God is the master. Thus the high standard of hard work would itself lead the pastor to holiness.

The requirement to lovingly shepherd individuals was sanctifying
No amount of hard work, however, can make a faithful shepherd if his work does not spring from the right motive: a fatherly love for the flock. "No one will ever be a good pastor, unless he shews himself to be a *father* to the Church that is committed to him."[197] Filled with the love of Christ,[198] the pastor has no room for avarice or ambition[199] but must prioritize the good of the church, in constant self-sacrifice.[200] This pastoral love is not a vague feeling but a compelling desire for the holiness of his people[201] that they may be offered to Christ as a pure bride.[202] The loving pastor then will "pine away with grief and sorrow"[203] if the church is in spiritual decay.[204]

Faithful pastors must also show this love in their personal conduct with the people by "their courtesy and their pleasing manner,"[205] such that they "allure people to kindness, rather than violently compel them."[206] Likewise in their preaching, pastors are to hold forth the love of Christ in their disposition. "A pastor's warmth must be sensed in his preaching."[207] He is not to alarm "with terrors" but to encourage the people by "means of a cheerful affability."[208]

Pastoral love was to work itself out, as a shepherd's love for his flock, both in providing good pasture—preaching the Word[209]—and in protecting the sheep[210] from wolves—false teachers.[211] This shepherd's love must be demonstrated for every individual sheep, not just generally,[212] and come through even while preaching to the entire flock.[213] This individual care meant that any member could seek out the pastor[214] and was demonstrated by the pastor's annual visit to every home in the parish.[215]

---

[197] *Commentary*, 1 Thess. 2:11.
[198] *Commentary*, John 21:15.
[199] *Commentary*, Jer. 23:1.
[200] *Commentary*, Acts 20:28.
[201] *Commentary*, 2 Cor. 11:2.
[202] *Commentary*, Acts 13:2.
[203] *Commentary*, 1 Thess. 3:8.
[204] *Commentary*, 2 Cor. 12:21.
[205] *Commentary*, Rom. 16:18.
[206] *Commentary*, 1 Thess. 4:1.
[207] Selderhuis, *Pilgrim Life*, 114; cf. *Commentary*, 2 Cor. 11:2.
[208] *Commentary*, 2 Cor. 2:2.
[209] *Commentary*, Jer. 23:4.
[210] Reid, *Treatises*, 224, "Reply to Sadolet."
[211] *Sermons on 2 Samuel*, 177; cf. *Commentary*, Ezek. 3:17.
[212] *Commentary*, 1 Thess. 2:11.
[213] Wallace, *Calvin and Geneva*, 172.
[214] Reid, *Treatises*, 216, "Necessity of Reforming the Church."
[215] *CO* 18:236, Calvin's letter to Olevianus, Nov. 1560; cf. Selderhuis, *Pilgrim Life*, 249.

Required to love to such a high standard, a pastor must either fail or in humility seek Christ to supply him with the love necessary to shepherd with such selfless diligence (Principle 3, God's Love).[216] Loving so as to place the church before himself was another exercise in self-denial (Principle 8), which would lead the pastor toward holiness.

The requirement to discipline the flock was sanctifying
Pastoral care was practiced as church discipline, perhaps more successfully in Geneva than elsewhere in the Reformation.[217] Discipline called for rebuking sin and calling the sinner to repent, or face excommunication,[218] and was done in tandem with the elders[219] and, in part, with the whole church.[220] The holy shepherd, who is in intimate contact with his sheep, knows who needs shepherding[221] and how best to approach each member.[222] Once the pastor is aware of sin in the life of a member, he must be diligent to confront the sin in their lives.[223] To confront resistant sinners effectively, the pastor must put aside his own emotions,[224] whether fear or hatred, and gently confront the sinner for his own good[225] and for the sake of the church.[226] If individual confrontation failed, the recalcitrant was brought before the weekly meeting of the Consistory.[227] Blind to their sin, even before the Consistory, church members would usually begin their interaction with the claim, "I am innocent."[228] Because the Consistory had real power to confront and excommunicate (since a decisive battle in 1555[229]), the sinner was forced to carefully count the cost for contumacy. Thus discipline was truly an instrument of the Holy Spirit to bring about repentance.[230]

This high standard of church discipline helped engender holiness in pastors. First, to have the moral authority to confront sin among his people, Calvin taught that the pastor must himself live a life of exemplary holiness (Principles

---

[216] *Commentary*, Jer. 1:17.
[217] S. Ozment, *The Age of Reform 1250-1550: An Intellectual and Religious History of Late Medieval and Reformation Europe* (New Haven, Conn.: Yale University Press, 1980), 367-68.
[218] *Commentary*, Hos. 9:5.
[219] *Institutes* 4.11.6, 4.11.2.
[220] McKee, *Elders and the Plural Ministry*, 30.
[221] Holder, "Pastoral Model," 289.
[222] *Commentary*, Tit. 3:11.
[223] Lobstein, *Die Ethik Calvins*, 130; *Commentary*, Gal. 6:1.
[224] Holder, "Pastoral Model," 291.
[225] *Commentary*, Gal. 4:12.
[226] *Commentary*, Gal. 6:1.
[227] W.G. Naphy, "Church and State in Calvin's Geneva," *Calvin and the Church, Calvin Studies Society Papers 2001* (Grand Rapids, Mich.: CRC Product Services, 2002), 18.
[228] *Sermons on Genesis 1-11*, 580.
[229] W.G. Naphy, *Calvin and the Consolidation of the Genevan Reformation* (Louisville, Ky.: Westminster/John Knox, 2003), 189.
[230] McKee, *Elders and the Plural Ministry*, 119.

4 and 5).[231] Second, the necessity of confronting sin in his church would force the opportunity for the pastor's own self-examination and repentance, the downward move of prostration (Principle 7).[232] Third, confronting a person with sin means the pastor might "lose their friendship,"[233] which was particularly dangerous when confronting the powerful.[234] Therefore the pastor must both deny his own self-interest and rely on God's love to make him secure (Principle 8 and 3), producing a holy boldness. Fourth, confronting sin requires faith, faith that God can change a person merely through the Word of God (Principle 2).[235] Fifth, the gentleness needed for a proper disciplinary confrontation is not a natural human attribute but must be sought from God, so as not "to appear to triumph over those whom they reprove, or to take delight in their disgrace" (Principle 4).[236] Finally, the call to discipline his flock is ultimately humbling for the pastor inasmuch as his work is always imperfect,[237] and he must await the return of the perfect Shepherd to finish the job he has only begun (Principles 1 and 4).[238] The call to discipline the flock leads the pastor himself toward holiness.

The high standard of administering sacraments enhanced holiness
The faithful administration of the sacraments would lead a pastor to further sanctification. First, Calvin was clear that a pastor must only use the sacraments precisely as they are given by Christ.[239] This restriction would lead a pastor toward humility in preventing him from embellishing on the sacraments in any way.[240] Second, a pastor must come to recognize his humble role,[241] since he is no priest offering Christ in sacrifice,[242] nor does he hold great power in his hands, for the sacrament is powerful only by the blessing of Christ (Principle 13, Sacraments).[243] Third, the pastor must work diligently to regularly offer the sacraments[244] and to prepare his flock to receive them.[245] The diligence in preparing the people to receive the sacrament, examining their faith, would encourage a pastor toward the *descensus in se*, to examine his own heart (Princi-

---

[231] *Commentary*, Phil. 4:9. Calvin reflects Gregory's sentiment. "It is necessary that the hand that aims at cleansing filth should itself be clean." (*Pastoral Care*, 46) Cf. *Institutes* 2.8.46; *Commentary*, Jer. 15:19.
[232] *Commentary*, Jer. 8:11.
[233] *Sermons on 2 Samuel*, 441.
[234] Bouwsma, *Sixteenth-Century Portrait*, 221.
[235] McKee, *Elders and the Plural Ministry*, 30; cf. *Institutes* 4.8.1.
[236] *Commentary*, 1 Cor. 4:14.
[237] *Commentary*, 1 Thess. 2:20.
[238] *Commentary*, Jer. 36:23; 1 Cor. 15:24.
[239] *Commentary*, John 1:31.
[240] *Commentary*, 1 Cor. 11:23.
[241] Niesel, *Theology of Calvin*, 223.
[242] Reid, *Treatises*, 240, "Reply to Sadolet."
[243] Steinmetz, *Context*, 72.
[244] Reid, *Treatises*, 49-50, "Articles Concerning the Organization of the Church," 1537.
[245] Reid, *Treatises*, 66, "Ecclesiastical Ordinances," 1541.

ples 7 and 6).[246] Fourth, in presenting the sacraments, he must teach on the meaning of the sacrament and the requirement of worthy receiving: knowing one's unworthiness.[247] The pastor would be humbled with his congregation and come to the table himself, a penitent sinner seeking grace (Principles 1, 7 and 13).[248] Fifth, in the right distribution of the elements, which requires that any member in good standing with the church be allowed to partake, the pastor would have his private judgment severely curtailed,[249] since he could not imperiously withhold the cup from those he dislikes.[250] Yet at the same time, the pastor must guard the table, boldly fencing it from the unworthy receiver, lest he admit one whom the Lord does not admit, a task which surely would leave a pastor trembling before God.[251] To faithfully administer the sacraments, a pastor would grow in holiness.[252]

The high standard of personal holiness enhanced holiness

Calvin called his pastors to another high standard: personal holiness. Though not formally listed by Calvin as a duty of the office, it was a clear expectation. Were a pastor to faithfully teach, administer the sacraments and shepherd the flock, yet fail in his personal holiness, he would have failed in his duty as a pastor.[253] In fact the typical pastor disciplined in Geneva was disciplined precisely because of a failure in holiness.[254] For example, Mathieu Issotier, who had misappropriated money in Provence, appeared before the Consistory in 1563, where it was decided that "qu'il est excommunié de ceste eglise et declaré scismatique au synode de Provence où il a faict de grandz troubles."[255] We find the Genevan pastor, Merlin, was dismissed for preaching against the Council.[256] Even the respected Chevalier was admonished by the Company of Pastors for being too concerned with his personal finances and was told that "he should not give priority to other considerations over the vocation which he had."[257]

Calvin would present to his students the highest standard of pastoral holiness in personal morality, purity of motive and dealing with money,[258] making "moral behavior the center of religious life"[259] to complement the high standard for education.[260] This high standard was unapologetically a double standard,

---

[246] *Commentary*, 1 Cor. 11:28.
[247] Reid, *Treatises*, 152, "Treatise on the Lord's Supper," 1541.
[248] *Institutes* 4.17.42.
[249] Reid, *Treatises*, 160, "Treatise on the Lord's Supper," 1541.
[250] *Commentary*, 1 Cor. 11:24.
[251] *Institutes* 4.17.43.
[252] Niesel, *Theology of Calvin*, 194.
[253] Witte, *Sex, Marriage and Family*, 88; cf. *Commentary*, 1 Tim. 6:12.
[254] Flaming, "The Apostolic and Pastoral Office," 155-56.
[255] *Registres du Consistoire*, XX, 127v, Sept. 2, 1563, Meeter Center transcripts.
[256] *RCP*, 371.
[257] *RCP*, 365.
[258] *Commentary*, 2 Cor. 12:14.
[259] Ozment, *The Age of Reform*, 379.
[260] Pettegree, "The Clergy and the Reformation," 9.

higher for the pastor than the people (Principle 5, Desire Holiness).[261] The higher standard for the pastors served both positively and negatively. Positively, pastoral holiness gives credibility to the message and serves as a visible sermon.[262] "Let them instruct the people not only through teaching, but also through example of life."[263] Negatively, when a pastor fails, he is judged more harshly in order to serve as a warning to the congregation that if even a pastor is disciplined for sin, then they should expect discipline.[264] Calvin reminds pastors that they are being watched by all with a hyper-critical, ever-vigilant eye to detect in them even the smallest failing.[265] With every eye upon them and such a daunting standard before them, the pastoral candidate would be motivated to flee to Christ for help (Principle 4).[266] Calvin prayed with his students: "May we learn to fight with ourselves and with our sins, and rely on thy word, until we gain the victory."[267]

The standard of moral purity enhanced holiness
Calvin set before his pastoral candidate a high standard for personal morality.[268] The pastor must not drink excessively nor have a temper,[269] the latter a continual problem for Calvin.[270] There must not be even a hint of sexual immorality.[271] "Nothing is more opposed to holiness than the defilement of *fornication*."[272] Calvin set forth this standard for moral purity both positively and negatively. Negatively, he would often, and lavishly, critique the morality of the Roman clergy.[273] "Today there is no order of men more notorious in excess, effeminacy, voluptuousness, in short, in all sorts of lusts; in no order are there masters more adept or skillful in every deceit, fraud, treason, and treachery; nowhere is there as great cunning or boldness to do harm. I say nothing about their arrogance, pride, greed, and cruelty."[274] Calvin would also critique the morality of his fellow Reformers, even those close to him. When Farel was 69 years of age, he declared to Calvin his intent to marry Marie Torel, likely in her late teens.[275]

---

[261] *Institutes* 4.12.22.
[262] *Commentary*, Jer. 42:5
[263] *Institutes* 2.8.46; cf. *Sermons on 2 Samuel*, 222; *Commentary*, Phil. 4:9; 1 Thess. 3:2; Tit. 2:7.
[264] *Commentary*, 1 Tim. 5:20.
[265] *Commentary*, Jer. 34:9; 1 Tim. 5:19.
[266] *Sermons on 2 Samuel*, 96.
[267] *Commentary*, Jer. 5:9.
[268] *Commentary*, 1 Tim. 3:2
[269] *Commentary*, 1 Tim. 3:3.
[270] In his farewell address to the Council of Geneva, Calvin expressed regret for his "natural disposition by far too vehement." *CSW*, Vol. 7, 370; *CO* 9:888.
[271] *Commentary*, Tit. 1:7.
[272] *Commentary*, 1 Thess. 4:3.
[273] *Institutes* 4.12.23.
[274] *Institutes* 4.5.14.
[275] D.N. Wiley, "Calvin's Friendship with Guillaume Farel," *Calvin and Spirituality, Calvin and His Contemporaries, Calvin Studies Society Papers, 1995, 1997* (Grand Rapids, Mich.: CRC Product Services, 1998), 202.

Calvin scolded Farel for even inviting him to participate in such an unseemly wedding, which would invite much "evil speaking."[276]

Positively, Calvin set forth a high standard for his fellow pastor's morality. "He shall be a man of unblemished reputation."[277] This high standard of moral conduct was enforced through the Company of Pastors.[278] Calvin found this policing especially important in the early years after his return to Geneva, for there was so much ungodliness rampant among the pastors he had inherited. Among the thirty-one pastors who served in Geneva from 1538-46, nine were deposed, one of whom was arrested for fornication with two women in the plague hospital and another for embezzlement.[279] Calvin would remind his students that such an unholy life disqualifies one for ministry. "Those are not God's instruments or ministers, nor are worthy of any honor, who so pervert vices and virtues as to say that light is darkness and that darkness is light."[280]

Such a high standard for moral purity would drive a pastor down in humility before God as they saw not only their own weakness but the high standard of office (Principles 1 and 5).[281] "Those who attain a place of honor should put all pride aside."[282] The high standard would also turn a pastor's gaze up toward God, seeking him for help to keep from falling (Principle 4). "When we see men fall like this, we...are therefore warned to remain modest and humble....Our attitude should be: 'Alas! The same could have happened to us, except that God wonderfully preserved us by his grace!'"[283] This dependence on Christ to strive toward the high standard of personal holiness would make a pastor humble in himself yet confident in what Christ could do through him. This is progress in holiness.

The standard of pure motives enhanced holiness
Nowhere was Calvin more strict and insistent when it came to the holiness of the pastor than in dealing with the pastor's motivation in ministering. There was absolutely no room allowed for personal ambition. "For it is certain that ambition is the most mortal evil that can possibly happen to the Church of God, when everyone wants to advance himself and wants to be seen by others."[284] The pastor must labor without desire for his own glory; for to desire advancement in the world means that the pastor must neglect the interests of Christ.[285]

---

[276] *CSW*, Vol. 6, 476, Calvin to Farel, Sept. 1558.
[277] *Commentary*, Tit. 1:6.
[278] Small, "A Company of Pastors," 11.
[279] W.G. Naphy, "The Renovation of the Ministry in Calvin's Geneva," *The Reformation of the Parishes* (ed. A. Pettegree; Manchester: Manchester University Press, 1993), 119-20.
[280] *Commentary*, Jer. 15:19.
[281] Schaff, *History of the Church*, Vol. 7, 24.
[282] *Sermons on the Beatitudes* (tr. R. White; Edinburgh: Banner of Truth Trust, 2006), 15.
[283] *Sermons on Beatitudes*, 14-15.
[284] *Sermons on 2 Samuel*, 125.
[285] *Commentary*, Phil. 2:21.

Chapter 5 - The Model of the Pious Pastor

When a pastor sets as his ambition getting ahead in the world, he will of necessity desire to please people, rather than God, and so pay better attention to the rich and powerful[286] and go easy on their vices.[287] To be a faithful pastor one cannot desire to please people but must please God.[288] "Ambitious persons, that is, those who hunt after the applause of men, cannot serve Christ."[289] Instead of pleasing people, the pastor is called to confront them all, even "kings and queens," with the claims of Christ.[290]

Calvin's pastors were to leave no room in their hearts for ambition but were rather to root it out constantly. Calvin held forth the pope as a bad example of ambition in ministry, who "arrogates...to himself alone" the seat of power.[291] When a Reformed pastor found any of the characteristics of the ambitious Roman clergy in his own ministry, he was called to immediate repentance and was to be humbled by his high calling.[292] "They are not to aspire to this office as many do, who...are guided by ambition."[293] Indeed, the pastor must never use ministry to fulfill his own desires[294] but make it his "sole object to promote, to the utmost of his power, the glory of God."[295] The pastor must be willing to cooperate with other ministers, rather than jealously compete, since their mutual cooperation is a demonstration of their unity and submission to Christ.[296] Calvin designed this cooperative stance into his practice at Geneva, rotating the pastors on a weekly basis, for the midweek services, through the principal Genevan parishes.[297]

In laying aside all desire for position and power, the faithful pastor must forego any desire to see his own name lifted up by others.[298] "If anyone is influenced by ambition, that man gathers disciples, not to Christ, but to himself."[299] The pastor must win followers for Christ, never taking the Bride for himself, which would be base immorality.[300] Calvin would strive to remind not only pastors, but the church, that they must not follow a pastor as their hero but

---

[286] *Commentary*, Jer. 1:10.
[287] *Commentary*, Jer. 15:19.
[288] *Commentary*, Dan. 6:17; 1 Thess. 2:4.
[289] *Commentary*, Gal. 1:10. Calvin echoes the sentiment of Gregory again, "For from love of himself, the ruler's mind is diverted into laxity, when he sees his subjects sinning and does not dare to correct them, lest their love of him grow weak." (*Pastoral Care*, 75).
[290] *Commentary*, Jer. 13:18.
[291] Reid, *Treatises*, 208, "Necessity of Reforming the Church;" cf. *Institutes* 4.7.21.
[292] *Sermons on 2 Samuel*, 534.
[293] *Commentary*, Jer. 17:16.
[294] *Commentary*, Jer. 11:19.
[295] *Commentary*, John 7:18.
[296] *Commentary*, John 4:37.
[297] McKee, "Calvin and His Colleagues," 21.
[298] *Commentary*, Jer. 26:7; Dan. 4:25; 1 Cor. 1:11.
[299] *Commentary*, 1 Cor. 1:12.
[300] *Commentary*, John 3:29.

only Christ.[301] One case in *The Register of the Company of Pastors* serves to illustrate the seriousness of Calvin's hatred of pastoral ambition. On Friday, June 19, 1562, some of the country pastors around Geneva requested that they be considered for a city parish. When this was denied, some of the country pastors declared, "They would have never entered the ministry if they had thought that they would be left in the country."[302] Calvin later chagrined, "What is this which I see before I die?"[303] He could neither believe nor tolerate, that so near the end of his life, his model and teaching had had so little effect.

This rooting out of all personal ambition and substituting for it the desire for Christ's glory is an opportunity to live out self-denial (Principle 8).[304] There is here an enforced necessity for pastors to deny themselves, for should they indulge in self-glorification, God will eventually humble them[305] by destroying their ministry and removing them from office,[306] "so that they shall cease to boast of their dignity."[307] The pastor who strives for faithfulness in his motives[308] is left with one route forward—self-denial—which would sanctify him.[309]

The standard of financial integrity enhanced holiness
Calvin saw avarice as a close and deadly twin to ambition in pastors, "since it results in the loss of justice and equity."[310] The love of money could only corrupt the pastor and his ministry.[311] "We know how very pestilent the disease is when prophets and teachers are addicted to gain, or easily receive the gifts offered them."[312] Not that Calvin would insist that his pastors take a vow of poverty, he meant for them to have no concern for money, though the Council was not as responsive to their needs.[313] Calvin, however, did insist that pastors must not set their hearts on acquiring more wealth.[314] "It is the part of a genuine and upright pastor, not to seek to derive gain from his sheep, but to endeavor to promote their welfare."[315] Calvin would hold up the Roman clergy, yet again, as the negative example to avoid. For they "first interpret title as meaning an income sufficient for their support."[316] The pastor who loves money will seek his gain rather than the flock's, thus neglecting the duty of preaching the hard

---

[301] McKee, "Calvin and His Colleagues," 10.
[302] *RCP*, 357.
[303] *RCP*, 357.
[304] *Sermons on 2 Samuel*, 73.
[305] *Commentary*, Jer. 23:21; cf. *Sermons on 2 Samuel*, 106.
[306] *Commentary*, 1 Thess. 2:5.
[307] *Commentary*, Hos. 4:10; cf. *Sermons on 2 Samuel*, 128.
[308] *Sermons on 2 Samuel*, 137.
[309] *Commentary*, Rom. 15:14.
[310] *Sermons on Micah*, 176.
[311] *Commentary*, Jer. 15:16.
[312] *Commentary*, Dan. 2:48.
[313] Naphy, *Calvin and the Consolidation*, 62.
[314] *Commentary*, 1 Tim. 6:9.
[315] *Commentary*, 2 Cor. 12:14.
[316] *Institutes* 4.5.4.

truths of the Word,[317] which might close the purses of those offended.[318] For Calvin this was simply axiomatic: to love money means to ignore God's Word in order to curry the favor of the rich[319] through "flattery, servile obsequiousness, and cunning of all kinds."[320] Love of money was a pestilence to faithful pastors. "Ministers who are given to self-gain…will inevitably compromise and falsify the Word of God."[321]

The pastor, therefore, must examine his heart for any desire to profit from his ministry, and he must destroy that desire through self-denial, faith and repentance (Principles 8, 6 and 7).[322] Denying oneself financially was an expectation, which Calvin modeled himself by owning no property.[323] "Neither the table at which we eat, nor the bed on which we sleep, is my own."[324] Here we find a practical exercise in self-denial,[325] aimed uniquely at pastors, who must constantly subjugate their desire to advance materially in this world.[326] At the same time, with each effort to turn from the love of money, the pastor must look reverentially upward to the Lord to meet his very real needs "as if from the hand of God,"[327] helping to build confidence in God's supply (Principle 11, Present Life). Together these two motions, prostration and reverence, applied to finances, led the pastor to Christ and to greater holiness.[328]

The standard of discipline for pastors enhanced holiness
Calvin understood that this pursuit of personal holiness in the pastor required the help of others.[329] Sinful human nature rendered the pastor, like every other sinner, blind to his own sin. Therefore, the pastor needed accountability—shepherding and discipline —to confront his sin.[330] "To obviate all scandals of living, it will be proper that there be a form of correction to which all submit themselves."[331] This accountability was to flow from the entire church. Parishioners should monitor the pastor's faithfulness to teaching but also his overall moral conduct.[332] This responsibility the citizens of Geneva seemed happy to fulfill, for example, pointing out that Pastor Cop had been "shopping in St.

---

[317] *Institutes* 4.5.6.
[318] *Sermons on Micah*, 178.
[319] *Commentary*, Tit. 1:11.
[320] *Commentary*, Dan 2:6; cf. *Commentary*, Jer. 15:10.
[321] *Sermons on Micah*, 178.
[322] *Commentary*, John 12:28.
[323] Selderhuis, *Pilgrim Life*, 220.
[324] *CSW*, Vol. 5, 106, Letter to Poulain, 1547.
[325] *Sermons on Micah*, 180.
[326] *Commentary*, 1 Thess. 2:9.
[327] *Sermons on Micah*, 180.
[328] Wallace, *Christian Life*, 52.
[329] Reid, *Treatises*, 60, "Ecclesiastical Ordinances," 1541.
[330] *Commentary*, 1 Cor. 4:3.
[331] Reid, *Treatises*, 60, "Ecclesiastical Ordinances," 1541.
[332] *Commentary*, 1 Cor. 4:3.

Gervais at the hour of prayers."[333] To be a pastor in Geneva meant that you were subject to lay correction.

In addition to the church's role in providing moral accountability for the pastor, the Company of Pastors served to promote the piety of pastors.[334] This was achieved with the weekly Friday morning meeting,[335] which performed once quarterly the *censura morum*.[336] "This was an open conversation where each pastor was free to say whether he had any problems with the life or doctrine of a colleague...so that they could be resolved."[337] One example of the Company at work involved the pastor, Philippe de Ecclesia. In 1552 he was charged with usury, disloyalty and bad doctrine. Unrepentant, he was eventually deposed by the Council, with undoubtedly a salutary effect on the rest.[338] Calvin, while subject to the Company, also maintained an informal accountability with a web of life-long friendships.[339] Writing of his friendship with Viret and Farel, Calvin emoted, "I think there has never been in ordinary life a circle of friends so heartily bound to each other as we have been in our ministry."[340]

Being confronted with one's sin meant that the pastor must be willing to accept rebukes "and profit from them."[341] This readiness to receive correction required the pastor to always occupy the posture of a learner. "While we are teachers, we ought at the same time to continue learners."[342] Part of what the pastor must learn is the true knowledge of himself, of his own sins, so that he might daily turn to grace, in order to lead others as well. "Here we see that no one can discharge the teacher's office, unless he be proficient in God's school."[343]

This direct dealing with a pastor's sin (Principle 14, Discipline) was designed not only to protect the churches from bad pastors but remedially to enhance the holiness of the pastor through faith and repentance (Principles 6 and 7). Confronted by his own failings, the pastor must humbly turn to Christ for help, reverentially worshipping his Savior.[344] The life of holiness grows as the

---

[333] McKee, "Calvin and His Colleagues," 39, note 93.
[334] Small, "A Company of Pastors," 12.
[335] *RCP*, 3. Cf. R.M. Kingdon, *Geneva and the Consolidation of the French Protestant Movement, 1564-1572* (Geneva: Droz, 1967), 21-22.
[336] Reid, *Treatises*, 61, "Ecclesiastical Ordinances," 1541. This practice spread to other institutions in Geneva as well, such as the deaconate and the City Council. Cf. J.E. Olson, "Calvin as Pastor-Administrator During the Reformation in Geneva," *Articles on Calvin and Calvinism*, Vol. 3, *Calvin's Work in Geneva* (ed. R.C. Gamble; Garland, New York, N.Y. and London, 1992), 8.
[337] Selderhuis, *Pilgrim Life*, 126.
[338] *RCP*, 202.
[339] Wiley, "Calvin's Friendship," 187.
[340] *Commentary*, Tit., Introduction.
[341] *Sermons on 2 Samuel*, 102.
[342] *Commentary*, Dan. 9:2. Cf. McKee, "Calvin and His Colleagues," 11; *Commentary*, 1 Cor. 14:31.
[343] *Commentary*, Ezek. 2:8.
[344] *Commentary*, Dan. 12:3.

pastor is shepherded away from his own sin and led to Christ by his fellow pastors and indeed the entire church.[345]

Conclusion: Calvin's model of the faithful pastor led toward holiness

Calvin's model of the pastor, truly called and faithful to that call, led his students toward increased piety as it required the engagement of his basic paradigm of sanctification: the two-fold knowledge of God and self, leading to a two-fold response of prostration and reverence before God. This holiness produced a pastor who was personally humble yet bold in proclaiming the Word of God and confronting. The necessity of a true call from God and church would promote both a careful self-examination and an even more careful examination by the church (Principles 7 and 14). This examination would lead to the exposure of failings and a turning to Christ for help (Principles 7 and 4). Recognizing that the true call was from God would promote the two-fold response of prostration and reverence (Principle 1), leaving a man humble as a servant but bold as a servant of God.[346]

The high standard of faithfulness would drive a pastor to God dependence, recognizing his own inability (Principles 4 and 5).[347] The call to faithfully preach the Word of God would both humble a pastor in submitting himself to teach only what is in the Word and lift him toward God (Principle 2).[348] The high call to faithfulness in shepherding the flock leads a pastor to examine his own heart for sin, while at the same time leading him to turn to God for love, in order to have the love necessary to herd a flock of sinful sheep (Principle 3).[349] The high call to faithfulness in administering the sacraments would call the pastor downward, as he was but a mere deliveryman for God's grace, who did not possess the authority to deny even one person, on his own power, admission to the Supper. The call to faithfulness in personal holiness would force pastoral candidates to examine their hearts and consciences on the deepest levels, as they sought to deny their own desires for respect and advancement in the world (Principles 1, 4 and 7).[350]

In all things Calvin's model of a good pastor, one truly called and faithful to that call, would force the pastor to either abandon the vocation or turn to God in humble dependence to make him stand. In following Calvin's prescription to rely on God to become a faithful pastor, a new kind of pastor would emerge, one humble yet bold. This was Calvin's persistent instruction to his pastoral students: cry out to God to make you a holy pastor. "By these words God exhorts his Prophet to prayer; for we know how dangerous is self-security to all the children of God, and especially to teachers. As then they have at all times

---

[345] *Commentary*, 1 Cor. 4:3.
[346] *Commentary*, Jer. 1:17.
[347] *Commentary*, 2 Tim. 1:7.
[348] *Commentary*, Dan. 9:22.
[349] *Commentary*, Jer. 2:1.
[350] *Commentary*, Ezek. 13:17.

need of God's aid, they are to be exhorted to have recourse to solitude and prayer."[351]

---

[351] *Commentary*, Jer. 15:20.

Chapter 6 - Calvin's Teaching to the Students of the Genevan Academy

"Nunc ergo videmus qualis sit vera ratio docendi, nempe dum humiliantur homines...deinde animantur ad bene sperandum."[1]

Calvin Aimed His Teaching toward the Sanctification of His Students

Introduction

We will advance in this chapter a simple proposition: Calvin regularly taught the principles of sanctification to the students of the Genevan Academy, in order to enhance their holiness. First, we will review Calvin's methods of teaching the students, along with dominant themes of that teaching. Second, we will demonstrate that the fourteen principles of sanctification, which we observed in Section One, were distinctly and consistently taught to the students. Finally, we will show how the fourteen principles interact in a "certain order."

We prioritize for our study the types of teaching Calvin offered to the students of the Academy, ranking his lectures, preserved in Old Testament commentaries,[2] over his sermons, since the lectures were focused upon the students. The sermons are valuable too, for since attendance at a Sunday worship was legally mandatory[3] and Calvin's teaching was generally enthusiastically attended,[4] we surmise that the students would have regularly heard the Sunday sermons and likely heard many of his midweek sermons. Though the *Institutes* were a staple of teaching at the Academy,[5] having relied on them heavily for the preceding chapters, we will not focus on them here.

Calvin's forms of teaching to the students of the Academy

Lectures

Calvin, originally called to Geneva as a Bible lecturer and not a pastor,[6] began lecturing "to the scholars, ministers, and other auditors,"[7] including the younger students trained under the guidelines of the *Ecclesiastical Ordinances*.[8] Follow-

---

[1] *CO* 39:520-21, *Commentary*, Lam. 1:9. "Now, therefore, we see what is the right way of teaching, even that men are to be humbled...and then they are to be encouraged to entertain hope."
[2] Not, however, his Commentaries on The Four Books of Moses, 1559-62, or Joshua, 1563-64, which were apparently delivered in the Congregation, where there is less evidence of mass student attendance. Parker, *Old Testament Commentaries*, 15; Boer, "The *Congrégation*," 59.
[3] Naphy, *Calvin and the Consolidation*, 123; cf. Reid, *Treatises*, 69; Burnett, "A Tale of Three Churches," 115.
[4] Kingdon, *Wars of Religion*, 15.
[5] Witte, *Sex, Marriage and Family*, 11.
[6] D.L. Puckett, "John Calvin as Teacher," *Southern Baptist Journal of Theology* 13 (2009), 46.
[7] *CO* 21:71, Colladon, *The Life of Calvin*.
[8] Parker, *Old Testament Commentaries*, 15.

ing 1559 the lectures, at either the *Auditoire* or the newly constructed Academy,[9] were given to an audience estimated at about 1000 during 1561,[10] which included those who had particularly come to the Genevan Academy, mostly as pastoral candidates.[11] While the lower school of the Academy, the *schola privita*, focused on younger students, the *schola publica* trained those older than 17 years of age, perhaps mostly in their early 20s but some in their 30s as well, who were prepared to accept pastorates upon graduation.[12] During our period of study, Calvin lectured three afternoons per week, on alternate weeks, expositing Daniel (1559), Jeremiah (1560-62), Lamentations (1562) and Ezekiel (1563-64).[13]

Calvin's well-preserved lectures[14] were delivered in Latin without notes, after perhaps one half-hour of preparation and lasted one hour.[15] The lectures followed a basic pattern. They began with a brief prayer, then presentation of the text (in Hebrew and Latin) along with explanatory glosses, an explanation of the important philological insights, the explication of the meaning of the text, an application to his hearers and a closing prayer, which acted as a summary of the application.[16] While scholarly, Calvin's lectures, simple and unembellished, were aimed at the final product of increased piety.[17] Blacketer makes a similar point about Calvin's Joshua Commentary: "Calvin will bring out the spiritual implications of the text, explaining the things the text teaches about what Christians should believe, what they should hope for, and how they should live."[18] His customary opening prayer for his lectures shows this desire to increase holiness by bringing to bear God's Word, "that our piety truly pro-

---

[9] There is some lack of clarity as to the precise location of Calvin's lectures for the Academy during 1559-62. After this time it seems clear his lectures were given at the *Auditoire*. While Borgeaud states that the lectures were moved to the *Auditoire* in 1562 (Borgeaud, *Histoire de l'Université*, 54), Wilcox concludes that Calvin simply continued to lecture from the pulpit of the *Auditoire*, so the lectures on Jeremiah (1560-62) were given there as well. (P. Wilcox, "The Lectures of John Calvin and the Nature of His Audience, 1555-1564," *Archiv für Reformationsgeschicte* 87, 1996, 139-140.) Calvin's introduction to the Jeremiah Commentary may confirm this, for he describes his lecture as given from the pulpit to a "medium auditory," (*mediocri auditorio*) *CO* 20:77.

[10] Kingdon, *Wars of Religion*, 15; cf. *CO* 19:10, Letter from Jean de Beaulieu to Farel, Oct. 3, 1561.

[11] Parker, *Old Testament Commentaries*, 16.

[12] Wilcox, "Lectures of Calvin," 146.

[13] Parker, *Old Testament Commentaries*, 29.

[14] Puckett, "John Calvin as Teacher," 48. See the Preface to *Commentary* on Hosea, by Jean Budé, for a description of the process.

[15] *CO* 42:189-90, Jean Crispin's Prologue to the Minor Prophets. Cf. *Commentary*, Lam. 3:23.

[16] Parker, *Old Testament Commentaries*, 34-38.

[17] Jean Budé, "Preface to Commentary on Hosea."

[18] R.A. Blacketer, "The Moribund Moralist: Ethical Lessons in Calvin's Commentary on Joshua," *Dutch Review of Church History/Nederlands Archief voor Kerkgeschiedenis* 85 (2005), 153.

gresses."[19] Calvin's closing prayers, unique to each lecture, show this same concern.[20] They typically pick up the chief theme of his teaching, and starting with the need of his hearers to repent of their sins, offer them hope in God's grace for renewal and new obedience.[21] Calvin's lectures, as with his commentaries in general, were often directed toward pastors, and served as a kind of "first seminary,"[22] hence our assigning them first priority here. Lecture by lecture Calvin meant his commentaries to help sanctify the pastors he hoped to send to his beloved French homeland.[23]

Sermons
During this period Calvin typically preached 10 times a fortnight, covering a series on the Harmony of the Gospels from 1559-64 on Sunday and covering an Old Testament series during midweek service, namely Genesis (1559-61), Judges (1561), 1 and 2 Samuel (1561-63) and 1 and 2 Kings (1563-4).[24] Calvin preached without notes,[25] after carefully exegeting the passage in the original language and consulting historical and contemporary interpretations. His sermons were typically an hour in length, in French, from either the Hebrew or Greek Bible.[26] While it varied he would generally expound two to four verses in a chapter, following the pattern of *lectio continua*,[27] as he worked his way through a book, "riveted to the biblical text."[28]

Calvin's sermons, also well-preserved,[29] followed a general pattern: an opening prayer, the reading of the text, a summary of the last sermon, exposition of a verse, followed by application, then exposition and application again, until the passage was complete, and finally a closing prayer which served as a summary of the sermon in application.[30] His style was lucid, fluid and uninterrupted by lengthy quotations or anecdotes, which was in sharp contrast to the Medieval style.[31] He aimed for an eloquence of substance and not style,[32] which

---

[19] *CO* 37:463.
[20] Jean Budé, "Preface to Commentary on Hosea."
[21] *Commentary*, Lam. 1:10.
[22] Holder, "Exegetical Understanding," 207-08. Pastors also perceived the value of these commentaries. Jean Chambeli, sent from Geneva in 1558, listed among his few books two commentaries by Calvin: Isaiah and Romans (Kingdon, *Wars of Religion*, 16).
[23] Wilcox, "Lectures of Calvin," 148.
[24] S.J. Lawson, "The Biblical Preaching Of John Calvin," *Southern Baptist Journal of Theology* 13 (2009), 23; Parker, *Oracles of God*, 162. Unfortunately we still lack the Judges and Kings series.
[25] Parker, *Oracles of God*, 30.
[26] Lawson, "Biblical Preaching," 22.
[27] T.H.L. Parker, *Calvin's Preaching* (Louisville, Ky.: Westminster/John Knox, 1992), 90.
[28] Holder, "Exegetical Understanding," 196.
[29] Parker, *Oracles of God*, 40.
[30] Parker, *Oracles of God*, 71.
[31] Parker, *Oracles of God*, 75.
[32] *Commentary*, 1 Cor. 1:17.

would bring the hearer to Christ, where Christ might move them toward holiness.[33] Certainly his intent in preaching was clear: the increased holiness of his hearers.[34] "For why has God appointed the ministers of his gospel, except to invite us to become partakers of his salvation, and thus sweetly to restore and refresh our souls?"[35] Preaching must impact the hearer, penetrating "into the consciences of men,"[36] awakening the hearer,[37] and making forceful application,[38] so they might be led to the solution of Christ, for growth in holiness.[39] In his prayers before and after the sermon, we see Calvin's intent to bring the congregation low in prostration and lifted up in reverence to God. He regularly used the same opening prayer, learned from his time in Strasbourg, which called on God to grant humility, the upward reverence to "trust only in him," and the call to obediently love God and neighbor, all based on the prior fact that God has been pleased "graciously to receive us." The aim was clearly for sanctification: "So that we may glorify his holy name in all our living and edify our neighbor by our good example, rendering to God the love and the obedience which faithful servants give their masters."[40] Consider in this typical closing prayer, unique to each sermon, the downward movement of prostration and the upward movement brought on by forgiveness and mercy. "Now let us prostrate ourselves before the Majesty of our good God in recognition of the infinite faults of which we are guilty....Thus may it be, that...we are yet assured of being absolved before God by his infinite goodness."[41]

Teaching emphases

We find some themes in Calvin's theology of sanctification occurring more frequently than others; we will highlight four of them. First, we should make note of a negative theme. Calvin repeatedly corrects errors in Roman theology and methods of sanctification, while showing the correctness of the Reformed views.[42] The root problem was bad Roman theology,[43] which attributed too much ability to human will,[44] allowing for human merit and thus satisfactions.[45] Calvin challenged Roman theology[46] by showing that the human will was

---

[33] Holder, "Exegetical Understanding," 198.
[34] Parker, *Oracles of God*, 43.
[35] *Commentary*, Jer. 5:14.
[36] *Commentary*, Gal. 3:1.
[37] *Commentary*, 1 Thess. 2:12.
[38] Lawson, "Biblical Preaching," 22; Parker, *Calvin's Preaching*, 81; Selderhuis, *Pilgrim Life*, 112.
[39] Bouwsma, *Sixteenth-Century Portrait*, 228.
[40] J. Calvin, *Songs of the Nativity, Selected Sermons on Luke 1 and 2* (tr. R. White; Edinburgh: Banner of Truth Trust, 2008), 3; *CO* 23:741-42.
[41] *Sermons on 2 Samuel*, 518.
[42] We found 274 direct corrections in the four commentaries: 162 in Jeremiah, 71 in Ezekiel, 41 in Daniel but interestingly none in Lamentations.
[43] *Sermons on 2 Samuel*, 575; *Commentary*, Dan. 4:27.
[44] *Commentary*, Ezek. 11:19.
[45] *Commentary*, Ezek. 16:63.
[46] *Sermons on 2 Samuel*, 435.

bound by sin,[47] and therefore humanity was entirely, not partly, justified *and* sanctified by grace alone,[48] with no human works added.[49] The faulty theology of Rome naturally led to faulty practices. The Roman sacraments were thought to offer assisting grace, particularly baptism and penance, which were sought to wash away original sin and deal with present sin, respectively.[50] Calvin denounced the Roman methods as spiritually destructive to holiness,[51] with their magical view of the sacraments[52] and an external, false and penitential system to acquire merit.[53] The bad theology and methods of sanctification naturally led to an unholy priesthood.[54] "So much for the Pope's men, who bravely preach about merit but whose lives are an affront to God!"[55] For Calvin the Roman system of sanctification was entirely a failure, from theology, to practices, to results, and he wanted his students to understand the superiority of the Reformed approach.

Second, it is clear by the frequency of repetition that Calvin believed that the human journey toward holiness started with a move away from pride and toward a true and realistic appraisal of the human condition as one of helpless sinner.[56] "Now as to pride, the first step we must take to overcome it is to acknowledge that we possess nothing good which does not come from God."[57] We must see God's greatness[58] and our littleness to be properly humbled[59] that prostrated before God we might find his grace to transform us more into the image of Christ.[60]

Third, nearly as often as he takes his hearers down in humility, he lifts them up again in reverence before God.[61] In order to help his hearers toward a proper reverence, Calvin will offer knowledge of God, showing his immense power

---

[47] *Commentary*, Ezek. 11:19.
[48] Battles, *Interpreting Calvin*, 134; *Sermons on Nativity*, 36-37; *Commentary*, Ezek. 16:51.
[49] *Commentary*, Lam. 3:41; cf. *Commentary*, Jer. 14:9; *Sermons on Beatitudes*, 76-77.
[50] Ozment, *The Age of Reform*, 29-30.
[51] *Commentary*, Dan.11:35; *Sermons on Nativity*, 90; *Sermons on 2 Samuel*, 269-70.
[52] *Commentary*, Ezek. 20:20.
[53] *Commentary*, Jer. 14:12; Ezek. 14:14; *Sermons on 2 Samuel*, 583-84.
[54] *Commentary*, Jer. 23:11.
[55] *Sermons on Beatitudes*, 76.
[56] B. Pitkin, "The Spiritual Gospel? Christ and Human Nature in Calvin's Commentary on John," *The Formation of Clerical and Confessional Identities in Early Modern Europe* (eds. W. Janse, B. Pitkin; Leiden: Brill, 2006), 203.
[57] *Sermons on Nativity*, Luke 1:49-51, 46. Cf. *Sermons on Nativity*, 16, 27, 49; *Sermons on Genesis 1-11*, 171, 194, 203, 390, 561, 852; *Sermons on 2 Samuel*, 53, 172, 192, 281, 510; *Commentary*, Jer. 5:25; 7:31; 4:23; 12:8; 13:18; Lam. 1:8, 20.
[58] *Sermons on 2 Samuel*, 391.
[59] *Commentary*, Jer. 9:23.
[60] *Sermons on Nativity*, 28.
[61] *Commentary*, Jer. 2:17; 4:2; 9:3; 13:16; 26:19; 33:9; 44:24; Lam. 1:5; 2:14; Ezek. 3:11; 11:12; 13:22; Dan. 2:27; 6:11; 8:27; *Sermons on Nativity*, 23, 35; *Sermons on Genesis 1-11*, 687, 838.

and goodness[62] and our utter dependence on him.[63] Seeing God's goodness in the face of human wickedness, the heart is filled, reverences God as Father and renders to him thankful worship[64] and the obedience of faith.[65]

Fourth, Calvin will return to the theme of the love and mercy of God[66] because he understood that it was God's love, and not his justice, which finally moved the prostrated sinner toward God in reverence.[67] God's love is seen in the promises of his Word,[68] in his gracious provision for his people[69] and most clearly in the offer of mercy through faith in his Son.[70] Perhaps the most stirring aspect of God's love is his pure affection for us, which he communicates to us as if to say, "I will not fail you in any way since I have given you such good testimony of the love I bear for you."[71] Seeing God's love in word, deed and in the very affection of his heart, the prostrated sinner is lifted up toward God, returning God's affection as worshipful reverence. These four themes are woven together consistently through Calvin's teaching to his students.

Calvin Repeatedly Taught the Principles of Sanctification to His Students

Principle 1: Two-fold Knowledge. Because God created us to lovingly revere him, therefore gain knowledge of God and self thus to offer God prostration and reverence.

At the very heart of Calvin's theology of sanctification, regularly preached and taught,[72] we find the two-fold knowledge of God and self.[73] This knowledge highlights humanity's hopelessness and God's great mercy, which leads to a two-fold response, a movement downward in prostration before God and upward toward God in reverence.[74] "The reaction is twofold: man stands awestricken in fear, and yet is drawn in love."[75] This movement of prostration

---

[62] Lawson, "Biblical Preaching," 30.
[63] *Commentary*, Jer. 13:16.
[64] *Sermons on Nativity*, 26.
[65] *Sermons on Beatitudes*, 1.
[66] *Sermons on Genesis 1-11*, 90, 112, 120; *Sermons on 2 Samuel*, 61, 162, 198, 395, 489, 535, 602; *Sermons on Nativity*, 11, 20, 81; *Commentary*, Jer. 2:1; 3:1; 6:8; 10:24; 12:10; Lam. 1:9; 2:9.
[67] Wallace, *Christian Life*, 35.
[68] *Commentary*, Jer. 11:4.
[69] *Sermons on Nativity*, 62-63.
[70] *Sermons on Election and Reprobation*, 266, 273.
[71] *Sermons on Genesis 1-11*, 112.
[72] For example, in his *Sermons on 2 Samuel*: 53, 74, 172, 194, 232, 172, 257, 281, 305, 357, 391, 510, 525, 537. Similarly, it is a frequent topic in his lectures; in just the first ten chapters of Jeremiah we find: 2:28, 4:22, 4:23, 5:19, 5:25, 9:22, 9:23, 9:24, 9:25, 10:2, 10:10, 10:11, 10:16, 10:23, 10:25.
[73] Dowey, *Knowledge of God*, 18-19.
[74] B.A. Gerrish, "Calvin's Eucharistic Piety," *Calvin and Spirituality, Calvin and His Contemporaries, Calvin Studies Society Papers, 1995, 1997* (Grand Rapids, Mich.: CRC Product Services, 1998), 59.
[75] Dowey, *Knowledge of God*, 30.

and reverence, the two must always come together, restores the person to their rightful place before God, a humble, thankful, beloved child of God, who is eager to serve God.[76]

Calvin taught his students that humanity was created good,[77] yet had in its pride rebelled against a good God,[78] rejecting and despising God,[79] while indulging itself in everything vile,[80] violating its own remaining sense of piety.[81] Humankind, blind to its own sin[82] and responsible for its own blindness,[83] is helpless to do anything about its sin[84] or to benefit itself[85] in its own power.[86] Calvin dwelt on the importance of knowing God,[87] for "to know God is the chief part of perfect wisdom."[88] We are to see God's greatness in his creation and providence,[89] and his holiness in his judgment,[90] all cause for human humility.[91] In nearly every message, Calvin exalted God's mercy in Christ, who stands ready to help all who turn to him,[92] then invited all to respond with repentant prostration before God.[93] Humankind must be prostrated before God.[94] "God then wanted to subdue all human glory, God wanted to reduce men to subjection."[95] Once humankind was prostrate, always prostration first,[96] Calvin would call them upward in reverence,[97] linking together the two-fold

---

[76] *Commentary*, Ezek. 1:13.
[77] Zachman, "Deny Yourself," 467.
[78] *Sermons on Nativity*, 46; *Commentary*, Ezek. 11:19.
[79] *Sermons on Genesis 1-11*, 190, 846.
[80] *Commentary*, Jer. 4:23.
[81] E.A. McKee, "Contacts, Contours, Contents: Towards a Description of Calvin's Understanding of Worship," *Calvin and Spirituality, Calvin and His Contemporaries, Calvin Studies Society Papers, 1995, 1997* (Grand Rapids, Mich.: CRC Product Services, 1998), 69.
[82] Pitkin, "The Spiritual Gospel," 193-95.
[83] *Commentary*, Ezek. 5:13.
[84] Dowey, *Knowledge of God*, 22.
[85] *Commentary*, Jer. 10:23.
[86] *Sermons on Genesis 1-11*, 171, 194, 390, 561, 827, 852; *Sermons on 2 Samuel*, 53, 185, 203, 232, 290; *Commentary*, Jer. 7:30; 10:23; 12:8; 13:18; Lam. 1:7, 20; 2:21; Ezek. 1:28; 9:10; 11:5, 19.
[87] *Sermons on Genesis 1-11*, 401, 562; *Sermons on 2 Samuel*, 74, 223, 286, 305, 356, 371, 396, 542; *Sermons on Nativity*, 27, 34; *Commentary*, Jer. 2:28; 4:22; 9:24; 10:10, 16, 23; Ezek. 1:28; 2:5; 6:10.
[88] *Commentary*, Jer. 9:24.
[89] *Commentary*, Jer. 10:2.
[90] *Sermons on 2 Samuel*, 257.
[91] Selderhuis, *Pilgrim Life*, 63; *Commentary*, Lam. 4:9; 5:16; Ezek. 15:6; 16:1; 18:25; Dan. 2:21; 4:31; 7:10; 9:4.
[92] E.D. Kraan, "Le Péché et la Repentance," *La Revue Reformée* 48 (1997), 44; *Sermons on Nativity*, 28.
[93] *Commentary*, Lam. 2:14; 3:42.
[94] *Commentary*, Ezek. 18:20; Dan. 9:7; 10:12; 11:37.
[95] "Sermon on Luke 1:1-4," *CO* 46:8.
[96] Wallace, *Christian Life*, 284.
[97] *Sermons on 2 Samuel*, 391.

knowledge of God with the two-fold response.[98] "That we may especially be humbled under thy mighty hand, and that being really prostrate through a deep feeling of repentance, we may raise our hopes to heaven."[99] He explains this two-fold response regarding prayer: "Repentance throws men downwards, and faith raises them upwards again."[100]

The two-fold knowledge and response bid a person to rely on God to save and help them.[101] "For those who cast their eyes down to the earth raise their eyes to heaven."[102] In order to come to this knowledge and response, one must listen to the Word preached,[103] which aids our struggle for more faith[104] and invites us to repentance[105] with the allure of God's love in Christ.[106] Calvin prayed for those "destined pastors" in his lectures that they would, through teaching the true knowledge of God and humanity, call sinners to repentance.[107] The students of the Genevan Academy would understand the need for the two-fold knowledge of God and self, leading to the two-fold response of prostration and reverence, in order to grow in holiness.

Principle 2: Bible Preaching. Because God has given his Word to lead us to life, therefore submit to the preaching of the Word of Christ.

Calvin would remind his hearers that submitting to Bible preaching is necessary because sanctification relies on the continuous exposure to God's Word,[108] brought by faithful preaching within the church.[109] One must hear and heed the Word,[110] fleeing to the grace of God offered in Christ.[111] The students were reminded that they must not only preach faithfully,[112] but that they too, as pastors, must sit under the preaching of the Word to grow in holiness.[113]

During sermons Calvin will remind all of the importance of heeding the sermon. God sends pastors to preach to the people,[114] so they must listen even to imperfect pastors, for God uses weak men, who preach with God's authori-

---

[98] *Commentary*, Ezek. 6:10; Dan. 4:16, 37; 8:18; 9:4, 21; 10:8.
[99] *Commentary*, Lam. 2:14.
[100] *Commentary*, Dan. 9:18.
[101] *Sermons on Genesis 1-11*, 827.
[102] *Commentary*, Dan. 4:34.
[103] *Sermons on Nativity*, 35.
[104] *Commentary*, Jer. 10:25.
[105] *Commentary*, Ezek. 6:10.
[106] *Commentary*, Jer. 9:25.
[107] *Commentary*, Ezek. 13:9.
[108] *Sermons on 2 Samuel*, 375; Wallace, *Christian Life*, 206; *Sermons on Election and Reprobation*, 299.
[109] Wallace, *Christian Life*, 207.
[110] Dowey, *Knowledge of God*, 38.
[111] *Sermons on Nativity*, 79.
[112] *Commentary*, Jer. 4:12, 27; 5:13; 8:21; 9:6, 11, 12, 21; 11:18; 15:1; 30:31; Lam. 1:2; 2:1; 4:13; Ezek. 3:17; 7:26; Dan. 7:6; 9:6; 10:7; 11:33-34.
[113] *Commentary*, Dan. 9:2.
[114] *Sermons on Genesis 1-11*, 394.

Chapter 6 - Calvin's Teaching to the Students of the Genevan Academy

ty.[115] It is God's voice they must hear,[116] for they can hear his voice nowhere else,[117] in order to find Christ,[118] who is all they need.[119] In his lectures his students were reminded that they must heed sermons,[120] from men sent by God,[121] as God's Word for them,[122] to bring judgment on sin[123] that they might repent[124] and through faith[125] find mercy and life in Jesus Christ.

Since no human could naturally deduce his lowliness and God's glory in such a way as to continuously find grace,[126] they must have the Word of God preached[127] to give them this knowledge. With God meeting them in the Word preached,[128] they repent, and God pours faith into the believers' hearts though the Word, which unites them to the sanctifying power[129] of Christ himself,[130] presented in the Word.[131] Submitting to biblical sermons was critical in Calvin's plan for enhancing the holiness of his pastoral candidates.

Principle 3: God's Love. Because God has elected us in love, therefore apprehend God's love to move us to love God in holiness.

Calvin believed that it was not knowledge of sin that finally moved the sinner to turn to God,[132] but the apprehension of the love and mercy of God as found in Christ.[133] Calvin taught that God loved us first, apart from any good in us or merit which might warrant his love, rendering moot the Roman claim to our meritorious love of God.[134] God's love stands alone in priority, and causality, that all might be of grace, not human effort.[135] Calvin will highlight God's love often,[136] showing it by God's provision in creation[137] and protection in provi-

---

[115] *Sermons on Election and Reprobation*, 252-53; "Sermon on Luke 1:1-4," *CO* 4:8.
[116] *Sermons on Nativity*, 70; *Sermons on Election and Reprobation*, 297-98.
[117] *Sermons on 2 Samuel*, 233.
[118] *Sermons on Election and Reprobation*, 208-09.
[119] "Sermon on Luke 1:1-4," *CO* 46:1-2.
[120] *Commentary*, Ezek. 10:15; Dan. 2:9; 3:7; 7:16.
[121] *Commentary*, Dan. 8:14.
[122] *Commentary*, Jer. 9:20.
[123] *Commentary*, Jer. 3:13.
[124] *Commentary*, Jer. 5:15.
[125] *Commentary*, Dan. 12:3.
[126] *Commentary*, Jer. 11:23.
[127] *Sermons on 2 Samuel*, 50; *Sermons on Genesis 1-11*, 545.
[128] *Commentary*, Jer. 7:23.
[129] Dowey, *Knowledge of God*, 10.
[130] Niesel, *Theology of Calvin*, 30; *Sermons on Nativity*, 8.
[131] *Commentary*, Jer. 12:2.
[132] *Sermons on 2 Samuel*, 162.
[133] *Sermons on Nativity*, 81.
[134] *Sermons on 2 Samuel*, 602. Calvin, contra Aquinas, followed Scotus, who taught that God, in choosing to love humans, made them lovable. Ozment, *The Age of Reform*, 34-35.
[135] *Commentary*, Ezek. 16:8.
[136] *Commentary*, Jer. 2:1.
[137] *Commentary*, Jer. 32:33; cf. *Sermons on Genesis 1-11*, 90, 112, 120.

dence,[138] where even our suffering[139] becomes a sign of God's "paternal love."[140]

One must perceive God's love to advance in holiness,[141] for once a sinner was brought low before a holy God, he must have the hope of God's love,[142] seen in Christ on the cross.[143] It was God's warm love, in his promise of forgiveness[144] through faith in Christ,[145] that served as the magnetic attractive force[146] to bring the Christian to repent of sin,[147] and turn toward God[148] in new obedience.[149]

Calvin constantly invites his hearers to marvel at the depth of God's love for us, who, unlike a normal husband, takes us back after our failures[150] and bids us tenderly to come to him.[151] In his sermons Calvin will remind his hearers that God's love is unconditional kindness,[152] like that of a Father,[153] which came to us before creation,[154] he takes us into his house and makes us his children,[155] so that we are drawn to him,[156] may rest in his love,[157] be assured in troubles[158] and bring him glory.[159] In his lectures he will emphasize to his students that God's love stands constant despite our sin,[160] restrains God's hand,[161] gives us hope in adversity[162] and invites us sweetly and daily to submission,[163] that we might "taste God's paternal goodness"[164] and be reconciled with our father.[165]

---

[138] *Sermons on 2 Samuel*, 226.
[139] *Commentary*, Lam. 4:21.
[140] *Commentary*, Jer. 10:24.
[141] *Commentary*, Lam. 3:32.
[142] *Sermons on 2 Samuel*, 489.
[143] *Sermons on 2 Samuel*, 400.
[144] *Commentary*, Jer. 14:22.
[145] *Sermons on Nativity*, 20.
[146] *Commentary*, Ezek. 7:26; 18:5; 20:11; Dan. 11:5.
[147] *Commentary*, Jer. 2:1.
[148] *Sermons on Genesis 1-11*, 547.
[149] *Commentary*, Jer. 11:4.
[150] *Commentary*, Jer. 3:1.
[151] *Sermons on Nativity*, 25.
[152] *Sermons on Beatitudes*, 4.
[153] *Sermons on 2 Samuel*, 603, 198.
[154] *Sermons on 2 Samuel*, 605.
[155] *Sermons on 2 Samuel*, 535.
[156] *Sermons on 2 Samuel*, 386.
[157] *Sermons on 2 Samuel*, 161.
[158] *Sermons on 2 Samuel*, 396.
[159] *Sermons on 2 Samuel*, 382.
[160] *Commentary*, Jer. 17:7.
[161] *Commentary*, Jer. 6:8.
[162] *Commentary*, Lam. 2:9.
[163] *Commentary*, Jer. 11:12; 12:10.
[164] *Commentary*, Lam. 1:9. Cf. *Commentary*, Jer. 14:22; Lam. 3:24; Ezek. 1:13; 3:18; Dan. 11:1.
[165] *Commentary*, Jer. 6:8.

Calvin will also instruct his students to be certain to preach on his mercy whenever sin is denounced.[166] The love of God, as the motive force in Calvin's theology of sanctification, received ample treatment in all of Calvin's teaching to the students of the Academy.

Principle 4: God Reliance. Because God is the one who sanctifies, therefore rely on God's powerful grace, and not yourself, to become holy.
Calvin wanted his hearers to abandon faulty Roman methods of self-improvement and instead rely on God for their progress in holiness.[167] "Let us be clear: our soul's eternal salvation depends on God's exercise of his marvelous power."[168] He would remind them that the Father sanctifies us through election,[169] the Son sanctifies us through union with us[170] and the Spirit quickens us to holiness.[171] People must believe entirely that God desires their holiness and will sanctify them to the uttermost, so that, disabused of the notion of self-help, they will actively turn to God for holiness,[172] resting from self-effort.[173] "We must always remind ourselves of this word: God must do it."[174]

Underscoring all his teaching was the powerful theme of grace, looking to and relying on the grace of God to save and sanctify his hearers.[175] "Not only has God's free grace raised us to such a height, but [it] also sustains us."[176] In his lectures he teaches that God shows us mercy,[177] circumcises our hearts,[178] refashions us,[179] gives us new hearts,[180] sanctifies even our prayers[181] and makes us holy.[182] In his sermons we hear that God pities us always,[183] raises us to new life,[184] offers us continual grace,[185] adopts us,[186] convicts us of sin,[187]

---

[166] *Commentary*, Jer. 26:6; Ezek. 1:1.
[167] *Commentary*, Jer. 4:14; Ezek. 16:30, 63; 18:30; Dan. 10:11, 19; *Sermons on 2 Samuel*, 620.
[168] *Sermons on Nativity*, 42.
[169] *Commentary*, Jer. 11:17.
[170] *Commentary*, Lam. 4:20. Wallace, *Christian Life*, 78; Wallace, *Geneva and the Reformation*, 177. Cf. M.A. Garcia, *Life in Christ, Union with Christ and Twofold Grace in Calvin's Theology*, Studies in Christian History and Thought (Waynesboro, Ga.: Paternoster, 2008), 125.
[171] *Sermons on 2 Samuel*, 528.
[172] *Sermons on Nativity*, 88; Wallace, *Christian Life*, 14.
[173] *Commentary*, Ezek. 20:12, 44.
[174] *Sermons on 2 Samuel*, 194.
[175] *Commentary*, Ezek. 16:60; 18:17; "Sermon on Matt. 14:14-18," *CO* 46:755.
[176] *Commentary*, Ezek. 15:6.
[177] *Commentary*, Jer. 10:23.
[178] *Commentary*, Jer. 4:4.
[179] *Commentary*, Ezek. 18:32.
[180] *Commentary*, Ezek. 11:19.
[181] *Commentary*, Jer. 14:12.
[182] *Commentary*, Jer. 2:3.
[183] *Sermons on Nativity*, 39; *Sermons on Genesis 1-11*, 559.
[184] *Sermons on Genesis 1-11*, 134-35.
[185] *Sermons on Beatitudes*, 1.
[186] *Sermons on 2 Samuel*, 400.

purifies us,[188] reforms his image in us,[189] molds and leads us.[190] Relying on God's grace to sanctify is essential to Calvin's theology of sanctification because people must be moved from willful self-reliance to the humility of depending on God for holiness.[191]

Principle 5: Desiring Holiness. Because God is holy and loves holiness therefore desire deeply to become holy.

To help his hearers desire to become more holy,[192] Calvin held up both the high standard of the law[193] and examples of holiness, such as God himself[194] and the Old Testament saints,[195] to contrast to his hearers' low expectations for holiness.[196] He persistently set these models before them, reminding them of the requirements of obedience within the covenant of grace,[197] to stir them up to strive to "attain to that perfect holiness."[198] He would call hearers to wholehearted obedience,[199] never just external conformity,[200] lived out in *pietas* and *caritas*,[201] a deep love for God culminated in true worship[202] and love for one's neighbor,[203] which translated into actual service.[204]

In his sermons Calvin constantly cajoled or warned that the people must keep themselves under strict control,[205] walk the narrow path,[206] in all modesty,[207] with whole hearts,[208] forgiving others,[209] doing deeds of mercy[210] and worshiping God aright.[211] Similarly, in his lectures Calvin called his students to obey the law,[212] worship honestly,[213] live with integrity[214] and attend to doc-

---

[187] *Sermons on 2 Samuel*, 455.
[188] *Sermons on 2 Samuel*, 328.
[189] *Sermons on Genesis 1-11*, 366.
[190] *Sermons on 2 Samuel*, 142.
[191] *Commentary*, Jer. 10:23.
[192] Wallace, *Christian Life*, 324.
[193] *Commentary*, Jer. 9:14.
[194] *Commentary*, Dan. 9:25.
[195] *Commentary*, Ezek. 14:14; Dan. 1:1.
[196] *Sermons on Genesis 1-11*, 578-79.
[197] *Commentary*, Jer. 13:25.
[198] *Commentary*, Jer. 23:24; cf. *Sermons on Genesis 1-11*, 851.
[199] *Sermons on Genesis 1-11*, 578; *Sermons on 2 Samuel*, 253; *Commentary*, Jer. 7:23; Wallace, *Christian Life*, 122.
[200] *Sermons on 2 Samuel*, 261.
[201] McKee, "Contacts, Contours, Contents," 73.
[202] *Commentary*, Jer. 11:4.
[203] *Sermons on Nativity*, 46.
[204] *Sermons on 2 Samuel*, 258.
[205] *Sermons on Beatitudes*, 43; *Sermons on 2 Samuel*, 73.
[206] *Sermons on 2 Samuel*, 91.
[207] *Sermons on 2 Samuel*, 63.
[208] *Sermons on Genesis 1-11*, 577.
[209] *Sermons on Beatitudes*, 54.
[210] *Sermons on Beatitudes*, 44.
[211] *Sermons on 2 Samuel*, 246.
[212] *Commentary*, Jer. 11:4.

Chapter 6 - Calvin's Teaching to the Students of the Genevan Academy

trine.[215] This desire for holiness was an essential part of Calvin's overall sanctification theology.[216] By showing God's holiness, God's desire for their holiness and their incredible need to become more holy, Calvin created in his hearers a hunger for holiness that would lead them to seek more the grace of God,[217] and thus become more holy.[218]

Principle 6: Faith. Because God sanctifies by giving more faith, therefore struggle daily for more faith to become more holy.

Although faith is a gift of God, coming though his Holy Spirit[219] by hearing of the Word,[220] the Christian must still struggle to increase his faith[221] toward greater assurance,[222] for faith is certainty,[223] which leads to holiness[224] by uniting us to Christ.[225] "That we may not be like the rose wobbling in every wind, but that we may have an assured faith."[226] The struggle for faith is always a struggle to believe the promises of God, which we hear over against life's visible trials,[227] by which the devil tempts us to unbelief.[228] Taking the struggles of the prophets in the texts,[229] Calvin will point out that such struggles are necessary because they force believers into periods where they see the weakness of their faith, leading them to desire more faith from God.[230] Believers must struggle for faith in trials[231] by accepting God's promises in his Word,[232] in order to repose in him[233] without fear or shame of the struggle, knowing God will give increased faith.[234]

To gain more faith in the struggle, the believer must come to a true knowledge of himself as weak in faith,[235] and to a true knowledge of God as the

---

[213] *Commentary*, Jer. 7:31.
[214] *Commentary*, Ezek. 14:14.
[215] *Commentary*, Jer. 11:6.
[216] Wallace, *Christian Life*, 325.
[217] *Commentary*, Ezek. 11:3; Wallace, *Christian Life*, 323.
[218] *Sermons on Genesis 1-11*, 571.
[219] Niesel, *Theology of Calvin*, 155.
[220] *Sermons on Nativity*, 8; "Sermon on Luke 1:1-4," *CO* 46:5.
[221] *Commentary*, Jer. 20:8; Lam. 3:15, 18, 54, 60; Dan. 7:2.
[222] Muller, *Unaccommodated*, 168.
[223] J.R. Beeke, "Making Sense of Calvin's Paradoxes on Assurance of Faith," *Calvin and Spirituality, Calvin and His Contemporaries, Calvin Studies Society Papers, 1995, 1997* (Grand Rapids, Mich.: CRC Product Services, 1998), 14.
[224] Wallace, *Christian Life*, 327.
[225] Wallace, *Christian Life*, 21.
[226] "Sermon on Luke 1:1-4," *CO* 46:6.
[227] Wallace, *Christian Life*, 251.
[228] *Commentary*, Lam. 3:54.
[229] *Commentary*, Lam. 3:55.
[230] *Commentary*, Lam. 3:18, 26.
[231] *Commentary*, Lam. 3:15, 60; Dan 7:5.
[232] *Commentary*, Jer. 22:5.
[233] *Commentary*, Jer. 6:16.
[234] Niesel, *Theology of Calvin*, 155; *Commentary*, Jer. 14:10; Lam. 3:20; 5:22.
[235] *Institutes* 3.2.18.

one who supplies faith.[236] It is the love of God, known through the promises of his Word,[237] which infuses the heart of the struggling believer with faith[238] and therefore assurance.[239] Calvin offered his students a particularly applicable example of how to struggle for faith: Jeremiah's struggle for faith to preach boldly to a world which rejects God's Word.[240] To be a student at the Genevan Academy was to understand the need to struggle for faith, even as a pastor.

Principle 7: Repentance. Because God gives grace to the lowly, therefore repent humbly to find more grace.
Calvin affirmed that the whole of the believer's life must be one of repentance,[241] since even the best of us sins continually.[242] Repentance, a gift of God's grace,[243] is necessary that we may continually obtain pardon as we turn from sin to God,[244] receiving new grace to walk in obedience.[245] Calvin typically ended his messages with prayers of repentance.[246] "Now let us let us cast ourselves down…conscious of our faults."[247]

Calvin would often teach on repentance, as though his hearers did not understand it, calling them to see their need for it.[248] He taught that repentance was not a ceremony but a turning of the heart from sin to God,[249] a divine opening of Satan-blinded eyes to the reality of sin,[250] along with the gift of admitting that one is wrong.[251] To see our sin properly, we must have God's Word to define our sin,[252] the church to confront us with conviction of the sin we would rather not see[253] and self-examination for sin;[254] for the moment must come when we look inward and see that we have sinned.[255] This recognition of sin

---

[236] *Commentary*, Dan. 7:2; "Sermon on Luke 1:1-4," *CO* 46:7.
[237] *Commentary*, Jer. 29:14; Beeke, "Assurance," 49-50.
[238] *Commentary*, Jer. 3:12.
[239] McWilliams, "Certainty," 514.
[240] *Commentary*, Jer. 20:9.
[241] *Commentary*, Jer. 14:20; Steinmetz, "Reformation and Conversion," 32.
[242] *Sermons on 2 Samuel*, 94.
[243] Kraan, "Le Péché et la Repentance," 47; *Sermons on 2 Samuel*, 488.
[244] *Sermons on 2 Samuel*, 491; *Commentary*, Dan. 9:9.
[245] *Commentary*, Ezek. 5:15; 18:22; Steinmetz, "Reformation and Conversion," 32.
[246] *Commentary*, Jer. 2:35.
[247] *Sermons on Nativity*, 151; cf. *Sermons on 2 Samuel*, 505; *Commentary*, Jer. 2:5; 8:5.
[248] *Sermons on 2 Samuel*, 544.
[249] The distinction between Roman ritual and real heart turning was a particular theme in his lectures on Jeremiah, see the *Commentary* at 3:10; 4:4, 14; 7:1, 5, 21; 11:11. Cf. *Sermons on 2 Samuel*, 540, 556.
[250] Selderhuis, "Faith Between God and the Devil," 201.
[251] *Commentary*, Jer. 8:5; 13:23; *Sermons on 2 Samuel*, 54.
[252] *Sermons on 2 Samuel*, 491.
[253] *Sermons on 2 Samuel*, 556.
[254] *Commentary*, Ezek. 13:9; 18:30; Dan. 3:1; 8:11; Wallace, *Christian Life*, 225.
[255] *Sermons on Genesis 1-11*, 379, 547, 554; *Sermons on 2 Samuel*, 188, 495, 512, 560, 632; *Sermons on Nativity*, 90; *Commentary*, Jer. 2:35; 8:6; Lam. 3:39. Cf. Beeke, "Assurance," 56.

Chapter 6 - Calvin's Teaching to the Students of the Genevan Academy

must contain a real heart-felt grief over sin,[256] followed by a sincere, not ritualistic, confession to God and any others who ought to hear our confession.[257] The turn from sin is always away from God's corrective hatred of sin[258] and toward God's mercy,[259] where one may find forgiveness[260] and all the grace needed[261] to walk in the obedience of faith.[262]

Repentance, a fruit of faith,[263] was central to sanctification, leading to the low point of the downward movement of prostration, as the full force of the two-fold knowledge of God and self brought the believer low, leading to the upward movement of reverence. Calvin will generally put these two motions together in order: go down in repentance[264] that you might be lifted up[265] by God's grace. Believers would find there the holiness that God required,[266] which they could never manufacture in themselves.[267] The students of the Genevan Academy were reminded that preaching must never tickle the ears but confront stony hearts with conviction of sin that they might repent and thus find holiness.[268]

Principle 8: Self-denial. Because God gives life to those who lose it, therefore deny yourself as a practice of faith and repentance.
Although Calvin did not use the term self-denial often in these commentaries,[269] if one considers his entire emphasis on pastoral holiness,[270] these commentaries drip with self-denial, the heart of all "true religion."[271] We must daily search for opportunities to deny self-love,[272] since we all seek to exalt ourselves over God and our neighbors,[273] and rather embrace God's will and

---

[256] *Commentary*, Ezek. 6:9; 20:43; *Sermons on 2 Samuel*, 521, 555, 656; *Sermons on Election and Reprobation*, 296.
[257] *Commentary*, Jer. 5:9; 10:19; *Sermons on 2 Samuel*, 488, 492, 514, 553, 654.
[258] *Commentary*, Jer. 15:10; Lam. 2:19.
[259] Kraan, "Le Péché et la Repentance," 41; *Commentary*, Lam. 2:14; Dan. 4:26.
[260] *Commentary*, Jer. 14:20.
[261] *Sermons on 2 Samuel*, 518.
[262] *Commentary*, Jer. 7:6.
[263] R.C. Gamble, "Calvin and Sixteenth-Century Spirituality: Comparison with the Anabaptists," *Calvin and Spirituality, Calvin and His Contemporaries, Calvin Studies Society Papers, 1995, 1997* (Grand Rapids, Mich.: CRC Product Services, 1998), 46, note 77.
[264] *Commentary*, Jer. 40:1.
[265] *Commentary*, Lam 3:40.
[266] *Commentary*, Lam. 1:9.
[267] *Sermons on Genesis 1-11*, 385.
[268] *Commentary*, Jer. 6:8; Lam. 2:14; Ezek. 13:22.
[269] *Commentary*, Jer. 4:4; 17:24; 31:33; Lam. 2:14; Ezek. 3:14; 20:12-13; Dan. 1:14; 6:23.
[270] See Chapter 5.
[271] *Commentary*, Jer. 4:4.
[272] Winecoff, "Mortification," 93.
[273] *Sermons on 2 Samuel*, 77.

grace to love our neighbor and God.[274] Self-denial is not an outward ritual but a surrendering of the heart to God's will, as when we rightly observe the Sabbath[275] and the sacraments.[276] While self-denial involves human will, it only follows our union with Christ and God's gracious work in the life of Christians.[277] Calvin would offer models of self-denial, notably Daniel and his three colleagues,[278] showing their willingness to die rather than worship falsely, a point with obvious applications for preachers facing the fury of persecution in France.[279]

Self-denial was the daily outworking of several key themes in Calvin's theology of sanctification. First, self-denial required submitting to God's Word, which would reveal the will of God to which one must be in subjection,[280] rather than trusting in one's own reason.[281] Second, self-denial required the believer to practice faith, believing that following God's will was best.[282] Third, self-denial was a clear call to repentance, to turn from self-will, which must be renounced for God to work in us.[283] Fourth, self-denial applied the two-fold knowledge in coming to see that God's will was best, which leads to a reverent embrace of God's will.[284] Fifth, cross-bearing forces the will of God upon us,[285] leading us to deny our own will[286] and conforming us to the image of Christ.[287] Finally, self-denial helps guide one in the right use of this life, enforcing a vocation-specific moderate use of this life[288] and a moderation of our emotions,[289] so that we might do good to those who hurt us.[290] It would be clear to any student at the Academy, for a pastor to advance in holiness, he must constantly deny himself.

Principle 9: Cross-bearing. Because God mortifies through suffering, therefore bear the cross to mortify our flesh.

In bearing the cross, Calvin wants his students to understand that all our suffering, no matter what the immediate source—people, nature or the devil—comes

---

[274] *Commentary*, Jer. 31:33.
[275] *Commentary*, Ezek. 20:13.
[276] *Commentary*, Jer. 4:4.
[277] *Commentary*, Ezek. 3:14; 20:12; Winecoff, "Mortification," 90.
[278] *Commentary*, Dan. 3:16.
[279] *Commentary*, Dan. 6:23.
[280] *Commentary*, Jer. 31:33.
[281] Zachman, "Deny Yourself," 471.
[282] *Sermons on 2 Samuel*, 231.
[283] *Commentary*, Jer. 17:24.
[284] *Commentary*, Lam. 2:14; Ezek. 9:9.
[285] *Sermons on 2 Samuel*, 321.
[286] *Sermons on 2 Samuel*, 523.
[287] Winecoff, "Mortification," 92; Wallace, *Christian Life*, 52.
[288] *Commentary*, Dan. 1:14.
[289] *Sermons on 2 Samuel*, 636-37.
[290] *Sermons on 2 Samuel*, 239.

at the hands of God's loving and wise providence,[291] such that we always "have to do with him."[292] We must all bear the cross, for there is no other way for the Father to kill off our flesh.[293] While there are various reasons we suffer the cross, sometimes as discipline for sin,[294] sometimes for righteousness' sake,[295] it always works to conform us to Christ.[296] So rather than fleeing the cross,[297] we must willingly submit to it, embracing it with patience,[298] even joy, knowing that God is at work for our salvation.[299]

Cross-bearing works toward our holiness by bringing us down, prostrate in humility,[300] forcing us to see the truth about ourselves; we are weak, finite creatures[301] who cannot stop even our own suffering,[302] and so must give up trusting ourselves.[303] Humbled by the true knowledge of our weakness, we are brought to repent of our prideful self-reliance,[304] as well as any immediate sin,[305] embracing the cross even more tightly.[306] Cross-bearing leads us to look upward to God for mercy, as the only one who can truly alleviate our pain,[307] because we know he only wounds in order to heal us.[308] Cross-bearing drives forward our daily struggle for faith, providing the tests where we come to believe that God, not fate, is at work in our suffering.[309] Finally, cross-bearing spurs us to think of the future life,[310] a day in which we will suffer no more.[311] Given the reality of the world in which Calvin was sending out his pastoral

---

[291] *Sermons on Genesis 1-11*, 599, 834; *Sermons on 2 Samuel*, 49, 68, 224, 441, 653, 829; *Sermons on Beatitudes*, 19; *Sermons on Nativity*, 73; *Commentary*, Jer. 3:37; 12:2; Ezek. 9:4, 9; 12:13; 14:21; Dan. 2:21. For an example of the frequency of this theme, consider these occurrences in just the first three chapters of the commentary on Lamentations: 1:17, 12, 21; 2:4, 17; 3:25-26, 30-32, 34.
[292] *Commentary*, Lam. 1:12; *CO* 39:523, "...quum sentimus nobis cum ipso esse negotium."
[293] *Sermons on 2 Samuel*, 343; *Commentary*, Lam. 4:21.
[294] *Commentary*, Jer. 10:24.
[295] *Sermons on Beatitudes*, 68.
[296] Garcia, *Life in Christ*, 141.
[297] *Commentary*, Ezek. 1:1.
[298] *Commentary*, Lam. 3:25.
[299] *Commentary*, Lam. 3:30.
[300] *Sermons on 2 Samuel*, 288.
[301] Zachman, "Deny Yourself," 475.
[302] *Sermons on 2 Samuel*, 336.
[303] Winecoff, "Mortification," 101.
[304] *Commentary*, Jer. 4:18.
[305] *Commentary*, Jer. 2:9, 18, 25; Lam.1:5; Ezek. 6:9; *Sermons on Election and Reprobation*, 142, 160; *Sermons on 2 Samuel*, 636.
[306] *Commentary*, Jer. 10:24.
[307] *Sermons on 2 Samuel*, 68, 147, 183, 478, 485, 532, 587, 593; *Commentary*, Jer. 1:16; 2:30.
[308] *Commentary*, Jer. 14:22; Dan. 4:25; "Sermon on Matt. 14:14-18," *CO* 46:749.
[309] *Commentary*, Lam. 1:21.
[310] *Sermons on 2 Samuel*, 411.
[311] *Commentary*, Jer. 2:11; Dan. 8:10.

candidates, it is natural that he would regularly remind them that faithful teachers, like the prophets of old, will always be attacked by the enemies of God, and in bearing the cross would grow in piety.[312]

Principle 10: Future Life. Because God grants us an eternal inheritance, therefore meditate on the future life with Christ.
Calvin would generally take up the subject of meditating on the future life when the passage spoke of trials in this life,[313] or during his closing prayers,[314] reminding his hearers that they will eventually have a place of rest.[315] "We shall at length enjoy thy full and perfect glory, when we shall be transformed into it in that inheritance."[316] Naturally it was the Word of God to which one should look for such hope and faith in the future life.[317] He encouraged the students to use times free of trials to meditate on heaven, in order to develop the constancy needed to "to pour forth our blood in testimony to the truth."[318] They were to remember that, as "pilgrims in the world,"[319] they were passing to their true home in heaven,[320] and so like the Old Testament saints,[321] they must aspire to "perpetual existence" rather than to "grovel upon earth,"[322] in order to not stumble by being too attached to this world.[323]

Meditation on the future life promotes holiness, first, as it relates to God's mercy. Since our future life is secured in our graceful adoption as God's children through Christ,[324] such that Christians already "bear within them heavenly life,"[325] we are able "always to aspire to this eternal rest."[326] Second, meditation on the future life helps us with the struggle for faith, by raising our eyes from the trials in this world upward to the hope that we have.[327] Third, it aids our self-denial, for by showing us the future glories that await us, we can more easily deny ourselves here.[328] Fourth, it allows us patience in bearing the

---

[312] *Commentary*, Jer. 37:17; 38:6; Ezek. 7:27; 17:20; Dan. 1:9; 6:24.

[313] *Commentary*, Dan. 3:19; *Sermons on 2 Samuel*, 508.

[314] Calvin drew attention to the future life in 57 of his 66 lectures on Daniel and 60 of his 65 lectures on Ezekiel. That Calvin retained a similar ratio of prayers on the future life in his lectures on Ezekiel, even as he himself drew near to death, may suggest that these prayers were a theological discipline more than a situational necessity.

[315] *Sermons on Beatitudes*, 20.

[316] *Commentary*, Jer. 10:16.

[317] "Sermon on Luke 1:1-4," *CO* 46:6.

[318] *Commentary*, Dan. 3:19.

[319] *Commentary*, Ezek. 6:9.

[320] *Sermons on Beatitudes*, 26.

[321] *Commentary*, Jer. 31:2.

[322] *Commentary*, Dan. Introduction by Calvin.

[323] *Sermons on Genesis 1-11*, 854.

[324] *Commentary*, Jer. 32:39; Ezek. 20:14.

[325] *Commentary*, Dan. 2:45.

[326] *Sermons on 2 Samuel*, 509.

[327] *Commentary*, Jer. 12:15; Lam. 1:9; Dan. 12:2-3.

[328] *Commentary*, Dan. 2:43; 3:19.

cross,[329] knowing that a better life awaits us,[330] so we may boldly endure trials here, even to martyrdom,[331] a real possibility for his students. "But when we understand our inheritance to be in heaven...[this prepares] the sons of God for martyrdom."[332] Calvin's students could not but help learn this lesson: meditation on the future life was essential for faithful living in this present world.

Principle 11: Present Life. Because God providentially guides all of life, therefore rightly use this present life to love others.
Calvin would often teach and preach on the right use of the present life,[333] with moderation as a favorite theme within the topic.[334] Moderation was more than restraining appetites or self-discipline, it was an inner spiritual state of trusting the Lord[335] rather than letting our fears drive us to immoderate passions.[336] Because the emotional life is one place where faith is most perfected,[337] believers were called first to moderate their emotions and desires[338] by looking to the Lord for the equilibrium of faith.[339] One is to be moderate in their use of food and drink,[340] their desire for money,[341] their use of material possessions,[342] even in their zeal for the Lord.[343] Second, as an exercise in devotion to God where obedience and faith grow,[344] one must embrace God's vocation, never rebelling from it[345] no matter the difficulties or results,[346] since God protects us within our vocation.[347] Nor should one grab for more than God provides,[348] lest he bring correction.[349] Third, we should be good stewards in this world so that we can love our neighbors well,[350] both by avoiding injury to them and by serving

---

[329] *Sermons on Beatitudes*, 66.
[330] Wallace, *Christian Life*, 316; *Commentary*, Dan. 8:10.
[331] *Sermons on Beatitudes*, 25, 28, 51; *Commentary*, Dan. 3:18.
[332] *Commentary*, Dan. 3:18.
[333] Zachman, "Deny Yourself," 480-81.
[334] Wallace, *Christian Life*, 170. There are, for example, 12 references to moderation in just the first four chapters of the Daniel Commentary: 1:4, 8, 14; 2:46; 3:13, 19; 4:2, 13, 16, 27, 28, 35.
[335] *Sermons on 2 Samuel*, 420.
[336] *Sermons on 2 Samuel*, 659.
[337] *Sermons on 2 Samuel*, 173, 252, 276, 452, 591.
[338] *Commentary*, Jer. 31:3; Lam. 3:19.
[339] *Commentary*, Jer. 48:37; Lam. 1:2.
[340] *Commentary*, Ezek. 16:20; Dan. 5:2.
[341] *Commentary*, Ezek. 18:8.
[342] *Sermons on Genesis 1-11*, 115.
[343] *Commentary*, Jer. 17:18.
[344] Wallace, *Christian Life*, 155; *Commentary*, Ezek. 15:8; *Sermons on 2 Samuel*, 246.
[345] Wallace, *Christian Life*, 181; *Commentary*, Dan. 5:20; 6:7.
[346] *Commentary*, Ezek. 12:3; *Sermons on Election and Reprobation*, 7.
[347] "Sermon on Matt. 4:5-7," *CO* 46:622.
[348] *Commentary*, Dan. 11:2.
[349] *Sermons on Nativity*, 52.
[350] *Commentary*, Dan. 6:17.

them freely.³⁵¹ Throughout this present life, the obedience of faith was to be rendered promptly and completely.³⁵²

The proper use of the present life served to integrate two major aspects of Calvin's theology of sanctification, humility and self-denial. Warring against pride in moderation,³⁵³ submitting to your God-given vocation³⁵⁴ and serving your neighbor as though as important as yourself are all exercises in applied humility.³⁵⁵ Self-denial is found in the moderation of emotions,³⁵⁶ remaining in one's vocation rather that reaching higher,³⁵⁷ and in caring for your neighbor.³⁵⁸ The students at the Genevan Academy would have learned that the right use of this present life was instrumental in their pursuit of piety.

Principle 12: Church. Because God sanctifies his church, therefore engage fully in the life of church.

God sanctifies the church,³⁵⁹ outside of which there is no ordinary hope of salvation,³⁶⁰ so the students were instructed to remain within³⁶¹ and participate fully in her life,³⁶² in order to be made holy.³⁶³ God establishes his church,³⁶⁴ directs and protects her³⁶⁵ with his providence,³⁶⁶ such that her course is more certain than "the fixed course of the sun."³⁶⁷ Because she is his beloved bride,³⁶⁸ God will purify his church,³⁶⁹ redeeming her entirely from sin,³⁷⁰ to his own glory³⁷¹ that we may repose³⁷² in his everlasting salvation.³⁷³ It is the church which is united to the life of Christ as a vine³⁷⁴ and to whom he has given his Word, teachers, discipline, the sacraments and true worship.³⁷⁵

---

[351] *Commentary*, Ezek. 18:7; Dan. 11:34; 12:3.
[352] "Sermon on Matt. 8:14-18," *CO* 46:759; *Commentary*, Ezek. 3:22; Dan 3:13.
[353] *Commentary*, Ezek. 16:15.
[354] *Sermons on Nativity*, 45.
[355] Wallace, *Christian Life*, 179.
[356] *Commentary*, Jer. 12:1.
[357] *Commentary*, Dan. 5:20.
[358] *Commentary*, Jer. 22:13.
[359] Wallace, *Christian Life*, 12.
[360] *Sermons on 2 Samuel*, 389.
[361] *Commentary*, Jer. 31:31.
[362] J. Calvin, *Sermons on the Deity of Christ* (tr. L. Nixon; Audubon, N.J.: Old Paths, 1997), 78.
[363] *Sermons on 2 Samuel*, 377; *Commentary*, Jer. 31:14.
[364] *Sermons on Election and Reprobation*, 8-9.
[365] *Commentary*, Jer. 24:7.
[366] *Commentary*, Dan. 7:27.
[367] *Commentary*, Jer. 31:35.
[368] *Commentary*, Ezek. 6:9.
[369] *Sermons on Election and Reprobation*, 234.
[370] *Commentary*, Jer. 31:32.
[371] *Commentary*, Ezek. 20:9.
[372] *Commentary*, Dan. 11:11.
[373] *Commentary*, Jer. 23:6.
[374] *Commentary*, Jer. 2:21; 11:17.
[375] *Commentary*, Jer. 15:2; 25:6.

Chapter 6 - Calvin's Teaching to the Students of the Genevan Academy

While exalting the value of the church, Calvin is frank about her failings and trials. Externally the world will "mock and deride" the church,[376] reduce her in number through blood shed,[377] exult over her calamities, such that she is small and despised.[378] Internally, because she is by nature a mixture of wheat and tares, there will always be in the church "the wicked who remain with the good,"[379] false professors of the faith who are disguised,[380] backsliders,[381] betrayers like Judas,[382] wolves in the place of pastors[383] and mercenaries who will fight against the progress of the true saints.[384] Calvin would urge his students to prepare for the unavoidable, internal battles against the false believers.[385] God uses both this internal warfare and external sufferings, disciplining first the church,[386] to separate out false from true believers[387] so as to make the church more pure, sparing the true remnant.[388] Yet his hearers were told that they should remain in the church, bearing "in patience the betrayals,"[389] preferring to be "connected to the children of God,"[390] even though the church is "yet sad and deformed,"[391] and praying that Christ will raise the church "out of its miserable afflictions."[392]

Calvin taught his students that the church was important for holiness first, because the church is united to Christ[393] whose sanctifying life flows into her[394] as does the Father's paternal love.[395] Second, in the heart of the church they come under the ministry of the Word[396] through true teachers,[397] a blessing from God.[398] Third, the church will offer them grace through her sacraments[399] and discipline.[400] Fourth, it is the church which will aid them in their struggle

---

[376] *Sermons on Election and Reprobation*, 5.
[377] *Sermons on 2 Samuel*, 73.
[378] *Commentary*, Lam. 1:7.
[379] *Sermons on 2 Samuel*, 90.
[380] *Sermons on Election and Reprobation*, 27.
[381] *Commentary*, Dan. 11:32.
[382] *Sermons on the Deity of Christ*, 76.
[383] *Commentary*, Jer. 18:18.
[384] *Commentary*, Jer. 15:16.
[385] *Sermons on 2 Samuel*, 87; *Commentary*, Jer. 23:16.
[386] *Sermons on the Deity of Christ*, 119; cf. *Commentary*, Jer. 25:18.
[387] *Commentary*, Jer. 12:14.
[388] *Commentary*, Jer. 23:3.
[389] *Sermons on the Deity of Christ*, 80.
[390] *Commentary*, Jer. 51:50.
[391] *Commentary*, Jer. 51:50.
[392] *Commentary*, Dan. 7:22; cf. *Commentary*, Lam. 4:2; Ezek. 11:20.
[393] *Commentary*, Jer. 33:16.
[394] *Commentary*, Dan. 7:27.
[395] *Sermons on the Deity of Christ*, 177.
[396] "Sermon on Luke 1:1-4," *CO* 46:5.
[397] *Commentary*, Dan. 7:1.
[398] *Commentary*, Jer. 3:15.
[399] *Commentary*, Ezek. 20:12.
[400] *Sermons on 2 Samuel*, 522.

for faith, through all her ministries.[401] Fifth, it is within the church that they will be called to repentance and to know the forgiveness and cleansing from God that follows.[402] Finally, it is only within the church, taught by the Word,[403] gathered for worship,[404] that they will be able to render the ultimate act of piety: true biblical worship.[405] Calvin's students could not emerge from the Academy without a deep confidence that in order to grow in holiness, they must continue to serve the church all their life, as Calvin prayed, "May we there join intelligence with zeal in building up thy Church."[406]

Principle 13: Sacraments. Because God offers grace sacramentally, therefore commune regularly with Christ through the sacraments.

Calvin will emphasize that the sacraments, rightly used, are effective means of grace, so he taught his hearers how they should be rightly understood and rightly administered.[407] They should understand that there are only two sacraments,[408] which are a visible Word of an invisible grace,[409] made visible in part as an accommodation to their weakness, since they need to see as well as hear of God's grace.[410] The sacraments are only for believers who can come with faith,[411] or in the case of baptism, for believers and their children.[412] The sacraments are more than a memorial or statement of faith;[413] they are an effective means of grace, despite their weak appearance,[414] because God does a mighty work through them to help us.[415] They are not effective *ex opere operato*, however, but only because God works through them in those who have faith,[416] such that Christ is really spiritually present.[417] To be administered properly, the sacraments must be offered with the spoken Word, to make sense of them,[418] without any pomp, which might distract the receiver from Christ.[419] Most im-

---

[401] *Commentary*, Lam. 1:20.
[402] *Commentary*, Jer. 3:14.
[403] *Commentary*, Jer. 7:22.
[404] *Commentary*, Lam. 1:4.
[405] *Commentary*, Jer. 11:13.
[406] *Commentary*, Dan. 11:34.
[407] Perhaps considering the sacraments were well covered in the *Institutes* and sermons, Calvin seldom touches on them in our commentaries, indeed, we could find only fifteen direct teachings. *Commentary*, Jer., Dedication, 4:4; 6:10; 9:25; 27:5; 28:10; 51:63; Ezek. 2:3; 4:1; 11:25; 16:20-21; 20:12, 20; Dan. 21:1.
[408] *Sermons on the Deity of Christ*, 175; *Commentary*, Jer. 51:63.
[409] *Commentary*, Ezek. 11:25; 20:12.
[410] Gerrish, "Calvin's Eucharistic Piety," 61.
[411] *Commentary*, Jer. 6:10.
[412] *Commentary*, Ezek. 16:21.
[413] *Commentary*, Ezek. 20:12.
[414] *Commentary*, Ezek. 4:1.
[415] *Sermons on Nativity*, 12, 43.
[416] *Commentary*, Jer. "Dedication;" *Sermons on the Deity of Christ*, 175.
[417] *Commentary*, Jer. "Dedication."
[418] *Commentary*, Ezek. 2:3; 4:1.
[419] *Commentary*, Jer. 28:10.

portantly they must be received with a faith which seeks to know Christ better in the sacrament.[420] Finally, the worthy receiver must come repenting of all sin, so as not to corrupt his communion with Christ.[421]

First, the sacraments rightly used helped advance holiness in the Lord's Supper by uniting the worthy receiver more to Christ's human body,[422] whose life flows into them to strengthen their faith for the daily struggle.[423] Second, the sacraments work to give us assurance that we are adopted children of God,[424] whom we can claim as Father,[425] since we are made Christ's brothers,[426] who are moved by this love to love and obey God.[427] Finally, by requiring repentance of sin in preparation,[428] the sacraments create a desire for holiness.[429] A student at the Academy would come to understand the vital role that rightly partaking of the sacraments would have for advancement in piety.[430]

Principle 14: Church Discipline. Because God shepherds us through his leaders, therefore seek pastoral care and church discipline.

Because sin blinds the sinner to its presence, the entire church is needed to help the believer see their sin through pastoral care and discipline and be brought to repentance. First, everyone needs correction, since preferring to consider ourselves sinless, we want to reject any reproof.[431] "Who is there that can bear to be admonished and reproved?"[432] The mighty,[433] whether kings[434] or princes[435] or popes,[436] need correction, and especially for the sake of the church, pastors[437] must be reproved, particularly by one another.[438] Second, we must accept correction, even if harsh, rather than being stiff-necked and self-justifying.[439] In fact we "ought to seek"[440] out this correction from others the better to be brought to repentance and grace.[441] Third, all, particularly teachers, must con-

---

[420] *Sermons on Election and Reprobation*, 244-45; *Commentary*, Ezek. 20:20.
[421] *Sermons on the Deity of Christ*, 196.
[422] Wallace, *Christian Life*, 18.
[423] *Sermons on Election and Reprobation*, 244-45; *Commentary*, Jer. 27:5.
[424] Gerrish, "Calvin's Eucharistic Piety," 61.
[425] *Sermons on the Deity of Christ*, 65.
[426] *Sermons on the Deity of Christ*, 195.
[427] *Sermons on the Deity of Christ*, 65.
[428] *Commentary*, Jer. 9:25.
[429] *Commentary*, Jer. 4:4.
[430] *Commentary*, Dan. 9:21.
[431] *Commentary*, Jer. 2:23.
[432] *Commentary*, Jer. 8:8.
[433] *Commentary*, Jer. 10:21.
[434] *Commentary*, Dan. 1:1.
[435] *Commentary*, Jer. 36:25.
[436] *Commentary*, Jer. 22:3.
[437] *Commentary*, Jer. 10:21.
[438] *Commentary*, Dan. 9:2.
[439] *Sermons on Genesis 1-11*, 548.
[440] *Sermons on 2 Samuel*, 522.
[441] *Commentary*, Ezek. 3:17; cf. *Commentary*, Jer. 36:32.

stantly offer this correction, preached or in person,[442] since everyone is always sinning and needs to be led back to God.[443] "The minister of the Church then must not cease to repeat these admonitions."[444]

Pastoral care advanced holiness by helping believers come to a true knowledge of their sin,[445] contrasted against both God's goodness and his judgment on sin,[446] in order to want to find forgiveness.[447] Once helped to see their sin, they are invited to the self-examination that leads to a deeper self-knowledge and repentance.[448] Brought down by the confrontation with sin, they are bid by pastoral care to look away from sin, and upward to see the love of God,[449] that they might be moved toward grace.[450] We see here the importance of living in open community within the church[451] so discipline flows from all to all. "When [we love one another] what will then happen is that instead of friends flattering one another…they will admonish one another."[452] The students of the Academy would learn that sanctification requires that each Christian be fully subject to the critiques of the whole church.

Calvin Taught Sanctification in a Right Order to His Students

As we examine these fourteen principles in Calvin's theology of sanctification, we find, first, that there is a general pattern, an order of teaching, which unsurprisingly roughly follows the *Institutes*, and second, that Calvin will make variations on this pattern dependent on the text and audience. Generally speaking, the true knowledge of God and self leads one to prostration and then, toward reverence in offering God all of one's life in service.[453] More specifically, progress in sanctification begins with knowledge of God and self (Book 1, Principle 1), which shows us both the holiness and graciousness of God, seen in contrast to our ungrateful hard-heartedness. He will then teach on the necessity of submission to the Word of God, to become convinced of God's greatness and our need (Book 1, Principle 2). Calvin will then typically detail knowledge of human pride, rebellion and blindness (Book 2, Principle 1). Next Calvin will expound the mercy of God in Christ, showing the hope of forgiveness and purity that might be gained if we rely on God (Book 3, Principles 3 and 4). He will then follow with the call to faith and repentance (Book 3, Principles 5, 6 and 7). Next Calvin will call his hearers to the upward journey, seeking to revere God

---

[442] *Commentary*, Ezek. 3:17.
[443] *Commentary*, Jer. 3:15; Ezek. 3:18.
[444] *Commentary*, Ezek. 3:18.
[445] *Commentary*, Lam 2:14.
[446] *Commentary*, Lam. 1:7.
[447] *Commentary*, Lam. 2:15.
[448] *Commentary*, Lam. 3:40.
[449] Wallace, *Geneva and the Reformation*, 176.
[450] *Commentary*, Ezek. 1:1.
[451] *Sermons on Beatitudes*, 50; *Sermons on 2 Samuel*, 144, 186.
[452] *Sermons on 2 Samuel*, 621.
[453] Wallace, *Christian Life*, 83; Bouwsma, *Sixteenth-Century Portrait*, 228.

Chapter 6 - Calvin's Teaching to the Students of the Genevan Academy

with all of life, helped on by the practical disciplines of self-denial, cross-bearing, meditation on the future life and use of this present life (Book 3, Principles 8, 9, 10 and 11). Finally comes engaging the church, receiving its sacraments and discipline (Book 4, Principles 12, 13 and 14).

We see this pattern of teaching, for example, in his lecture on Lamentations 1:5-10. He will teach that the people "added sins to sins," giving knowledge of self.[454] Next he offers knowledge of God and humanity together, pointing out that the Jews did not see "the benefits which God had bestowed."[455] He turns to the need for repentance from the sin of not appreciating God.[456] There follows an explanation of the need for self-examination leading to prostration.[457] Calvin then teaches that struggle for faith is helped by looking to the future life.[458] He concludes by pointing out that his hearers' hope for holiness was found in turning to God.[459]

One might object that this teaching reveals nothing of Calvin's own plan but has him only following the text. Calvin himself addresses this objection by pointing out to his students that this order is, in fact, the "right way of teaching," (*vera ratio docendi*), that individuals must be humbled before they can be shown that a "hand is to be stretched out to them."[460] Here he highlights the certain order of sanctification: "Thus our Prophet prescribes to us a certain order [*certum ordinem*],—that we are to examine our whole life, and that, being influenced by the fear of God, we are to return to him."[461]

We find this pattern, for another example, demonstrated in the sermon on Luke 1:74-76. He begins with the knowledge of self,[462] then calls his hearers to repentance while relying on God's mercy,[463] which can be trusted[464] because of God's great love in Christ. "He will always be good and gracious to us when we seek him, pleading the name of his beloved Son."[465] After warning against the uselessness of trying to become holy the Roman way, he will emphasize the upward movement of reverence in our need to struggle for holiness "all the days of our lives."[466] He instructs in the right use of this life that one cannot live as though "there were no difference between good and bad."[467] He will then go on to show the importance of the church since God "fills all things and

---

[454] *Commentary*, Lam. 1:5.
[455] *Commentary*, Lam. 1:7.
[456] *Commentary*, Lam. 1:7.
[457] *Commentary*, Lam. 1:8.
[458] *Commentary*, Lam. 1:9.
[459] *Commentary*, Lam. 1:9.
[460] *Commentary*, Lam. 1:9.
[461] *Commentary*, Lam. 3:40.
[462] *Sermons on Nativity*, 96.
[463] *Sermons on Nativity*, 96.
[464] *Sermons on Nativity*, 97.
[465] *Sermons on Nativity*, 99.
[466] *Sermons on Nativity*, 103.
[467] *Sermons on Nativity*, 104.

governs his church through the pastors."[468] He closes with an exhortation to live all of our lives for Christ, because Christ came to "rule us and govern us."[469]

Calvin's model of teaching was fluid and dynamic, yet while generally following this pattern, he will make variations. For example his prayers, which generally follow the certain order of sanctification, show also his variations. At the end of Ezekiel 1:16, having just made the lecture point that life is changeable, he prays about humanity's fallen condition in a world "subject to so many changes," then immediately focuses attention toward the future life, followed by inviting his hearers to struggle for faith. There follows knowledge of God and reliance upon his love to us. He finishes with a reminder of the certainty of heaven, which comes from the mercy of God in Christ. We see here how Calvin will vary on the general pattern of prostration leading to reverence by emphasizing the theme of heaven. Yet still the right order of teaching remains; the human condition is miserable (prostration), so we must look to God to deliver us to heaven (reverence).

In the end we see that Calvin carefully taught the students of the Academy through his right order of instruction, all fourteen of the principles of sanctification, with great clarity and constant repetition, helping them grow in holiness into the bold yet humble pastors France required.

---

[468] *Sermons on Nativity*, 106.
[469] *Sermons on Nativity*, 108.

Chapter 7 - The Structures of the Genevan Academy which Enhanced Sanctification

"Sapiens et eloquens pietas."[1]

The Educational Context of the Genevan Academy

In Chapter 7 we will define the structures of the Genevan Academy which enhanced the students' holiness. We will argue simply that the theology of sanctification which was taught to the students was also structured for them in the processes, methods and relationships within the context of the Academy. We will show in this first section how movements in higher education during this period helped to shape the distinctive characteristics of the Academy. In the second part, we will show how each of 10 structures of the Academy were incarnations of various aspects of the fourteen principles of sanctification, serving to reinforce through experience what was taught in the classroom. In that section we will particularly investigate the correspondence to, from and about the students for evidences of the impact of these structures.

One must recognize, however, that the nature of historical research into the causes of sanctification is inherently limited by the type and quantity of historical data available after five centuries. In order to prove that these structures of the Academy were the primary instrument used in the life of any student to enhance their sanctification, we would have to be able to demonstrate 1) their level of sanctification before attending the Academy, 2) their level of sanctification after attending the Academy and then also 3) prove that the particular structure was conclusively the agent which brought about the observable progress in holiness. The historical material available will not allow this type of proof. However, while we cannot prove that the Genevan Academy was the efficient cause of any student's sanctification, we can demonstrate that 1) these educational structures were utilized, and 2) the students after attending the Academy either recognized the helpful influence of those structures for their holiness or reflected the holiness intended in the design of those structures. Yet even here, since we have letters from only a small minority of the students, we must take the correlations between the structures of the Academy and the students growth in holiness as suggestive of their effectiveness, rather than as incontrovertible evidence. Of course even relatively scant evidence could easily falsify a theory, as the proverbial appearance of one black swan negates the statement "all swans are white." Finding in the letters no falsification, but rather general confirmation that these 10 structures were at work, we offer them as illustrations of the effectiveness of the structures.

---

[1] "Wise and eloquent piety," Johann Sturm's educational motto which was adopted in principle in Geneva. L.W. Spitz and B.S. Tinsley, *Johann Sturm on Education* (St. Louis, Mo.: Concordia, 1995), 28.

Education in the Reformation

The Genevan Academy came to fruition in the midst of an educational revolution, which deeply affected how the students of the Academy were to be taught. During the late Middle Ages, the old Greek method of classical education, with its Trivium[2] (grammar, logic and rhetoric) and the following Quadrivium[3] (music, arithmetic, geometry and astronomy), emphasized mastery of material produced by prior scholars through logical analysis. In the medieval system logic, or dialectics, which focused on the precise definitions of terms and the validity of propositions, had become a central coordinating subject, queen above all others.[4] In theological education, this medieval approach was practiced by the polemical mastery of Lombard's *Sentences*.[5] The Trivium, and its medieval tendency toward abstract scholarship, was challenged by a new approach to education, which depended more on the humanistic skill of direct inquiry into primary sources. By 1518 Erasmus had published *Ratio seu methodus compendio perveniendi ad veram theologiam*, calling for a reformation of education, which set aside much of scholastic inquiry and returned to direct study of original source material, in particular the Bible.[6] Good education, in his view, was not abstract, logical argumentation but rather good biblical exegesis.[7] "I have sought to call back theology...to the sources and to its original simplicity...and good literature, before practically pagan, I have taught to speak of Christ."[8] Logic became a supporting discipline to aid biblical interpretation, which relied more heavily on philology and rhetoric for expression. In addition to this *ad fontes* aspect of the new educational model, there developed a renewed understanding that education ought to lead to piety. For Erasmus education was essentially "implanting the seeds of piety."[9] While Lutheran education focused on the pious individual, the Reformed version focused on the individual as a part of the larger society, an important distinguishing characteristic in Geneva.[10]

---

[2] Borgeaud, *Histoire de l'Université*, 14.

[3] Bell, *Many Mansions*, 85.

[4] A.N. Burnett, "The Educational Roots of Reformed Scholasticism: Dialectic and Scriptural Exegesis in the Sixteenth Century," *Dutch Review of Church History/Nederlands Archief voor Kerkgeschiedenis* 84 (2004), 301.

[5] A. Siedlecki, "Protestant Theological Education in German Universities in the Sixteenth Century," *American Theological Library Association Summary of Proceedings* 62 (2008), 252.

[6] Siedlecki, "Protestant Theological Education," 252.

[7] Burnett, "Reformed Scholasticism," 300.

[8] D. Erasmus, *Opus epistolarum Desiderii Erasmi Roterodami*, Vol. 7 (eds. P.S. Allen and H.M. Allen; Oxford: Oxford University Press, 1928), 208, Epistle 1891, lines 185-91.

[9] R.A. Faber, "Humanitas as Discriminating Factor in the Educational Writings of Erasmus and Luther," *Dutch Review of Church History/Nederlands Archief voor Kerkgeschiedenis* 85 (2005), 27-30.

[10] Ehrenpreis, "Reformed Education," 42.

Chapter 7 - The Structures of the Genevan Academy which Enhanced Sanctification

This new, back-to-the-sources-for-the-sake-of-piety method, a new biblical humanism, began to spread in the Universities of Europe in the 1520s.[11] By 1543 even foundational assumptions, such as Aristotle's approach to logic, came under attack by the educational reformer Peter Ramus.[12] Maturin Cordier, an early advocate of the new method, had been Calvin's Latin professor at the *Collège de la Marche*[13] and greatly influenced Calvin. "Providence so ordered it that I had, for a short time, the privilege of having you as my instructor, that I might be taught by you the true method of learning."[14] Johann Sturm, another early practitioner of the new educational method, was educated at the College of St. Jerome at Liège, which had been founded by the Brethren of the Common Life. The Brethren emphasized personal piety and good scholarship,[15] and had already begun the careful systematic examination of their pastors.[16] Sturm's use of the new method focused on the complete mastery of basic material (for example, the Latin grammar) and progression through logical steps to higher and higher levels of mastery (for example, Latin rhetoric), always aimed toward growth in piety.[17] Called to establish the Strasbourg Academy in 1538, Sturm's motto for the Academy, *sapiens et eloquens pietas*, "wise and eloquent piety," would become influential for Geneva as well.

Education in Geneva

During the struggle for the Reformation, the Roman Catholic College of Versonnex, which had been established in 1502, ceased to operate and was replaced in 1536 by a distinctly Reformed effort, *Collège de la Rive*.[18] Under the direction first of Antoine Saunier, then in 1537 of Cordier,[19] the *Collège de la Rive* offered Latin along with rudimentary Greek and Hebrew,[20] which was taught by Calvin and Farel. However, this secondary school served only a limited function, giving "the sons of the rich local bourgeois a smattering of culture."[21] Calvin wanted a more systematic and pure institution, dedicated more to pastoral training[22] and under the control of the Company of Pastors.[23] Calvin

---

[11] Burnett, "Reformed Scholasticism," 301.
[12] J. Murphy (ed.), C. Newlands (tr.), *Arguments in Rhetoric Against Quintilian: Translation and Text of Peter Ramus's Rhetoricae Distinctiones in Quintilianum (1549)* (DeKalb, Ill.: Northern Illinois University Press, 1986), 11-15.
[13] Ganoczy, *Young Calvin*, 57; cf. Borgeaud, *Histoire de l'Université*, 24.
[14] *Commentary*, 1 Thess., Dedication by Calvin.
[15] P. Mesnard, "The Pedagogy of Johann Sturm (1507-1589) and its Evangelical Inspiration," *Studies in the Renaissance* 13 (1966), 201.
[16] W.S. Reid, "Calvin and the Founding of the Academy of Geneva," *Westminster Theological Journal* 18 (1955), 3.
[17] Mesnard, "The Pedagogy of Johann Sturm," 209-10.
[18] Borgeaud, *Histoire de l'Université*, 15-16.
[19] Reid, "The Academy of Geneva," 7.
[20] Borgeaud, *Histoire de l'Université*, 17.
[21] Kingdon, *Wars of Religion*, 14.
[22] C. Borgeaud, *Calvin, Fondateur de l'Académie de Genève* (Paris: Armand Colin, 1897), 15.
[23] Borgeaud, *Histoire de l'Université*, 18.

had desired to establish an academy at least from the time of his return from Strasbourg in 1541, where he had lectured in their flourishing Academy.[24] This desire was clearly indicated in his 1541 *Ecclesiastical Ordinances*.

> But since it is possible to profit from such teaching only if in the first place there is instruction in the languages and humanities, and since also there is need to raise up seed for the future so that the church is not left desolate to our children, it will be necessary to build a college for the purpose of instructing them, with a view to preparing them both for the ministry and the civil government.[25]

In 1550 we see Calvin's dream for the Academy was still alive in his correspondence with Claude Baudel, who had gone to Nîmes to start a school along the lines of Sturm's model.[26] It appears that a strong stimulus to action occurred in 1556 when, on a brief visit to Strasbourg, Calvin discussed educational plans with his colleagues there, saw the growth of nearly 20 years of their Academy and offered a lecture at the Academy, which was received with a standing ovation.[27] By January 1558 the city began searching for a suitable building site,[28] and by October formal plans for the building were drawn up.[29]

Providentially, in the spring of 1559 the Lausanne Academy was torn asunder by tensions with Berne over the Lord's Supper, and many of their faculty suddenly became available, joining Beza who had departed the year before.[30] On May 22, 1559 Calvin and Viret proposed to the Small Council that "it has become necessary to publish the ordinances of the college,"[31] which were written by Calvin and modeled after the Lausanne by-laws.[32] The new faculty was organized. Beza was Rector and taught theology, Antoine Le Chevalier was professor of Hebrew, Calvin taught theology in the form of Old Testament lectures[33] and "François Béraud pour le grec, Jean Tagaut pour la philosophie."[34] Everything was approved at a May 29, 1559 meeting of the Council[35] just in time for a June 5 formal inauguration of the Academy at St. Pierre.[36] At the inauguration Beza gave a speech in which he outlined the purpose of the Academy, expressing the grand hopes of the founders. "You have not come here as most of the Greeks of old went to their gymnasia to watch vain wrestling matches. Instead, prepared by the knowledge of the true religion and all scienc-

---

[24] Reid, "The Academy of Geneva," 8.
[25] *RCP*, 41.
[26] Letter of Baduel to Calvin, June 10, 1550; *CO* 13:589.
[27] Borgeaud, *Fondateur*, 17.
[28] Maag, *Genevan Academy*, 9.
[29] Borgeaud, *Fondateur*, 22.
[30] H. Meylan, *La Haute École de Lausanne*, 1537-1937 (University of Lausanne, 1986), 26-27.
[31] *Annales, CO* 21:717.
[32] L. Junod and H. Meylan (eds.), *L'Académie de Lausanne au XVIe Siècle* (Lausanne: F. Rouge, 1947), 15.
[33] Borgeaud, *Fondateur*, 23; cf. Maag, "Education and Training," 134.
[34] *Annales, CO* 21:716.
[35] *Annales, CO* 21:716; Borgeaud, *Fondateur*, 24.
[36] Reid, "The Academy of Geneva, 10.

Chapter 7 - The Structures of the Genevan Academy which Enhanced Sanctification

es, you can contribute to the glory of God and become the honor of your homeland and the support of your family."[37]

The Genevan Academy was more than a school, it was meant to be the training center for the Reformed movement in Europe.[38] While Beza had hoped to add law and medicine to the theological training offered at the Academy,[39] this did not happen in Calvin's lifetime, and the purpose of the Academy clearly remained the training of pastors,[40] with religious-minded civil servants as a secondary emphasis.[41] The start of the Academy was the final piece of Calvin's master plan of changing not only Geneva, but reforming the European pastorate.[42]

The Genevan Academy consisted of two schools, the *schola privata*, for the younger students, and the *schola publica*, for those over age 17 who were preparing for ministry or civil service.[43] It is the Public School with which we are primarily concerned. The Academy was housed in its new facility in 1559 overlooking the lake, built under the watchful eye of Jean Budé,[44] primarily with money raised from private sources. The lectures were given here until the large number of students required that Calvin's lectures be moved to the *Auditoire* in 1562.[45] Unlike the Private School with its carefully age-segregated curriculum,[46] the Public School had no class levels and offered no diplomas.[47] Students were simply required to enter their names with the Rector and sign a statement of faith, and were then free to attend as many lectures as they chose.[48] There were about 27 hours of classes offered each week: three in Hebrew, three in Greek, five each in Old and New Testament interpretation, three in theology, three in logic and five in rhetoric.[49] The theology lectures, which in the *ad fontes* model were Bible studies, were given each Monday, Tuesday and Wednesday from 2:00-3:00 by either Calvin or Beza, who alternated weeks.[50] The Academy's daily schedule began at 6:00 AM in the summer and 7:00 in the winter,[51] with the worship services of the city churches followed by lectures.[52]

---

[37] Maag, *Genevan Academy*, 15-16.
[38] S. Cornut, *L'Académie de Calvin* (Geneva: H. George, 1902), 12.
[39] Borgeaud, *Fondateur*, 32.
[40] Borgeaud, *Histoire de l'Université*, 51.
[41] *RCP*, 41.
[42] Naphy, "The Renovation of the Ministry," 127.
[43] Reid, "The Academy of Geneva," 11.
[44] J.E. Olson, "The Friends of John Calvin: The Budé Family," *Calvin and Spirituality, Calvin and His Contemporaries, Calvin Studies Society Papers, 1995, 1997* (Grand Rapids, Mich.: CRC Product Services, 1998), 165.
[45] Borgeaud, *Histoire de l'Université*, 54. Or perhaps Calvin's lectures were always given at the *Auditoire*, see Chap. 6, footnote 9.
[46] Battles, *Interpreting Calvin*, 261.
[47] Maag, *Genevan Academy*, 116.
[48] Borgeaud, *Fondateur*, 25.
[49] Borgeaud, *Fondateur*, 32.
[50] *CO* 10:87, "Le Ordre du Collège de Genève;" Borgeaud, *Fondateur*, 32.
[51] Cornut, *L'Académie de Calvin*, 7.

Fridays the students were encouraged to attend both the Congregation and the Company.[53] Saturdays had no lectures but were reserved for prospective pastors to preach trial sermons before members of the Company.[54] Sundays also had no classes but were to be "used to hear sermons."[55] Students were to finally pass an exam from their Regent to be considered graduates, who were announced each year in St. Pierre during May.[56]

In addition to the formal classes, the students were trained through an informal mentoring system by living and learning in close proximity to the professors of Geneva, with whom they commonly boarded.[57] The basic training model for pastoral students, normal for Reformed training,[58] included apprenticeships in the local churches, particularly the rural churches, where they were supervised by the Company.[59] Since the professors during this period were typically pastors,[60] the student would find himself interacting with his professors, who were as interested in their piety as their theology,[61] in the classroom, at home, at church, in the Congregation and the Company. The students were also fully integrated into the life of the city, becoming "habitants" and therefore coming under the authority of the Consistory and Councils, with an eye to their piety.[62]

The students who attended the Public School were primarily French refugees, with others coming from places such as the Netherlands, Catalonia, Scotland and Venice.[63] Surprisingly, only eight Genevans attended the Public

---

[52] *CO* 10:85, "Le Ordre du Collège de Genève." Cf. Borgeaud, *Histoire de l'Université*, 165.
[53] *CO* 10:85, "Le Ordre du Collège de Genève."
[54] *CO* 10:87, "Le Ordre du Collège de Genève." Cf. Selderhuis, *Pilgrim Life*, 239.
[55] *CO* 10:85, "Le Ordre du Collège de Genève."
[56] Borgeaud, *Fondateur*, 25.
[57] Carrington, "Calvin and Erasmus," 138.
[58] Maag, "Preaching Practice,"134-35. Cf. Maag, "Education and Training," 149.
[59] Maag, *Genevan Academy*, 118.
[60] Of the ten professors in the Public School during our years of study, five were clearly pastors, Calvin, Beza, Chevalier, Baduel and Colladon. Two apparently belonged to the *Compagnie*, Scrimger and Simonius. Three apparently were not pastors but may have had some status as Doctors of the Church, the Greek Professors Bérauld and Portus, and the Arts Professor, Tagaut. See R.W. Henderson, "The Teaching Office in Reformed Tradition," *The Genevan Reform in School and Church* (Philadelphia, Pa.: Westminster, 1962), 66-67.
[61] Maag, "Education and Training," 139.
[62] *CO* 10:81, "Le Ordre du Collège de Genève." There were three classifications for residents in Geneva, *citoyen*, who had full voting rights, *bourgeois*, who either bought or were granted this status and could vote in certain elections, and *habitants*, who were legal residents but had no voting rights. Calvin himself only obtained *bourgeois* status on Christmas Day, 1559. Cf. McGrath, *Life of John Calvin*, 109.
[63] Selderhuis, *Pilgrim Life*, 217.

Chapter 7 - The Structures of the Genevan Academy which Enhanced Sanctification

School in the first twenty years.[64] Many of the students had previously been monks or priests with some prior theological training.[65] Nearly half of those eventually sent out to pastoral posts came from the nobility.[66] A majority of the early students became pastors; for example, of the 68 students who enrolled in 1559, 37 are known to have become pastors.[67]

The Genevan Academy combined a high degree of academic rigor, requiring excellence in the biblical languages, along with Latin and French, theological and rhetorical precision, with careful guidance in piety. Truly Sturm's model had found a home, *sapiens et eloquens pietas* had arrived in Geneva with the Academy, a uniquely powerful tool for shaping the holiness of its students.

The Educational Structures of the Genevan Academy

Structure 1: The Academy was integrated into the city

To understand the sanctifying impact of the Genevan Academy, one must come to understand that it stood as an integral part of the entire system of the city of Geneva, with its Church, Consistory, Congregation, Company of Pastors and Council. We will explore here how each part in turn contributed to make Geneva a complex integrated system which would enhance the students' piety.

Geneva was a city whose life was dominated by her churches. Sunday would begin with a service at 4:00 AM (5:00 in winter) for travelers and servants,[68] followed by the principle morning service at 8:00, a noon Catechism and then a 3:00 Vespers service, in all three churches.[69] Wednesday had a two hour prayer service which would start at 7:00 AM (8:00 in winter) and was second in importance to Sunday.[70] The other week days would begin with a 6:00 AM worship service (7:00 in winter) at each church.[71] This meant that over twenty worship services were offered weekly among the three parishes.[72] Additionally, refugee churches worshipped in Italian, Spanish and English.[73] While residents were required by law to attend only one Sunday service[74] plus the noon catechism service for families with young children,[75] the church had a far greater impact than an hour or two a week in Genevan life.

---

[64] F. Scholl, *Professions et Quelques Aspects Généalogiques des Étudiants Genevois Inscrits A L'Académie de Genève 1559-1878* (Geneva: University of Geneva, 1986), 6.
[65] Maag, *Genevan Academy*, 105-07.
[66] Kingdon, *Wars of Religion*, 6.
[67] Maag, "Education and Training," 150, footnote 8.
[68] McKee, "Calvin and His Colleagues," 18.
[69] McKee, "Calvin and His Colleagues," 19.
[70] McKee, *Pastoral Piety*, 135.
[71] "Ecclesiastical Ordinances," 1561, *OS* 2:337.
[72] McKee, "Calvin and His Colleagues," 18-19.
[73] Selderhuis, *Pilgrim Life*, 217.
[74] Burnett, "A Tale of Three Churches," 115.
[75] Parker, *Calvin's Thought*, 140.

The spirituality of Geneva was a corporate spirituality, with baptisms, weddings, funerals and the Lord's Supper spilling over from the four walls of the church and touching family, business and leisure.[76] The singing of Psalms would be heard throughout the city each day.[77] The bells of the city's churches were constantly calling her people to worship. The bell of St. Pierre's North Tower, known as *La Clémence*, carried the revealing inscription: "I praise the true God, I summon the people, I assemble the clergy, I weep for the dead, I chase the plague away, I embellish feast days. My voice is the terror of all devils."[78] Indeed the voice of the church could not be ignored in Geneva. It was into this church-rich environment that the students of the Academy would step and be encouraged, obliged rather, to participate fully in worship, sacraments, singing, preaching, catechizing, visiting, disciplining and mentoring by her pastors. This could not help but enforce the students' commitment to the church (Principle 12) and help them grow in piety.

The Consistory of Geneva included all of the pastors along with twelve lay elders, who were appointed by the Small Council: six from the Council of Two Hundred, four from the Council of Sixty, and two from the Small Council.[79] Working in subordination to the authority of the Small Council, this body of about 20 men[80] met weekly, on Thursday mornings, for nearly half a day to consider all matters of church order and discipline in Geneva, often referring to the Small Council for physical discipline.[81] The Consistory's work began with informal watch over the residents in assigned districts, where elders would confront any suspected sinner[82] and, failing repentance, bring the offender before the entire Consistory,[83] who ordered their repentance.[84] The Consistory increasingly turned to excommunication to help engender this repentance. While there were only four excommunications in 1551, by 1564 the number had grown to about 300.[85]

---

[76] J.D. Witvliet, "The Spirituality of the Psalter: Metrical Psalms in Liturgy and Life in Calvin's Geneva," *Calvin and Spirituality, Calvin and His Contemporaries, Calvin Studies Society Papers, 1995, 1997* (Grand Rapids, Mich.: CRC Product Services, 1998), 117.

[77] Witvliet, "The Spirituality of the Psalter," 108-09.

[78] E.W. Monter, *Calvin's Geneva* (Eugene, Oreg.: Wipf & Stock, 2012), 13.

[79] Selderhuis, *Pilgrim Life*, 56-57.

[80] E.W. Monter, "The Consistory of Geneva, 1559-1569," *Bibliothèque d'Humanisme et Renaissance* 3 (1976), 469. Although the pastors of Geneva might outnumber the elders, through absences the average meeting of the Consistory had about ten pastors and ten elders.

[81] R.M. Kingdon, "Calvin and the Family: the Work of the Consistory in Geneva," *Articles on Calvin and Calvinism*, Vol. 3, *Calvin's Work in Geneva* (ed. R.C. Gamble; New York, N.Y. and London: Garland, 1992), 95.

[82] S.M. Manetsch, "Pastoral Care East of Eden: The Consistory of Geneva, 1568-82," *Church History* 75 (2006), 278.

[83] Kingdon, "Calvin and the Family," 95.

[84] *Registres du Consistoire*, XIX, 13v, Mar. 5, 1562; XIX 18v, Mar. 12, 1562; XIX, 23, Mar. 24, 1562, Meeter Center transcripts.

[85] Monter, "Consistory," 476.

Chapter 7 - The Structures of the Genevan Academy which Enhanced Sanctification

Yet the Consistory's true genius may have been in its function as an authoritative shepherding and counseling body,[86] concerned with "educating the unlearned, defending the weak, and mediating interpersonal conflicts."[87] Indeed, two-thirds of those appearing before the Consistory in this period were dismissed with reprimands and advice,[88] such as, that "he may have leisure to think better in his conscience."[89] Even when excommunication was used, it was short-term, expecting that the guilty party would repent before the next communion within a few months.[90] The students of the Academy would live under the watchful eyes of Consistory elders in their own neighborhoods, an aid to holiness (Principle 14). At least one student, Christophe Bertrand, stood before the Consistory, accused of stealing 1000 Florins from his parents.[91]

Having experienced its benefits, the students would go on to replicate the Consistory's structure.[92] Claude Courtois wrote during his first year in the Tarentaise after leaving Geneva, "We have now created deacons and elders and formed a Consistory from them."[93] Philippe Birgan, later to become a lecturer in Hebrew at Cambridge, demonstrated his approval of Consistory discipline when he commended a man to Calvin with these words, "He truly submits himself through the grace of God to ecclesiastical corrections."[94]

The Company of Pastors, which consisted of all the pastors and assistant pastors in and around Geneva[95] (numbering 19 in 1564[96]), including the Academy professors,[97] met on Friday mornings after the Congregation. The Company was responsible for nominating pastors,[98] examinations, ordinations, oversight of pastors[99] and missionary work.[100] These pastors had a collegial approach to ministry, exchanging pulpits, conducting baptisms and weddings in

---

[86] Kingdon, "The Geneva Consistory," 34.
[87] Manetsch, "Pastoral Care," 275.
[88] Monter, "Consistory," 471.
[89] *Registres du Consistoire*, XI, 3, Feb. 24, 1556, Meeter Center transcripts.
[90] Monter, "Consistory," 477.
[91] Maag, *Genevan Academy*, 104.
[92] R.M. Kingdon, "The Control of Morals in Calvin's Geneva," *Articles on Calvin and Calvinism*, Vol. 3, *Calvin's Work in Geneva* (ed. R.C. Gamble; New York, N.Y. and London: Garland, 1992), 44.
[93] Letter of Claude Courtois to Calvin, Dec. 17, 1563; *CO* 20:215. The author is indebted to Dr. David Butterfield for his kind assistance in clarifying some translations of the Latin letters used in this chapter and the next.
[94] Letter of Philippe Birgan to Calvin, Apr. 2, 1564; *CO* 20:285-87. Cf. Borgeaud, *Histoire de l'Université*, 65.
[95] Burnett, "A Tale of Three Churches," 113.
[96] Kingdon, "Calvin and the Family," 94.
[97] Backus, "Calvin's Patristic Models," 25.
[98] Bouwsma, *Sixteenth-Century Portrait*, 226.
[99] Oversight was shared with the Consistory, see *Registres du Consistoire*, XIX, 178v, Nov. 26, 1562, Meeter Center transcripts, where a pastor was rebuked for serving the Lord's Supper without preaching the Word.
[100] Small, "A Company of Pastors," 11. Cf. Backus, "Calvin's Patristic Models," 25.

each other's churches and correcting one another.[101] The Company also worked to develop the pastoral candidates of the Academy, mentoring, coaching and correcting them.[102] To become a student at the Academy was to find one's self engaged with the entire Company, which would deeply affect the piety of the students through close pastoral care and discipline (Principle 14).

The Congregation, an open meeting of the pastors along with lay leaders, city visitors, Council members and students, numbered about 50-60 in total attendance[103] and occurred on Friday mornings for two hours, after the sermon and before the Company.[104] Its primary purpose was to maintain purity and unity of doctrine by training in biblical exegesis, as a kind of in-service training.[105] Each week one of the pastors in turn would expound a pre-assigned text, a second would comment critically on points of doctrine (commonly Calvin would open this), and then the entire group was invited to comment, correcting arguments, exposition, teaching method or any "vice that needs reproach."[106] Calvin wanted his students, who attended occasionally, to understand that proper biblical interpretation required the humility to be correctable and submission to communal exegesis,[107] another lesson in church commitment and discipline (Principles 12 and 14).

As we consider the sanctifying structures of the Genevan Academy, we must not neglect the city councils. Geneva had several related Councils, beginning with the annual General Council, which consisted of all the citizens and bourgeois, who elected members to the other councils. The Council of Two Hundred handled appeals from the other councils. The Council of Sixty handled foreign affairs. Smallest, and perhaps most powerful, was the Petit Council, whose 25 members were responsible for the daily operations of Geneva, including the morality of its citizens.[108]

Naphy and others have explored the tensions between the City Council and the clergy of Geneva, highlighting in particular the fight over the ultimate locus of authority concerning the power to excommunicate.[109] However, in examining the political tensions, one may lose sight of one critical point: Calvin and the pastors of Geneva counted on the state to enforce piety and faith,[110] with physical force not available to the church,[111] the Middle Age ideal.[112] "Yet civil government has as its appointed end…to cherish and protect the outward wor-

---

[101] McKee, "Calvin and His Colleagues," 20-21; *RCP*, 202.
[102] Maag, "Education and Training," 139.
[103] Boer, "The *Congrégation*," 81.
[104] Selderhuis, *Pilgrim Life*, 125-26.
[105] Boer, "The *Congrégation*," 57.
[106] Boer, "The *Congrégation*," 69.
[107] *Institutes*, 6, Calvin's Preface to 1560 French Edition.
[108] Selderhuis, *Pilgrim Life*, 56-57; *RCP*, 38-39.
[109] Naphy, *Calvin and the Consolidation*, 32-33.
[110] *Commentary*, Dan. 4:2; Lobstein, *Die Ethik Calvins*, 120.
[111] *Institutes* 4.11.16; Wendel, *Origins*, 65.
[112] M.J. Larson, "John Calvin and Genevan Presbyterianism," *Westminster Theological Journal* 60 (1998), 65.

Chapter 7 - The Structures of the Genevan Academy which Enhanced Sanctification

ship of God, to defend sound doctrine of piety and the position of the church...to form our social behavior to civil righteousness...and to promote general peace and tranquility."[113] While there may have been tension over precisely who would control which behaviors, both parties expected the State to exercise significant control over morality, even to enforcing confessions of faith[114] and intimate details of life,[115] such as controlling dancing.[116] Thus the city had its hand in nearly every aspect of the Academy, from hiring decisions,[117] to salaries,[118] to regulating student marriages,[119] to the graduation ceremony.[120]

The integration of Academy into the city was helpful for student sanctification. Student Charles Parrot described Geneva by saying, "Yet everything endures in unbroken tranquillity through divine goodwill–especially through the work of the magistrates."[121] The students would be helped to grow in the moderate use of the present life (Principle 11) under the strict moral laws of Geneva.[122] For example, regulations in 1560 decreed that one may not "commit any excess in food, either at weddings, banquets, feasts or otherwise, or in clothing and apparel."[123] As habitants the students had duties and relationships which aided their self-denial (Principle 8). The students were obliged to serve as night watchmen for the city,[124] they worked as tutors to children of prominent families[125] and lived as boarders in the homes of professors or city leaders,[126] subject to their host's schedules,[127] each of these a mundane self-denial.

Geneva was more than a city; as Calvin and the other leaders had constructed it, it was designed to be a unified system working toward the piety of each resident.[128] The church taught and fed the people on God's Word. The Council enforced moral discipline. The Consistory shepherded the people of the city. The Company shepherded the pastors of the city who mentored the students.

---

[113] *Institutes* 4.20.2.
[114] Selderhuis, *Pilgrim Life*, 76-77.
[115] Wendel, *Origins*, 72-73.
[116] Witte, *Sex, Marriage and Family*, 475.
[117] *Annales*, Sept. 25, 1561; *CO* 21:761. Portus is presented as the new Greek Professor.
[118] *Annales*, Apr. 23, 1562; *CO* 21:778.
[119] *Annales*, Oct. 21, 1561; *CO* 21:763. The Council required that students have parental consent for marriage.
[120] *Annales*, Apr., 21, 1561; *CO* 21:747.
[121] Letter of Charles Perrot to his brother Daniel, Feb. 25, 1564; *CO* 20:258-60.
[122] *Commentary*, Jer. 32:32; Borgeaud, *Histoire de l'Université*, 165; Maag, *Genevan Academy*, 29, note 66.
[123] E. Rivoire and V. van Berchem (eds.), *Les sources du droit du canton du Genève* (Geneva 1911-1940) as cited by Witte, *Sex, Marriage and Family*, 454-55.
[124] Borgeaud, *Histoire de l'Université*, 171.
[125] Kingdon, *Wars of Religion*, 18. Cf. *CO* 21:736, student Jean Blanchard served as a family tutor.
[126] Carrington, "Calvin and Erasmus," 138.
[127] T. Bodley, *The Life of Sir Thomas Bodley* (Chicago, Ill.: A.C. McClurg, 1906), 35-36.
[128] Eby, *Early Protestant Educators*, 235.

The Congregation controlled the theology of the pastors, and therefore of the city. To enroll in the Academy of Geneva meant that one was involved not simply with one Genevan institution, but with the entire unified city system.

Modern critical evaluations of Geneva

Many question the methods and organization used in Geneva to promote piety. Where Calvin saw growing holiness, others may see oppression by Calvin, Consistory and Council. While Genevan authorities were certainly intrusive by modern standards, one must, however, guard against anachronism. When understood within the context of sixteenth-century social structures the Genevan approaches may become more reasonable.

Calvin clearly desired to replace pastors he considered to be inadequate, yet some see Calvin's treatment of the pastor Henri de la Mare, for example, as almost a personal vendetta.[129] Naphy recognizes, however, that the pastors from De la Mare's time lacked "education or expertise," showed "scandalous behavior" and were replaced with pastors who had a "high level of learning, expertise and quality."[130] These facts support another possible conclusion: could it not be that Calvin, as Moderator of the Company of Pastors, was properly executing his professional duty to replace incompetent pastors with more competent ones?

Calvin's sermons could certainly be pointed. Naphy writes that Calvin, "voiced specific, personal attacks."[131] Yet even the most extreme examples of Calvin's sermons, while forceful, seem to fall within the standards for effective preaching modeled by Christ.[132] "Let it be known that even those who are pillars of the church are wanton like dogs chasing after dogs in heat."[133] Calvin was only twice admonished by the Council for naming particular sins, a common practice of Reformed preachers.[134] Since Calvin preached over 4000 sermons,[135] it appears he was temperate in using this rhetorical device. When one takes Calvin's sermons on the whole, it becomes clear that he was not a pulpit bully, but an effective preacher, therefore pointed in describing sin and clear in prescribing its cure, the love of God in Christ.

The divorce of Calvin's brother, Antoine, from his wife, Anne, has been offered as an example of Calvin harshly using his influence to "drive her out of a

---

[129] Naphy, *Calvin and the Consolidation*, 67.

[130] Naphy, *Calvin and the Consolidation*, 72.

[131] Naphy, *Calvin and the Consolidation*, 154.

[132] Manetsch, *Company of Pastors*, 160; cf. Matt. 12:3, "You brood of vipers."

[133] *Supplementa Calviniana* (eds. H. Ruckert, E. Mulhaupt, G. Barrois, et al; Neukirchener-Vluyn: Neukirchener Verlag, 1936), 6:111; Naphy, *Calvin and the Consolidation*, 159. Calvin's rhetoric may have been further softened by his use of humorous alliteration, a common preaching device, the pillars of the church, *pilliers*, he called *paillars*, wanton.

[134] Naphy, *Calvin and the Consolidation*, 160.

[135] Manetsch, *Company of Pastors*, 150.

household."[136] The record of the case, however, such as the witness who saw one of the accused, "hastily pulling on his pants, after spending some time with Anne in a closed room"[137] so strongly suggested adultery, that the Small Council was convinced of her guilt. While even Calvin would admit that he was at times too harsh, it is not unreasonable in this instance to suggest that Calvin appropriately helped his brother to obtain a rightful divorce from a serial adulteress.

The Consistory has been accused, by critics both ancient and modern, of being heavy-handed in providing moral oversight.[138] As one contemporary said: "Satan would not be so harsh."[139] Clearly the Consistory was deeply involved in the daily lives of those in Geneva. However, we must recognize that controlling morality was the norm for church and state across Europe.[140] Catholic Geneva had a Peace Council in 1527 to redress wrongs.[141] Strasbourg closely regulated the details of students' lives, forbidding joking and prohibiting entry into another's bedroom "except from an honest reason."[142] While intrusive, overall the work of the Consistory was done with fairness and equity[143] and focused on "getting people to treat each other better."[144] As Manetsch notes, "Consistory members served as helpers for the poor, advocates for the weak, mediators for the estranged, and defenders of the exploited and abused."[145]

The Consistory is criticized for propagating hatred of Catholic doctrine.[146] While it is true that faithful Reformed pastors, in an effort to obey their understanding of Scripture,[147] taught their congregations to hate "error," one must remember that during this period hatred was engendered and lives were commonly taken over doctrine. For example, Protestants were killed by Catholics in 1560 in Rouen for failing to decorate their homes in honor of the feast of Corpus Christi.[148] While modern sensibilities dictate that religious viewpoints are an inappropriate reason to hate, we must avoid the cultural parochialism of making this an absolute standard by which to overly condemn the Consistory.

---

[136] R.M. Kingdon, *Adultery and Divorce in Calvin's Geneva* (Cambridge, Mass.: Harvard University Press, 1995), 94.
[137] Kingdon, *Adultery and Divorce*, 82.
[138] Kingdon, *Adultery and Divorce*, 180-81; R.M. Kingdon and T.A. Lambert, *Reforming Geneva, Discipline, Faith and Anger in Calvin's Geneva* (Geneva: Droz, 2012), 138.
[139] *Registres du Consistoire*, VIII, 78v, Dec. 21, 1553, Meeter Center transcripts.
[140] Naphy, *Calvin and the Consolidation*, 108.
[141] Kingdon, *Reforming Geneva*, 119.
[142] Fournier, *Les statuts*, "Leges Collegii Praedicatorum," 28-29.
[143] Kingdon, *Adultery and Divorce*, 181-82.
[144] Kingdon, *Reforming Geneva*, 101.
[145] Manetsch, *Company of Pastors*, 219.
[146] Kingdon, *Reforming Geneva*, 121-22.
[147] Cf. Ps. 31:6, "I hate those who regard vain idols."
[148] Kingdon, *Reforming Geneva*, 125.

The Geneva Council is criticized for the use of torture as a "rite of violence."[149] While admittedly shocking to modern Western sensibilities, torture was only used as a final recourse in the Genevan criminal justice system. This system was not based upon the adversarial system popular today in Great Britain and the United States, but on the inquisition system more common to the Continent.[150] The inquisition system, relying heavily upon the accused's confession, utilized increasingly close examination by experts to uncover the truth from often evasive defendants, wherein torture became a final resort.[151] Torture, based in Roman law, was not unique to Geneva, but was used in France and the Continent before and after the Reformation.[152] It was, however, used with great caution in Geneva, where it was conscientiously administered and well supervised.[153] Controlled by the Council not the Consistory,[154] torture was reserved for those accused of serious crimes, vetted by a legal scholar and required the later repetition of any confessions.[155] When properly understood within context, the use of torture in Geneva, while perhaps not commendable, should neither be held particularly condemnable.

Geneva's use of the death penalty for adultery has been described as "cruel and barbaric."[156] However, this practice, also controlled by the Council not the Consistory,[157] was based on Roman law and Scripture[158] and occurred in France as well.[159] Moreover, the Genevan laws provided some equality between the sexes[160] and in practice often resulted in a life sentence being commuted to a few months.[161] When seen in its broader historical context this suggests a degree of moderation and equity rather than extremism.

While life in Geneva was certainly more closely controlled than in the modern Western world, it was not an unfair, totalitarian existence. Rather, taken in context, Geneva was a city deeply concerned with, and carefully and realistically working toward, the moral holiness of its residents, which in turn, benefited its students.

---

[149] S. Beam, "Rites of Torture in Reformation Geneva," *Past and Present* 214 (2012), 217.
[150] M. Jones and P. Johnstone, *History of Criminal Justice* (Waltham, Mass.: Anderson/Elsevier, 2012), 63-66.
[151] Kingdon, *Adultery and Divorce*, 21-30.
[152] Beam, "Rites of Torture," 199-200; Jones, *History of Criminal Justice*, 66.
[153] Beam, "Rites of Torture," 201.
[154] Beam, "Rites of Torture," 214.
[155] Kingdon, *Adultery and Divorce*, 25-30.
[156] Kingdon, *Reforming Geneva*, 138.
[157] Kingdon, *Adultery and Divorce*, 119.
[158] Kingdon, *Adultery and Divorce*, 116-18.
[159] Kingdon, *Adultery and Divorce*, 179.
[160] Kingdon, *Adultery and Divorce*, 117.
[161] Kingdon, *Adultery and Divorce*, 59, 61.

Chapter 7 - The Structures of the Genevan Academy which Enhanced Sanctification

Structure 2: The Academy was integrated with the church

The Academy was integrated with the church through the Company of Pastors,[162] which would enhance the students' sanctification in several ways. First, as the students daily attended sermons,[163] they would have lived out a submission to biblical preaching (Principle 2), which would also enhance their twofold knowledge of God and self (Principle 1).[164] Second, attending church, thus rightly observing the Sabbath and giving God his due, was a practice of self-denial (Principle 8).[165] Third, engaging fully in the church would promote their sanctification as God made the church holy (Principle 12).[166] Fourth, the students' true call to pastoral work was discerned by the Company as they observed them in trial ministries, thus encouraging their holiness through right use of the present life regarding vocation (Principle 11).[167] Fifth, participation in the sacraments, particularly the Lord's Supper, would promote their holiness (Principle 13).[168]

We find good evidence that the integration of church and Academy had the desired effect in the students, creating a high commitment to serve the church and thus become more holy themselves. When Birgan writes from Vannes in 1564, his commitment to the church is clearly evident. "Everywhere do churches in our own Brittany flourish through the deepest goodwill of God and our eternal Lord Jesus Christ. But many churches are without pastors."[169] When Courtois writes Calvin from the Tarentaise in 1563, his satisfaction at the progress of the church is seen. "Know this then, reverend father, that although the people here are hard and (so to speak) stony, it nevertheless happens that through God's favor the number grows each day."[170] Paul Dotaeus, writing in 1560 from Castelmoron, reveals his love for the church in his affectionate term "sheepfold." "Sent on 25 September from Castelmoron, whose church (I call it my sheepfold) sends warmest greetings to you."[171] Bon Dupre reports on the progress of his church shortly after departing from Geneva, reflecting the importance placed upon the sacrament. "We are now pursuing to examine for the Supper."[172] The students lived out what Calvin had taught in the *Institutes*, the need to cling to the church to become holy.[173]

---

[162] Reid, "The Academy of Geneva," 11.
[163] *CO* 10:85, "Le Ordre du Collège de Genève."
[164] *Sermons on 2 Samuel*, 391.
[165] *Commentary*, Jer. 17:24.
[166] *Commentary*, Jer. 31:31; *Institutes* 4.1.4.
[167] Selderhuis, *Pilgrim Life*, 239; Maag, *Genevan Academy*, 121.
[168] *Sermons on Election and Reprobation*, 244-45; *Commentary*, Ezek. 20:20.
[169] Birgan to Calvin, Apr. 2, 1564.
[170] Courtois to Calvin, Dec. 17, 1563.
[171] Letter of Paul Dotaeus to Calvin, Oct. 20, 1560; *CO* 18:225.
[172] Letter of Bon Dupre to Calvin, Dec. 23, 1561; *CO* 19:193-94.
[173] *Institutes* 4.1.4.

Structure 3: The students were closely mentored by pastors

The students were closely mentored by the Company, who worked to produce godly students who would "come peacefully and in all modesty and honesty to honor God for the benefit and repose of the city."[174] The pastors taught them in classroom lectures, discussed with them over meals in their homes, encouraged or corrected them in private conversations, critiqued their sermons and theological treatises, guided them in their apprenticeships in rural churches and finally examined them to judge them ready for the pastorate. We see an example of how closely the students were mentored in Calvin's letter to the father of student François Daniel, detailing his spiritual development. He writes, "I shall make it my business to watch over him and prevent him from overstepping the limits of authority at the caprice of his own will."[175] Beza, who had lived with his Greek professor while a student,[176] showed this same close mentoring as he wrote Johann Wolf, assuring him that the two Zurich students in Geneva would be carefully trained in the holy life. "We shall…give to these young men all the assistance needed for their studies and for their instruction in the holy life."[177] The churches and pastors recommending students to the Genevan Academy expected this hands-on approach to training. "I implore you therefore to encourage him and according to your good and holy custom to watch over him."[178]

From the student perspective we can see the presence of the close mentoring. In the letter of Birgan, who apparently went through a spiritual upheaval during his studies in Geneva, even doubting his own salvation, we see he was counseled back to stability by Calvin. He writes, "You certainly were a help and consolation to me not only in your writings but also in conversation (which indeed has greater effect through the working of the Spirit within) to prevent me from falling into desperation, tested as I was by various afflictions of the spirit."[179] We can see a similar impact in the life of the student Bon Dupre from the pastoral care Calvin showed. "I have occasion to praise God every time I remember the holy exhortation that you gave me on my departure."[180] The Company of Pastors would continue to offer this close pastoral oversight even after the students left the Academy, sometimes recalling their former students

---

[174] S. and S. Stelling-Michaud (eds.), *Le Livre du Recteur de l'Académie de Genève*, Vol. 1 (Geneva: Droz, 1959-89), 73-74.

[175] Letter of Calvin to François Daniel père, Nov. 26, 1559; *CSW*, Vol. 7, 77-78; *CO* 17:680-81.

[176] R.D.C. Robbins, "Life and Character of Theodore Beza," *Bibliotheca Sacra* 7 (1850), 504-05. Beza cherished his relationship with Melchior Wolmar, with whom he lived from ages 10-17.

[177] As cited by Maag, *Genevan Academy*, 140.

[178] Letter of Pierre Bise to the Ministers of Geneva, Sept. 15, 1561; *CO* 18:716-17.

[179] Birgan to Calvin, Apr. 2, 1564.

[180] Dupre to Calvin, Dec. 23, 1561.

Chapter 7 - The Structures of the Genevan Academy which Enhanced Sanctification

for failures in ministry,[181] as was the case with de la Faverge, who did not satisfy the church to which he was assigned.[182]

This close mentoring would encourage the holiness of the students by applying several of the principles of sanctification. First, the close supervision would provide ample opportunity to impress on the students the need for the two-fold knowledge of God and the two-fold response of prostration and reverence, with particular emphasis on humility (Principle 1).[183] Note the lessons of humility reflected in the letter from Dupre. "I hope that the good God will so govern me by his Spirit, who is the Spirit of littleness and humility, that he will give me the grace to strive for his glory, for I estimate it sacrilege if I retain some opinion of myself."[184] Consider as well the case of Nicolas Le More, a young student sent out, apparently too quickly, to be a pastor in France. He wrote to the Company requesting that they recall him for further study and evidences a correctable humility. "Besides, if I am not as patient as is required, I would beg you to support me in my weakness. Consider that I am still learning and still very young, and that I have great need to return to my studies."[185]

Second, the close mentoring would underscore the love of God for the students (Principle 3). The pastors were to evidence love and care for the students, which would assist them in apprehending God's love,[186] an awareness which would draw them toward God for greater holiness.[187] Calvin, known for his warm friendships,[188] showed a particular shepherd's touch. "With what gentleness he comforted the afflicted and cheered those who were faint and sorrowful."[189] Love was shown not only in attitude, but in caring for the students' daily needs, a proof of God's providential love.[190] The Academy provided for the students by offering the courses free of charge,[191] by taking the students in as boarders[192] or finding lodging for them,[193] by offering scholarships for the poor[194] and by providing them with work in the city.[195] Beza demonstrated such

---

[181] Kingdon, *Wars of Religion*, 49.

[182] Letter of the Company of Pastors to Gaspard de la Faverge, Aug. 11, 1561; *CO* 18:605-06.

[183] "Sermon on Gen. 25:24-28," *CO* 58:72.

[184] Dupre to Calvin, Dec. 23, 1561.

[185] N. Le More, "Letter to the Church of Geneva," Nov. 1, 1561, *Bulletin de la Société de l'Histoire du Protestantisme Français* 46 (1897), 466-68.

[186] Selderhuis, *Pilgrim Life*, 114; *Commentary*, 2 Cor. 11:2; 1 Thess. 4:11.

[187] *Sermons on Nativity*, 20.

[188] R.D. Linder, "Brothers in Christ: Pierre Viret and John Calvin as Soul-mates and Co-laborers in the Work of the Reformation," *Calvin and Spirituality, Calvin and His Contemporaries, Calvin Studies Society Papers, 1995, 1997* (Grand Rapids, Mich.: CRC Product Services, 1998), 157.

[189] *Commentary*, Preface to Isaiah by Nicolas des Gallars.

[190] *Sermons on Genesis 1-11*, 90.

[191] Maag, "Education and Training," 146.

[192] Borgeaud, *Histoire de l'Université*, 54.

[193] Letter of Calvin to Peter Martyr, May 11, 1560; *CO* 18:81-83.

[194] Borgeaud, *Histoire de l'Université*, 141-42.

[195] Kingdon, *Wars of Religion*, 18.

material love in his close association with his students, supplying the dowry for a poor refugee girl who wanted to marry an Academy student.[196] Daniel reveals Calvin's love, thanking Calvin for his "goodwill and very great kind deeds towards me."[197] The students clearly felt this love and appreciated it. When Charles Perrot described Calvin to his brother, he used a very affectionate term typical among the students: "our good master and common father."[198] Perrot goes on to describe Beza as "our Theodore," again with clear affection. Young Daniel was unafraid to call upon Calvin's affection for a favor. "It seemed a good idea, most humane of men, to ask you by this letter to display in the present day the same love that you made clear to me beforehand in many ways."[199]

Third, close pastoral supervision would help the students practice a life of continual repentance (Principle 7).[200] This mentoring toward repentance appears evident in the student letters. Dupre, for example, appears to have benefited from such direct calls to repentance by Calvin. "I thank you for so holy a warning, for it has taught me to walk in the greatest solicitude ever, so that to not fall in such evil, of which, I feel only too inclined."[201] Birgan as well admits that after an initial unwillingness to see how his constant studying had actually hurt his spiritual life, he had come to see his own sin. "Many people...said that I brought that pain upon myself through reading papers through the night....Though I thought otherwise, through the grace of God, now I do too."[202]

Fourth, through close pastoral supervision, the students were encouraged to turn to God for help in holiness (Principle 4).[203] Calvin, in his direct counsel, would emphasize this need to turn from seeing one's sin to God for help.[204]

Fifth, in requiring the students to submit entirely to the leadership of the pastors for their typical one to three year sojourn in Geneva,[205] there was an encouragement to self-denial (Principle 8). This would be lived out through their subjection to the Genevan statement of faith[206] and conformity to the standards of preaching for the Company.[207] The confession was particularly lengthy and rigorous, requiring them to submit to the doctrine and discipline of Geneva, taking on a "yoke of subjection" to all in authority over them.[208]

Sixth, through close supervision in their apprenticeships, the students learned the importance of church discipline as an aid to sanctification (Principle

---

[196] Kingdon, *Wars of Religion*, 17.
[197] Letter of François Daniel to Calvin, Aug. 2, 1561; *CO* 18:588-89.
[198] Perrot to his brother Daniel, Feb. 25, 1564.
[199] Letter of François Daniel to Calvin, Apr. 6, 1561; *CO* 18:414-16.
[200] *Commentary*, Lam. 2:14.
[201] Dupre to Calvin, Dec. 23, 1561.
[202] Birgan to Calvin, Apr. 2, 1564.
[203] *Commentary*, Jer. 10:23.
[204] Wallace, *Geneva and the Reformation*, 176.
[205] Maag, *Genevan Academy*, 20-21.
[206] *Le Livre du Recteur*, Vol. 1, 73.
[207] *Le Livre du Recteur*, Vol. 1, 72-73.
[208] "Formulaire de Confession de Foy," *CO* 9:729.

Chapter 7 - The Structures of the Genevan Academy which Enhanced Sanctification

14).[209] The practice of the *censura morum*, which began in the Company of Pastors,[210] eventually spread to the deacons and even the City Council with good effect.[211] This same close supervision, and willingness to confront sins, was practiced with the students, giving them the opportunity to experience church discipline/pastoral care first hand, just as they had been taught.[212] The former student Lacombe recognized this value as he recommended a new student, who apparently required some work in sanctification. "I hope in God that having to remain some time [in Geneva] that God will make him to know his past faults, which are not small, all the more that he has been a papal priest....God show him grace that he goes to the place where he will be polished."[213]

Seventh, the students were encouraged to bear the cross (Principle 9) through the personal counsel of the pastors in one-on-one meetings. Calvin frequently advised his counselees to bear the cross. To French Christians suffering persecution he wrote, "But since it is our duty to suffer, we ought humbly to submit; as it is the will of God."[214] In his letter to François Daniel's father, Calvin explained that he had instructed young Daniel to submit to the burden of legal studies, in effect, taking it as a cross. "After I had reminded him of his duty...he promised that he would submit to whatever by your orders I should prescribe."[215] This was a cross which Daniel, at least initially, bore. "It was my first plan when I was leaving you to devote my energies, on your encouragement, to Roman Law."[216]

Eighth, the close pastoral supervision and counsel would encourage the students to meditate on the future life (Principle 10). Calvin frequently reminded those under his care of the importance of looking to the future life. "Whatever difficulties we may have to encounter, the promise given us that God will...teach us to think more wisely, fixing our hearts, upon that life which is in heaven, so that the world shall seem nothing to us."[217] Courtois in turn praises meditation on the future life in his church members. "Certainly this church has many noble and faithful members: those who not only despise earthly goods for the name of Christ but also of their own accord promise to hand over their bodies to death."[218]

Ninth, the close pastoral supervision would be an aid to the proper use of this present life through moderation and vocational guidance (Principle 11). We

---

[209] Maag, "Education and Training," 149. Cf. Kingdon, *Wars of Religion*, 20.
[210] Small, "A Company of Pastors," 11.
[211] Olson, "Calvin as Pastor-Administrator," 8.
[212] Reid, "The Academy of Geneva," 11; Kingdon, *Wars of Religion*, 17.
[213] Letter of Ennemond Lacombe to Calvin, Mar. 5, 1562; *CO* 19:322-23.
[214] Letter of Calvin to the faithful in France, Nov. 1559; *CSW*, Vol. 7, 84; *CO* 17:681-87.
[215] Calvin to François Daniel père, Nov. 26, 1559.
[216] François Daniel to Calvin Apr. 6, 1561.
[217] Letter of Calvin to Madame de Coligny, Feb. 27, 1559; *CSW*, Vol. 7, 30-31; *CO* 17:458-60.
[218] Letter of Claude Courtois to Calvin, Jan. 2, 1564; *CO* 20:225-226.

may see this watchfulness for moderation in Calvin's reflections on young François Daniel père, when he notes: "here he conducts himself with modesty."[219] We can see that the students absorbed the lesson to remain in their vocations despite difficulties. Colliod wrote of the troubles he faced on the field in France, but concluded that he would remain fast. "They have assigned me to remain in this city, where I may be more useful to them than there where I was."[220] Thus it appears that the close mentoring by the pastors was a leading structural contributor to the students' growth in piety.

Structure 4: The professors served as models of piety
The Genevan Academy used the professors as models of holiness, in order to enhance the students' holiness. Sturm's educational model emphasized the necessity of teachers serving as holy examples. "For many may bear certain marks of distinction and teaching, but nonetheless possess faulty habits that make them unfit role models."[221] Calvin and Beza understood the importance of godly examples and lived as models themselves.[222] "Whenever God exalts us, he does so that we might become examples for others."[223] Calvin dedicated his Ezekiel commentary to de Coligny, Beza explained, so that his example might excite others "to true piety and to other virtues."[224] The desire for pious pastoral models led Calvin to replace the low quality pastors of early Geneva with the outstanding examples who served as professors.[225] Calvin commended Chevalier as a professor, calling him "a pious brother."[226] Viret recommended Jacques des Bordes as a professor for his "pious affections" and zeal for pure religion.[227]

The professors' example would help the holiness of the students, first, by modeling the humility found in the two-fold knowledge (Principle 1), through their mutual submission to the Company and their cooperative ministry.[228] "We cannot otherwise discharge our duty to God and his Church unless we [ministers] mutually extend our hands to each other."[229] Second, the professors' model of holiness would naturally stimulate the students to desire such holiness themselves (Principle 5). Daneau highlights the importance of the professors as models, describing them as "men of greatest merit, and highest renown."[230] We

---

[219] Letter of Calvin to François Daniel père, July 25, 1559; *CO* 17:585-86.
[220] Letter of Pierre Colliod to Calvin, Sept. 5, 1561; *CO* 18:677-79.
[221] Spitz, *Johann Sturm*, 74, "Opening of Elementary Schools."
[222] *Commentary*, Beza's Dedication to Ezek.
[223] *Sermons on Micah*, 12.
[224] *Commentary*, Beza's Dedication to Ezek.
[225] Letter of Calvin to Myconius, Mar. 14, 1542, *CSW*, Vol. 4, 314; *CO* 11:376-81. Cf. Pettegree, "The Clergy and the Reformation," 9.
[226] Letter of Calvin to Francis Bosinormand, Mar. 27, 1559, *CSW*, Vol. 7, 36; *CO* 17:477.
[227] Borgeaud, *Histoire de l'Université*, 77; *CO* 19:379.
[228] McKee, "Calvin and His Colleagues," 13, 40.
[229] *Commentary*, Ezek. 11:3.
[230] Address of Lambert Daneau to the Council of Geneva; Borgeaud, *Histoire de l'Université*, 52.

Chapter 7 - The Structures of the Genevan Academy which Enhanced Sanctification

can hear the impact of these models in Perrot's letter to his brother. "And indeed, both the continuous hearing of the Word of God, and the singular public example of this city, keep us in a wonderful way."[231]

Third, the professors served as models of cross-bearing (Principle 9), which would lead the students to bear their crosses and thus grow in holiness. The professors bore daily burdens in their extraordinary schedules, since most of them were also full-time pastors.[232] With a day starting at 6:00 AM, preaching during the week and on Sundays,[233] Consistory meetings for half the day Thursdays, Congregation and Company on Fridays,[234] and hearing and critiquing students' sermons on Saturdays,[235] there was scarce leisure in their typical week.[236] Calvin recognized this burden in a letter he wrote to Mercer in an effort to recruit him as a pastor/professor, after an unsuccessful effort two years prior. "It was certainly a laborious and modest situation to which I called you."[237] Beyond the daily burden, we find examples of cross-bearing among the professors, beginning with those who had been exiled from the Academy of Lausanne.[238] Many of the professors suffered from serious health problems, as Calvin noted, "Diseases have been raging among our townsmen since your departure, two of them are dead, Tagaut and Gaspar; in fine that most excellent man Macar to the great sorrow of all has been taken from us....Baduel drags on as well as he can. Bernard and Chevalier have got rid of their fever."[239] The ill health of Calvin of course is famous, but he labored under a burden noticed by the students. "[Calvin] can scarcely manage to take his turn regularly because of illness, especially in the winter, in the summer he is a little better."[240] The pastors also suffered from low and often irregular remuneration, Beza even at times teaching gratis.[241]

Fourth, the students would learn about faithfulness in pastoral vocation (Principle 11) from their professors' lives. The students noticed their steadiness. "Theodore [Beza] bears almost the entire burden of the school, a man whose obvious hardiness is in evidence from the fact that, where there is a large crop of listeners, the strength of the ox should necessarily appear."[242] Dotaeus noticed that same faithfulness in Calvin. "Your...diligence to God by virtue of

---

[231] Perrot to his brother Daniel, Feb. 25, 1564.
[232] Henderson, "The Teaching Office," 66-67.
[233] Parker, *Calvin's Thought*, 139.
[234] Boer, "The *Congrégation*," 66.
[235] *Le Livre du Recteur*, Vol. 1, 73.
[236] Borgeaud, *Histoire de l'Université*, 53.
[237] Letter of Calvin to Mercer, Oct. 23, 1563, *CSW*, Vol. 7, 341-42.
[238] Meylan, *La Haute École de Lausanne*, 26-27. Cf. *Annales, CO* 21:716.
[239] Letter of Calvin to Nicolas des Gallars, Oct. 3, 1560, *CSW*, Vol. 7, 141; *CO* 18:212-14.
[240] Perrot to his brother Daniel, Feb. 25, 1564.
[241] H.M. Baird, *Theodore Beza the Counsellor of the French Reformation, 1519-1605* (Eugene, Oreg.: Wipf & Stock, 2004), 108.
[242] Perrot to his brother Daniel, Feb. 25, 1564.

which you came to church every day, so far as you were able."[243] Courtois replicated the perseverance he saw modeled ministering to crowds, even while "embroiled in danger."[244] The example set by the pastors and professors of Geneva seemingly served to enhance the piety of the students.

Structure 5: The Academy maintained a reputation for piety
The Genevan Academy gained a reputation for piety, which served to enhance the students' holiness. The Colloquy of Aulnis recognized this reputation. "Your holy zeal and pious devotion…are well known to us, shown especially in that from your hand, as from a holy seminary of piety have come…people who are well-trained and ready."[245] Aware of this reputation, those who wrote recommending candidates often mentioned their piety. "We have good testimony of his piety and zeal."[246] Students were inspired by Geneva's reputation, as if by a "new and invisible spirit" to study there.[247] This reputation for piety would serve as both a filter, screening out those who wished to cling to their sins, and a magnet, attracting those who wanted holiness, thus increasing the desire for holiness of those matriculating (Principle 5).

The desire to maintain the Academy's reputation for holiness would lead the professors to discipline the students carefully (Principle 14). Geneva's reputation was important to its success, as a Genevan magistrate noted to the Small Council while he traveled to raise money for the city. "The renown that Geneva has acquired for the good order and discipline that prevails there is not small….Therefore it is the good discipline that has occasioned fathers and parents to send their children here."[248] The leaders of the Academy would be careful to guard its reputation by ensuring good discipline, and thus piety, among their students, the export of whom was so central to the city's position in the world.[249]

Structure 6: The Academy required a high standard of personal piety
The students were held to a very high standard for personal holiness, which would increase their piety. Everyone in the city was to be an example of piety to the world in every minute detail of life.[250] "People today marvel at us, and say that the city of Geneva not only *possesses* the Gospel, but *professes*

---

[243] Dotaeus to Calvin, Oct. 20, 1560.
[244] Courtois to Calvin, Dec. 17, 1563.
[245] Aulnis to the Company of Pastors, as cited by Maag, *Genevan Academy*, 108.
[246] Bise to the Ministers of Geneva, Sept. 15, 1561. For another example see, *CO* 19:399-400.
[247] K. Maag, "Calvin and Students," *The Calvin Handbook* (ed. H.J. Selderhuis; Grand Rapids, Mich.: Eerdmans, 2009), 168.
[248] J. Anjorrant, Letter to the Genevan Magistrates, in *Mémoires et Documents publiés par la Société d'Histoire et d'Archéologie de Genève*, Vol. 11 (Geneva: Chez Jullien Frères, 1859), 168-71.
[249] Maag, "Education and Training," 139.
[250] For example, May 15, 1561, the Consistory forbade playing quits the day of the Lord's Supper; *CO* 21:749.

Chapter 7 - The Structures of the Genevan Academy which Enhanced Sanctification

it....Our lives ought so to become shining examples."[251] The students' holiness was particularly charged to the Rector, who should "diligently inquire of their life and knowledge."[252] Pastors, and therefore pastoral candidates, were held to the higher standards outlined in the Ecclesiastical Ordinances.[253] The "intolerable" sins for pastors included: "heresy, schism, rebellion against ecclesiastical order, blasphemy...simony...leaving one's church without lawful leave...lewdness...usury."[254] Those lesser crimes, which merited "direct fraternal admonitions," included: "injurious words...avarice...undisciplined anger, quarrels and contentions."[255] Sinful pastors were regularly disciplined in Geneva, which would also serve as a sanctifying warning to the students.[256] Witness again the concern, not only for outward behavior but internal motivation, as Calvin shepherds young François Daniel. "You judge wisely that the disposition of the young man requires the rein to prevent it from being carried away hither and thither by its natural facility."[257]

This high standard of personal holiness would enhance the students' piety, first, by giving them knowledge of a standard by which to measure their own conduct and therein come to a true knowledge of their sin (Principle 1). Colliod understood from the Genevan pastoral model that it was a pastoral failing to leave a flock without a shepherd, so he appealed for a replacement before he had to leave, "so that if I was forced to leave them they should not remain devoid, this may return great damage to this church."[258] Birgan recognized that his peering into the mysteries of election was a yielding to temptation by Satan since he desired "to enter into the eternal plan of God with Satan as my leader and to penetrate it with blind impetus."[259]

Second, having learned from the high standard where they have failed, they would be encouraged to rely on God to meet that standard (Principle 4). The students demonstrated this desire to rely on God in their persistent requests for prayer. "We are forced to ask for your help so that by receiving from the Lord the richest fruits of your prayers we can drag the devil, the earth and death with our Christ into triumph."[260] Birgan showed an awareness of his need to rely on God for holiness. "Therefore Satan was defeated finally at that time and always thereafter through God's will."[261]

Third, the high standard of holiness had the effect of increasing the students' desire for holiness (Principle 5). This occurred in part because the school *re-*

---

[251] *Sermons on Micah*, 12-13.
[252] *Le Livre du Recteur*, Vol. 1, 71.
[253] Kingdon, *Wars of Religion*, 27.
[254] Reid, *Treatises*, 60-61, "Ecclesiastical Ordinances," 1541.
[255] Reid, *Treatises*, 61, "Ecclesiastical Ordinances," 1541.
[256] Naphy, *Calvin and the Consolidation*, 70.
[257] Letter of Calvin to François Daniel père, Feb. 13, 1560, *CSW*, Vol. 7, 89-90; *CO* 18:16-17.
[258] Colliod to Calvin, Sept. 5, 1561.
[259] Birgan to Calvin, Apr. 2, 1564.
[260] Dotaeus to Calvin, Oct. 20, 1560.
[261] Birgan to Calvin, Apr. 2, 1564.

quired growth toward the Genevan standard of holiness in order to graduate.[262] Dotaeus evidences this desire for holiness as he writes about the Satanic attack on the pastors in his region, knowing he must rise on grace superior to them. "But also the devil, the implacable enemy of peace and harmony, never ceased to attack the...pastors....But by the grace of God it happened that, the more serious the insults were up to this point, the more superior in strength we were."[263] The high standard of personal holiness appears to have assisted the students in their growth in piety as new pastors.

Structure 7: The Academy held a high standard for biblical fidelity
The Academy began with a high standard of biblical knowledge and theological purity, which it maintained for many years.[264] To help assure this high standard, the students were required to sign an extensive statement of faith,[265] to master the biblical languages,[266] to preach using those languages, following Calvin's *lectio continua* style,[267] and to pass a theological exam for graduation. Most of the weekly lectures (19 of 27) and most of the professors (4 out of 5) were devoted to maintaining this purity by work in the biblical text and languages.[268] While the Academy may not have been seen as a highly academic environment compared to some of the great universities of the day,[269] it was nevertheless considered a source of pure learning, as Lambert Daneau notes.

> In 1560 I arrived at your Academy, heart full of enthusiasm, not because it was next to our France, for there were others near, but because it offered me the purest source of that heavenly doctrine.... So many world lights, so many men of greatest merit and highest renown, in all the branches of learning were in this city, it appeared to me, what seemed to be one of the richest intellectual markets in the world.[270]

The high standard of biblical knowledge and doctrinal purity worked simultaneously in two ways to enhance the holiness of the students. In requiring them to submit to biblical teaching (Principle 2), the students were forced to deny themselves (Principle 8). The core of self-denial is giving up our will and substituting God's will as revealed in his Word.[271] The students were constantly required to submit their will to the Word. This submission began with signing the statement of faith. "I confess that the rule of right living and the instruction of faith are so contained in the Holy Scripture, even in all perfection, such that

---

[262] Maag, "Education and Training,"139; Kingdon, *Wars of Religion*, 25-26.
[263] Dotaeus to Calvin, Oct. 20, 1560.
[264] M. d'Aubigné, *La Pierre sur Laquelle L'Académie de Genève Fut Posée en Juin 1559* (Geneva: Chez E. Beroud, 1859), 14.
[265] Maag, *Genevan Academy*, 16.
[266] Battles, *Interpreting Calvin*, 261.
[267] Kingdon, *Wars of Religion*, 14.
[268] Borgeaud, *Fondateur*, 23; Maag, "Education and Training," 134.
[269] Maag, *Genevan Academy*, 111.
[270] Borgeaud, *Histoire de l'Université*, 52.
[271] *Commentary*, Jer. 31:33.

nothing can be lawfully added or subtracted."[272] The submission to the Word continued in their daily studies,[273] their preaching,[274] their closely watched monthly theological papers[275] and their carefully guarded lives.[276] Birgan reflects this submission to Scripture, telling Calvin that it was his teaching on Romans which had helped him to escape the trap of the devil. "In this whirlpool of trial I was delighted by your commentaries on the meaning of the seventh chapter of the Epistle to the Romans."[277] This subjection to the Word of God was an enforced self-denial in yielding their thoughts, beliefs and actions totally to God's Word, which would have the effect of increasing holiness.

Structure 8: The professors used a hortatory teaching style
Rather than simply presenting information, the teaching under which the students sat was persistently sermonic in nature, applying the biblical truths to the hearers and exhorting them toward repentance. Calvin's sermons were calls to believe and repent, which ended with prayers of repentance. "Now let us cast ourselves down before the majesty of our good God, conscious of our faults."[278] Calvin would typically call his students to repent after his lectures as well. "Grant, also, that we may beg pardon of thee, and resolve upon a true repentance."[279] The worship services themselves required a response of repentance, since the Genevan Psalter tended toward songs of penitence.[280] "For well aware am I of my great shame; these evil deeds upon my heart are weighing. Thus have I erred and now deserve your blame, since your commands I have not been obeying."[281] These Psalms were joined with the confession of sin. "Lord God...we confess and acknowledge...that we are poor sinners...[who] ceaselessly transgress your holy commandments."[282] Both the Wednesday prayer meeting and the quarterly celebration of the Lord's Supper emphasized this call to repentance.[283]

Additionally, in most lectures Calvin sought to apply the text directly to his hearers that they might grasp "what Christians should believe, what they should hope for and how they should live."[284] In his lectures he regularly reminded the students that they must obey, exhorting them with the phrase "let us learn"

---

[272] "Formulaire de Confession de Foy," *CO* 9:727.
[273] Borgeaud, *Histoire de l'Université*, 53.
[274] *Le Livre du Recteur*, Vol. 1, 73.
[275] Maag, *Genevan Academy*, 116.
[276] Maag, "Education and Training," 149.
[277] Birgan to Calvin, Apr. 2, 1564.
[278] *Sermons on Nativity*, 166.
[279] *Commentary*, Dan. 4:27. Cf. *Commentary*, Dan. 4:37; 9:7.
[280] Witvliet, "The Spirituality of the Psalter," 98.
[281] D.T. Koyzis, ed., *The 1562 Genevan Psalter*, Genevan Psalter web site, (http://genevanpsalter.redeemer.ca/psalm_texts.html#psalm51; accessed Aug. 23, 2011).
[282] "La Forme Des Prieres," *CO* 6:173.
[283] Pitkin, "Redefining Repentance," 281.
[284] Blacketer, "The Moribund Moralist," 153. Cf. *Commentary*, Budé's Preface to Hosea; Holder, "Exegetical Understanding," 207.

(*discamus*).[285] Let us learn to appreciate the blessings of God,[286] let us learn to flee to God,[287] let us learn that God punishes ingratitude,[288] let us learn to examine ourselves.[289] The Bible is a word which must be taken to heart and acted upon,[290] first with repentance.[291]

The persistent hortatory style of communicating the Scriptures, in sermon, prayer, praise, confession, sacrament and lecture, would confront the students with sin and call them to repentance, which would lead them toward holiness (Principle 7). Dupre understood that he must repent. "I do not want to excuse myself all the time, the Lord, by his grace, has made me daily to ask that he will grant me humility and will remove all arrogance from my heart."[292] Dotaeus understood that his teaching of the Word was to be more than just information, but must actually feed the flock. "When we had been waited for by the hungry sheep for a long time…we offered heavenly food to them."[293] The hortatory seems to have found its mark.

Structure 9: The professors closely critiqued students' preaching and theology
To help the students grow in holiness through a right understanding and application of Scripture, the Company carefully critiqued the students' weekly practice preaching sessions and monthly theological papers.[294] The Saturday sermons were critiqued by the presiding member of the Company and then any others present, provided this was done "modestly and in fear of the Lord."[295] The theological papers, which must contain no "curiosities, sophistries, or…false doctrines," were presented in a forum, followed with public critique by the pastors and fellow students. The presiding pastor was expected to resolve on the spot, "by the Word of God," any theological disputes which arose.

The students were also invited to watch the Congregations, where they would see their professors receive critical feedback from other pastors.[296] Apparently aware that sharpening was available through the critical feedback of the Academy, churches would write asking that their candidates receive such help.[297] "The aforementioned Mr. Raillet has asked time in order to go study to take advantage by conversing with you to better fashion himself."[298]

---

[285] For example, we found 89 occurrences in the *Commentary* on Jeremiah.
[286] *Commentary*, Lam. 1:7.
[287] *Commentary*, Lam. 3:20.
[288] *Commentary*, Ezek. 7:26.
[289] *Commentary*, Ezek. 13:9.
[290] *Commentary*, Ezek. 7:26.
[291] *Commentary*, Lam. 2:14.
[292] Dupre to Calvin, Dec. 23, 1561.
[293] Dotaeus to Calvin, Oct. 20, 1560.
[294] *Le Livre du Recteur*, Vol. 1, 73.
[295] *CO* 10:87, "Le Ordre du Collège de Genève."
[296] Maag, "Preaching Practice," 137.
[297] Maag, *Genevan Academy*, 116.
[298] Letter from the Church of Annonay to Calvin; *CO* 19:399-400.

Chapter 7 - The Structures of the Genevan Academy which Enhanced Sanctification

This critical feedback would advance the students' holiness, first, by helping them come into submission to the preaching of the Word (Principle 2), requiring them to humbly submit to the plain meaning of Scripture, banishing all "sophistry, impudent curiosity and audacity to corrupt the Word."[299] The students evidenced this submission to Scripture. Perrot shows this in describing his studies. "I have embarked seriously upon Hebrew, and if the Lord is willing, will persevere in it with great pleasure. I am working at Theology, both in the School and on my own. Our good master and common father [Calvin] is giving us lessons on the Book of Ezekiel."[300] Birgan had been distressed, because he feared that he had peered into election contrary to God's Word and heard Satan accusing him. "You, not content with the rule of sacred Scripture, sinned against the Holy Spirit."[301] When Dupre wrote, asking Calvin to send additional pastoral help, his chief criterion was that they send someone who had "great affection for the Word."[302] The students apparently had learned, in part from the critical feedback given to them, the importance of conforming all their lives to the Word of God.

Second, the critical feedback would have the effect of giving the students a true knowledge of their weakness and thus humbling them (Principle 1). Calvin, aware that preachers are prone to self-aggrandizement, structured a system in which all preachers would be regularly critiqued by others, sounding out errors, thus proving their fallibility and their continued need for the humility to rely only on the power of the Word, rather than native abilities. It was perhaps from this practice of critical feedback that Le More found it so easy to write to the Company of his failures as a preacher. "I recognize a vice in me that I speak too quickly, and because I am in a place where they understand French with difficulty, they do not profit much [from my sermons]."[303] Dupre demonstrated a similar humility in response to a reprimand from Calvin. "For knowing how I am easily in such vice this will teach me to control myself in fear."[304] The critical feedback given to the students would advance their holiness, as it lead them to submit themselves more fully to Scripture and to realize that they were imperfect pastors, always in need of correction.

Structure 10: The students faced dangers in France

While the dangerous situation in France was not properly a structure of the Academy, when one considers Calvin's theology of sanctification, it becomes apparent that those very dangers were a contributor to the students' growth in holiness. Although the *Registers of the Company of Pastors* lists 88 pastors sent to France during 1555-62, Kingdon surmises that this was a low count, and in reality as many as 142 pastors went out in 1561 alone.[305] This flood of

---

[299] *CO* 10:87, "Le Ordre du Collège de Genève."
[300] Perrot to his brother Daniel, Feb. 25, 1564.
[301] Birgan to Calvin, Apr. 2, 1564.
[302] Dupre to Calvin, Dec. 23, 1561.
[303] N. Le More, Letter to the Church of Geneva, Nov. 1, 1561.
[304] Dupre to Calvin, Dec. 23, 1561.
[305] Kingdon, *Wars of Religion*, 2, 79.

Protestant pastors from Geneva did not go unnoticed. King Charles IX wrote to the senate of Geneva in January of 1561, accusing the Genevan-trained pastors of "open sedition," and asking the senate to recall them and send no more.[306] This prompted the less than candid reply from the senate, penned by Calvin on their behalf, explaining that "it will be found that no one, with our knowledge and permission, has ever gone from here to preach."[307] Even as he wrote, the Company was besieged by requests for pastors, which they scrambled to meet. "From all quarters demands for ministers are addressed to us, and though we have no more to send, yet such is the importunity of those who ask, that we must choose certain ministers from the lower ranks of the people."[308] As the Huguenot Church grew to its height in 1562, with an estimated three million members in 2150 churches, persecution intensified,[309] leading to the slaughter of a Calvinist congregation in Vassy by the Guise forces in March of 1562 and the start of the Wars of Religion.[310] Of the 88 named pastors sent to France during 1555-62, 10 would eventually be killed, and another six would die untimely deaths.[311]

First, for those students studying in the relative safety of Geneva, most of whom were from France and planning to return there,[312] news of persecutions would have the uniquely sanctifying effect of causing them to struggle for more faith (Principle 6). Dotaeus reported the typical dangers of travel in France. "On 20 September we set out from here on the course of our journey–not indeed without danger but at least without any harm, and through the grace of God we travelled and reached Nerac on 7 October safe and unharmed."[313] Courtois arrived at his new assignment, Moutier, in 1564, only to discover a number of plots underway to harm the church. "Meanwhile, however, I see a small gathering of plots that has scarcely been stable up to this point, for, as I learned from one of the faithful, the enemy are working at new plots."[314] Lacombe found trouble as well. "The churches of Dauphine and of Lyonaise

---

[306] Letter of Charles IX to the Senate of Geneva, Jan. 22, 1561; *CO* 18:337-39.
[307] Letter of the Genevan Senate to the King of France, Jan. 28, 1561; *CSW*, Vol.7, 168; *CO* 18:343-45. This troubling reply might be explained by two factors: first, the city had truthfully not sent any *seditious* pastors to France, the essential charge against them; second, Calvin and the Company had consistently counseled against seditious activity on the part of their pastors. Hence they sincerely declared their innocence even among themselves: "But regarding the disturbances which happened in France, they are not at all guilty there." (*Annales*, Jan. 28, 1561; *CO* 21:742)
[308] Letter of Calvin to Ambrose Blaurer, May, 1561; *CSW*, Vol. 7, 191; *CO* 18:474-75.
[309] Kingdon, *Wars of Religion*, 79.
[310] Kingdon, *Wars of Religion*, 106.
[311] Kingdon, *Wars of Religion*, 144.
[312] In 1563 79 out of the 94 matriculating students were from France; Maag, *Genevan Academy*, 30.
[313] Dotaeus to Calvin, Oct. 20, 1560.
[314] Courtois to Calvin, Jan. 2, 1564.

are assembled here to celebrate the synod, but the governor of the country blocks us and does not provide that we may assemble."[315]

Anticipating being sent into battle, these young recruits would endure an intense struggle for faith. Calvin, who was teaching during this time on the prophets Jeremiah, Daniel and Ezekiel, all of whom faced opposition that produced real struggles of faith, put these words in the mouth of Jeremiah, "There is then no reason for you to think that I speak so boldly, because I feel nothing human; but I have done so after a hard struggle, after all those things came into my mind, which are calculated to weaken the courage of my heart; yet God stretched forth his hand to me."[316] It was God who had given Jeremiah faith after the struggle to preach in the midst of his persecution and danger, and God who would give the students faith to face persecution in France. "Although a hundred deaths may threaten us, they must not weaken our faith."[317]

Second, the violence in France, and the likelihood of persecution, would serve as an aid to holiness by encouraging the students to think on the future life (Principle 10). While the dangers in France were not part of the structure of the Academy, Calvin apparently made free use of them. Consider this mention of the danger of "urgent perils" and the future life in this typical closing prayer: "Grant, Almighty God, since our life is only for a moment…that we may learn to cast all our care upon thee, and so to depend upon thee, as not to doubt thee as our deliverer from all urgent perils….May the hope of eternal life be so fixed in our hearts, that we may willingly leave this world."[318] This was a lesson not lost on the students, as we have seen in their readiness to pastor even in the face of danger. Facing opposition to his ministry, Colliod persevered because "the Lord has shown to my eye that he wants to do grace and mercy to this people."[319] Practically speaking, the persecution awaiting the pastoral students when they left Geneva would be one of the most effective possible inducements to meditate on the future life, which in turn, would advance their holiness.

Conclusion

The Genevan Academy not only offered teaching that was calculated by Calvin to advance the students' holiness, but its educational structures, modeled after the new methods of education, which focused on mastery of the biblical texts and languages while aiming at piety, were thoughtfully arranged so as to reinforce the basic biblical principles of sanctification working toward the rapid advance of piety. Though not proven conclusively, the evidence does suggest that this combination was effective, producing *sapiens et eloquens pietas*. Certainly this was the conclusion drawn by some of those who employed the Academy to shape their pastors. "We suggested to him to go to your Academy, as it is the best place we know of to be healthily and solidly taught about the

---

[315] Lacombe to Calvin, Mar. 5, 1562.
[316] *Commentary*, Jer. 20:9.
[317] *Commentary*, Dan. 3:7.
[318] *Commentary*, Dan. 3:25.
[319] Colliod to Calvin, Sept. 5, 1561.

mysteries of divine knowledge and to be directed always, either by good teachings or by pious examples, toward holiness of life."[320]

---

[320] Aulnis to the Company of Pastors, as cited by Maag, *Genevan Academy*, 109.

Chapter 8 - Comparing the Academies of Lausanne and Strasbourg with Geneva

"Das ym selbs niemant, sonder anderen leben soll."[1]

Introduction

In this chapter we will compare the two Academies of Lausanne and Strasbourg with the Genevan Academy, in order to discover both the similarities and differences among them. We will advance the theory that while Geneva had similarities with the other Academies, it had certain unique characteristics, which conformed more closely to what Calvin considered to be a good environment for enhancing holiness. To compare the three Academies, we will examine two aspects: their educational structures and their teaching regarding sanctification. To compare the educational structures, we will examine the foundational documents of each Academy. To compare the teaching, we will examine some representative teaching of Pierre Viret and Martin Bucer, the principle professors at Lausanne and Strasbourg respectively. In comparing both the structures and teaching of these other Academies in such a limited space, we do not pretend to take nearly as in depth a view as we have with either Calvin's teachings or the inner-workings of the Genevan Academy. However, even a summary comparison of some key structures and teachings could prove illuminating. Before we compare the Academies, however, a word of introduction to the schools will be helpful.

Lausanne

The Lausanne Academy, under the watchful eye of Bern, began meeting in the Cathedral and nearby buildings in January 1537,[2] with Viret serving as the initial director.[3] It was not until 1547, however, that its governing document, *Leges Scholae Lausannensis*, was written.[4] The school grew to 700 students in 1558,[5] while the city had only 5000 inhabitants.[6] The Academy attracted outstanding professors, including the young Theodore Beza and Maturin Cordier,

---

[1] "That no one should live for himself but for others," the title of Martin Bucer's tract on Christian love.
[2] A. Gindroz, *Histoire de l'instruction publique dans le Pays de Vaud* (Lausanne: Georges Bridel, 1853), 28-29.
[3] J. Cart, *Pierre Viret, le Réformateur Vaudois* (Lausanne: Librairie de Louis Meyer, 1864), 99-100.
[4] M. Campiche, *La Réforme en Pays de Vaud, 1528-1619* (Lausanne: L'Aire, 1985), 195-96. For the Latin text of the *Leges* see: J. Le Coultre, *Maturin Cordier et les origines de la pédagogie de protestante dans les pays de langue française (1530-1564)* (Neuchâtel: Mémoires de l'Université de Neuchâtel, 1926), 482-89.
[5] Baird, *Theodore Beza*, 96.
[6] M.W. Bruening, *Calvinism's First Battleground: Conflict and Reform in the Pays de Vaud, 1528-1559* (Dordrecht: Springer, 2005), 10.

Calvin's old Latin professor.[7] Sadly, the Academy would flounder in 1559 over a long simmering dispute with Bern concerning church discipline. Viret and the other pastors, refusing to administer the Lord's Supper at Christmas 1558, were summarily dismissed, many of them finding their way to the Genevan Academy.[8] Beza, having seen the handwriting on the wall, had already left for Geneva in summer of 1558.[9]

Strasbourg

Strasbourg, a city of 20,000 people, had welcomed Bucer's return in 1523,[10] shortly after the start of the Reformation there.[11] Strasbourg had inconsistent success with educational reform before its Academy was begun. Informal classes for reading and writing occurred in 1480.[12] Two Latin schools were founded in 1524.[13] Bucer expanded his lectures begun in 1523[14] to include Greek and Hebrew instruction.[15] In 1531, after urging by Bucer,[16] schools were established in each of the city's nine parishes.[17] In 1534 a school for younger students was opened, the *Collegium Praedicatorum*,[18] which was later absorbed by the Academy.[19] By 1535 there were 15 separate schools in the city.[20]

In 1536 the town council invited Johann Sturm to lay the groundwork for a new Academy.[21] He would complete two foundational documents in 1538: the brief and philosophical, *Advice on What Organization to Give the Gymnasium in Strasbourg*, and the longer more detailed, *The Correct Opening of Elementary Schools of Letters*.[22] These two works, supplemented by the *Leges et Statu-*

---

[7] Borgeaud, *Histoire de l'Université*, 38.
[8] Gindroz, *Histoire de l'instruction*, 37-38.
[9] H. Meylan, *La Haute École de Lausanne, 1537-1937* (Université de Lausanne, 1986), 26-27.
[10] D. Lawrence, *Martin Bucer: Unsung Hero of the Reformation* (Nashville, Tenn.: Westview, 2008), 45.
[11] H. Eells, "The Contributions of Martin Bucer to the Reformation," *Harvard Theological Review* 24 (1931), 30.
[12] M.U. Chrisman, *Strasbourg and the Reform: a Study in the Process of Change* (New Haven, Conn.: Yale University Press, 1967), 45.
[13] M. Lienhard (ed.), *La faculté de théologie protestante de Strasbourg—Hier et Aujourd'hui* (Strasbourg: Oberlin, 1988), 15.
[14] Lienhard, *La faculté de Strasbourg*, 15.
[15] Chrisman, *Strasbourg*, 266.
[16] A.H. Gilbert, "Martin Bucer on Education," *The Journal of English and Germanic Philology* 18 (1919), 326.
[17] Chrisman, *Strasbourg*, 268.
[18] E-W. Kohls, *Die Schule bei Martin Bucer in ihrem Verhältnis zu Kirche und Obrigkeit* (Heidelberg: Quelle & Meyea, 1963), 80.
[19] Lienhard, *La faculté de Strasbourg*, 17.
[20] Kohls, *Die Schule*, 76.
[21] Borgeaud, *Histoire de l'Université*, 25.
[22] Spitz, *Johann Sturm*, 61-67, "Advice," 71-118, "Opening of Elementary Schools." Kohls disputes Sturm's principal authorship of these documents, though he offers little proof. Kohls, *Die Schule*, 88.

Chapter 8 - Comparing the Academies of Lausanne and Strasbourg with Geneva

ta den Schulern,[23] served as the Academy's initial governing documents. Later, in 1545, Bucer created an important addendum to the Statutes.[24] Together these four documents will comprise the material for examining the structures of the Strasbourg Academy.

Sturm, hired as the Rector on June 24, 1538, by the *Scholarchen*, the city councilmen who comprised the board of education,[25] consolidated the educational system of Strasbourg in one central location. The new school, which opened formally on December 29, 1538,[26] had two parts: a preparatory school, which came to be known as the *Gymnasium*, and a public school for the study of Law, Arts and Theology,[27] for students aged 16-21.[28] The combined institutions were generally referred to as the *Hochschule*.[29]

Lausanne and Genevan Academies were seminaries, Strasbourg a university
When one examines the foundational purposes of our three Academies, one may see that while each was designed to inculcate a Reformed view of Scripture and to raise educational standards,[30] both Lausanne and Geneva were primarily conceived as training schools for pastors, while Strasbourg was designed to be a city university. We have already seen the Genevan Academy's aim to educate clergy.[31] Viret, despite his desire for universal literacy,[32] was principally concerned for the education of clergy; hence he served as the sole professor of theology for the first nine years of the Lausanne Academy.[33] We find this in the opening paragraphs of the *Leges*: "The very first elements of religion should be taught daily in the vernacular language in the afternoon hours."[34] Baird,[35] Gindroz, Le Coultre,[36] Junod and Martin all concur, the Lausanne Academy was "less an institution for science and literature"[37] but was founded to train

---

[23] M. Fournier and C. Engel (eds.), *Les statuts et privilèges des universités françaises depuis leur fondation jusqu'en 1789, tome 4/1: Gymnase, Académie, Université de Strasbourg* (Paris: L. Larose et Forcel, 1894) "Leges et Statuta den Schulern so in Classibus Anfengklichs Gegeben," 25-28. The author gratefully acknowledges the assistance of Mrs. Ella Shultz Hudson and Mr. Johannes Solf in the translation of this and a following German document, any errors, however, remain the author's own.
[24] Fournier, *Les statuts*, "Statuts du Gymnase," 48-53.
[25] Spitz, *Johann Sturm*, 14-15.
[26] Kohls, *Die Schule*, 89.
[27] Lienhard, *La faculté de Strasbourg*, 17.
[28] Kohls, *Die Schule*, 90.
[29] Chrisman, *Strasbourg*, 271.
[30] Gindroz, *Histoire de l'instruction*, 28-29.
[31] Reid, *Treatises*, 63, "Ecclesiastical Ordinances," 1541.
[32] R.D. Linder, "Pierre Viret's Ideas and Attitudes Concerning Humanism and Education," *Church History* 34 (1965), 31.
[33] Meylan, *La Haute École de Lausanne*, 17.
[34] Le Coultre, *Maturin Cordier*, "Leges Scholae," 482.
[35] Baird, *Theodore Beza*, 46.
[36] Le Coultre, *Maturin Cordier*, 209.
[37] Gindroz, *Histoire de l'instruction*, 29.

"faithful ministers with evangelistic zeal,"[38] particularly pastors for the French world.[39]

Defining the primary aim of the Strasbourg Academy is less simple. There are some historians, such as Lienhard[40] and Amos,[41] who would say that it too aimed primarily at training pastors. This, coupled with Bucer's life-long concern to develop pastors,[42] might lead one to assume the *Hochschule* shared this purpose. Kohls, however, reveals Bucer's desire to see a true university begun in Strasbourg,[43] evident in the foundational documents, which call for broader classical education and not ministerial preparation in particular.

The schedules of the three Academies reflect this different emphasis. Geneva offered all its students 19 hours of Bible, biblical languages and theology out of 27 hours of courses, and Lausanne offered 20 hours out of 30.[44] Sturm divided the *Hochschule* into Medicine, Law and Theology and expected the students to attend courses from all three disciplines. Those in Medicine and Law received little Bible training, and even pastoral students would have to subtract from their 20 hours of classes[45] to attend lectures in other disciplines.[46]

The curriculum for the upper school reflects Sturm's emphasis on a university education. "The poets who are arduous and hard to understand should be examined after Vergil and Homer are well understood."[47] After he describes the classical authors in great detail, Sturm then offers the theology students this: "Thus…the theologian, shall not be ignorant of the knowledge of distinctions [logic] and of speaking [rhetoric], and should be acquainted with," history and law.[48] Sturm appears to be driven by the conviction that classical education, even more than Scripture, would produce a godly individual. "There is nothing in the nature of the universe that cultivates morality as does the study of letters."[49] Sturm, "restrained in his method of communicating the Christian Gospel,"[50] appears to have been shaped more by Aristotle than Augustine.[51]

---

[38] H. Martin, *Les Cinq Étudiants de L'Académie de Lausanne* (Lausanne: Georges Bridel, 1863), 6.
[39] Junod, *L'Académie de Lausanne*, 12.
[40] Lienhard, *La faculté de Strasbourg*, 18.
[41] N.S. Amos, "Bucer Among the Biblical Humanists: The Context for His Practice in the Teaching of Theology in Strasbourg, 1523-1548," *Reformation & Renaissance Review* 6 (2004), 143-45.
[42] W. Pauck (ed.), *Melanchthon and Bucer* (Philadelphia, Pa.: Westminster, 1969) *De Regno Christi*, 274.
[43] Kohls, *Die Schule*, 79-80, 91.
[44] Le Coultre, *Maturin Cordier*, "Leges Scholae," 486-89.
[45] Fournier, *Les statuts,* "Leges et Statuta," 28.
[46] Spitz, *Johann Sturm*, "Opening of Elementary Schools," 112.
[47] Spitz, *Johann Sturm*, "Opening of Elementary Schools," 106-07.
[48] Spitz, *Johann Sturm*, "Opening of Elementary Schools," 111.
[49] Spitz, *Johann Sturm*, "Opening of Elementary Schools," 72.
[50] Chrisman, *Strasbourg*, 272.
[51] Aristotle, *Politics*, Book VIII, Section 1, 1337, "The neglect of education does harm to the constitution."

Chapter 8 - Comparing the Academies of Lausanne and Strasbourg with Geneva

A Comparison of the Structures

Structure 1: The Academy integrated into the city

All three of our Academies had a degree of integration into the life of the city. For example, in all three towns the city councils exercised some control over the Academies. Strasbourg, with its complex structure of six councils,[52] was ruled by the *Ratsherren*,[53] which created a special committee of three of its members in 1526, the *Scholarchen*, to direct all the city's educational affairs.[54] Although Bucer would have preferred church control,[55] the Academy maintained an independent constitution.[56] The Bernese City Council initially created the Lausanne Academy and continued to exercise control,[57] purchasing its buildings,[58] appointing Viret and other professors[59] and requiring the students to vow loyalty to the "magnificent state of Bern."[60] Bern did allow the Lausanne council to select the president of the Academy.[61] While the Genevan Academy was technically under the overall direction of the City Council, it was really the Company of Pastors who ran the school, selecting the rector and teachers, with the Council ratifying their decisions.[62] The Genevan Academy, therefore, had a greater emphasis on the training of pastors and the purity of doctrine and discipline, sources of frustration for the pastors of Lausanne and Strasbourg.

In all three cities, the city councils watched over the morals and religious life of the city. Bucer fully expected the state to "propagate the Kingdom of Christ also by the power of the sword,"[63] to punish unbelievers[64] or to help recover lost sheep.[65] The *Kirchenpfleger*, or church caretakers, similar to elders in Geneva, watched directly over the morals of the city.[66] Its 21 members, appointed for life from various city councils, were assigned in teams of three to the seven

---

[52] Lawrence, *Martin Bucer*, 47.
[53] S.F. Nelson and J. Rott, "Strasbourg: The Anabaptist City in the Sixteenth Century," *Mennonite Quarterly Review* 58 (1984), 230.
[54] Chrisman, *Strasbourg*, 263-65.
[55] Kohls, *Die Schule*, 82.
[56] Kohls, *Die Schule*, 95-98.
[57] Junod, *L'Académie de Lausanne*, 12.
[58] Gindroz, *Histoire de l'instruction*, 32.
[59] Campiche, *Pays de Vaud*, 195-96.
[60] Le Coultre, *Maturin Cordier*, "Leges Scholae," 489.
[61] Le Coultre, *Maturin Cordier*, "Leges Scholae," 489.
[62] CO 10:65-89, "Le Ordre du Collège de Genève." English translations used in this chapter are from Eby, *Early Protestant Educators*, 252-69.
[63] Pauck, *Bucer, De Regno Christi*, 272.
[64] M. Greschat, "The Relation Between Church and Civil Community in Bucer's Reforming Work," *Martin Bucer Reforming Church and Community* (ed. D.F. Wright; Cambridge: Cambridge University Press, 1994), 29.
[65] M. Bucer, *Concerning the True Care of Souls* (tr. P. Beale; Edinburgh: Banner of Truth Trust, 2009), 80.
[66] R.E.H. Uprichard, "The Eldership in Martin Bucer and John Calvin," *Irish Biblical Studies* 18 (1996), 139.

parishes of the city[67] and watched even over the pastors.[68] Both the City Council and the *Kirchenpfleger* wished to retain final control over the spiritual discipline[69] and theology[70] of the city, such that Bucer would fail repeatedly to win the pastoral right to exercise church discipline, particularly to fence the table.[71] Bucer even attempted to institute voluntary discipline in "Christian Fellowships" during 1547, but the City Council ordered him to cease.[72]

The Lords of Bern, who controlled Lausanne from 1536, asserted moral authority over the city, generating ordinances and catechisms and requiring pastoral visitations.[73] From 1538 through 1558 Viret fought with Bern,[74] particularly demanding the right to excommunicate the openly sinful,[75] but Bern consistently refused.[76] In 1558 Viret submitted a formal request to Bern for the creation of a Geneva-like Consistory, enumerating "the proper duty of the ministers and elders over their flocks."[77] The Bernese did not care to be lectured by Lausanne and flatly rejected this request. In response Viret refused to serve communion on Christmas of 1558. The Bernese had had enough and immediately dismissed both Viret and his cohorts.[78]

What Lausanne and Strasbourg lacked, Geneva supplied fully, a City Council which worked in harmony with the pastors to supervise the morals of the city. By waiting until 1559 to found the Academy, Calvin's battles had been fought and won, so that the integration of Academy with city and Consistory was nearly seamless, essential to creating Calvin's ideal environment for enhancing holiness and key to Calvin's genius.[79]

Structure 2: The Academy integrated with the church

Each of our cities had some integration of Academy and church. In Strasbourg it was not until Bucer's additions to the school rules (1545) that any real integration with the church was mandated, Sturm having neglected this nearly entirely. Professors vowed to be "faithful to the School and to the church" and were to regularly attend church services.[80] The Professors of Theology were to

---

[67] A.N. Burnett, *The Yoke of Christ: Martin Bucer and Christian Discipline* (Kirksville, Mo.: Sixteenth Century, 1994), 66-67.
[68] Burnett, *The Yoke of Christ*, 191-92.
[69] Burnett, *The Yoke of Christ*, 106.
[70] Greschat, "Church and Civil Community," 18.
[71] D. Engelsma, "Martin Bucer: Reformed Pastor of Strasbourg," *Mid-America Journal of Theology* 3 (1987), 50-51.
[72] Burnett, *The Yoke of Christ*, 193.
[73] Bruening, *Calvinism's First Battleground*, 160.
[74] Meylan, *La Haute École de Lausanne*, 26-27.
[75] Bruening, *Calvinism's First Battleground*, 164-68.
[76] Gindroz, *Histoire de l'instruction*, 37-38.
[77] M.W. Bruening, "'La nouvelle réformation de Lausanne': The Proposal by the Ministers of Lausanne on Ecclesiastical Discipline (1558)," *Bibliothèque d'Humanisme et Renaissance* 68 (2006), 33.
[78] Gindroz, *Histoire de l'instruction*, 37-38.
[79] Eby, *Early Protestant Educators*, 235.
[80] Fournier, *Les statuts*, "Statuts du Gymnase," 48.

urge the students "to work God-fearingly in the community of the church."[81] Yet full integration of the church and Academy was hindered by the continuous tensions between the pastors and the City Council and by Bucer's own desire to keep the *Hochschule* separate from the state.[82] In Strasbourg the church appears to be more of an appendage to the Academy, an afterthought to Sturm's magnificent classical education.

Lausanne integrated the church and Academy more, requiring that the Rector of the school be chosen from among the city ministers and professors.[83] Viret, a pastor, served as Rector from 1537 until 1547,[84] followed by Pastor Andre Zébédée, who was replaced by Beza in 1552.[85] The sermons were considered part of the daily curriculum.[86] The pastors and professors chose those who could board students; these landlords were to take their boarders to church and "notify the pastors" of any character issues.[87] Even the Liberal Arts Professor was to take his boarders to sermons on ceremonial days.[88] The Theology Professor was to apply lessons that built up the church. "He should show its use both for personal progress and for the institution and activity of the Church."[89]

In Geneva the Rector and teachers were chosen from among the pastors by a board of pastors and professors.[90] Each academic day began with the morning sermon, and "Sundays [were] devoted to attending religious services."[91] The students were invited to attend the weekly *Congregation* where the pastors preached and were to preach weekly under the watchful eyes of the pastors; neither of these disciplines were featured in Lausanne or Strasbourg. Thus Geneva more thoroughly integrated church and Academy than Strasbourg or Lausanne.

Structure 3: The students were closely mentored by pastors
In Strasbourg both Sturm[92] and Bucer[93] understood the importance of teachers serving as mentors for their students. Bucer wrote, "If he observes that any of them ceases from learning, he privately corrects him, and warns him of his duty."[94] The Rector, taking a close interest in the students, was to lead them in

---

[81] Fournier, *Les statuts*, "Statuts du Gymnase," 50.
[82] Kohls, *Die Schule*, 95-97.
[83] Le Coultre, *Maturin Cordier*, "Leges Scholae," 489.
[84] Cart, *Pierre Viret*, 99.
[85] Meylan, *La Haute École de Lausanne*, 22-23. However, of the ten professors at the Lausanne public school from 1547 until 1558, only Viret and Zébédée were fully pastors. Henderson, "The Teaching Office," 54.
[86] Le Coultre, *Maturin Cordier*, "Leges Scholae," 486-88.
[87] Le Coultre, *Maturin Cordier*, "Leges Scholae," 488.
[88] Le Coultre, *Maturin Cordier*, "Leges Scholae," 487.
[89] Le Coultre, *Maturin Cordier*, "Leges Scholae," 488.
[90] Eby, *Early Protestant Educators*, 253, 262; *CO* 10:85.
[91] Eby, *Early Protestant Educators*, 265; *CO* 10:85.
[92] Spitz, *Johann Sturm*, "Opening of Elementary Schools," 72-73.
[93] Gilbert, "Bucer on Education," 325-26.
[94] *Martini Buceri Scripta Anglicana* (Basel: Petri Pernae Officina, 1577), 563.

learning and piety, hearing reports on matters, "especially concerning the Christian religion and discipline."[95]

Lausanne called for careful mentoring by the Rector and professors who often held classes in their homes.[96] The Rector was to provide close supervision.[97] "[The students] should show the rector honesty in their character and keenness in their letters…one who is headstrong, or seriously delinquent or prone to crime should be punished."[98] The students from Bern were to be housed with the Professor of Arts, who was similarly charged: "He should attend to their domestic studies and characters."[99] The landlords, chosen from those "of good testimony," were to "give careful observation to the character and studies of his lodgers."[100] In the residential dormitory for scholarship students, *L'Escholiers de Messieurs*, the tutor was responsible for the students' moral, intellectual and spiritual development.[101]

The system in Geneva, perhaps benefiting from the models in the other cities, provided a somewhat more intense pastoral mentoring experience. Not only did pastors take in students as boarders and serve as their mentors, but they also guided them in apprenticeships, examined their readiness for ministry and supervised their practice sermons. The cooperation and control exerted by the Company of Pastors delivered a more thorough pastoral mentoring experience for the students of Geneva.

Structure 4: The professors served as models of piety

Johann Sturm was adamant that professors must serve as examples of the very scholarship and virtues which they wished to teach.[102] "If ever there were times in which religion demanded outstanding models…our times demand them most."[103] Bucer, too, was careful to underscore the importance of the professors' example of holiness[104] and so was personally involved in the effort to recruit honorable teachers.[105] Teachers must "vow to live in Christian love and community" and were to "serve as a good Christian example for the others in school."[106] They were to model a godly scholarship, disciplined and diligent in all their personal and professional conduct. The Law Professor, for instance, was to "truly motivate the students to follow our Christian religion and disci-

---

[95] Fournier, *Les statuts*, "Statuts du Gymnase," 49.
[96] Gindroz, *Histoire de l'instruction*, 33.
[97] Meylan, *La Haute École de Lausanne*, 20.
[98] Le Coultre, *Maturin Cordier*, "Leges Scholae," 489.
[99] Le Coultre, *Maturin Cordier*, "Leges Scholae," 487.
[100] Le Coultre, *Maturin Cordier*, "Leges Scholae," 488.
[101] Meylan, *La Haute École de Lausanne*, 17.
[102] Kohls, *Die Schule*, 76.
[103] Spitz, *Johann Sturm*, "Opening of Elementary Schools," 116-17; cf. 74.
[104] W.P. Stephens, *The Holy Spirit in the Theology of Martin Bucer* (Cambridge: Cambridge University Press, 1970), 177.
[105] Kohls, *Die Schule*, 91.
[106] Fournier, *Les statuts*, "Statuts du Gymnase," 48.

Chapter 8 - Comparing the Academies of Lausanne and Strasbourg with Geneva

pline, in his teaching as well as in his exemplary daily living."[107] The Rector was to serve as the ultimate model of Christian care and learning, not only for the students but for the other teachers.[108]

The concept of teaching by example was present in Lausanne as well, though perhaps to a lesser degree. For Viret the pastor was to lead the way in church discipline by his own good example[109] and not to be a "dishonor to the Gospel."[110] Those who offered lodging to the students were to be examples as men of "good testimony."[111] It seems apparent from his efforts to recruit Beza from Geneva that Viret admired Beza for his well-known example of holiness and erudition,[112] and thus considered him an "honor and ornament" for the school.[113]

Geneva, built on modeling holiness, expected the Rector to be "a man of conspicuous piety and learning,"[114] while Lausanne was perhaps more oriented toward his academic side, seeking a rector of "authority and learning."[115] Geneva and Strasbourg then would seem to have emphasized more thoroughly than Lausanne the role of professors as models of holiness.

Structure 5: The Academy maintained a reputation for piety
Since our study of both Strasbourg and Lausanne was limited, and did not comprise any significant correspondence, we cannot adequately judge their reputations for holiness. Once Beza was a professor in Lausanne, its fame appeared to spread more quickly than Strasbourg's.[116] While Bucer was known as a man "deeply learned in the principles of theology and philosophy,"[117] his reputation suffered from his unwise choice of sanctioning the secret bigamy of Phillip of Hesse in 1539.[118] Certainly the piety of Lausanne must have been broadcast most loudly by the martyrdom of its famed five students, who were executed in Lyon in 1553, singing as they faced the flames: "With all my heart I will exalt you, Lord, and will tell all your unmatched works which are worthy of great wonder."[119] Overall, given the general respect which the Academies of Lausanne and Strasbourg enjoyed with Geneva, we would conjecture that these were roughly equivalent.

---

[107] Fournier, *Les statuts*, "Statuts du Gymnase," 50.
[108] Fournier, *Les statuts*, "Statuts du Gymnase," 48.
[109] Bruening, "Ecclesiastical Discipline," 44.
[110] P. Viret, *Du devoir et du besoing qu'ont les hommes à s'enquerir de la volonté de Dieu par sa parole* (Geneva: Jean Girard, 1551), 35.
[111] Le Coultre, *Maturin Cordier*, "Leges Scholae," 488.
[112] Robbins, "Life of Beza," 533.
[113] Letter of Viret to Calvin, Aug. 29, 1549; *CO* 13:369-72.
[114] Eby, *Early Protestant Educators*, 262; *CO* 10:81.
[115] Le Coultre, *Maturin Cordier*, "Leges Scholae," 489.
[116] Robbins, "Life of Beza," 530.
[117] Lawrence, *Martin Bucer*, 97.
[118] Lawrence, *Martin Bucer*, 115.
[119] Martin, *Les Cinq Étudiants*, 57-59.

Structure 6: The Academy required a high standard of personal piety
All three of our schools established a high standard for personal holiness. In Strasbourg Sturm, influenced by the Brethren of the Common Life,[120] demanded discipline toward godliness. "Let piety and religion be set forth in schools."[121] Bucer, trained in a system where piety and education were synonymous,[122] declared that "men of outstanding piety" should be chosen to teach the youth.[123] He required pastors and church officers to be "holy in their personal lives,"[124] serving as examples to the flock.[125] The Theology Professor was to aim toward piety, not just imparting knowledge, "so that godliness and Christian discipline may increase."[126] The Music Professor was to teach Christian songs "because of the positive effect that has on the youth."[127] Both the *Gymnasium* and the *Collegium Praedicatorum* required rigorous attention to holiness.[128] Among our cities Strasbourg is unequaled in their explicit and concrete standards for personal holiness.

The Lausanne Academy was dedicated to promoting holiness, "mores pietatemque."[129] The students were to vow their piety before the Rector of the school.[130] The student boarders were to be carefully watched by their hosts, who were to report any misbehavior to the pastors.[131] The Arts Professor was to see that there was suitable piety in daily prayers.[132] The Professor of Theology was to make application of the text in such a way that it would advance the holiness of the students.[133]

The *Order* of the Genevan Academy demonstrates a somewhat lesser stated concern with the piety of the students than Strasbourg. There is a general statement regarding the public students: "Public scholars...shall...conduct themselves with piety and decorum."[134] The Rector vowed to see that the students would "hold themselves in obedience and respect to our lords" and was not to "tolerate immoral or licentious students." The professors vowed to see to

---

[120] K.A. Strand, "John Calvin and the Brethren of the Common Life: The Role of Strassburg," *Andrews University Seminary Studies* 15 (1977), 44.
[121] Spitz, *Johann Sturm*, "Opening of Elementary Schools," 73.
[122] Amos, "Bucer Among the Humanists," 137.
[123] Pauck, *Bucer, De Regno Christi*, 335.
[124] Bucer, *True Care of Souls*, 42.
[125] Bucer, *True Care of Souls*, 52.
[126] Fournier, *Les statuts*, "Statuts du Gymnase," 50.
[127] Fournier, *Les statuts*, "Statuts du Gymnase," 51-52.
[128] For example, at the "Preacher's College," the students were required to attend evening prayer, avoid jesting or disparaging speech, injure no one, cause no discord and shun taverns. Fournier, *Les statuts,* "Leges Collegii Praedicatorum" 28-29. At the *Gymnasium* students were disciplined for neglecting studies, missing classes, fighting or failing to show respect. Fournier, *Les statuts*, "Leges et Statuta," 26.
[129] Junod, *L'Académie de Lausanne*, 22.
[130] Le Coultre, *Maturin Cordier*, "Leges Scholae," 489.
[131] Le Coultre, *Maturin Cordier*, "Leges Scholae," 488.
[132] Le Coultre, *Maturin Cordier*, "Leges Scholae," 487.
[133] Le Coultre, *Maturin Cordier*, "Leges Scholae," 488.
[134] Eby, *Early Protestant Educators*, 266; *CO* 10:87.

Chapter 8 - Comparing the Academies of Lausanne and Strasbourg with Geneva

it that the "students live peacefully, honorably, and with decorum."[135] While Geneva had a better overall system for disciplining and enforcing holiness, with the superior clarity of expectations for holiness in its foundational documents, Strasbourg would seem to exceed Geneva and Lausanne in this category.

Structure 7: The Academy held a high standard for biblical fidelity
Each of our Academies intended to have a relatively high standard of Bible knowledge. In Strasbourg we find that the Hebrew Professor was to teach by reading and interpreting the Old Testament.[136] The Theology Professors were to teach the Bible from the original languages.[137] The students of theology were expected to read the Bible in its entirety and to partake in bi-weekly theological disputes based on biblical teaching.[138] However, unlike in Geneva and Lausanne, the Bible was not extensively taught to the students who majored in law or medicine. Moreover, unlike Geneva, the students were not required to submit to a confession of faith.

In Lausanne the Greek Professor was to teach from both the Bible and the classics,[139] unlike in Strasbourg and Geneva, where Greek was taught only from the classics.[140] The Theologian was to read the biblical text "with as much faith and earnestness as he can" and to expound the Bible from the original languages.[141] The theology lectures were mostly preaching designed to be spiritually nourishing.[142] There were regular theological papers presented on biblical themes for debate.[143] Yet the Academy did not require the students to submit to a statement of faith.[144]

An examination of the actual weekly schedule of each Academy reveals that while Geneva had 19 hours dedicated to biblical subjects, and Lausanne had 20, we would calculate that in Strasbourg even the pastoral students, after fulfilling their obligations to attend lectures on medicine and law, as well as rhetoric and philosophy, might have had only five to eight hours of Bible training, less than half that of the others.[145]

Each of the Academies also required an examination of biblical knowledge, which would raise the overall standards. Geneva and Lausanne, with no set duration of study, held these exams when student and Rector agreed they were

---

[135] Eby, *Early Protestant Educators*, 269; *CO* 10:89.
[136] Fournier, *Les statuts*, "Statuts du Gymnase," 51.
[137] Fournier, *Les statuts*, "Statuts du Gymnase," 50.
[138] Fournier, *Les statuts*, "Statuts du Gymnase," 50.
[139] Le Coultre, *Maturin Cordier*, "Leges Scholae," 486.
[140] Fournier, *Les statuts*, "Statuts du Gymnase," 51; Eby, *Early Protestant Educators*, 266; *CO* 10:85.
[141] Le Coultre, *Maturin Cordier*, "Leges Scholae," 487.
[142] Gindroz, *Histoire de l'instruction*, 34.
[143] Le Coultre, *Maturin Cordier*, "Leges Scholae," 488.
[144] Meylan, *La Haute École de Lausanne*, 21.
[145] Spitz, *Johann Sturm*, "Opening of Elementary Schools," 110-12; Fournier, *Les statuts*, "Leges et Statuta," 28.

well-prepared. Strasbourg, with an expectation of five years of attendance,[146] would give a lengthy test after that time.[147]

We would conclude that Strasbourg trailed both Lausanne and Geneva in this category. Geneva's standard exceeded even Lausanne's with the additional requirements of the statement of faith[148] and weekly preaching practice.

Structure 8: The professors used a hortatory teaching style

We find evidence that the teaching at all our Academies was delivered in a hortatory manner, offering exhortation and application, not just information. Bucer would begin his lectures with a prayer, calling for the training to promote piety, not just knowledge. "Father, Thou wantest us to come together in Thy name and have pious meetings, Thou wantest also that among your children there are schools that serve to keep and promote your law and doctrine."[149] The Hebrew Professors in Strasbourg were to focus on those passages of Scripture which provided "short admonitions aimed at piety."[150] The Theologians were to teach "so that godliness and Christian discipline may increase."[151] The Law Professor was to apply his lectures for the students' personal growth.[152] During his tenure as a professor in Strasbourg, Peter Vermigli's lectures "sometime exhorted to godly life, sometime by a sharp rebuking...stirred up to repentance."[153] One of Bucer's students in Cambridge described the sermonic nature of his lectures, a style he would have likely carried over from his lengthy ministry in Strasbourg. "Dr. Bucer cries incessantly now in daily lectures, now in frequent sermons that we should practice penitence...be more frequent in having and hearing sermons, constrain ourselves to some sort of discipline."[154]

In Lausanne lectures were to have an immediate sanctifying impact. The Theologian was to bring his lectures to a sharp point so as to make practical application for "personal progress."[155] Viret wanted teaching that would ultimately "edify the house of God,"[156] which must be applied to the heart, "but it

---

[146] Spitz, *Johann Sturm*, "Opening of Elementary Schools," 108.
[147] Wright, *Common Places*, "The Restoration of Lawful Ordination," 257-58.
[148] Eby, *Early Protestant Educators*, 266; *CO* 10:87.
[149] From his lectures in Cambridge; presumably he would have preserved this practice from his long career in Strasbourg. Cf. H. Selderhuis, "Vera Theologia Scientia Est: Bucer and the Training of Ministers," *Reformation and Renaissance Review: Journal of the Society of Reformation Studies* 3 (2001), 139.
[150] Fournier, *Les statuts*, "Statuts du Gymnase," 51.
[151] Fournier, *Les statuts*, "Statuts du Gymnase," 50.
[152] Fournier, *Les statuts*, "Statuts du Gymnase," 50.
[153] W.J.T. Kirby, "From Florence to Zurich via Strasbourg and Oxford: The International Career of Peter Martyr Vermigli (1499-1562)," *Bewegung und Beharrung: Aspekte des reformierten Protestantismus, 1520-1650* (Leiden: Brill, 2009), 137.
[154] Lawrence, *Martin Bucer*, 204.
[155] Le Coultre, *Maturin Cordier*, "Leges Scholac," 488.
[156] Bruening, "Ecclesiastical Discipline," 33.

Chapter 8 - Comparing the Academies of Lausanne and Strasbourg with Geneva

is God alone who can accomplish it."[157] It is no surprise then that the lectures were largely sermons with pointed application.[158]

Since the lectures in Strasbourg and Lausanne were as hortatory as those in Geneva we could discover no appreciable difference in their approach to education in this matter, all three tended to aim at transformation of the heart, not just filling the head.

Structure 9: The professors closely critiqued the students' preaching and theology

All three Academies utilized student theological disputations, accompanied with critical feedback from professors, pastors and others students. Though this was a standard tool of scholasticism,[159] it appears our leaders sought to reform it by making Scripture, and not Lombard's *Sentences*, the point of debate. The disputations occurred every two weeks in Lausanne and Strasbourg, while Geneva had them only monthly but also uniquely offered weekly preaching practice with critical feedback. In each Academy the disputations were held on some important theological topic, not something controversial or silly (*keine absurda proposita*), and were conducted by a lead pastor or theologian who was to settle any disputes on the spot.[160] In Strasbourg the topics, which must have sound arguments on both sides,[161] were introduced through the teaching of the Professor of Theology.[162] In Lausanne the disputations were presented by one student, rebutted by another and then discussed by all.[163] The Theologian was always present to solve any controversies and to teach the students how to frame arguments from Scripture.[164] As in Geneva great care was to be given to control the debate so that feedback was offered "with moderation and without contention and shouting."[165]

In comparing the three Academies, we find some nuanced differences. Strasbourg tended more toward teaching rhetoric and logic than theology or Bible knowledge. "The pupils shall faithfully participate and practice dialectics in these debates as opponents and respondents, based on what they have learned in Sturm's *Partitiones* [Sturm's work on logic]."[166] Strasbourg also gave no caution against an uncivil tone in debate; perhaps it was either allowed in the German context, or it was assumed that the students would conduct themselves civilly. The major difference among the Academies is the presence of the weekly sermon presentations at Geneva, which would have afforded its pastoral stu-

---

[157] P. Viret, *L'Interim fait par dialogues* (New York, N.Y.: Peter Lang, 1985), 135.
[158] Gindroz, *Histoire de l'instruction*, 34.
[159] Amos, "Bucer Among the Humanists," 149.
[160] Fournier, *Les statuts*, "Statuts du Gymnase," 50; Le Coultre, *Maturin Cordier*, "Leges Scholae," 488; Eby, *Early Protestant Educators*, 267; *CO* 10:87.
[161] Spitz, *Johann Sturm*, "Opening of Elementary Schools," 115.
[162] Fournier, *Les statuts*, "Statuts du Gymnase," 50.
[163] Meylan, *La Haute École de Lausanne*, 20.
[164] Le Coultre, *Maturin Cordier*, "Leges Scholae," 488.
[165] Le Coultre, *Maturin Cordier*, "Leges Scholae," 488.
[166] Fournier, *Les statuts*, "Statuts du Gymnase," 50.

dents the advantage of greater frequency and scope for receiving critical feedback.

Structure 10: The students faced dangers in France/Germany
When the Strasbourg school was founded in 1538, it was just over a decade after the Peasant Wars (1524-25) had cost some 100,000 lives, and just prior to the Protestants' defeat in the Schmalkaldic League Wars (1546-47). However, by the time of the focus of our study, 1559-1564, Germany was under the sway of the Augsburg Peace (1555), which provided for freedom of religion within each ruler's territory, "cuius regio, eius religio."[167] Strasbourg was also a city of tolerance, which invited different sects to live side by side in relative peace.[168] As a result, the students of German-speaking Strasbourg during this period would have less imminent threat of danger to aid their progress in holiness.

In Lausanne most of the students were from France, hence all the dangers facing the students in Geneva were present to those of Lausanne.[169] Perhaps the dangers to the Lausanne students and the courage that they exhibited are best demonstrated in the five martyrs of Lausanne, who declaring their readiness to die, demonstrated the sanctifying lesson of suffering. "For you know better than we, that it is nothing to begin [well] if one does not remain constant and firm to the end. And for this you hold the honor of God in such high esteem, and only for this do we suffer."[170]

While we cannot count the environmental dangers as a formal aspect of the Academies' educational plans, we do see in the cases of Lausanne and Geneva that these dangers were a pressing reality, whereas they were not in Strasbourg. Even though the precise impact of these dangers would be hard to quantify, certainly Calvin believed they would benefit the holiness of his students and put them to that use in his lectures.

Summary of comparison of the educational structures of the Academies
In comparing the educational structures at our three Academies, we have observed that:

1. With the exception of the lack of danger in Strasbourg, each of the educational structures in Geneva was present to some degree in each of the other Academies.

2. Nine of the ten educational structures (excepting the environmental dangers) were intended by the leaders of the schools to in some way enhance the piety of the students. That is, the structures were not accidental or incidental but intentionally used to be helpful to the holiness of their students.

---

[167] T.A. Brady, Jr., *German Histories in the Age of Reformations, 1400-1650* (New York, N.Y.: Cambridge University Press, 2009), 220-31.

[168] R.E. McLaughlin, "The Politics of Dissent: Martin Bucer, Caspar Schwenckfeld and the Schwenckfelders of Strasbourg," *Mennonite Quarterly Review* 68 (1994), 78.

[169] Meylan, *La Haute École de Lausanne*, 18.

[170] Martin, *Les Cinq Étudiants*, 47.

Chapter 8 - Comparing the Academies of Lausanne and Strasbourg with Geneva

3. While all three Academies strove to excel in these areas, Geneva had a clear advantage in five of the ten areas: Academy Integrated with the City, Academy Integrated with the Church, Close Mentoring by Pastors, High Standard of Biblical Fidelity and Critical Feedback on Preaching and Theology.

4. There was one area where Strasbourg exceeded the standard set even by Geneva: High Standard for Personal Piety.

5. Strasbourg tied Geneva in one category: Professors Serving as Models. Lausanne tied Geneva in another category: Facing Dangers in France.

6. In two areas, Reputation for Piety and Hortatory Teaching Style, we could find no appreciable differences.

7. As to stated purposes of the Academies, both Lausanne and Genevan Academies had the purpose of training pastors, while Strasbourg was primarily for classical education.

Hence we draw the conclusion from this examination of the educational structures that while all three schools used very similar structures, the Genevan Academy, on the aggregate, exceeded the other two schools in the implementation of these structures, and Strasbourg exceeded Lausanne.

In an effort to summarize the differences in the educational structures we offer the chart below.

Educational Structure	Lausanne	Strasbourg	Geneva
1. Academy integrated into city	Present some	Present some	Present fully
2. Academy integrated with Church	Present some	Present some	Present fully
3. Close mentoring by pastors	Present some	Present some	Present fully
4. Professors serving as models	Present some	Present fully	Present fully
5. Reputation for piety	Present fully	Present fully	Present fully
6. High standard of personal piety	Present fully	Exceeds Geneva	Present fully
7. High standard of biblical fidelity	Present some	Present some	Present fully
8. Hortatory teaching style	Present fully	Present fully	Present fully
9. Critical feedback on preaching and theology	Present some	Present some	Present fully
10. Facing dangers in France/Germany	Present fully	Not present	Present fully

A Comparison of the Teaching Regarding Sanctification

In order to compare the efforts of our three Academies to foster holiness, we might also compare the teaching that occurred there. To do so we will compare some of the teaching of Bucer and Viret, the principle theologians at Strasbourg and Lausanne, to the teaching of Calvin in Geneva. To narrow the focus of this comparison, we will only compare the fourteen points proposed as elements of Calvin's theology of sanctification. Our purpose in the comparison is not to demonstrate that Calvin taught more like Calvin than say Martin Bucer did, an obvious conclusion. Rather the comparison will serve to show where the Reformers had similar emphases, and more importantly perhaps what, if anything, made Calvin's teaching on sanctification distinct.

We do not have a record of the lectures given by either Viret or Bucer as we have preserved in some of Calvin's Commentaries, therefore, we cannot assert that their representative teaching was directly delivered to their students. However, it seems reasonable to suppose that their classroom lectures would be reflected by their overall theology delivered in sermons, books and treatises. For Bucer's teachings we will look primarily at his *De Regno Christi*,[171] *The True Care of Souls*,[172] *Instruction in Christian Love*[173] and some collected works from Wright's *Common Places of Martin Bucer*. For Viret we will examine

---

[171] Pauck, *Bucer, De Regno Christi*.
[172] Bucer, *True Care of Souls*.
[173] M. Bucer, *Instruction in Christian Love* (tr. P.T. Fuhrmann; Eugene, Oreg.: Wipf & Stock, 2008), translation of *Das ym selbs niemant, sonder anderen leben soll*.

Instruction Chrétienne,[174] *The Proposal by the Ministers of Lausanne for Ecclesiastical Discipline*,[175] a *Sermon on Isaiah 65*,[176] *Du devoir et du besoing qu'ont les hommes à s'enquerir de la volonté de Dieu par sa parole*[177] and some other works.

Principle 1: Two-fold knowledge

Viret's teaching on the knowledge of God and self asserts that one's true happiness, and God's honor, is to be found in knowing God. "The true knowledge of Him...leads man to honor Him as his God and Creator with the true honor due Him."[178] One may find this knowledge as they look inward,[179] seeing God's glory in creating humanity[180] contrasted with humanity's own depravity. "We ourselves may be grouped with Satan, our mortal enemy, for aiding him to ruin ourselves."[181] Ultimately to understand God, necessary for joy,[182] and to understand ourselves, we need God's Word,[183] which reveals our sin and leads us to God.[184] The law informs us that we must first focus on God, since he is the primary source of both knowledge of self and God.[185] "For this reason there is nothing that they ought to fear more than ignorance of that heavenly and Divine knowledge."[186] We must be humbled before God by this knowledge. "Knowing our faults and imperfections we humble ourselves."[187]

Bucer follows Calvin, or rather anticipates him, more closely than Viret. From the Word we gain knowledge of God's holiness and our depravity, "to introduce the person to a deeper, but believing contemplation of his evil and what it means in terms of serious offense to God's goodness and his own undoing."[188] Sunken low in transgressions, and all creation with us,[189] we are enemies of God until he opens our eyes through true repentance. "This medicine is nothing else than getting the one who has sinned to recognize his sin sufficiently to cause and move them to a position of true acknowledgment, regret and

---

[174] P. Viret, *Instruction Chrétienne* (Lausanne: L'Age d'Homme, 2008).
[175] Bruening, "Ecclesiastical Discipline."
[176] C. Schnetzler, H. Vuilleumier and A. Schroeder (eds.), *Pierre Viret d'après lui-même* (Lausanne: Georges Bridel, 1911), 182-208.
[177] P. Viret, *Du devoir et du besoin*.
[178] Viret's Catechism of 1541, accessed July 19, 2012 from: http://www.pierreviret.org/theology-catechetical.php
[179] P. Viret, *Métamorphose chrétienne, faite par dialogues* (Geneva: Jacques Bres, 1561), 4.
[180] Schnetzler, *Pierre Viret*, 191.
[181] Viret, *La volonté de Dieu*, 4.
[182] Schnetzler, *Pierre Viret*, 187.
[183] Viret, *Instruction Chrétienne*, 255; cf. Schnetzler, *Pierre Viret*, 189.
[184] E. Grin, "Deux Sermons de Pierre Viret," *Theologische Zeitschrift* 8 (1962), 124.
[185] R.D. Linder, *The Political Ideas of Pierre Viret* (Geneva: Droz, 1964), 135.
[186] Viret, *Instruction Chrétienne*, 97-98.
[187] Schnetzler, *Pierre Viret*, 180-81.
[188] Bucer, *True Care of Souls*, 127.
[189] Bucer, *Instruction in Christian Love*, 27.

sorrow for his sin."[190] Struck low in repentance we are then lifted up by God, and returned to live according to our original "primeval and godly disposition."[191]

While both Bucer and Viret taught on the two-fold knowledge, based upon our limited sample of their teaching, we do not find it as prevalent as in Calvin. We would conjecture therefore that the students in Geneva would have heard this paradigm more regularly.

Principle 2: Bible preaching

Given the Reformation emphasis on *sola scriptura*, it is unsurprising that we find all three of our pastors taught this with remarkable consistency. Bucer agreed that the preaching of the Word was equivalent to hearing from God and should contain conviction of sin, a presentation of Christ and an announcement of judgment.[192] "It is impossible to come to faith and eternal life unless you hear the gospel and that administered by a man."[193] Preaching, the delivery of God's Word through sinful men, is itself humbling.[194] God's Word, as empowered by him,[195] was effective in all that it set out to accomplish,[196] producing faith and righteousness.[197] The Word, quickened by the Spirit, would be sufficient to restore the erring to the way of righteous living.[198]

Viret taught that God had given his Word as "a perfect Law by which we are truly enabled to govern ourselves."[199] While we naturally despise his Word, considering listening to a sermon the waste of an hour, but gladly wasting 12 hours in banquets or games, we must submit to preaching,[200] for nothing is more "harmful than ignorance of the Law."[201] His Word must be studied and heeded, for it is the final authority for all things regarding human life and religious practice.[202] When we hear the Bible preached, we hear God's accommo-

---

[190] Bucer, *True Care of Souls*, 101.
[191] Bucer, *Instruction in Christian Love*, 48.
[192] Stephens, *Theology of Bucer*, 200.
[193] Engelsma, "Martin Bucer," 53.
[194] W.P. Stephens, "The Church in Bucer's Commentaries on the Epistle to the Ephesians," *Martin Bucer Reforming Church and Community* (ed. D.F. Wright; Cambridge: Cambridge University Press, 1994), 57.
[195] Stephens, *Theology of Bucer*, 198.
[196] D. Timmerman, "Martin Bucer as Interpreter of the Old Testament: A Reexamination of Previous Scholarship in Light of Bucer's *Enarrationes in librum Iudicum* (ca. 1540)," *Reformation and Renaissance Review* 9 (2007), 35.
[197] Bucer, *Instruction in Christian Love*, 16, 51.
[198] Bucer, *True Care of Souls*, 169.
[199] J-M. Berthoud, "Pierre Viret and the Sovereignty of the Word of God Over Every Aspect of Life," *A Comprehensive Faith* (San Jose, Calif.: Friends of Chalcedon, 1996), 98-99.
[200] Viret, *La volonté de Dieu*, 53.
[201] Viret, *La volonté de Dieu*, 17.
[202] Viret, *La volonté de Dieu*, 26, 64, 94, 99; cf. Linder, *Political Ideas*, 55.

Chapter 8 - Comparing the Academies of Lausanne and Strasbourg with Geneva

dating voice speaking to us directly.[203] Therefore one must not neglect but submit to the Word preached each Sabbath,[204] the first mark of a true church.[205] Created through the Word, humans must be restored to uprightness by it,[206] an uprightness which is seen in the very image of the law.[207] The doctrine that the preaching of God's Word must be heard and submitted to for growth in holiness was taught as clearly by Bucer and Viret as it was by Calvin.

Principle 3: God's love

Bucer gave emphasis to the importance of God's love for us. Christians can know the love of God, "whose love for them is infinitely greater than the love which any earthly father could have for his only child."[208] The Lord's Supper is given to us as a tangible demonstration of God's "great and ineffable love."[209] Faith leads us to know God's love for us, and then this love overflows our heart so that we desire to love God and our neighbor. "What good could he withhold from us? His love is too great. Hence as soon as, through faith the heart recognizes and holds this truth, so soon the heart is overflowing with love and thereby completely made ready to do good to all men."[210] While Bucer teaches this transformative nature of apprehending God's love, he does not teach it with the same frequency as Calvin. More often he will speak of our love as a basis for our duty, the mark of our sanctification.[211] "No one should live for himself but each man should out of love for God live for his neighbor and by all means be of service to him."[212]

Viret would certainly speak of God's love for us. God loves us as a "good father, gentle amiable and gracious," and so is "moved by his own goodness, grace and mercy," to bless us and to "defend us against our enemies."[213] This love is most easily seen in Christ. "If you want to see the heart of the heavenly Father entirely open, you may see that in his son Jesus Christ."[214] In Christ we hear the voice of God, a gentle voice, which calls us in love "so amiable."[215] However, in Viret we did not find the connection between God's love and our movement toward him.

While both Bucer and Viret taught on the love of God for us, and Bucer even taught on its strategic connection to sanctification as the magnetic force

---

[203] P. Viret, *La vertu et usage du ministere la parolle de Dieu* (Geneva: Jean Girard, 1548), 7-8, 14.
[204] Schnetzler, *Pierre Viret*, 242, 308, 314, 316.
[205] Grin, "Deux Sermons," 118.
[206] Viret, *La vertu et usage*, 5.
[207] Viret, *Instruction Chrétienne*, 121.
[208] Wright, *Common Places*, "A Brief Summary of Christian Doctrine," 80.
[209] Wright, *Common Places*, "Visitation of the Sick," 433.
[210] Bucer, *Instruction in Christian Love*, 45.
[211] Stephens, *Theology of Bucer*, 91.
[212] Bucer, *Instruction in Christian Love*, 40.
[213] Schnetzler, *Pierre Viret*, 186-88.
[214] Schnetzler, *Pierre Viret*, 193.
[215] Schnetzler, *Pierre Viret*, 285.

which drives us toward God, yet still this teaching does not occur as frequently as in Calvin.[216]

Principle 4: God reliance

Here we find another major reformation theme, *sola gratia*: people must rely on God to make them holy, hence we find our Reformers again in harmony. Viret is clear that all of holiness, justification and sanctification, must come from God. "We are not able to find this perfection except in Jesus Christ, through faith in him, through which we are justified and sanctified."[217] The believer must look to God's grace in order to have his conscience freed from his own sin[218] and have a heart "renewed in order to see and know God in his Word."[219] God actively works faith, and thus salvation, in the heart of the believer.[220] Our sanctification is his work, a miracle no less than making the lame to walk.[221] Since our holiness must come from God, the Christian is called to live by faith in him[222] who "sanctifies us also, communicating to us the gifts and graces which are the fruits of faith."[223]

Bucer taught the necessity of the Christian's perpetual reliance on God. "For as the sun in the world [gives] the day, so God gives and works in us piety. Forever the sun must shine, so must the children of God forever be guided and driven by the spirit of God, that is, taught and inclined and made ready to do good."[224] It is the Holy Spirit who produces faith in those who "truly believe in our Lord Jesus Christ."[225] "Certainly, nothing good can be done by us, unless the spirit of God effects it in us."[226] The Holy Spirit, and not works of penance,[227] mortifies the old nature and enlivens the new,[228] creating a new will.[229] "We teach that the same spirit of divine sonship...effects in all who are Christ's a continual mortifying and crucifying of their flesh."[230] While effected by the

---

[216] Calvin would dwell on God's love as an attractive power in many sermons, for example: *Sermons on Genesis 1-11*, 547; *Sermons on 2 Samuel*, 198, 535, 603.
[217] Schnetzler, *Pierre Viret*, 264.
[218] Grin, "Deux Sermons," 131.
[219] Schnetzler, *Pierre Viret*, 189.
[220] Viret, *L'Interim fait par dialogues*, 135-37.
[221] Schnetzler, *Pierre Viret*, 194-95.
[222] Schnetzler, *Pierre Viret*, 264.
[223] Schnetzler, *Pierre Viret*, 288.
[224] M. Bucer, *Handlung inn dem offentlichen gesprech zu Straßburg* (Strasbourg, 1533), G.2.A.10-23.
[225] Wright, *Common Places*, "A Brief Summary of Christian Doctrine," 80.
[226] M. Bucer, *In sacra quatuor Evangelia enarrationes perpetuae secundum recognitae* (Basel: Johann Herwagen, 1536), 350.D.12-14.
[227] Stephens, *Theology of Bucer*, 75.
[228] Stephens, *Theology of Bucer*, 74.
[229] Lawrence, *Martin Bucer*, 186.
[230] Wright, *Common Places*, "A Brief Summary of Christian Doctrine," 80-81.

Holy Spirit, our sanctification is secured by our union with Christ.[231] All three of our pastors seemed to teach with equal clarity the need for *sola gratia*.

Principle 5: Desiring holiness

Bucer taught that the Word of God holds forth the standard of holiness, toward which believers should strive[232] through dependence on the power of Christ.[233] Christian rulers, pastors and teachers were to lead all toward pious living.[234] The purpose of schooling was to advance holiness.[235] The call to holiness was directed to the heart, to truly love God[236] and neighbor,[237] never just aimed at outward conformity.[238] The believer must long for greater holiness[239] and thus seek more grace from God in order to be made more holy.[240]

Viret also taught that God's law was the holiness toward which each believer must aspire.[241] Pastors must be examples of holiness.[242] True holiness, which must flow from the heart,[243] is lived out as love for God and neighbor, which must be both physical and spiritual care.[244] Viret called his hearers to desire holiness in order to be like their Lord. "Remember always that you are called to sanctification and holiness and purity."[245] The believer should develop a deep hunger for growth in holiness, to be always "consecrated to him."[246]

We find in our three Reformers remarkably similar teaching on the need to desire holiness: the law set the high standard of holiness, only God's grace can produce such holiness, pastors must embody holiness, holiness proceeds from the heart and finds its fulfillment in love of God and neighbor.

Principle 6: Faith

Bucer saw faith as the essential ingredient to wholeness for the Christian soul. "The health and life of the inner man consists in the true living faith in the mercifulness of God."[247] All "sickness and weakness"[248] stems from lack of faith,

---

[231] W. van 't Spijker, "The Influence of Bucer on Calvin as Becomes Evident from the Institutes," *John Calvin's Institutes: His Opus Magnum* (ed. B.J. van der Walt; Potchefstroom, South Africa: Potchefstroom University for Christian Higher Education, 1986), 121-22.
[232] Bucer, *True Care of Souls*, 169.
[233] Timmerman, "Martin Bucer as Interpreter," 42.
[234] Pauck, *Bucer, De Regno Christi*, 186-87, 335.
[235] Selderhuis, "Bucer and the Training of Ministers," 139.
[236] Engelsma, "Martin Bucer," 49-50.
[237] Bucer, *True Care of Souls*, 46-47.
[238] Bucer, *True Care of Souls*, 126; Wright, *Common Places*, "Visitation of the Sick," 431.
[239] Burnett, *The Yoke of Christ*, 35.
[240] Wright, *Common Places*, "A Brief Summary of Christian Doctrine,"80-81.
[241] Viret, *Instruction Chrétienne*, 121.
[242] Schnetzler, *Pierre Viret*, 291.
[243] Schnetzler, *Pierre Viret*, 260-63.
[244] Viret, *La volonté de Dieu*, Preface.
[245] Viret, *La volonté de Dieu*, Preface.
[246] Schnetzler, *Pierre Viret*, 288.
[247] Bucer, *True Care of Souls*, 103.

while faith's presence leads one to surrender to God.[249] Increased faith in the Word,[250] aided by pastors called to deliver the pure Word,[251] strengthens the union with Christ, whose benefits flow more freely to produce holiness.[252]

Viret taught that our sanctification progresses according to our faith in Christ, which unites us to him. "We are made participants of the blessings of Jesus Christ by faith."[253] This faith requires that we put our trust in God and all his promises.[254] Faith cannot be manufactured by humans but must come from God, through his Word preached within the Church[255] and quickened by the Holy Spirit.[256]

All our Reformers taught, similarly, that to grow in holiness is to grow in faith, which unites us to Christ and comes by hearing the Word. There is, however, one distinction which appears in our brief comparison. While both Viret[257] and Bucer[258] teach that the acquisition of faith is a struggle, neither of them, at least in our sample, has as clear a paradigm as Calvin, who presents the struggle for faith as an active warfare with the devil himself, who would have us look at circumstances while God bids us to hear his promise.[259]

Principle 7: Repentance

Both Viret and Bucer taught the importance of repentance for progress in holiness. Viret argued that the first purpose of church discipline was to bring the sinner "back to repentance and amendment."[260] Recognizing that the average congregant desired a "gospel without repentance,"[261] Viret taught that they must come to a knowledge of their own sinfulness[262] and repent after each disobedience[263] in order to be made holy by Christ.[264]

Bucer lamented the historical abuses of penance, calling for a heartfelt, rather than ritualistic, repentance.[265] True repentance emerges from an accurate two-fold knowledge of God and self,[266] leading one to properly fear God[267] and

---

[248] Bucer, *True Care of Souls*, 167.
[249] Lawrence, *Martin Bucer*, 53.
[250] Timmerman, "Martin Bucer as Interpreter," 40.
[251] Stephens, *Theology of Bucer*, 94.
[252] Bucer, *True Care of Souls*, 179.
[253] Schnetzler, *Pierre Viret*, 288.
[254] Schnetzler, *Pierre Viret*, 264.
[255] Viret, *L'Interim fait par dialogues*, 246-47.
[256] Schnetzler, *Pierre Viret*, 296.
[257] Schnetzler, *Pierre Viret*, 168.
[258] Bucer, *True Care of Souls*, 179.
[259] *Commentary*, Lam. 3:18.
[260] Bruening, "Ecclesiastical Discipline," 42.
[261] Schnetzler, *Pierre Viret*, 242.
[262] Bruening, "Ecclesiastical Discipline," 38.
[263] Grin, "Deux Sermons," 126.
[264] Schnetzler, *Pierre Viret*, 241.
[265] Bucer, *True Care of Souls*, 124-26.
[266] Lawrence, *Martin Bucer*, 184.
[267] Bucer, *True Care of Souls*, 127.

then to look towards God's mercy in Christ.[268] "True repentance must result from faith in Christ."[269] Repentance must be daily and life-long,[270] leading to forgiveness[271] and transformation into the image of God.[272] While using language that sounds almost Roman,[273] "the practice of penance is to be most strictly observed,"[274] Bucer's penance was entirely an evangelical ordinance. "Since God grants contrition and sorrow, in such things nothing fruitful can be accomplished by human commandments."[275] Repentance is the work of the entire church, pastor and members, helping each other move toward holiness.[276] All three of our Reformers taught that repentance was the heartfelt move away from sin and toward the mercy of God in Christ, which led to their forgiveness and the reformation of their character.

Principle 8: Self-denial
While Viret uses slightly different terminology, such as "renounce yourself,"[277] he appears to teach the same concept of self-denial.[278] "God requires of us...abjection and despising of ourselves."[279] Self-denial has the familiar two-fold movement, denying one's will in order to "consecrate ourselves entirely to the Lord."[280] Self-denial includes a renouncing of one's reason and being subject to the Scriptures.[281] Surrendering confidence in ourselves, we embrace God's will, "rendering to him obedience that we owe him."[282]

Bucer not only taught the same concepts but used very similar terms as Calvin. His 1523 tract, *Das ym selbs nieman*, was instruction in self-denial that we might "live a good and pious life in service to others."[283] Self-denial grows with faith. "Faith brings self-denial...forgetfulness of self and living wholly for others to the glory of God."[284] Penance and church discipline are aids that Christians may "learn to deny themselves more."[285] Both Sabbath worship[286] and

---

[268] Burnett, *The Yoke of Christ*, 106.
[269] Bucer, *True Care of Souls*, 127.
[270] Bucer, *True Care of Souls*, 121.
[271] Timmerman, "Martin Bucer as Interpreter," 35.
[272] Bucer, *True Care of Souls*, 101, 119-20, 160-61.
[273] Burnett, *The Yoke of Christ*, 108.
[274] Bucer, *True Care of Souls*, 114.
[275] Burnett, *The Yoke of Christ*, 51, citing R. Stupperich (ed.), *Martin Bucers Deutsche Schriften*, Vol. 3: *Confessio Tetrapolitana und die Schriften des Jahres 1531* (Gütersloh: Gütersloher Verlagshaus, 1969), 143.20-145.35.
[276] Bucer, *True Care of Souls*, 210; Burnett, *The Yoke of Christ*, 39.
[277] Schnetzler, *Pierre Viret*, 189.
[278] Viret, *La volonté de Dieu*, 54.
[279] Viret, *La volonté de Dieu*, 21-22.
[280] Schnetzler, *Pierre Viret*, 206.
[281] Schnetzler, *Pierre Viret*, 189.
[282] Schnetzler, *Pierre Viret*, 263.
[283] Timmerman, "Martin Bucer as Interpreter," 42.
[284] Bucer, *Instruction in Christian Love*, 48.
[285] Bucer, *True Care of Souls*, 9, 127.
[286] Wright, *Common Places*, "Ordination," 264.

providential suffering[287] help in denying pleasures and being drawn toward God.

Although Viret may have used somewhat different terminology, it appears that the students of Geneva, Strasbourg and Lausanne would have benefited equally from teaching on the role of self-denial in holiness, as offered from our three Reformers.

Principle 9: Cross-bearing

Bucer taught that the trials of life were God's providential discipline for us, which must be born with patience.[288] Illnesses are given to draw us to God. "By means of an illness [God] often urges the whole family to repentance."[289] Difficult providences are to be interpreted in light of God's fatherly love that we might bear the cross willingly,[290] with the full knowledge "that our dear God's intentions towards them are entirely fatherly."[291]

Viret taught on the need to accept God's providences, since God rules intimately over us.[292] He wrote to the Lausanne students imprisoned in Lyon, "God by his providence has led you to this that you are detained as prisoners....Whether you live or whether you die, you live and die to the Lord."[293] However, we did not discover the clear teaching on cross-bearing evident in both Bucer and Calvin. Hence we would conjecture, based on our limited study, that the students of Strasbourg and Geneva were more regularly taught to bear the cross.

Principle 10: Future life

Bucer taught occasionally on the longing for the future life. "He heightens the effect of the groaning with which the sons of God long for glory, so that he may show how great...is that glory of theirs for which they groan."[294] Though Bucer taught that faith rids of us a love for this present life, contrasted to Calvin, he did so less with an eye to the future as on present service. "Faith, finally, takes away from us love for the present life...which hinders so many from exercising a true love and service to their neighbor."[295]

Viret touches on the concept of heavenly bliss, where all our true longings will be found, and how that thought helps us today.[296] We must live in this broken world, knowing that "the Lord has ordained a place and a time of which he

---

[287] Wright, *Common Places*, "Visitation of the Sick," 431.
[288] Wright, *Common Places*, "A Brief Summary of Christian Doctrine," 76.
[289] Wright, *Common Places*, "Visitation of the Sick," 431.
[290] Lawrence, *Martin Bucer*, 148.
[291] Bucer, *True Care of Souls*, 169.
[292] Schnetzler, *Pierre Viret*, 277.
[293] Schnetzler, *Pierre Viret*, 166-68.
[294] M. Bucer, *Metaphrasis et enarratio in Epist. D. Pauli apostoli ad Romanos* (Basel: Peter Perna, 1562), 390.
[295] Bucer, *Instruction in Christian Love*, 47.
[296] Schnetzler, *Pierre Viret*, 283.

will put an end to all this disorder and will restore all things in their true state."²⁹⁷

Though our study is limited, it appears that neither Bucer nor Viret taught as regularly concerning meditation on the future life as Calvin, therefore we would conjecture that the students of Geneva received a more steady diet of heavenly thoughts.²⁹⁸

Principle 11: Present life

While Bucer taught infrequently on moderation,²⁹⁹ he did teach often on vocation and loving one's neighbor.³⁰⁰ Because each individual is uniquely called,³⁰¹ they are given a particular role in the church³⁰² and their profession.³⁰³ Loving one's neighbor is central for Bucer's theology.³⁰⁴ We are created by God to serve others³⁰⁵ by meeting their physical and spiritual needs,³⁰⁶ so we must all work productively to have something to offer, which will be "fruitful to [our] neighbors."³⁰⁷

Viret did not emphasize moderation, but he too taught on vocation and loving one's neighbor. Vocation depends on the gifting of God,³⁰⁸ and every legitimate calling, from prince to farmer, must submit to God through his Word.³⁰⁹ One must love his neighbor by supplying his material and spiritual needs.³¹⁰ "The Lord our God who has commanded us all to love our neighbor as ourselves, has declared...which love is required of us toward them."³¹¹

While all three Reformers taught the necessity of vocation and love of neighbor, it would appear from our short survey that neither Bucer nor Viret offered the same intensity of teaching that Calvin delivered on moderation in this present life.

Principle 12: Church

Given the ecclesial focus of the Reformation, it is no surprise to find in all three Reformers a high value on commitment to the church. Bucer taught that Chris-

---

²⁹⁷ Schnetzler, *Pierre Viret*, 279.
²⁹⁸ *Commentary*, Ezek. 1:16.
²⁹⁹ I. Backus, "Church, Communion and Community in Bucer's Commentary on the Gospel of John," *Martin Bucer Reforming Church and Community* (ed. D.F. Wright; Cambridge: Cambridge University Press, 1994), 69.
³⁰⁰ Stephens, *Theology of Bucer*, 92.
³⁰¹ Spijker, "The Influence of Bucer on Calvin from the Institutes," 126-27.
³⁰² Bucer, *True Care of Souls*, 2.
³⁰³ Pauck, *Bucer, De Regno Christi*, 335.
³⁰⁴ Lawrence, *Martin Bucer*, 61; cf. Bucer, *Instruction in Christian Love*, 22, 26, 28-30, 40, 48.
³⁰⁵ Burnett, *The Yoke of Christ*, 84.
³⁰⁶ Bucer, *True Care of Souls*, 53.
³⁰⁷ Pauck, *Bucer, De Regno Christi*, 334; cf. Stephens, *Theology of Bucer*, 93.
³⁰⁸ Berthoud, "Pierre Viret and the Sovereignty of the Word of God," 98-99.
³⁰⁹ Linder, *Political Ideas*, 59.
³¹⁰ Schnetzler, *Pierre Viret*, 185.
³¹¹ Viret, *La volonté de Dieu*, Preface.

tian growth directly correlated to participation in the life of the church. "When people are lax about church practices there is to be found weakness in their Christian lives."[312] The pastor was then to encourage the people to be "joyful and passionate"[313] about church involvement, so they are "diligent in attendance at divine assemblies," participating fully in church life.[314] "The church of Christ where I am...I ought to esteem and hold as precious, as being that through which the Lord wishes to grant me his word and spirit, forgiveness of sins and all good. I am to give myself wholly to such a congregation."[315] The church officers[316] help members' holiness by providing "all counsel and help in things both corporal and spiritual."[317]

Viret was emphatic about the necessity of commitment to the church for spiritual growth. "The [church is the] means by which God leads us to faith and communion."[318] The church holds the keys of the kingdom, entrusted to her officers[319] who govern and minister, "to edify the house of God."[320] To fully participate in the life of the church, one must be a member, sign a confession of faith and vow to submit to her with one's work and worship.[321] Safe within the church, God's providence works to build up the saints, even when enemies rage.[322] We discovered no significant differences among the three Reformers concerning the church's role in holiness.

Principle 13: Sacraments

The teaching regarding the use of the sacraments was remarkably similar in all three Reformers, in part due to Bucer's influence upon Calvin.[323] While Bucer attempted to maintain somewhat of a reconciling position between Luther and Zwingli regarding Christ's presence,[324] he taught that God works through the sacraments to make us holy by faith,[325] uniting us to Christ[326] who is truly present.[327] "Christ effects our salvation by his sacraments of baptism and Eucha-

---

[312] Bucer, *True Care of Souls*, 168.
[313] Bucer, *True Care of Souls*, 168.
[314] Engelsma, "Martin Bucer," 49.
[315] Bucer, *Catechism* (1534) as cited by Stephens, *Theology of Bucer*, 161.
[316] Calvin had the same four offices as Bucer. Lawrence, *Martin Bucer*, 176.
[317] Bucer, *True Care of Souls*, 211.
[318] Schnetzler, *Pierre Viret*, 265.
[319] Viret, *Instruction Chrétienne*, 27.
[320] Bruening, "Ecclesiastical Discipline," 33.
[321] J-M. Berthoud, *Des Actes de L'Eglise* (Lausanne: L'Age d'Homme, 1993), 67, 72-73.
[322] Berthoud, *Des Actes de L'Eglise*, 150.
[323] Spijker, "Bucer's Influence on Calvin," 34.
[324] Lawrence, *Martin Bucer*, 78.
[325] Stephens, *Theology of Bucer*, 214-15.
[326] Wright, *Common Places*, "Visitation of the Sick," 433.
[327] Lawrence, *Martin Bucer*, 208.

rist."[328] To be faithful as a pastor, one must administer the sacraments properly,[329] allowing only the repentant to partake.[330]

Viret taught that the sacraments, as the visible Word,[331] unite us to the life of Christ that we may have full communion with him.[332] The elements truly present to us Christ[333] nourishing us for eternal life and showing we are God's children.[334] "He gives us there…the true bread of life so to nourish us."[335] To receive worthily one must come repenting, therefore the pastor must rightly fence the table.[336]

We find little difference in the teachings concerning the sacraments. We have noted, however, that Calvin was successful, as Bucer and Viret were not, in gaining the power to thoroughly fence the table, hence, the teaching in Geneva was enhanced by this better practice.

Principle 14: Church discipline

Viret wanted to establish church discipline, which would reflect that of the New Testament. "La discipline très simple et très pure des temps apostoliques."[337] Ideally he wanted a Geneva-like Consistory,[338] which using the keys[339] would restrict access to the Lord's Supper[340] and increase the holiness of the people.[341] While the pastors were uniquely charged to offer correction,[342] the entire congregation was to take part.[343] Discipline, from admonition to excommunication, would force the sin-blinded to see his sin and, convinced of his fault,[344] repent, finding new holiness.[345]

Bucer saw church discipline as essential to the health of the church. "Where discipline is dormant, men are asleep and the devil sows tares."[346] Elders and pastors together were to administer discipline[347] by using the keys[348] toward the

---

[328] Wright, *Common Places*, "Ordination," 262.
[329] Bucer, *True Care of Souls*, 21.
[330] Burnett, *The Yoke of Christ*, 193.
[331] Viret, *La vertu et usage*, 10.
[332] Schnetzler, *Pierre Viret*, 266.
[333] Schnetzler, *Pierre Viret*, 298.
[334] Schnetzler, *Pierre Viret*, 197, 202.
[335] Schnetzler, *Pierre Viret*, 300.
[336] Schnetzler, *Pierre Viret*, 204-05.
[337] O. Favre, "Pierre Viret (1511-1571) et la discipline ecclésiastique," *La Revue Reformée* 49 (1998), 56.
[338] Bruening, "Ecclesiastical Discipline," 32-33.
[339] Schnetzler, *Pierre Viret*, 293.
[340] Baird, *Theodore Beza*, 98-99.
[341] Viret, *Instruction Chrétienne*, 27.
[342] Bruening, "Ecclesiastical Discipline," 33.
[343] Viret, *La volonté de Dieu*, Preface.
[344] Bruening, "Ecclesiastical Discipline," 40-42; cf. Favre, "La discipline ecclésiastique," 68-71.
[345] Viret, *L'Interim fait par dialogues*, 248.
[346] Engelsma, "Martin Bucer,"54.
[347] Engelsma, "Martin Bucer," 50-51.

recovery of sinners and the purity of the church.[349] Bucer expected the entire church to engage in discipline,[350] but realizing that the people were hesitant to do so, he focused on stirring up pastors[351] who "more than anyone else are to be diligent" and loving in discipline.[352] Church discipline, which replaced the Roman penitential system,[353] was needed because of natural human blindness to sin.[354] Yielding to discipline the penitent would find grace and be healed by Christ.[355]

The teaching on church discipline by all three Reformers, while similar, revealed minor differences. Bucer allowed excommunication for fewer grounds[356] and only barred from the table, not worship.[357] Viret[358] and Bucer[359] included discipline as a mark of the true church. The main difference in the cities, however, was their relative success in implementing a city-wide system of discipline, meaning Geneva would have had greater effectiveness in teaching on discipline, inasmuch as the theory was reinforced by the model of discipline.

Summary of the comparison of teaching on sanctification by three Reformers
Comparing the teaching samples of Bucer and Viret to the fourteen principles from Calvin's theology of sanctification, we note the following similarities and differences:
1. There were eight topics, which all three Reformers taught clearly: Bible Preaching, God Reliance, Desiring Holiness, Repentance, Self-denial, Church Life, Sacraments and Discipline. Geneva, however, more effectively implemented the sacraments and church discipline, which perhaps aided the teaching of these topics by example.
2. There were three topics which Bucer and Viret taught only partly: Two-fold Knowledge, Faith and Present Life. Calvin taught the two-fold knowledge more frequently. He taught that faith was a struggle between God and the devil. He taught that moderation was key to using the present life well.
3. God's Love was taught only partly by Viret and not as frequently by Bucer as by Calvin.
4. Viret and Bucer taught less frequently than Calvin on the Future Life.
5. Viret taught only partly on Cross-bearing.

---

[348] Burnett, *The Yoke of Christ*, 32.
[349] Bucer, *True Care of Souls*, 157.
[350] Bucer, *True Care of Souls*, 98.
[351] Burnett, *The Yoke of Christ*, 95.
[352] Bucer, *True Care of Souls*, 100.
[353] Burnett, *The Yoke of Christ*, 10-16.
[354] Bucer, *True Care of Souls*, 203-04.
[355] Bucer, *True Care of Souls*, 100-04.
[356] Burnett, *The Yoke of Christ*, 221.
[357] Burnett, *The Yoke of Christ*, 39.
[358] Schnetzler, *Pierre Viret*, 293.
[359] Lawrence, *Martin Bucer*, 133.

Chapter 8 - Comparing the Academies of Lausanne and Strasbourg with Geneva

It would appear then that Calvin's teaching was most distinct for its regularity in presenting the Two-fold Knowledge of God and self, the frequency of teaching on God's Love, the unique presentation of Faith as a struggle between God and the devil, the frequency of teaching on the Future Life and the emphasis on the moderate use of all things in the Present Life. Do these differences mean that that the students in Geneva had a better teaching environment in which to grow in holiness? One could not assert this with confidence. However one may say that: 1) *If* Calvin's approach to sanctification is assumed to be effective at producing holiness and 2) *if* our limited sampling of the teaching of Bucer and Viret represents what was taught to the students of their Academies, 3) *then* the students of Geneva would have theoretically received teaching which was slightly more helpful to enhance one's sanctification. Perhaps it is safest to conclude that it is likely that the students in Geneva received teaching that was in most ways similar to the teachings offered in the other Academies, with the exception of these few particular emphases distinct to Calvin.

To see the difference of the teaching of the Reformers in summary we have displayed them in a table.

Teaching Topic	Viret/Lausanne	Bucer/Strasbourg	Geneva
1.Two-fold knowledge	Taught Partly	Taught Partly	Taught Clearly
2. Bible Preaching	Taught Clearly	Taught Clearly	Taught Clearly
3. God's Love	Taught Partly	Taught Clearly	Taught Clearly
4. God Reliance	Taught Clearly	Taught Clearly	Taught Clearly
5. Desiring Holiness	Taught Clearly	Taught Clearly	Taught Clearly
6. Faith	Taught Partly	Taught Partly	Taught Clearly
7. Repentance	Taught Clearly	Taught Clearly	Taught Clearly
8. Self-denial	Taught Clearly	Taught Clearly	Taught Clearly
9. Cross-bearing	Taught Partly	Taught Clearly	Taught Clearly
10. Future Life	Taught Partly	Taught Partly	Taught Clearly
11. Present Life	Taught Partly	Taught Partly	Taught Clearly
12. Church Life	Taught Clearly	Taught Clearly	Taught Clearly
13. Sacraments	Taught Clearly	Taught Clearly	Taught Clearly
14. Church Discipline	Taught Clearly	Taught Clearly	Taught Clearly

Conclusion

Our three Academies are probably more remarkable for their similarities than their distinguishing characteristics. For example, we found evidence of nine of the ten educational structures at each Academy. This should come as no surprise, both because they were created in the midst of the educational reforms that accompanied the Reformation[360] and because of their interdependence: Calvin's early years teaching at Strasbourg, the dismissal of the Lausanne professors to Geneva, the use of the *Leges Scholae Lausannesis* as Calvin prepared the *Leges Academiae Genevensis* and Calvin's return visit to Strasbourg just prior to starting the Genevan Academy.

---

[360] Kirby, "Vermigli," 136.

Given these natural similarities, the differences perhaps become even more significant. Regarding the educational structures, Geneva was distinguished by: 1) the Integration of the Academy with the City, 2) the Integration of the Academy with the Church, in particular the control of the Academy by the *Compagnie* and 3) the highest standards of Biblical Fidelity, with its focus on doctrine, preaching and its confession of faith. Added to this was the fact that both Geneva and Lausanne, but not Strasbourg, had as their primary aim the training of pastoral candidates. In terms of teaching toward sanctification, while many of the emphases of the Reformation were taught by all three Reformers, Calvin's teaching was distinct in the emphasis given to the Two-fold Knowledge, Love of God, Faith, Present Life and Future Life.

While there are striking similarities, the differences discovered in our research suggest that a pastoral candidate at the Genevan Academy would have more consistently experienced education structures which were intended to be holiness-enhancing than at our two other contemporary Academies. They would also have received teaching on sanctification, which was in some ways distinct from that of some other Reformers, emphasizing Calvin's doctrines of sanctification. The students would have experienced what was, from Calvin's understanding of sanctification, a distinctly excellent environment for enhancing their holiness.

Conclusion

Reviewing the goals of this work

As we began our research for this book, we had a central question: How did John Calvin encourage the sanctification of the candidates for pastoral office at the Genevan Academy? In addressing that question we desired to advance the premise that Calvin's great concern for developing the holiness of the pastors at the Genevan Academy was shown by the way he used his theology of sanctification to shape the teaching and educational structures of the Academy. To explore the central question we asked more narrowly in Section One: What are the key elements of Calvin's theology of sanctification which bear on the process of progressive sanctification? In Section Two we focused on the application of that theology: What were the specific teachings and educational structures utilized by Calvin to enhance the *pietas* of the pastoral candidates he trained in the Genevan Academy? We have found distinct answers to each of these questions.

Summary of Section One: Theology of Sanctification

As we explored the elements of Calvin's theology of sanctification in Section One, we uncovered both the picture of the pious pastor, which Calvin hoped to help produce and the key elements of his teaching on sanctification. We found that Calvin described the pious Christian in these broad terms:

A summary of the sanctified person

1. **Fulfilling the true order.** Calvin described the goal of sanctification variously as being transformed into the image of Christ, the image of God, the image of the law or as being restored to the true order of creation; each one is equivalent to the other.

2. **Loving God.** Sanctification means to love God with a whole or round heart. One renders him heartfelt thanks, generous worship and filial loyalty, all to magnify and serve his glory.

3. **Loving neighbor.** Holiness means to love one's neighbor, refraining from doing him any harm, regarding his needs and wishes before one's own, caring for his soul and helping to meet his material needs.

4. **Moderation.** Holiness is a moderating of all emotions, appetites and desires, such that one is not carried to excess even while rejoicing or weeping, and one may enjoy the bounty of life while still having their hopes firmly fixed on heaven.

5. **Living within vocation.** The holy person understands God's call on their life and humbly submits to it, joyfully bearing any difficult providence as a cross.

6. Rendering the obedience of faith. Humankind is to render to God neither a legalistic nor a human-powered obedience, but an obedience which is by grace through faith and which makes use of all the ordinary means of grace within the life of the church.

Understanding the goal of sanctification, we also discovered the key elements of Calvin's theology of progressive sanctification:

Principles from Calvin's theology of progressive sanctification
Principle 1: Two-fold Knowledge. Because God created us to lovingly revere him, therefore gain knowledge of God and self thus to offer God prostration and reverence. The two-fold knowledge, of God's greatness and of human depravity and inability to improve itself, leads the believer to respond to God with the two-fold motion of faith: downward in humble prostration before God and upward in thankful and loving reverence to God.

Principle 2: Bible Preaching. Because God has given his Word to lead us to life, therefore submit to the preaching of the Word of Christ. Bible preaching proclaims both God's judgment on sin, and an offer of God's grace in Christ, calling the believer to turn in faith and repentance to the grace of God, who makes them holy for the obedience of faith.

Principle 3: God's Love. Because God has elected us in love, therefore apprehend God's love to move us to love God in holiness. Knowledge of God's paternal love, most clearly seen in Christ and presented in covenant promises, serves as a primary motive force behind the believer's submission to God in sanctification.

Principle 4: God Reliance. Because God is the one who sanctifies, therefore rely on God's powerful grace, and not yourself, to become holy. God is the author of sanctification, working through the election of the Father, union with the Son and the indwelling of the Spirit to make the believer holy, as he continuously relies on the grace of God and stops relying on his goodness or his own ability to improve himself.

Principle 5: Desiring Holiness. Because God is holy and loves holiness, therefore desire deeply to become holy. The believer must see God's intention to conform his people to the Scriptural standard of holiness and thus desire to become more holy, rendering the obedience of faith from a heart of integrity.

Principle 6: Faith. Because God sanctifies by giving more faith, therefore struggle daily for more faith to become more holy. Holiness grows with faith, and faith, as a gift of God, arises from hearing the Word of God, while also ignoring the world, the flesh and the devil, which all bid us to doubt God by focusing on negative circumstances.

Principle 7: Repentance. Because God gives grace to the lowly, therefore repent humbly to find more grace. The grace of God for sanctification only flows to the humble penitent who, through self-examination, based on the Word preached, read and held forth by others in the church, seeks out all sin in his life, so that in seeing his sin, he will ask God for the humility to turn from sin to Christ and there receive forgiveness and grace to make him holy.

Principle 8: Self-denial. Because God gives life to those who lose it, therefore deny yourself as a practice of faith and repentance. To progress in holiness, the believer must practice faith and repentance by constantly considering the interests of God and others before his own and yielding to God's will, as it is revealed in Scripture, through his neighbor's needs and to his conscience.

Principle 9: Cross-bearing. Because God mortifies through suffering, therefore bear the cross to mortify our flesh. God sanctifies the believer by providentially bringing him the sufferings of the cross, which he should bear with joy and patience, as he submits to God in difficult providences.

Principle 10: Future Life. Because God grants us an eternal inheritance, therefore meditate on the future life with Christ. The believer progresses in holiness as he is constantly drawn through public preaching and private meditation to contemplate the heavenly life with God, away from an inordinate desire for the world.

Principle 11: Present Life. Because God providentially guides all of life, therefore rightly use this present life to love others. God produces holiness as the believer practices the obedience of faith in the schoolroom of this daily life: enjoying life without lusting, being moderate within his vocation and benefiting others as a steward of his resources.

Principle 12: Church. Because God sanctifies his church, therefore engage fully in the life of church. The believer is sanctified by Christ only as he fully participates in the life of the church, in its preaching of the Word, its right administration of the sacraments and its shepherding through discipline.

Principle 13: Sacraments. Because God offers grace sacramentally, therefore commune regularly with Christ through the sacraments. The sacraments, properly administered and worthily received, communicate the grace of Christ, which actually puts to death sin and engenders faith, by which Christ is received more and more.

Principle 14: Church Discipline. Because God shepherds us through his leaders, therefore seek pastoral care and church discipline. Church discipline and pastoral care, when received in submission, confront the believer with particular sins to which he is blind and leads him toward the cure of Christ.

We have seen that the essence of Calvin's view of progressive sanctification is this: sanctification progresses as we gain an accurate two-fold knowledge of God and self, and respond to this knowledge with the two-fold motion of grace, downward in humble prostration before God, and at the same time, upward before him in thankful reverence.

Summary of Section Two: Training of Pastors

In Section Two, informed by the principles discovered in Calvin's theology of progressive sanctification, we asked: What were the specific teachings offered and the educational structures utilized by Calvin to enhance the *pietas* of the pastoral candidates he trained in the Genevan Academy? However, before we explored this question, we first had to ask the question of Calvin's goal: What is the model of the pious pastor toward which Calvin would train?

The model of the pious pastor operative at the Genevan Academy

A. **One who is truly called to the pastoral office**

1. **Truly called by God.** No man can be a real pastor unless God has called him into ministry, both by giving the requisite gifts for the office and by granting an internal sense of call.

2. **Truly called by the church.** A true call must proceed from the church, which is to select, train, examine and ordain those she knows God has prepared for pastoral work.

B. **One who is faithful to the true pastoral call**

1. **Faithful to the pastoral office.** The pastor must dedicate himself to his office, laboring long and hard, with great diligence and love, while always relying on the grace of God to do through him what he cannot do himself.

2. **Faithful in preaching the Word.** The pastor must always accurately preach the Word of God, neither adding to, nor subtracting from it. He must preach Christ boldly to confront sin, calling people to repentance and faith, never backing down from opposition in order to gain admirers or wealth.

3. **Faithful in shepherding the flock.** The pastor must dedicate himself to one flock, where he will remain, to labor lovingly and diligently on behalf of the sheep. When the flock is attacked, he will lovingly sacrifice himself to protect it. When the flock is sin-sick, he will bring the healing remedy of church discipline, without delay or favoritism, but with fatherly gentleness.

4. **Faithful in administering the sacraments**. The pastor must faithfully administer the sacraments by preparing his people to receive them, by teaching of their proper use and power, by warning of the dangers of their abuse and by calling the people to their regular use.

5. **Faithful in personal holiness.** The pastor must be pure in his morality, without the least hint of sexual impurity or drunkenness. He must be pure in his motivation; neither avarice nor ambition can enter his heart. The pastor must be accountable to other pastors and his own flock in order to discover his own blindness to sin.

Educational structures present at the Genevan Academy
Having elucidated Calvin's model of the pious pastor, we then answered our central question: How did John Calvin encourage the sanctification of the candidates for pastoral office at the Genevan Academy? We found he did this both through the repetitive teaching of the fourteen elements of progressive sanctification and through the use of the ten educational structures, which effectively applied Calvin's theology of sanctification. We have seen that Calvin, while never offering a summary of these fourteen principles, clearly repeated these doctrines in his lectures with a view toward enhancing the students' holiness. We have discovered that the ten educational structures were intentionally used, not only to give ministry skills and knowledge, but also to shape the piety of the pastoral candidates. Thus we have demonstrated our central thesis that Calvin's great concern for developing the holiness of the pastors at the Genevan Academy was shown by the way he used his theology of sanctification to shape the teaching and educational structures of the Academy.

Ten educational structures present at the Genevan Academy
Structure 1: The Academy was integrated into the city. Geneva itself was developed as a complex system to encourage piety, where church and state worked in harmony to produce sanctification among all its members, including the students.

Structure 2: The Academy was integrated with the church. The Academy was integrated with, and under the authority of, the church of Geneva, which would bring the students under the Word, sacraments and discipline.

Structure 3: The students were closely mentored by pastors. The students were closely mentored and supervised by the Company of Pastors, who worked to produce not only skilled but godly pastors.

Structure 4: The professors served as models of piety. The professors of the Academy served as models of holiness, setting a standard toward which the students might strive.

Structure 5: The Academy maintained a reputation for piety. This reputation for piety would serve both as a filter, screening out those who wished to cling to their sins, and as a magnet, attracting those who wanted to grow in holiness.

Structure 6: The Academy required a high standard of personal piety. The students were held accountable for a very high standard for personal holiness, encouraging their desire and effort toward piety.

Structure 7: The Academy held a high standard for biblical fidelity. The students were encouraged to hold the Bible in highest regard and to master its teachings in concept and practice, thus enhancing their holiness.

Structure 8: The professors used a hortatory teaching style. Rather than simply presenting information, the teaching at the Academy was persistently sermonic in nature, applying the biblical truths to the hearers and exhorting them toward repentance.

Structure 9: The professors closely critiqued students' preaching and theology. The Company carefully critiqued the students' weekly practice preaching sessions and monthly theological papers, helping the students grow in holiness through a right application of Scripture.

Structure 10: The students faced dangers in France. While not properly a structure of the Academy, Calvin used the awareness of the dangers in France to move the students toward self-denial and meditation on the future life, in order to enhance their holiness.

The comparison of Academies

In Section Two we also compared the Academy of Geneva with those in Strasbourg and Lausanne. While we found many similarities, due to the interdependence of the Academies, we nevertheless discovered that there were certain features unique to Geneva. In Geneva the Academy was more completely integrated with the city and the church, and the students were more closely mentored by the pastors. Geneva maintained the highest standard of biblical fidelity, evidenced by the lengthy confession of faith that students were required to adopt. Geneva taught more clearly and more often on Calvin's essential paradigm of the need for the two-fold knowledge of God and self, on the struggle for faith in all of life as a struggle between God and the devil and on the full-orbed use of this present life as the arena in which calling, moderation and love for neighbor are to be lived.

Calvin's Success at Preparing Pious Pastors

How are we to evaluate the effectiveness of the Genevan Academy? Not all of its graduates were exemplary pastors, indeed some were notorious failures. Pierre Des Préaux demonstrated a failure to care for his flock, abandoning them when the plague struck and again when he had family business. He was finally encouraged to resign in 1576 after just five years.[1] Jean Le Gaigneux spoke so strongly against both the City Council and Beza's leadership that he was de-

---

[1] Manetsch, *Company of Pastors*, 68-69.

Conclusion

posed in 1571.² Even while attending the Academy some students showed troubling signs. Michael Cop's own son, Lucas, was publicly flogged in 1570 for lying to the ministers and reading "several profane books."³

Despite a number of failures, most of the pastors who prepared at the Academy served admirably. Charles Perrot, known for his compassion toward the poor and his personal holiness, ministered for 40 years beginning in 1567 as a faithful associate in St. Pierre.⁴ Jean Gervais faithfully endured Roman Catholic oppression for 18 years while pastoring the country parish of Bossey before being called to serve in St. Gervais in 1612.⁵ Simon Goulart pastored St. Gervais from 1571 for more than 50 years, while also writing over 65 works.⁶ Theodore Tronchin became professor of Hebrew in 1606 at age 24 and then served Geneva for 50 years as professor, school rector and pastor.⁷

Perhaps a more reliable way to evaluate the effectiveness of the Genevan Academy is a statistical examination. We may compare the rate at which pastors who studied in Geneva were deposed from ministry with the deposition rates for pastors from other areas. During the 50 years after the founding of the Academy in 1559, Geneva was served by 105 pastors, 47 of whom studied at the Academy. Out of the 47 only 5 were deposed, or approximately 10.6%.⁸ That rate is similar to or lower than the deposition rate for Reformed pastors in some other areas which have been studied.⁹

While this rate speaks favorably of the effectiveness of the Genevan Academy one may wonder why it was not even lower. Part of the answer certainly lies in what we have observed in Chapter 8: other Reformed academies used many of the same approaches to sanctification as did Geneva. However, could it not also be that in Geneva, with its more thorough supervision, fewer breaches of conduct would pass undetected? Perhaps this rate of deposition might have been even lower were the supervision of Genevan pastors more nearly equivalent to that in other places.

We may also see Geneva's effectiveness in training godly pastors in 1) the demand for a high quantity of Geneva graduates, 2) the high quality of the personal holiness in the graduates and 3) the great effectiveness of these men in furthering the Reformation in France.

---

² Manetsch, *Company of Pastors*, 64.
³ Manetsch, *Company of Pastors*, 225.
⁴ Manetsch, *Company of Pastors*, 53-54.
⁵ Manetsch, *Company of Pastors*, 142-43.
⁶ Manetsch, *Company of Pastors*, 54-55.
⁷ Manetsch, *Company of Pastors*, 61.
⁸ Manetsch, *Company of Pastors*, 309-16.
⁹ Manetsch, *Company of Pastors*, 365, note 70: 17% in the duchy of Deux-Pons, 1557-1619; 14% in the County of Sponheim, 1557-1619; 10% in the South of France, 1559-1598.

The high quantity of the pastors sent from Geneva

As the Reformation progressed in France, the number of congregations exploded such that there were about 2150 congregations in 1562.[10] As evidence that others judged its graduates worthy, Geneva was asked to supply many of these pastors, sending out as many as 142 in 1561 alone.[11] Calvin would complain in 1561 of this incessant request for pastors from Geneva: "From all quarters demands for ministers are addressed to us, and though we have no more to send, yet such is the importunity of those who ask, that we must choose certain ministers from the lower ranks of the people."[12] The flood of pastors from Geneva was so great that the King of France wrote to the town fathers of Geneva in 1561 asking them to stem the tide.[13] While sheer quantity cannot prove the overall effectiveness of the Academy, the high demand for pastors from Geneva certainly suggests that the Academy's men were welcomed by the churches of France.

The high quality of the pastors sent from Geneva

The students went out with a holy humility, learned in their prostration before God. One former student, Bon Dupré, would write Calvin, "I hope that…the Spirit of smallness and humility will give me the grace to strive for his glory."[14] Dupré had learned his lessons well. The students went out with a holy boldness as well, learned in their reverent worship of God. They endured hardship and battles all around them with courage, as Calvin wrote to Bullinger, "At Montpelier, Nîmes, and other cities, our brethren are still in possession of the churches, because no one of the opposite party ventures to claim them."[15] They were still in possession of those churches, for no one else was bold enough to demand them (*repetere audet*). Those brethren had learned their lessons, too.

One of the clearest virtues displayed by the pastors from Geneva was their great courage. While many would eventually die in the line of duty, most of them faced difficulties and persecution.[16] Operating often in secret[17] the pastors perceived themselves as missionaries to a hostile land[18] who were unafraid to hold up the truth to "friend and foe alike," just as the prophets of the Old Testament had done.[19] Calvin compared the courage of the graduates of Geneva favorably against the followers of Heshusius while disputing with him over the

---

[10] Kingdon, *Wars of Religion*, 79.
[11] Kingdon, *Wars of Religion*, 79.
[12] Calvin to Ambrose Blaurer, May 1561, *CSW*, Vol. 7, 191; cf. Calvin to Bullinger, Mar. 12, 1562, *CSW*, Vol. 7, 263; Calvin to the Queen of Navarre, June 1, 1563, *CSW*, Vol. 7, 319.
[13] *CO* 18:337-39.
[14] Letter of Dupré to Calvin, Dec. 1561; *CO* 19:193-94.
[15] Letter of Calvin to Bullinger, July 19, 1563; *CO* 20:64-65.
[16] During the early years of the Academy ten former students were killed and another six had untimely deaths. Kingdon, *Wars of Religion*, 144.
[17] Kingdon, *Wars of Religion*, 56-57.
[18] Carrington, "Calvin and Erasmus," 138.
[19] Selderhuis, *Pilgrim Life*, 242.

Lord's Supper in 1561. "It is of no consequence to observe what kind of pupils his own school has produced. It is certain that the pigsty of Epicurus does not send forth men who boldly offer their lives in sacrifice, that they may confirm the ordinance of the Supper by their own blood."[20]

The great effectiveness of the pastors sent from the Academy
One last indicator of the effectiveness of the Academy was the impact of its students. Broadly speaking these men were highly effective at advancing the Reformation in the various parishes to which they were deployed, introducing Geneva-like teaching and ecclesial structures.[21] While eager to send men out to many locales,[22] Calvin and the Company deployed them with greater concentration in certain cities and provinces so as to multiply their effectiveness in the more influential areas.[23] Surveying the impact of these men in organizing such a massive groundswell of Reformed congregations all over France, Kingdon concludes, "The training that the men received in Geneva must have been exceptionally effective in teaching them not only how to do their pastoral work well, but also how to cooperate with one another with uncommon efficiency."[24] As we tally the quantity, the quality and the effectiveness of the graduates of the Academy of Geneva, we come to conclude that it was highly successful in helping to produce the pious pastor which Calvin had longed to see.

A final word

Calvin had lived to see his dream, at least in part, fulfilled. Godly and well-trained men streamed from his little Academy to reform the churches of France. Geneva, a city on a hill, had become a complex and coordinated system for promoting piety, which with the combined help of State, Church and Academy, produced a new kind of pastor, one who was humble regarding himself but bold in preaching the Word of God. Their piety was exemplary. Having learned humility, born out of prostration won through the two-fold knowledge of God and self, they practiced self-denial before a holy and gracious God. Having learned boldness, born out of reverence won through the same two-fold knowledge of God and self, they fearlessly declared God's Word. The Genevan Academy mightily added to the advance of the Reformation in France, and Calvin must certainly have been able to approach his end with real satisfaction. His prayer, offered to close his lecture to the Academy on Jeremiah 1:17, reflects his desire to send out pastors both humble and bold. A desire, as we have seen, his gracious God had, in some measure at least, granted.

---

[20] Reid, *Treatises*, 321, "Partaking of the Flesh and Blood."
[21] G.S. Sunshine, "Pastors in the French and Hungarian Reformation," *Calvin and the Company of Pastors, Calvin Studies Society Papers 2003* (Grand Rapids, Mich.: CRC Product Services, 2004), 229.
[22] Wallace, *Geneva and the Reformation*, 158.
[23] Kingdon, *Wars of Religion*, 55.
[24] Kingdon, *Wars of Religion*, 14.

Grant, Almighty God, that as thou hast been once pleased to fortify thy servant Jeremiah with the invincible power of thy Spirit,—O grant that his doctrine may at this day make us humble, and that we may learn willingly to submit to thee...and that we, relying on thy power and protection, may fight against the world and against Satan, while each of us, in his vocation, so recumbs on thy power, as not to hesitate, whenever necessary, to expose our very life to dangers: and may we manfully fight and persevere in our warfare to the end, until having finished our course we shall at length come to that blessed rest which is reserved for us in heaven, through Christ our Lord.[25]

---

[25] *Commentary*, Jer. 1:17.

Bibliography

Primary Sources

Anjorrant, J. Letter to the Genevan Magistrates. *Mémoires et Documents publiés par la Société d'Histoire et d'Archéologie de Genève*, Vol. 11. Geneva: Chez Jullien Frères, 1859, 168-71.
Anselm. *Cur Deus Homo*. Translated by S.N. Deane. Fort Worth, Tex.: RDMc, 2005.
Benedict of Nursia. *The Rule of St. Benedict*. Edited by T. Fry. New York, N.Y.: Random House, 1998.
Bernard of Clairvaux. *On the Love of God*. Translated by T.L. Connolly. New York, N.Y.: Spiritual Books Assoc., 1937.
Beza, T. *The Life of John Calvin*. Durham, England: Evangelical, 1997.
Bucer, M. *Common Places of Martin Bucer*. Edited and translated by D.F. Wright. Appleford, England: Sutton Courtenay, 1972.
— *Concerning the True Care of Souls*. Translated by P. Beale. Edinburgh: Banner of Truth Trust, 2009.
— *Enarrationes perpetuae in sacra quatuor Evangelia, recognitae nuper et locis compluribus auctae*. Strasbourg: Georg Ulricher, 1530.
— *In sacra quatuor Evangelia enarrationes perpetuae secundum recognitae*. Basel: Johann Herwagen, 1536.
— *Handlung inn dem offentlichen gesprech zu Straßburg*. Strasbourg, 1533.
— *Instruction in Christian Love*. Translated by P.T. Fuhrmann. Eugene, Oreg.: Wipf & Stock, 2008.
— *Martin Bucers Deutsche Schriften*. Edited by R. Stupperich. 17 vols. Gütersloh: Gütersloher Verlagshaus, 1960.
— *Martini Buceri Scripta Anglicana*. Basel: Peter Perna, 1577.
— *Metaphrasis et enarratio in epistolam D. Pauli Apostoli ad Romanos*. Basel: Peter Perna, 1562.
— *Praelectiones doctiss, in epistolam D. P. ad Ephesios*. Basel: Peter Perna, 1550-51.
Calvin, J. *The Bondage and Liberation of the Will*. Edited by A.N.S. Lane. Translated by G.I. Davies. Grand Rapids, Mich.: Baker, 2002.
— *Calvin's Commentaries*. The Calvin Translation Society. 22 vols. Grand Rapids, Mich.: Baker, 2005.
— *Calvin: Theological Treatises*. Edited by J.K.S. Reid. Louisville, Ky.: Westminster/John Knox, 2006.
— *Institutes of the Christian Religion*. Edited by J.T. McNeill. Translated by F.L. Battles. Philadelphia, Pa.: Westminster, 1960.
— *Instruction in Faith (1537)*. Edited and translated by P.T. Fuhrmann. Louisville, Ky.: Westminster/John Knox, 1977.

— *Ioannis Calvini opera quae supersunt omnia.* Edited by G. Baum, E. Cunitz, and E. Reuss. 59 vols. Brunswick: C.A. Schwetschke and Son, 1863-1900.
— *Ioannis Calvini opera selecta.* Edited by P. Barth, W. Niesel, and D. Scheuner. 5 vols. Munich: Christian Kaiser, 1926-52.
— *John Calvin, Tracts and Letters.* Edited by H. Beveridge and J. Bonnet. 7 vols. Edinburgh: Banner of Truth Trust, 2009.
— *Sermons on 2 Samuel Chapters 1-13.* Edited by D. Kelly. Edinburgh: Banner of Truth Trust, 1992.
— *Sermons on the Beatitudes.* Translated by R. White. Edinburgh: Banner of Truth Trust, 2006.
— *Sermons on the Book of Micah.* Edited and translated by B.W. Farley. Phillipsburg, N.J.: P&R, 2003.
— *Sermons on the Deity of Christ.* Translated by L. Nixon. Audubon, N.J.: Old Paths, 1997.
— *Sermons on Election and Reprobation.* Translated by J. Fielde. Willowstreet, Pa.: Old Paths, 1996.
— *Sermons on Ephesians.* Translated by A. Golding. Edinburgh: Banner of Truth Trust, 1998.
— *Sermons on Galatians.* Translated by A. Golding. Audubon, N.J.: Old Paths, 1995.
— *Sermons on Genesis Chapters 1-11.* Translated by R.R. McGregor. Edinburgh: Banner of Truth Trust, 2009.
— *Sermons on Job.* Translated by A. Golding. Edinburgh: Banner of Truth Trust, 1993.
— *Sermons on the Ten Commandments.* Edited and translated by B.W. Farley. Grand Rapids, Mich.: Baker, 1980.
— *Songs of the Nativity, Selected Sermons on Luke 1 and 2.* Translated by R. White. Edinburgh: Banner of Truth Trust, 2008.
— *Supplementa Calviniana.* Edited by H. Ruckert, E. Mulhaupt, G. Barrois, et al. Neukirchener-Vluyn: Neukirchener Verlag, 1936.
Erasmus, D. *Opus epistolarum Desiderii Erasmi Roterodami,* Vol. 7. Edited by P.S. Allen and H.M. Allen. Oxford: Oxford University Press, 1928.
Fournier, M. and C. Engel, eds. *Les statuts et privilèges des universités françaises depuis leur fondation jusqu'en 1789, tome 4/1: Gymnase, Académie, Université de Strasbourg.* Paris: L. Larose et Forcel, 1894.
Gregory the Great. *Pastoral Care.* Edited and translated by H. Davis. New York, N.Y.: Newman, 1950.
Hughes, P.E., ed. and tr. *The Register of the Company of Pastors of Geneva in the Time of Calvin.* Eugene, Oreg.: Wipf & Stock, 2004.
Knox, J. *The Works of John Knox, Volume 4: Writings from Frankfurt and Geneva by John Knox.* Edited by D. Laing. Eugene, Oreg.: Wipf & Stock, 2004.
Le More, N. "Letter to the Church of Geneva," Nov. 1, 1561. *Bulletin de la Société de l'Histoire du Protestantisme Français* 46 (1897), 466-68.

Luther, M. *Luther's Works, American Edition.* Edited by J. Pelikan and H.T. Lehmann. 55 vols. Philadelphia, Pa.: Muehlenberg and Fortress, and St. Louis, Mo.: Concordia, 1955-86.

— *Commentary on Galatians.* Translated by E. Middleton. Grand Rapids, Mich.: Kregel, 1979.

Pauck, W., ed. *Melanchthon and Bucer.* Philadelphia, Pa.: Westminster, 1969.

Registers of the Consistory of Geneva in the Time of Calvin. Edited by R.M. Kingdon. Vol. 1: 1542-1544. Grand Rapids, Mich.: Eerdmans, 2000.

Registres de la Compagnie des Pasteurs de Genève, au temps de Calvin. Edited by R.M. Kingdon and J.F. Bergier. 11 vols. Geneva: Droz, 1962.

Registres du Consistoire. Unpublished transcriptions available in the Meeter Center, Calvin College and Seminary, Grand Rapids, Mich.

Registres du Consistoire de Genève au temps de Calvin. Edited by T.A. Lambert, I.M. Watt, and J.R. Watt under the direction of R.M. Kingdon. Geneva: Droz, 1996.

Roberts, A. and J. Donaldson, eds. *The Ante-Nicene Fathers.* 10 vols. Peabody, Mass.: Hendrickson, 1994.

Schaff, P., ed. *The Nicene and Post-Nicene Fathers.* 28 vols. Peabody, Mass.: Hendrickson, 1994.

Schroeder, H.J., tr. *The Canons and Decrees of the Council of Trent.* Rockford, Ill.: Tan Books and Publishers, 1978.

Seneca, L.A. *Moral Epistles.* Translated by R.M. Gummere. 3 vols. The Loeb Classical Library. Cambridge, Mass.: Harvard University Press, 1917-25.

Thomas à Kempis. *The Imitation of Christ.* Translated by A. Croft and H.F. Bolton. Milwaukee, Wis.: Bruce, 1962.

Viret, P. *Instruction Chrétienne.* Lausanne: L'Age d'Homme, 2008.

— *Du devoir et du besoing qu'ont les hommes à s'enquerir de la volonté de Dieu par sa parole.* Geneva: Jean Girard, 1551.

— *La vertu et usage du ministère la parolle de Dieu.* Geneva: Jean Girard, 1548.

— *L'Interim fait par dialogues.* New York, N.Y.: Peter Lang, 1985.

— *Métamorphose chrétienne, faite par dialogues.* Geneva: Jacques Bres, 1561.

— *Pierre Viret d'après lui-même.* Edited by C. Schnetzler, H. Vuilleumier, and A. Schroeder. Lausanne: Georges Bridel, 1911.

Secondary Sources

Amos, N.S. "Bucer Among the Biblical Humanists: The Context for His Practice in the Teaching of Theology in Strasbourg, 1523-1548." *Reformation & Renaissance Review* 6 (2004), 134-154.

Aubigné, M. d'. *La Pierre sur Laquelle L'Académie de Genève Fut Posée en Juin 1559.* Geneva: Chez E. Beroud, 1859.

Backus, I. "Calvin's Patristic Models for Establishing the Company of Pastors." *Calvin and the Company of Pastors, Calvin Studies Society Papers 2003.* Grand Rapids, Mich.: CRC Product Services, 2004, 25-51.

— "Church, Communion and Community in Bucer's Commentary on the Gospel of John." *Martin Bucer Reforming Church and Community*. Edited by D.F. Wright. Cambridge: Cambridge University Press, 1994, 61-71.

—"L'Enseignement de la Logique à l'Académie de Genève Entre 1559 et 1565." *Revue de Théologie et de Philosophie* 3 (1979), 153-163.

Baird, H.M. *Theodore Beza the Counsellor of the French Reformation, 1519-1605*. Eugene, Oreg.: Wipf & Stock, 2004.

Barth, K. *The Theology of John Calvin*. Grand Rapids, Mich.: Eerdmans, 1995.

—*The Word of God and the Word of Man*. Translated by D. Horton. Grand Rapids, Mich.: Zondervan, 1935.

Battles, F.L. *Interpreting John Calvin*. Edited by R. Benedetto. Grand Rapids, Mich.: Baker, 1996.

—*The Piety of John Calvin: An Anthology Illustrative of the Spirituality of the Reformer of Geneva*. Grand Rapids, Mich.: Baker Book House, 1978.

Bauke, H. *Die Probleme der Theologie Calvins*. Leipzig: J.C. Hinrichs, 1992.

Baur, F.C. "Über Princip und Charakter des Lehrbegriffs der reformirten Kirche in seinem Unterschied von dem der lutherischen, mit *Rücksicht* auf A. Schweizer's Darstellung der reformirten Glaubenslehre." *Theologische Jahrbücher* 6 (1847), 309-89.

Beam, S. "Rites of Torture in Reformation Geneva." *Past and Present* 214 (2012), 197-219.

Beeke, J.R. "Does Assurance Belong to the Essence of Faith? Calvin and the Calvinists." *The Master's Seminary Journal* 5 (1994), 43-71.

— "Making Sense of Calvin's Paradoxes on Assurance of Faith." *Calvin and Spirituality, Calvin and His Contemporaries, Calvin Studies Society Papers, 1995, 1997*. Grand Rapids, Mich.: CRC Product Services, 1998, 13-30.

Bell, D.N. *Many Mansions, An Introduction to the Development and Diversity of Medieval Theology West and East*. Kalamazoo, Mich.: Cistercian, 1996.

Benedict, P. *Christ's Churches Purely Reformed: A Social History of Calvinism*. New Haven, Conn.: Yale University Press, 2002.

Berthoud, J-M. *Des Actes de L'Eglise*. Lausanne: L'Age d'Homme, 1993.

— "La Formation des Pasteurs et la Prédication de Calvin." *La Revue Réformée* 49 (1998), 19-44.

— *Pierre Viret: A Forgotten Giant of the Reformation*. Tallahassee, Fla.: Zurich, 2010.

— "Pierre Viret and the Sovereignty of the Word of God Over Every Aspect of Life." *A Comprehensive Faith*. San Jose, Calif.: Friends of Chalcedon, 1996, 93-106.

Blacketer, R.A. "The Moribund Moralist: Ethical Lessons in Calvin's Commentary on Joshua." *Dutch Review of Church History/Nederlands Archief voor Kerkgeschiedenis* 85 (2005), 149-168.

Bodley, T. *The Life of Sir Thomas Bodley*. Chicago, Ill.: A.C. McClurg, 1906.

Boer, E.A. de. "Calvin and Colleagues: Propositions and Disputations in the Context of the *Congrégations* in Geneva." *Calvinus Praeceptor Ecclesiae*. Edited by H.J. Selderhuis. Geneva: Droz, 2004, 331-42.

— "The *Congrégation*: An In-service Theological Training Center for Preachers to the People of Geneva." *Calvin and the Company of Pastors, Calvin Studies Society Papers, 2003*. Grand Rapids, Mich.: CRC Product Services, 2004, 57-87.

— "The Presence and Participation of Lay People in the *Congrégations* of the Company of Pastors in Geneva." *Sixteenth Century Journal* 35 (2004), 651-70.

Boisset, J. "Justification et Sanctification chez Calvin." *Calvinus Theologus*. Neukirchen: Neukirchener Verlag, 1974, 131-148.

Borgeaud, C. *Calvin, Fondateur de l'Académie de Genève*. Paris: Armand Colin, 1897.

—*Histoire de l'Université de Genève. Tome 1: L'Académie de Calvin 1559-1798*. Geneva: Georg, 1900.

Bouwsma, W.J. *John Calvin: A Sixteenth-Century Portrait*. New York, N.Y.: Oxford University Press, 1988.

Bouyer, L. "The Calvinist Doctrine of Sanctification." *A History of Christian Spirituality*. London: Burns & Oates, 1969, 85-89.

Brady, T.A., Jr. *German Histories in the Age of Reformations, 1400-1650*. New York, N.Y.: Cambridge University Press, 2009.

Bray, J.S. *Theodore Beza's Doctrine of Predestination*. Nieuwkoop: B. De Graaf, 1975.

Brockliss, L.W.B. *French Higher Education in the Seventeenth and Eighteenth Centuries*. Oxford: Clarendon, 1987.

Bruening, M.W. *Calvinism's First Battleground: Conflict and Reform in the Pays de Vaud, 1528-1559*. Dordrecht: Springer, 2005.

—"'La nouvelle réformation de Lausanne': The Proposal by the Ministers of Lausanne on Ecclesiastical Discipline (1558)." *Bibliothèque d'Humanisme et Renaissance* 68 (2006), 21-50.

Burnett, A.N. "The Educational Roots of Reformed Scholasticism: Dialectic and Scriptural Exegesis in the Sixteenth Century." *Dutch Review of Church History/Nederlands Archief voor Kerkgeschiedenis* 84 (2004), 299-317.

— "A Tale of Three Churches." *Calvin and the Company of Pastors, Calvin Studies Society Papers 2003*. Grand Rapids, Mich.: CRC Product Services, 2004, 95-124.

— *The Yoke of Christ: Martin Bucer and Christian Discipline*. Kirksville, Mo.: Sixteenth Century, 1994.

Campbell, C.R. *Paul and Union with Christ*. Grand Rapids, Mich.: Zondervan, 2012.

Campiche, M. *La Réforme en Pays de Vaud, 1528-1619*. Lausanne: L'Aire, 1985.

Carrington, L. "Calvin and Erasmus on Pastoral Formation." *Calvin and the Company of Pastors, Calvin Studies Society Papers 2003*. Grand Rapids, Mich.: CRC Product Services, 2004, 129-47.

Cart, J. *Pierre Viret, le Réformateur Vaudois*. Lausanne: Librairie de Louis Meyer, 1864.

Chrisman, M.U. *Strasbourg and the Reform: a Study in the Process of Change.* New Haven, Conn.: Yale University Press, 1967.

Cornut, S. *L'Académie de Calvin.* Geneva: H. George, 1902.

Cottret, B. *Calvin: A Biography.* Translated by M.W. McDonald. Grand Rapids, Mich.: Eerdmans, 2000.

Courvoisier, J. "Les Catéchismes de Genève et de Strasbourg." *Société de l'Histoire du Protestantisme Français* 84 (1935), 105-121.

Davis, T.J. "A Response to the Apostolic and Pastoral Office." *Calvin and the Company of Pastors, Calvin Studies Society Papers 2003.* Grand Rapids, Mich.: CRC Product Services, 2004, 173-78.

Derksen, J. "The Schwenckfeldians in Strasbourg, 1533-1562: A Prosopographical Survey," *Mennonite Quarterly Review* 74 (2000), 257- 294.

DeVries, D. *Jesus Christ in the Preaching of Calvin and Schleiermacher.* Columbia Series in Reformed Theology. Louisville, Ky.: Westminster/John Knox, 1996.

Diefendorf, B. *Beneath the Cross: Catholics and Huguenots in Sixteenth Century Paris.* Oxford: Oxford University Press, 1991.

Dixon, S.C. and L. Schorn-Schutte, eds. *The Protestant Clergy of Early Modern Europe.* New York, N.Y.: Palgrave Macmillan, 2003.

Doumergue, E. *Jean Calvin: Les Hommes et les Choses de Son Temps.* 7 vols. Lausanne: Georges Bridel, 1899-1927.

— *Le caractère de Calvin.* Paris: Editions de Foi et Vie, 1921.

Dowey, E.A., Jr. *The Knowledge of God in Calvin's Theology.* New York, N.Y.: Columbia University Press, 1965.

Eby, F. *Early Protestant Educators.* New York, N.Y.: McGraw Hill, 1931.

Eells, H. "The Contributions of Martin Bucer to the Reformation." *Harvard Theological Review* 24 (1931), 29-42.

Ehrenpreis, S. "Reformed Education in Early Modern Europe: A Survey." *Dutch Review of Church History/Nederlands Archief voor Kerkgeschiedenis* 85 (2005), 39-51.

Engelsma, D. "Martin Bucer: Reformed Pastor of Strasbourg." *Mid-America Journal of Theology* 3 (1987), 35-63.

Faber, R.A. "Humanitas as Discriminating Factor in the Educational Writings of Erasmus and Luther." *Dutch Review of Church History/Nederlands Archief voor Kerkgeschiedenis* 85 (2005), 25-37.

Favre, O. "Pierre Viret (1511-1571) et la discipline ecclésiastique." *La Revue Reformée* 49 (1998), 55-76.

Ferguson, S.B. "The Reformed View." *Christian Spirituality: Five Views of Sanctification.* Edited by D.L. Alexander. Downers Grove, Ill.: InterVarsity, 1988, 47-76.

Fesko, J.V. "Sanctification and Union with Christ: A Reformed Perspective." *Evangelical Quarterly* 82 (2010), 197-214.

Flaming, D.K. "The Apostolic and Pastoral Office: Theory and Practice in Calvin's Geneva." *Calvin and the Company of Pastors, Calvin Studies Society Papers, 2003.* Grand Rapids, Mich.: CRC Product Services, 2004, 149-72.

Gaffin, R.B., Jr. "Calvin's Soteriology: The Structure of the Application of Redemption in Book Three of the *Institutes*." *Ordained Servant* 18 (2009), 68-77.

Gamble, R.C. "Calvin and Sixteenth-Century Spirituality: Comparison with the Anabaptists." *Calvin and Spirituality, Calvin and His Contemporaries, Calvin Studies Society Papers, 1995, 1997*. Grand Rapids, Mich.: CRC Product Services, 1998, 31-51.

Ganoczy, A. *The Young Calvin*. Philadelphia, Pa.: Westminster, 1987.

— *Calvin, Théologien de l'Eglise et du Ministère*. Paris: Ed. du Cerf, 1964.

— *La Bibliothèque de l'Académie de Calvin*. Geneva: Droz, 1969.

Garcia, M.A. "Life in Christ—The Function of Union with Christ in the Unio - Duplex Gratia Structure of Calvin's Soteriology with Special Reference to the Relationship of Justification and Sanctification in Sixteenth-Century Context." PhD. thesis, University of Edinburgh, 2004.

— *Life in Christ, Union with Christ and Twofold Grace in Calvin's Theology*. Studies in Christian History and Thought. Waynesboro, Ga.: Paternoster, 2008.

— "Imputation and the Christology of Union with Christ: Calvin, Osiander, and the Contemporary Quest for a Reformed Model." *Westminster Theological Journal* 68 (2006), 219-251.

Gerrish, B.A. *Grace and Gratitude, the Eucharistic Theology of John Calvin*. Eugene, Oreg.: Wipf & Stock, 2002.

— "The Gift of Saving Faith." *Christian Century* 116 (1999), 968-71.

— "Calvin's Eucharistic Piety." *Calvin and Spirituality, Calvin and His Contemporaries, Calvin Studies Society Papers, 1995, 1997*. Grand Rapids, Mich.: CRC Product Services, 1998, 52-65.

Gilbert, A.H. "Martin Bucer on Education." *The Journal of English and Germanic Philology* 18 (1919), 321-345.

Gindroz, A. *Histoire de l'instruction publique dans le Pays de Vaud*. Lausanne: Georges Bridel, 1853.

Gleason, R.C. *John Calvin and John Owen on Mortification: A Comparative Study in Reformed Spirituality*. New York, N.Y.: Peter Lang, 1995.

Godfrey, W.R. "Faith Formed by Love or Faith Alone? The Instrument of Justification." *Covenant, Justification, and Pastoral Ministry: Essays by the Faculty of Westminster Seminary California*. Phillipsburg, N.J.: Presbyterian & Reformed, 2007, 267-84.

Graves, F.P. *Peter Ramus and the Educational Reformation of the Sixteenth Century*. New York, N.Y.: Macmillan, 1912.

Greengrass, M. "The French Pastorate: Confessional Identity and Confessionalization in the Huguenot Minority, 1559-1685." *The Protestant Clergy of Early Modern Europe*. Edited by C.S. Dixon. New York, N.Y.: Palgrave Macmillan, 2003, 176-95.

Greef, W. de. *The Writings of John Calvin: An Introductory Guide*. Grand Rapids, Mich.: Baker, 1993.

Greschat, M. "The Relation Between Church and Civil Community in Bucer's Reforming Work." *Martin Bucer Reforming Church and Community.* Edited by D.F. Wright. Cambridge: Cambridge University Press, 1994, 17-31.

Grin, E. "Deux Sermons de Pierre Viret." *Theologische Zeitschrift* 18 (1962), 116-32.

Holder, R.W. "Calvin's Exegetical Understanding of the Office of Pastor." *Calvin and the Company of Pastors, Calvin Studies Society Papers 2003.* Grand Rapids, Mich.: CRC Product Services, 2004, 179-209.

— "Paul as Calvin's (Ambivalent) Pastoral Model." *Dutch Review of Church History/Nederlands Archief voor Kerkgeschiedenis* 84 (2004), 284-98.

Horton, M. *Covenant and Salvation.* Louisville, Ky.: Westminster/John Knox, 2007.

— *The Christian Faith.* Grand Rapids, Mich.: Zondervan, 2011.

Janse, W. "Calvin's Eucharistic Theology: Three Dogma-Historical Observations." *Calvinus sacrarum literarum interpres. Papers of the International Congress on Calvin Research.* Edited by H.J. Selderhuis. Göttingen: Vandenhoeck & Ruprecht, 2008, 37-69.

Jones, M. and P. Johnstone. *History of Criminal Justice.* Waltham, Mass.: Anderson/Elsevier, 2012.

Jones, S. *Calvin and the Rhetoric of Piety.* Louisville, Ky.: Westminster/John Knox, 1995.

Junod, L. and H. Meylan, eds. *L'Académie de Lausanne au XVIe Siècle: Leges scholae Lausannensis 1547, Lettres et documents inédits.* Lausanne: F. Rouge, 1947.

Karp, A. "John Calvin and the Geneva Academy: Roots of the Board of Trustees." *History of Higher Education Annual* 5 (1985), 3-41.

Kingdon, R.M. *Geneva and the Coming of the Wars of Religion in France, 1555-1563.* Geneva: Droz, 1956.

— *Adultery and Divorce in Calvin's Geneva.* Cambridge, Mass.: Harvard University Press, 1995.

— "Calvin and the Family: the Work of the Consistory in Geneva." *Articles on Calvin and Calvinism.* Vol. 3, *Calvin's Work in Geneva.* Edited by R.C. Gamble. New York, N.Y. and London: Garland, 1992, 93-106.

— "The Control of Morals in Calvin's Geneva." *Articles on Calvin and Calvinism.* Vol. 3, *Calvin's Work in Geneva.* Edited by R.C. Gamble. New York, N.Y. and London: Garland, 1992, 43-56.

— *Geneva and the Consolidation of the French Protestant Movement, 1564-1572.* Geneva: Droz, 1967.

— "The Geneva Consistory in the Time of Calvin." *Calvinism in Europe, 1540-1620.* Edited by A. Pettegree, A. Duke, and G. Lewis. Cambridge: Cambridge University Press, 1996, 21-34.

Kingdon, R.M. and T.A. Lambert. *Reforming Geneva, Discipline, Faith and Anger in Calvin's Geneva.* Geneva: Droz, 2012.

Kirby, W.J.T. "From Florence to Zurich via Strasbourg and Oxford: The International Career of Peter Martyr Vermigli (1499-1562)." *Bewegung und Be-*

harrung: Aspekte des reformierten Protestantismus, 1520-1650. Leiden: Brill, 2009, 135-45.

Kohls, E-W. *Die Schule bei Martin Bucer in ihrem Verhältnis zu Kirche und Obrigkeit*. Heidelberg: Quelle & Meyea, 1963.

Kolfhaus, W. *Christusgemeinschaft bei Johannes Calvin*. Beiträge zur Geschichte und Lehre der Reformierten Kirche, Vol. 3. Neukirchen: Buchhandlung des Erziehungsvereins, 1938.

Koyzis, D.T., ed. *The 1562 Genevan Psalter*. Genevan Psalter web site. (http://genevanpsalter.redeemer.ca/psalm_texts.html#psalm51; accessed Aug. 23, 2011).

Kraan, E.D. "Le Péché et la Repentance." *La Revue Reformée* 48 (1997), 39-49.

Lane, A.N.S. *John Calvin: Student of the Church Fathers*. Grand Rapids, Mich.: Baker, 1999.

— "Calvin's Doctrine of Assurance." *Vox Evangelica* 11 (1979), 32-54.

— "Anthropology." *The Calvin Handbook*. Edited by H.J. Selderhuis. Grand Rapids, Mich.: Eerdmans, 2009, 275-288.

Larson, M.J. "John Calvin and Genevan Presbyterianism." *Westminster Theological Journal* 60 (1998), 43-69.

Lawrence, D. *Martin Bucer: Unsung Hero of the Reformation*. Nashville, Tenn.: Westview, 2008.

Lawson, S.J. "The Biblical Preaching Of John Calvin." *Southern Baptist Journal of Theology* 13 (2009), 18-32.

Le Coultre, J. *Maturin Cordier et les origines de la pédagogie de protestante dans les pays de langue française (1530-1564)*. Neuchâtel: Mémoires de l'Université de Neuchâtel, 1926.

Leith, J.H. *John Calvin's Doctrine of the Christian Life*. Louisville, Ky.: Westminster/John Knox, 1989.

Leithart, P.J. "Stoic Elements in Calvin's Doctrine of the Christian Life, Part 2: Mortification." *Westminster Theological Journal* 55 (1993), 192-208.

Lewis, G. "The Geneva Academy." *Calvinism in Europe, 1540-1620*. Edited by A. Pettegree, A. Duke, and G. Lewis. Cambridge: Cambridge University Press, 1996, 35-63.

Lienhard, M., ed. *La faculté de théologie protestante de Strasbourg—Hier et Aujourdhi*. Strasbourg: Oberlin, 1988.

Linder, R.D. "Brothers in Christ: Pierre Viret and John Calvin as Soul-Mates and Co-Laborers in the Work of the Reformation," *Calvin and Spirituality, Calvin and His Contemporaries, Calvin Studies Society Papers, 1995, 1997*. Grand Rapids, Mich.: CRC Product Services, 1998, 134-58.

— "Pierre Viret's Ideas and Attitudes Concerning Humanism and Education." *Church History* 34 (1965), 25-35.

— *The Political Ideas of Pierre Viret*. Geneva: Droz, 1964.

Lobstein, P. *Die Ethik Calvins in Ihren Grundzügen Entworfen*. Strasbourg: C.F. Schmidt's, 1877.

Maag, K. *Seminary or University? The Genevan Academy and Reformed Higher Education, 1560-1620.* Aldershot, England: Scolar, 1995.
— "Called to Be a Pastor: Issues of Vocation in the Early Modern Period." *Sixteenth Century Journal* 35 (2004), 65-78.
— "Calvin and Students." *The Calvin Handbook.* Edited by H.J. Selderhuis. Grand Rapids, Mich.: Eerdmans, 2009, 165-171.
— "Education and Training for the Calvinist Ministry: The Academy of Geneva, 1559-1620." *The Reformation of the Parishes.* Edited by A. Pettegree. Manchester: Manchester University Press, 1993, 133-52.
— "Preaching Practice: Reformed Students' Sermons." *The Formation of Clerical and Confessional Identities in Early Modern Europe.* Edited by W. Janse and B. Pitkin. Leiden: Brill, 2005, 133-46.
Manetsch, S.M. "Pastoral Care East of Eden: The Consistory of Geneva, 1568-82." *Church History* 75 (2006), 274-313.
—*Calvin's Company of Pastors: Pastoral Care and the Emerging Reformed Church, 1536-1609.* New York, N.Y.: Oxford University Press, 2013.
Marcel, P. "The Relation Between Justification and Sanctification in Calvin's Thought." *Evangelical Quarterly* 27 (1955), 132-45.
Martens, H. "Hutterite Melodies from the Strassburg Psalter." *Mennonite Quarterly Review* 48 (1974), 201-214.
Martin, H. *Les Cinq Étudiants de L'Académie de Lausanne.* Lausanne: Georges Bridel, 1863.
McGrath, A.E. *A Life of John Calvin: A Study in Shaping of Western Culture.* Malden, Mass.: Blackwell, 1990.
McKee, E.A. *Elders and the Plural Ministry.* Geneva: Droz, 1988.
— "Calvin and His Colleagues as Pastors: Some New Insights into the Collegial Ministry of Word and Sacraments." *Calvinus Praeceptor Ecclesiae.* Geneva: Droz, 2004, 9-42.
— "Contacts, Contours, Contents: Towards a Description of Calvin's Understanding of Worship." *Calvin and Spirituality, Calvin and His Contemporaries, Calvin Studies Society Papers, 1995, 1997.* Grand Rapids, Mich.: CRC Product Services, 1998, 66-92.
—*John Calvin, Writings on Pastoral Piety.* New York, N.Y.: Paulist, 2001.
— "Spirituality." *The Calvin Handbook.* Edited by H.J. Selderhuis. Grand Rapids, Mich.: Eerdmans, 2009, 465-71.
McKim, D., ed. *The Cambridge Companion to John Calvin.* Cambridge: Cambridge University Press, 2004.
McLaughlin, R.E. "The Politics of Dissent: Martin Bucer, Casper Schwenckfeld and the Schwenckfelders of Strasbourg." *Mennonite Quarterly Review* 68 (1994), 59-78.
McWilliams, D.B. "Calvin's Theology of Certainty." *Resurrection and Eschatology: Theology in Service of the Church, Essays in Honor of Richard B. Gaffin Jr.* Phillipsburg, N.J.: Presbyterian & Reformed, 2008, 513-33.
Mesnard, P. "The Pedagogy of Johann Sturm (1507-1589) and its Evangelical Inspiration." *Studies in the Renaissance* 13 (1966), 200-19.

Meylan, H. *La Haute École de Lausanne, 1537-1937*. University of Lausanne, 1986.

Monter, E.W. *Calvin's Geneva*. Eugene, Oreg.: Wipf & Stock, 2012.

— "The Consistory of Geneva, 1559-1569." *Bibliothèque d'Humanisme et Renaissance* 3 (1976), 467-84.

Moore, T.M. "Some Observations Concerning the Educational Philosophy of John Calvin." *Westminster Theological Journal* 46 (1984), 140-55.

Muller, R.A. *The Unaccommodated Calvin*. New York, N.Y.: Oxford University Press, 2000.

— *Calvin and the Reformed Tradition*. Grand Rapids, Mich.: Baker Academic, 2012.

Murphy, J., ed. and C. Newlands, tr. *Arguments in Rhetoric Against Quintilian: Translation and Text of Peter Ramus's Rhetoricae Distinctiones in Quintilianum (1549)*. DeKalb, Ill.: Northern Illinois University Press, 1986.

Naphy, W.G. *Calvin and the Consolidation of the Genevan Reformation*. Louisville, Ky.: Westminster/John Knox, 2003.

— "Church and State in Calvin's Geneva." *Calvin and the Church, Calvin Studies Society Papers 2001*. Grand Rapids, Mich.: CRC Product Services, 2002, 13-28.

— "The Renovation of the Ministry in Calvin's Geneva." *The Reformation of the Parishes*. Edited by A. Pettegree. Manchester: Manchester University Press, 1993, 113-32.

Nelson, S.F. and J. Rott. "Strasbourg: The Anabaptist City in the Sixteenth Century." *Mennonite Quarterly Review* 58 (1984), 230–40.

Niesel, W. *The Theology of Calvin*. Translated by H. Knight. Philadelphia, Pa.: Westminster, 1956.

Olson, J.E. "Calvin as Pastor-Administrator During the Reformation in Geneva." *Articles on Calvin and Calvinism*. Vol. 3, *Calvin's Work in Geneva*. Edited by R.C. Gamble. New York, N.Y. and London: Garland, 1992, 2-9.

— "The Friends of John Calvin: The Budé Family." *Calvin and Spirituality, Calvin and His Contemporaries, Calvin Studies Society Papers, 1995, 1997*. Grand Rapids, Mich.: CRC Product Services, 1998, 159-68.

Ong, W.J. *Ramus: Method, and the Decay of Dialogue / from the Art of Discourse to the Art of Reason*. Cambridge, Mass.: Harvard University Press, 1958.

Osmer, R.R. "The Teaching Office in the Thought and Practice of John Calvin." *A Teachable Spirit. Recovering the Teaching Office in the Church*. Louisville, Ky.: Westminster/John Knox, 1990, 107-135.

Ozment, S. *The Age of Reform 1250-1550: An Intellectual and Religious History of Late Medieval and Reformation Europe*. New Haven, Conn.: Yale University Press, 1980.

Parker, T.H.L. *Calvin's Doctrine of the Knowledge of God*. Grand Rapids, Mich.: Eerdmans, 1959.

— *Calvin, An Introduction To His Thought*. Louisville, Ky.: Westminster/John Knox, 1995.

— *Calvin's Old Testament Commentaries*. Louisville, Ky.: Westminster/John Knox, 1986.
— *Calvin's Preaching*. Louisville, Ky.: Westminster/John Knox, 1992.
— *John Calvin, a Biography*. Philadelphia, Pa.: Westminster, 1975.
— *The Oracles of God*. Cambridge: James Clarke, 2002.
Pettegree, A. "The Clergy and the Reformation: from 'Devilish Priesthood' to New Professional Elite." *The Reformation of the Parishes*. Edited by A. Pettegree. Manchester: Manchester University Press, 1993, 1-21.
Pettegree, A., A. Duke and G. Lewis, eds. *Calvinism in Europe, 1540-1620*. Cambridge: Cambridge University Press, 1997.
Pitkin, B. "Redefining Repentance: Calvin and Melanchthon." *Calvinus Praeceptor Ecclesiae*. Edited by H.J. Selderhuis. Geneva: Droz, 2004, 275-86.
— "Sermons sur le Genèse chapitres 1, 1-11, 4/Sermons sur la Genèse chapitres 11, 5-20, 7/Sermons on the Acts of the Apostles, Chapters 1-7." *Dutch Review of Church History/Nederlands Archief voor Kerkgeschiedenis* 81 (2001), 219-220.
— "The Spiritual Gospel? Christ and Human Nature in Calvin's Commentary on John." *The Formation of Clerical and Confessional Identities in Early Modern Europe*. Edited by W. Janse and B. Pitkin. Leiden: Brill, 2006, 187-204.
Puckett, D.L. "John Calvin as Teacher." *Southern Baptist Journal of Theology* 13 (2009), 44-50.
Rainbow, J.H. "Double Grace: John Calvin's View of the Relationship of Justification and Sanctification." *Ex Auditu* 5 (1989), 99-105.
Raynal, C.E. "The Place of the Academy in Calvin's Polity." *John Calvin and the Church: A Prism of Reform*. Edited by T. George. Louisville, Ky.: Westminster/John Knox, 1990, 120-134.
Reid, W.S. "Calvin and the Founding of the Academy of Geneva." *Westminster Theological Journal* 18 (1955), 1-33.
— *John Calvin: His Influence on the Western World*. Grand Rapids, Mich.: Zondervan, 1982.
Richard, L.J. *The Spirituality of John Calvin*. Atlanta, Ga.: John Knox, 1974.
Robbins, R.D.C. "Life and Character of Theodore Beza." *Bibliotheca Sacra* 7 (1850), 501-33.
Schaff, P., ed. *The Creeds of Christendom*. 3 vols. Grand Rapids, Mich.: Baker Book House, 1977.
— *History of the Christian Church*. 8 vols. Peabody, Mass.: Hendrickson, 2002.
Scholl, F. *Professions et Quelques Aspects Généalogiques des Étudiants Genevois Inscrits A L'Académie de Genève 1559-1878*. Geneva: University of Geneva, 1986.
Schreiner, S. "Calvin's Concern with Certainty in the Context of the Sixteenth Century." *Calvin, Beza and Later Calvinism, John Calvin and the Interpretation of Scripture, Calvin Studies Society Papers 2005, 2000, 2002*. Grand Rapids, Mich.: CRC Product Services, 2006, 113-131.

Selderhuis, H.J. "Faith Between God and the Devil: Calvin's Doctrine of Faith as Reflected in his Commentary on the Psalms." *Calvin, Beza and Later Calvinism, John Calvin and the Interpretation of Scripture, Calvin Studies Society Papers 2005, 2000, 2002.* Grand Rapids, Mich.: CRC Product Services, 2006, 188-205.

— *A Pilgrim's Life.* Downers Grove, Ill.: InterVarsity, 2009.

— "Vera Theologia Scientia Est: Bucer and the Training of Ministers." *Reformation and Renaissance Review: Journal of the Society of Reformation Studies* 3 (2001), 125-140.

Shepherd, V.A. "Calvin's Doctrine of Sanctification." *The Bulletin: Committee on Archives and History of the Church of Canada* 29 (1980-1982), 93-101.

— *The Nature and Function of Faith in the Theology of John Calvin.* Macon, Ga.: Mercer University Press, 1983.

Shin, K.Y. "Calvin's Theology of Holiness." PhD. thesis. University of Aberdeen, 2002.

Siedlecki, A. "Protestant Theological Education in German Universities in the Sixteenth Century." *American Theological Library Association Summary of Proceedings* 62 (2008), 250-64.

Small, J.D. "A Company of Pastors." *Calvin and The Company of Pastors, Calvin Studies Society Papers 2003.* Grand Rapids, Mich.: CRC Product Services, 2004, 9-15.

Smith, S.F. "The Genevan School of Theology." *Christian Review* 12 (1847), 321-359.

Spijker, W. van 't. "Bucer's Influence on Calvin: Church and Community." *Martin Bucer Reforming Church and Community.* Edited by D.F. Wright. Cambridge: Cambridge University Press, 1994, 32-44.

— *Calvin: Biographie und Theologie. Die Kirche in ihrer Geschichte.* Göttingen: Vandenhoeck und Ruprecht, 2001.

— "Calvin's Friendship with Martin Bucer: Did it Make Calvin a Calvinist?" *Calvin and Spirituality, Calvin and His Contemporaries, Calvin Studies Society Papers, 1995, 1997.* Grand Rapids, Mich.: CRC Product Services, 1998, 169-86.

— "The Influence of Bucer on Calvin as Becomes Evident from the Institutes." *John Calvin's Institutes: His Opus Magnum.* Edited by B.J. van der Walt. Potchefstroom, South Africa: Potchefstroom University for Christian Higher Education, 1986, 106-132.

— "The Influence of Luther on Calvin According to the Institutes." *John Calvin's Institutes: His Opus Magnum.* Edited by B.J. van der Walt. Potchefstroom, South Africa: Potchefstroom University for Christian Higher Education, 1986, 83-105.

Spitz, L.W. and B.S. Tinsley. *Johann Sturm on Education.* St. Louis, Mo.: Concordia, 1995.

Steinmetz, D.C. *Calvin in Context.* New York, N.Y.: Oxford University Press, 1995.

— "Reformation and Conversion." *Theology Today* 35 (1978-79), 25-32.

Stelling-Michaud, S. and S. *Le Livre du Recteur de l'Académie de Genève.* 6 vols. Geneva: Droz, 1959-89.

Stephens, W.P. *The Holy Spirit in the Theology of Martin Bucer.* Cambridge: Cambridge University Press, 1970.

— "The Church in Bucer's Commentaries on the Epistle to the Ephesians." *Martin Bucer Reforming Church and Community.* Edited by D.F. Wright. Cambridge: Cambridge University Press, 1994, 45-60.

Strand, K.A. "John Calvin and the Brethren of the Common Life: The Role of Strassburg." *Andrews University Seminary Studies* 15 (1977), 43-56.

Sunshine, G.S. "Pastors in the French and Hungarian Reformation." *Calvin and the Company of Pastors, Calvin Studies Society Papers 2003.* Grand Rapids, Mich.: CRC Product Services, 2004, 217-36.

— *Reforming French Protestantism: The Development of Huguenot Ecclesiastical Institutions, 1557-1572.* Kirksville, Mo.: Truman State University Press, 2003.

Tamburello, D.E. *Union with Christ: John Calvin and the Mysticism of St. Bernard.* Louisville, Ky.: Westminster/John Knox, 1994.

Timmerman, D. "Martin Bucer as Interpreter of the Old Testament: A Re-examination of Previous Scholarship in Light of Bucer's *Enarrationes in librum Iudicum* (ca. 1540)." *Reformation and Renaissance Review* 9 (2007), 27-44.

Torrance, T.F. *Calvin's Doctrine of Man.* Westport, Conn.: Greenwood, 1997.

— "The Eldership in the Reformed Church." *Scottish Journal of Theology* 37 (1984), 503-18.

Uprichard, R.E.H. "The Eldership in Martin Bucer and John Calvin." *Irish Biblical Studies* 18 (1996), 136-55.

Venema, C.P. *Accepted and Renewed in Christ: The "Twofold Grace of God" and the Interpretation of Calvin's Theology.* Göttingen: Vandenhoeck & Ruprecht, 2007.

Walker, W. *John Calvin, the Organizer of Reformed Protestantism, 1509-1564.* New York, N.Y.: Putnam, 1906.

Wallace, R.S. *Calvin, Geneva and the Reformation.* Eugene, Oreg.: Wipf & Stock, 1998.

— *Calvin's Doctrine of the Christian Life.* Edinburgh: Oliver and Boyd Ltd., 1959.

Wendel, F. *Calvin: Origins and Development of His Religious Thought.* New York, N.Y.: Harper & Row, 1963.

Wenger, T.L. "The New Perspectives on Calvin: Responding to Recent Calvin Interpretations." *Journal of the Evangelical Theological Society* 50 (2007), 311-28.

White, J.F. *Protestant Worship: Traditions in Transition.* Louisville, Ky.: Westminster/John Knox, 1989.

Wilcox, P. "The Lectures of John Calvin and the Nature of His Audience, 1555-1564." *Archiv für Reformationsgeschichte* 87 (1996), 136-48.

Wiley, D.N. "Calvin's Friendship with Guillaume Farel." *Calvin and Spirituality, Calvin and His Contemporaries, Calvin Studies Society Papers, 1995, 1997*. Grand Rapids, Mich.: CRC Product Services, 1998, 187-204.

Winecoff, D.K. "Calvin's Doctrine of Mortification." *Presbyterion* 13 (1987), 85-101.

Witte, J., Jr. and R.M. Kingdon. *Sex, Marriage, and Family in John Calvin's Geneva: Courtship, Engagement, and Marriage*. Grand Rapids, Mich.: Eerdmans, 2005.

Witvliet, J.D. "The Spirituality of the Psalter: Metrical Psalms in Liturgy and Life in Calvin's Geneva." *Calvin and Spirituality, Calvin and His Contemporaries, Calvin Studies Society Papers, 1995, 1997*. Grand Rapids, Mich.: CRC Product Services, 1998, 93-117.

Zachman, R.C. "'Deny Yourself and Take up Your Cross': John Calvin on the Christian Life." *International Journal of Systematic Theology* 11 (2009), 466-82.

— "Restoring Access to the Fountain: Melanchthon and Calvin on the Task of Evangelical Theology." *Calvin and Spirituality, Calvin and His Contemporaries, Calvin Studies Society Papers 1995, 1997*. Grand Rapids, Mich.: CRC Product Services, 1998, 205-27.

Author Index

Amos, N.S. 200.
Anselm 42, 46, 61.

Backus, I. 6.
Baird, H.M. 199.
Battles, F.L. 9, 20, 23, 37, 39, 50, 81.
Bauke, H. 5.
Baur, F.C. 5.
Beeke, J.R. 66.
Benedict of Nursia 91.
Bernard of Clairvaux 47, 55, 91, 187.
Beza, T. 99, 170-171, 182-184, 186-187, 197-198, 203, 205, 232-233.
Blacketer, R.A. 142.
Boer, E.A. de. 10.
Borgeaud, C. 11.
Bouwsma, W.J. 47-48.
Bucer, M. 6, 24, 30, 40, 89, 111, 116, 197-206, 208, 212-225.

Cottret, B. 13, 45.

Doumergue, E. 6.
Dowey, E.A., Jr. 7, 64.

Eby, F. 12.
Ehrenpreis, S. 12.
Erasmus, D. 38, 168.

Flaming, D.K. 10.

Gaffin, R.B., Jr. 26-27.
Ganoczy, A. 18, 45, 114.
Gerrish, B.A 77-78.
Gindroz, A.199.
Godfrey, W.R. 68.
Gregory the Great 91, 111.

Holder, R.W. 10.
Horton, M. 27.

Janse, W. 6.
Jones, S. 36, 39.
Junod, L. 199.

Kingdon, R.M. 10, 193, 235.

Lane, A.N.S. 6, 40, 91.
Le Coultre, J. 199.
Leith, J.H. 5, 7, 9, 21, 55, 95.
Leithart, P.J. 95.
Le More, N. 183, 193.
Lienhard, M., 200.
Lobstein, P. 7, 9, 16.
Luther, M. 6, 17, 86, 222.

Maag, K. 10-11.
Manetsch, S.M. 11, 179.
Marcel, P. 3, 14.
McKee, E.A. 8, 10.
McWilliams, D.B. 87.
Moore, T.M. 12.
Muller, R.A. 8, 28, 33, 40, 45.

Naphy, W.G. 176, 178.
Niesel, W. 5, 8-9, 13, 15, 23, 33, 46, 48, 53, 91.

Pettegree, A. 10.
Pitkin, B. 9.

Richard, L.J. 7, 9, 36, 91.

Selderhuis, H.J. 9, 70, 78.
Seneca, L.A. 111.
Spijker, W. van 't. 6, 17, 25, 40.
Steinmetz, D.C. 48, 80.

Tamburello, D.E. 8, 33, 59.
Thomas à Kempis 7, 91.
Torrance, T.F. 7-9, 36, 38, 44, 58-59, 78.

Viret, P. 138, 170, 186, 197-199, 201-203, 205, 208, 212-216, 218-225.

Wallace, R.S. 3, 6-7, 9, 22, 24, 93.
Wendel, F. 13, 35, 45, 54.

www.ingramcontent.com/pod-product-compliance
Lightning Source LLC
Chambersburg PA
CBHW050438240426
43661CB00055B/2425